Lecture Notes in Computer Science 10034

Commenced Publication in 1973
Founding and Former Series Editors:
Gerhard Goos, Juris Hartmanis, and Jan van Leeuwen

More information about this series at http://www.springer.com/series/7409

Ioana Ciuciu · Christophe Debruyne
Hervé Panetto · Georg Weichhart
Peter Bollen · Anna Fensel
Maria-Esther Vidal (Eds.)

On the Move to Meaningful Internet Systems: OTM 2016 Workshops

Confederated International Workshops:
EI2N, FBM, ICSP, Meta4eS, and OTMA 2016
Rhodes, Greece, October 24–28, 2016
Revised Selected Papers

 Springer

Editors

Ioana Ciuciu
University Babes-Bolyai
Cluj-Napoca
Romania

Christophe Debruyne
ADAPT Centre
Trinity College Dublin
Dublin 2
Ireland

Hervé Panetto
University of Lorraine
Vandoeuvre-les-Nancy
France

Georg Weichhart
Profactor GmbH and Johannes Kepler
University Linz
Linz
Austria

Peter Bollen
Maastricht University
Maastricht
The Netherlands

Anna Fensel
University of Innsbruck
Innsbruck
Austria

Maria-Esther Vidal
Universidad Simón Bolívar
Caracas
Venezuela

ISSN 0302-9743　　　　　　　　ISSN 1611-3349　(electronic)
Lecture Notes in Computer Science
ISBN 978-3-319-55960-5　　　　ISBN 978-3-319-55961-2　(eBook)
DOI 10.1007/978-3-319-55961-2

Library of Congress Control Number: 2017935842

LNCS Sublibrary: SL3 – Information Systems and Applications, incl. Internet/Web, and HCI

Printed on acid-free paper

This Springer imprint is published by Springer Nature
The registered company is Springer International Publishing AG
The registered company address is: Gewerbestrasse 11, 6330 Cham, Switzerland

General Co-chairs' Message for OnTheMove 2016

The OnTheMove 2016 event held October 24–28 in Rhodes, Greece, further consolidated the importance of the series of annual conferences that was started in 2002 in Irvine, California. It then moved to Catania, Sicily, in 2003, to Cyprus in 2004 and 2005, Montpellier in 2006, Vilamoura in 2007 and 2009, in 2008 to Monterrey, Mexico, to Heraklion, Crete, in 2010 and 2011, Rome in 2012, Graz in 2013, Amantea, Italy, in 2014, and to Rhodes in 2015 as well.

This prime event continues to attract a diverse and relevant selection of today's research worldwide on the scientific concepts underlying new computing paradigms, which of necessity must be distributed, heterogeneous, and supporting an environment of resources that are autonomous yet must meaningfully cooperate. Indeed, as such large, complex, and networked intelligent information systems become the focus and norm for computing, there continues to be an acute and increasing need to address the software, system, and enterprise issues involved and discuss them face to face in an integrated forum that covers methodological, semantic, theoretical, and application issues too. As we all realize, e-mail, the Internet, and even video conferences are not by themselves optimal or even sufficient for effective and efficient scientific exchange.

The OnTheMove (OTM) International Federated Conference series was created to cover the scientific exchange needs of the communities that work in the broad yet closely connected fundamental technological spectrum of Web-based distributed computing. The OTM program every year covers data and Web semantics, distributed objects, Web services, databases, information systems, enterprise workflow and collaboration, ubiquity, interoperability, mobility, as well as grid and high-performance computing.

OnTheMove is proud to give meaning to the "federated" aspect in its full title: It aspires to be a primary scientific meeting place where all aspects of research and development of Internet- and intranet-based systems in organizations and for e-business are discussed in a scientifically motivated way, in a forum of interconnected workshops and conferences. This year's 15th edition of the OTM Federated Conferences event therefore once more provided an opportunity for researchers and practitioners to understand, discuss, and publish these developments within the broader context of distributed, ubiquitous computing. To further promote synergy and coherence, the main conferences of OTM 2016 were conceived against a background of their three interlocking global themes:

- Trusted Cloud Computing Infrastructures Emphasizing Security and Privacy
- Technology and Methodology for Data and Knowledge Resources on the (Semantic) Web
- Deployment of Collaborative and Social Computing for and in an Enterprise Context

Originally the federative structure of OTM was formed by the co-location of three related, complementary, and successful main conference series: DOA (Distributed Objects and Applications, held since 1999), covering the relevant infrastructure-enabling technologies, ODBASE (Ontologies, Databases and Applications of Semantics, since 2002) covering Web semantics, XML databases, and ontologies, and of course CoopIS (Cooperative Information Systems, held since 1993), which studies the application of these technologies in an enterprise context through, e.g., workflow systems and knowledge management. In the 2011 edition issues of security aspects, originally started as topics of the IS workshop in OTM 2006, became the focus of DOA as secure virtual infrastructures, further broadened to cover aspects of trust and privacy in so-called cloud-based systems. As this latter aspect came to dominate agendas in this and overlapping research communities, we decided in 2014 to rename the event as the Cloud and Trusted Computing (C&TC) Conference, and originally launched it in a workshop format.

These three main conferences specifically seek high-quality contributions of a more mature nature and encourage researchers to treat their respective topics within a framework that simultaneously incorporates (a) theory, (b) conceptual design and development, (c) methodology and pragmatics, and (d) application in particular case studies and industrial solutions.

As in previous years we again solicited and selected additional quality workshop proposals to complement the more mature and "archival" nature of the main conferences. Our workshops are intended to serve as "incubators" for emergent research results in selected areas related, or becoming related, to the general domain of Web-based distributed computing. This year this difficult and time-consuming job of selecting and coordinating the workshops was brought to a successful end by Ioana Ciuciu, and we were very glad to see that our earlier successful workshops (EI2N, Meta4eS, FBM) re-appeared in 2016, in some cases in alliance with other older or newly emerging workshops. The Fact-Based Modeling (FBM) Workshop in 2015 succeeded and expanded the scope of the successful earlier ORM Workshop. The Industry Case Studies Program, started in 2011 under the leadership of Hervé Panetto and OMG's Richard Mark Soley, gained further momentum and visibility in its sixth edition this year.

The OTM registration format ("one workshop or conference buys all workshops or conferences") actively intends to promote synergy between related areas in the field of distributed computing and to stimulate workshop audiences to productively mingle with each other and, optionally, with those of the main conferences. In particular EI2N continues to create and exploit a visible cross-pollination with CoopIS.

We were very happy to see that in 2016 the number of quality submissions for the OnTheMove Academy (OTMA) noticeably increased. OTMA implements our unique, actively coached and therefore very time- and effort-intensive formula to bring PhD students together, and aims to carry our "vision for the future" in research in the areas covered by OTM. Its 2016 edition was organized and managed by a dedicated team of collaborators and faculty, Peter Spyns, Maria-Esther Vidal, and Anja Metzner, inspired as always by the OTMA Dean, Erich Neuhold.

In the OTM Academy, PhD research proposals are submitted by students for peer review; selected submissions and their approaches are to be presented by the students in front of a wider audience at the conference, and are independently and extensively analyzed and discussed in front of this audience by a panel of senior professors. One may readily appreciate the time, effort, and funds invested in this by OnTheMove and especially by the OTMA faculty.

As the three main conferences and the associated workshops all share the distributed aspects of modern computing systems, they experience the application pull created by the Internet and by the so-called Semantic Web, in particular the developments of big data, the increased importance of security issues, and the globalization of mobile-based technologies. For ODBASE 2016, the focus somewhat shifted from knowledge bases and methods required for enabling the use of formal semantics in Web-based databases and information systems to applications, especially those within IT-driven communities. For CoopIS 2016, the focus as before was on the interaction of such technologies and methods with business process issues, such as occur in networked organizations and enterprises. These subject areas overlap in a scientifically natural and fascinating fashion and many submissions in fact also covered and exploited the mutual impact among them. For our event C&TC 2016, the primary emphasis was again squarely put on the virtual and security aspects of Web-based computing in the broadest sense. As with the earlier OnTheMove editions, the organizers wanted to stimulate this cross-pollination by a program of engaging keynote speakers from academia and industry and shared by all OTM component events. We are proud to list for this year:

- François Vernadat, LGIPM and EU Institutions, Luxemburg
- Giancarlo Fontino, University of Calabria, Italy
- Patrick McLaughlin, ORACLE, Ireland
- Sotiris Ioannidis, Foundation for Research and Technology Hellas, Greece

The general downturn in submissions observed in recent years for almost all conferences in computer science and IT has also affected OnTheMove, but this year the harvest again stabilized at a total of 133 submissions for the three main conferences and 58 submissions in total for the workshops. Not only may we indeed again claim success in attracting a representative volume of scientific papers, many from the USA and Asia, but these numbers of course allowed the respective Program Committees to again compose a high-quality cross-section of current research in the areas covered by OTM. Acceptance rates vary but the aim was to stay consistently at about one accepted full paper for two to three submitted (nearly one in three for CoopIS), yet as always these rates are subject to professional peer assessment of proper scientific quality.

As usual we separated the proceedings into two volumes with their own titles, one for the main conferences and one for the workshops and posters. But in a different approach to previous years, we decided the latter should appear after the event and thereby allow workshop authors to improve their peer-reviewed papers based on critiques by the Program Committees and on interactions at OTM. The resulting additional complexity and effort of editing the proceedings were professionally shouldered by our leading editor, Christophe Debruyne – with the general chairs for the conference volume, and with Ioana Ciuciu and Hervé Panetto for the workshop volume. We are again most grateful to the Springer LNCS team in Heidelberg for their professional support, suggestions, and meticulous collaboration in producing the files and indexes ready for downloading on the USB sticks. It is a pleasure to work with staff that so deeply understands the scientific context at large, and the specific logistics of conference proceedings publication.

The reviewing process by the respective OTM Program Committees was performed to professional quality standards: Each paper review in the main conferences was assigned to at least three referees, with arbitrated e-mail discussions in the case of strongly diverging evaluations. It may be worth emphasizing once more that it is an explicit OnTheMove policy that all conference Program Committees and chairs make their selections in a completely sovereign manner, autonomous and independent from any OTM organizational considerations. As in recent years, proceedings in paper form are now only available to be ordered separately.

The general chairs are once more especially grateful to the many people directly or indirectly involved in the set-up of these federated conferences. Not everyone realizes the large number of qualified persons that need to be involved and the huge amount of work, commitment, and financial risk in the uncertain economic and funding climate of 2016 that are entailed by the organization of an event like OTM. Apart from the persons in their roles mentioned earlier, we therefore wish to thank in particular explicitly our main conference Program Committee chairs:

- CoopIS 2016: Eva Kühn, Frank Leymann, and Willem-Jan van den Heuvel
- ODBASE 2016: Declan O'Sullivan, Joseph Davis, and Satya Sahoo
- C&TC 2016: Claudio Ardagna and Nils Gruschka

And similarly we thank the Program Committee (co-)chairs of the 2016 ICSP, OTMA, and Workshops (in their order of appearance on the website): Peter Spyns, Maria-Esther Vidal, Mario Lezoche, Ovidiu Noran, Eduardo Portela, Georg Weichhart, Peter Bollen, Hans Mulder, Maurice Nijssen, Anna Fensel, Ioana Ciuciu.

Together with their many Program Committee members, they performed a superb and professional job in managing the difficult yet existential process of peer review and selection of the best papers from the harvest of submissions. We all also owe a serious debt of gratitude to our supremely competent and experienced conference secretariat and technical administration staff in Guadalajara and Dublin, respectively, Daniel Meersman and Christophe Debruyne, with the occasional valuable support by Jan Demey while passing through Fiumicino, Zaventem, and Schiphol airports.

The general conference and workshop co-chairs also thankfully acknowledge the academic freedom, logistic support, and facilities they enjoy from their respective institutions—Technical University of Graz, Austria; Université de Lorraine, Nancy, France; Latrobe University, Melbourne, Australia; and Babes-Bolyai University, Cluj, Romania—and without which such a project quite simply would not be feasible. Reader, we do hope that the results of this federated scientific enterprise contribute to your research and your place in the scientific network... and we hope to welcome you at next year's event!

September 2016   Robert Meersman
                                                         Hervé Panetto
                                                         Ioana Ciuciu

Organization

OTM (On The Move) is a federated event involving a series of major international conferences and workshops. These proceedings contain the papers presented at the OTM 2016 Federated Conferences, consisting of CoopIS 2016 (Cooperative Information Systems), C&TC 2016 (Cloud and Trusted Computing), and ODBASE 2016 (Ontologies, Databases, and Applications of Semantics).

Executive Committee

General Co-chairs

Robert Meersman	TU Graz, Austria
Tharam Dillon	La Trobe University, Melbourne, Australia
Hervé Panetto	University of Lorraine, France
Ernesto Damiani	Politecnico di Milano, Italy

EI2N Program Co-chairs

Mario Lezoche	University of Lorraine, France
Ovidiu Noran	Griffith University, Australia
Eduardo Portela	Pontifical Catholic University of Parana, Curitiba, Brazil
Georg Weichhart	Profactor GmbH, Steyr, Austria
	Johannes Kepler University, Linz, Austria

FBM Program Co-chairs

Robert Meersman	T.U. Graz, Austria
Peter Bollen	University of Maastricht, The Netherlands
Hans Mulder	University of Antwerp, Belgium
Maurice Nijssen	PNA, The Netherlands

Industry Case Studies Program Chairs

Hervé Panetto	University of Lorraine, France

Meta4eS Program Co-chairs

Anna Fensel	STI Innsbruck, University of Innsbruck, Austria
Ioana Ciuciu	University of Babes-Bolyai Cluj-Napoca, Romania

OnTheMove Academy Dean

Erich Neuhold	University of Vienna, Austria

OnTheMove Organizing Chairs

Peter Spyns   Flemish Department of Economy, Science and Innovation,
                   Belgium
Maria-Esther Vidal Fraunhofer IAIS, Sankt Augustin, Germany
                   Universidad Simon Bolivar, Caracas, Venezuela

Local Organization Chair

Stefanos Gritzalis University of the Aegean, Greece

Publication Chair

Christophe Debruyne Trinity College Dublin, Ireland

Logistics Team

Daniel Meersman

EI2N 2016 Program Committee

Agostino Villa
Alexis Aubry
Andres Garcia Higuera
Angel Ortiz Bas
Cesare Fantuzzi
Charlotta Johnsson
David Chen
David Romero Diaz
Dimitris Askounis
Eduardo Rocha Loures
Erik Proper
Esma Yahia
Fenareti Lampathaki
François B. Vernadat
Georg Grossmann
Georg Weichhart
Hamideh Afsarmanesh
Hervé Panetto
Istvan Mezgár
Ivan Lukovic
Janusz Szpytko
Juan-Carlos Mendez
Julio Cesar Nardi
Lea Kutvonen
Luis Camarinha-Matos

Marek Wegrzyn
Mario Lezoche
Martin Zelm
Michele Dassisti
Milan Zdravkovic
Miroslav Trajanovic
Nacer Boudjlida
Nenad Stefanovic
Ovidiu Noran
Peter Bernus
Qing Li
Qing-Shan Jia
Radu Emil Precup
Rafael Batres
Raul Poler
Ricardo Jardim Goncalves
Richard Soley
Ted Goranson
Udo Kannengiesser
Ulrich Jumar
Ulrike Lechner
Vincent Chapurlat
Xiaofan Wang
Yannick Naudet
Yannis Charalabidis

FBM 2016 Program Committee

Roel Baardman
Ed Barkmeyer
Roel Baardman
Herman Balsters
Ed Barkmeyer
Hans van Bommel
Peter Bollen
Cory Casanave
Matthew Curland
David Cuyler
Robert van Doesburg
Diederik Dulfer
Harald Eisenmann
Tom van Engers
Gordon Everest
William Frank
Pat Hallock
Terry Halpin
Clifford Heath
Stijn Hoppenbrouwers
Paul Iske
Mustafa Jarrar
Inge Lemmens
Dirk van der Linden
Mariette Lokin
Robert Meersman

Tony Morgan
Hans Mulder
Ellen Munthe-Kaas
David Newman
Maurice Nijssen
Sjir Nijssen
Leo Obrst
Baba Piprani
Erik Proper
Mark von Rosing
Jos Rozendaal
Pierre Schlag
Robert Schmaal
Hayo Schreijer
John Sowa
Peter Spyns
Peter Straatsma
Serge Valera
Jan Vanthienen
Jos Vos
Adrian Walker
Matthew West
Jan Pieter Wijbenga
Yan Tang
Martijn Zoet

Meta4eS 2016 Program Committee

Adrian M.P. Brasoveanu
Andrea Ko
Anna Fensel
Camelia-M. Pintea
Christophe Debruyne
Christophe Roche
Constantin Orasan
Fouad Zablith

Ioana Ciuciu
Jorge Martinez-Gil
Magali Séguran
Maria Poveda Villalón
Peter Spyns
Vikash Kumar
Vladimir Alexiev

ICSP 2016 Program Committee

Vasco Amaral
Gash Bhullar
Christoph Bussler
Luis Camarinha-Matos
Yannis Charalabidis
Francesco Danza
Michele Dassisti
Giancarlo Fortino
Andres Garcia Higuera
Pascal Gendre
Ricardo Goncalves
Ted Goranson
Mattew Hause
Mathias Kohler

Peter Loos
Eduardo Loures
Juan-Carlos Mendez
Arturo Molina
Yannick Naudet
Hervé Panetto
Sobah Abbas Pertersen
Joe Salvo
Daniel Sáez Domingo
Jean Simao
François B. Vernadat
Lawrence Whitman
Milan Zdravkovic

OTMA 2016 Program Committee

Christoph Bussler
Claudia d'Amato
Claudia Jiménez
Erich J. Neuhold
Erik Proper
Frédéric Le Mouël
Galia Angelova

Hervé Panetto
Manu De Backer
Maria-Esther Vidal
Paolo Ceravolo
Peter Spyns
Rik Eshuis
Rudi Studer

Keynotes

Challenges and Trends for Next Generation Enterprise Information Systems

François Vernadat[1,2]

[1] LGIPM, University of Lorraine, Nancy, France
[2] European Institutions, Luxembourg, Luxembourg

Short Bio

Dr François Vernadat has been a research officer, first at the National Research Council of Canada (NRCC), Ottawa, in the 80's and then at the Institut National de Recherche en Informatique et Automatique (INRIA), France, in the 90's. Since 1995 he has been a professor at the University of Metz in France in automatic control and industrial engineering. At the end of 2001, he joined the European Commission, DG Eurostat in Luxemburg, as project manager in the IT Directorate and then DG Informatics (DIGIT). In 2008 he moved to the European Court of Auditors in Luxemburg, another European institution, where he is currently the head of the Information Systems and Methods (ISM) unit. His research work has been dealing with enterprise architectures, enterprise modelling and integration, information systems design and analysis, CIM and various aspects of industrial engineering (facility layout, performance evaluation, cost estimation, competency modelling and value-risk management). He has lectured in many countries in Europe, North, Latin and South America, China and North Africa. He has consulted several large and medium-sized companies in France and Canada (automotive industry, aeronautics industry, and software houses). He is the author of over 285 scientific papers in journals, conferences, and edited books. He is the author of the textbook "Enterprise Modeling and Integration: Principles and Applications", co-author of the book "Practice of Petri nets in Manufacturing" and co-editor of the book "Integrated Manufacturing Systems Engineering", all published by Chapman & Hall. He is adviser for International Journal of Computer Integrated Manufacturing, associate editor for Computers in Industry, International Journal of Production Research, Enterprise Information Systems, and is on the editorial board of Computers and Industrial Engineering. He served as vice-chairman several technical committees of the IFAC, has been a member of IEEE and ACM and he has been chairman or vice-chairman of several international conferences on industrial engineering.

Talk

Since year 2000, nearly all corporate software vendor packages, many international research projects and a growing number of practical implementations have shown considerable progress in the area of Enterprise Information Systems, but such advances have also come with new challenges for the scientific community, especially regarding Information and Communication Technologies (ICTs), which are at the core of new developments and digital megatrends.

Indeed, SOA and Internet technologies, Enterprise Architecture Frameworks, Enterprise Modelling frameworks and tools as well as Enterprise Integration, Interoperability and Networking approaches and now Cloud Computing solutions have been continuously and rapidly evolving. The main driver has been to cope with emerging collaborative organizations in the industry and society, from the intra-organizational level to the inter-organizational level and up to the global landscape. In addition, future developments of Enterprise Information Systems in different emerging domains and application environments require the identification well in advance of challenges and trends to establish timely research roadmaps for researchers and a sound business vision for top managers and leading practitioners to enable the development of efficient EIS solutions in practice.

The next generation of Enterprise Information Systems will continue emphasizing the need for scalable, reliable, extensible, flexible, highly available and maintainable system architectures with new technologies, models and solutions. The aim is to provide ubiquitous, plug-and-play and secure integration, interoperability and networking solutions to realize collaborative systems, platforms and ICT infrastructures for all entities operating in a common business ecosystem.

The talk will present a synthesis of future trends and emerging key research challenges identified in the preparation of a Special Issue on Next Generation Enterprise Information Systems recently published in Computers in Industry.

Towards Multi-layer Interoperability of IoT Platforms: The INTER-IoT Approach

Giancarlo Fortino

University of Calabria, Rende, Italy

Short Bio

Giancarlo Fortino (SM'12) received the Laurea (B.S and M.S) and Ph.D in computer engineering from the University of Calabria, Italy, in 1995 and 2000, respectively. He is currently an Associate Professor of Computer Engineering (since 2006) with the Department of Informatics, Modeling, Electronics and Systems (DIMES), University of Calabria. He holds the Scientific Italian Habilitation for Full Professor and he is also Adjunct Full Professor of Computer Engineering at Wuhan University of Technology in the framework of High-End Foreign Experts in China and adjunct senior researcher at Italian National Research Council. He authored about 300 publications in journals, conferences, and books. He is currently the Scientific and Technical Project Manager of the EU-funded H2020 INTER-IoT project on heterogeneous IoT platform interoperability. His research interests include distributed computing, wireless sensor networks, body area networks, software agents, IoT technology, cloud computing. He is an associate editor of IEEE Trans. on Affective Computing, IEEE Trans. on Human-Machine Systems, Information Fusion, Engineering Application of Artificial Intelligence, Journal of Network and Computer Applications. He is founding co-chair of SMC TC on Interactive and Wearable Computing and Devices and is the Chair of the Italian Chapter of the IEEE SMC Society. He is co-founder and CEO of SenSysCal S.r.l., a spin-off of University of Calabria, engaged in advanced applied research and development of IoT systems.

Talk

While still in his infancy, the IoT domain already lists a number of solutions implemented, ranging from simple devices to full-fledged platforms. However, the heterogeneity at all levels (device, networking, middleware, services, data and semantics) of those solutions is preventing different systems to interoperate effectively, despite significant efforts in the development of a unique reference standard for IoT systems technology. The situation is likely to worsen in the near future, as lack of interoperability will cause major technological and business-oriented issues such as impossibility to plug non-interoperable IoT devices into heterogeneous IoT platforms, impossibility to develop IoT applications exploiting multiple platforms in homogeneous and/or cross domains, slowness of IoT technology introduction at large-scale, discouragement in adopting IoT technology, increase of costs, scarce reusability of technical solutions, and user dissatisfaction. This keynote will aim at analyzing such lack of interoperability in the IoT realm by proposing, as effective solution, the INTER-IoT approach that is being developed in our EU-funded H2020 project. In particular, first the keynote will provide the state-of-the-art of research- and standard-oriented approaches (including AIOTI and IEEE P2413); then, it will focus on the current status of the "products" of INTER-IoT granting multi-layer interoperability and IoT platform integration: INTER-LAYER, INTER-FW, and INTER-METH. Finally, we present two case studies in which our solutions will be tested: INTER-Health (interoperability among e-Health platforms) and INTER-LogP (interoperability in port logistics).

Data Processing in the Cloud:
Current Solutions and Future Challenges –
An Industry Perspective

Patrick McLaughlin

Oracle, Galway, Ireland

Short Bio

Patrick McLaughlin is an Oracle Fellow specialising in Information Security for Oracle across EMEA. He has over fifteen years experience in IT security. He is responsible for promoting Oracle's security offerings and enterprise solutions architecture, internally across the Oracle pre-sales, sales and consulting, and externally with major customers and partners across EMEA. Most recently he has been working on security of Cloud, Mobile and Big data.

Prior to this role Patrick was CTO at Baltimore Technologies, where he was product architect for Baltimore's PKI product and cryptographic toolkits. He also had responsibility for company R&D, technology partnering and working with lead customers in government and finance. Patrick has worked as an independent consultant for several years and has extensive experience in the distributed systems and telecoms management areas, having worked for Broadcom Éireann Research and Ericsson for ten years.

Talk

There is no doubt that significant amounts of data processing are moving from on-premise data-centers to using public cloud services. This is especially true for new "digital" applications that aim to deliver a great and compelling customer experience. At the same time we are living in an era of mega-databreaches and increasing regulations coming from industries and from government organisations.

This presentation will talk about what Oracle's experience is in relation to cloud in general and cloud security specifically outlining how we secure IAAS and PAAS, including the split of responsibilities with our customers. The talk will conclude by setting some challenges for the research community in relation to data technology in general and discuss the Nirvana for cyber-security in particular.

Security Applications of GPUs

Sotiris Ioannidis

Institute of Computer Science,
Foundation for Research and Technology – Hellas, Crete, Greece

Short Bio

Dr. Sotiris Ioannidis received a BSc degree in Mathematics and an MSc degree in Computer Science from the University of Crete in 1994 and 1996 respectively. In 1998 he received an MSc degree in Computer Science from the University of Rochester and in 2005 he received his PhD from the University of Pennsylvania. Ioannidis held a Research Scholar position at the Stevens Institute of Technology until 2007 and since then he is a Principal Researcher at the Institute of Computer Science of the Foundation for Research and Technology - Hellas. His research interests are in the area of systems and network security, security policy, privacy and high-speed networks. Ioannidis has authored more than 100 publications in international conferences and journals, as well as book chapters, and has both chaired and served in numerous program committees in prestigious conferences, such as ACM CCS, IEEE S&P, etc. Ioannidis is a Marie-Curie Fellow and has participated in numerous international and European projects. He has coordinated several European and National projects (e.g. PASS, EU-INCOOP, GANDALF, etc.), and is currently the coordinator of SHARCS, a H2020 European project.

Talk

Modern graphics processors have been traditionally used for gaming, but in the last few years they have been used more and more in the area of high performance computing. In this talk we will explore alternate uses of graphics processors, in the area of security. We will discuss how a defender can use graphics hardware to bolster system defenses, and how miscreants can exploit them to build better and stealthier malware.

Contents

Fact Based Modeling (FBM) 2016

Industry Case Studies Program (ICSP) 2016

International Workshop on Methods, Evaluation, Tools and Applications for the Creation and Consumption of Structured Data for the e-Society (Meta4eS) 2016

OnTheMove Academy (OTMA) 2016

International Workshop on Enterprise Integration, Interoperability and Networking (EI2N) 2016

EI2N 2016 PC Co-chairs' Message

In 2016 the 11th edition of the Enterprise Integration, Interoperability and Networking workshop (EI2N'2016) has been organised as part of the On The Move Federated Conferences (OTM'2016) in Rhodes, Greece. The workshop has established itself as a major interactive event for researchers exchanging ideas in the context of organisations and information technologies. This is shown by the long list of groups and committees that support this event.

This year, the workshop is co-sponsored by IFAC and supported by IFIP. In particular, IFIP's Technical Committee 5.3 "Enterprise Integration and Networking" (main sponsor) and IFAC TC 3.1, 3.2, 3.3, 5.2, 5.4 and 9.5 have shown their interest in this workshop. Also a number of IFIP Work Groups 8.1, 5.12, 5.8 support this workshop. Additionally, the SIG INTEROP Grande-Région on "Enterprise Systems Interoperability", the French CNRS National Research Group GDR MACS, the Greek Centre on Interoperability, and the industrial internet consortium have announced their interest in EI2N and support.

Today's rapidly evolving global economy has reiterated the urgent need to achieve dynamic, efficient and effective cooperation of partner organizations within networks of enterprises. Enterprises must collaborate and adapt in order to prosper in the current dynamic and heterogeneous business environment while meeting the sustainability requirements of present times. This in turn requires a substantial improvement of existing frameworks and technologies, along with the exploration of innovative theories and the development of new methods enabling the interaction of the emerging adaptive organisational and technical systems. Enterprise integration, interoperability and networking are major disciplines studying collaborative and communicative enterprise systems. Enterprise Modelling Techniques, Next Generation Computing Architectures and Socio-technical Platforms along with Semantic Interoperability approaches are essential pillars supporting the networked and adaptive enterprise system.

For EI2N'2016 19 papers have been received. After a rigorous review process 10 papers have been accepted. Every submitted paper was evaluated by at least two members of the program committee. Due to the quality, we have decided to include all 10 papers as long papers in the proceedings. For the first time, accepted papers will be made available in pre-proceedings. After the OTM workshops authors are able to revise their papers and include feedback from the interactive sessions in their work.

With respect to interactivity, EI2N will host a highly interactive session called "Workshop Café". This special session is now an integral part of EI2N since many years. The outcomes of these discussions will be reported during a plenary session jointly organized with the CoopIS and the OTM Industry Case Studies Program, in order to share topics and issues for future research with a larger group of experts and scientists.

We would like to thank the authors, international program committee, sponsors, supporters and our colleagues from the OTM organising team who have together contributed to the continuing success of this workshop. We welcome all attendees and participants and look forward to an enthusiastic exchange of ideas and thoughts for the progress of science at the workshop.

October 2016

Mario Lezoche
Ovidiu Noran
Eduardo Portela
Georg Weichhart

Service Oriented Collaborative Simulation in Concept and Design Stages: Framework and Enabling Technologies

Qing Li[✉], Dachuan Li, and Zhichao Cao

Department of Automation, Tsinghua University, Beijing 100084, People's Republic of China
liqing@tsinghua.edu.cn

Abstract. With the continually reducing of research and development time and cost, large-scale complex products design and development depends on powerful and flexible tools to validate, verify and test its results. A flexible and scalable simulation framework is needed to support research, design, test, function extension and new technology implementation, especially for the product definition, system definition and equipment definition stages in complex product development projects. To address these requirements, the service oriented simulation framework is developed. Some enabling technologies including simulation unit service, simulation orchestration, simulation process monitoring and control are developed. The prototype implementation of the simulation system and the simulation results of an AFMS/Autoflight system are given. Both the effectiveness and flexibility of the technology developed in the paper are confirmed.

Keywords: Service oriented, cloud computing · Collaborative simulation · Research and development

1 Introduction

High fidelity simulation is an important way to test product, system, equipment and component designs and interrelated technologies prior to their deployment in real hardware and real operation environments. However, complex products usually include plenty of complex equipment and components, and these equipment and components interact with each other tightly and complicatedly. Because these functions are developed by different design teams, how to design and simulate their relation logics becomes a great challenge. Currently, modelling and simulations of complex products meet the following requirements:

(1) Concept and definition stage supported.
(2) Scalability and flexibility.
(3) Reusability and reconfiguration capability.
(4) Technological secrets protection.

Due to the complexity of large scale complex products, and the requirement to have a high fine-gained, high–fidelity simulation, applying distributed simulation architecture and technologies to product and system simulations have become the trend.

I. Ciuciu et al. (Eds.): OTM 2016 Workshops, LNCS 10034, pp. 5–15, 2017.
DOI: 10.1007/978-3-319-55961-2_1

Currently, the DIS (distributed interactive simulation) and HLA (high level architecture) are the most widely used schemes for complex system simulation. However, the DIS/HLA does not prescribe any specific implementation of federations with particular software or programming language. Therefore, the DIS/HLA is more applicable for discrete-event-based, loosely-coupled, functionally- and regionally-distributed simulation problems. In contrast, simulations of product systems have functionally distributed architecture with both loosely-coupled and tightly-coupled continuous components. Furthermore, the DIS/HLA does not provide enough support for the description and modelling of complex, intelligent simulation entities. Therefore, applying DIS/HLA to the simulation of complex products, especially in the stage of specification may cause additional complexity and extra efforts on the design and description of simulation federations and RTI (Run Time Interface) protocols.

SOA, as an enterprise application integration (EAI) pattern and infrastructure, is developed to solve some problems of enterprise infrastructure, as well as ASP (application service provider). Cloud computing is the extension of ASP and SOA. It is Internet-based computing, with which resources, software, and information are shared among computers and other devices based on their demand. As shown in Fig. 1, comparing large scale product simulation requirements with characteristics of cloud computing, some combination points can be concluded. Cloud computing can present a high reliable and available environment for complex product development. Taking an AFMS/Autoflight system simulation as the example, comparisons between different system architectures are outlined in Table 1.

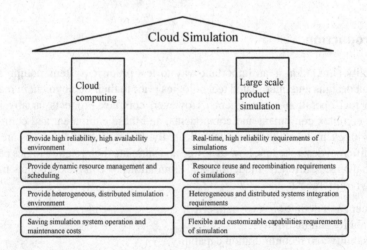

Fig. 1. Comparison of cloud computing and complex product simulation

Table 1. Comparisons of simulation architectures in the field of AFMS/Autoflight systems

System architecture	Advantages	Disadvantages	Fields of application
Flight-qualified components based architecture	●High compatibility ●High fidelity	●Low flexibility ●Low scalability ●Low reusability	Integration and testing of new hardware and prototypes
DIS/HLA	●Interoperability ●Scalability ●Reusability	●Deficiency in description and modelling of complex simulation entities ●Low reconfiguration capability	Large scale, discrete-event- based, loosely-coupled, functionally and regionally distributed simulation scenarios
Cloud simulation	●Flexibility ●Scalability ●Reusability ●Reconfiguration capability ●Standardised communication and platform	Cloud computing does not consider about real time requirements	Simulation blocks can be encapsulated as service and reduce cost of stimulators development. Simulation can be constructed in design and development stages

This paper presents a simulation architecture for complex products design and development based on cloud computing and service oriented technology. Firstly, a service and cloud computing based simulation architecture is developed. Secondly, two key enabling technologies are discussed in detailed: simulation unit service and simulation orchestration. Finally, an AFMS/Autoflight system simulation is discussed as the cases study.

2   Service and Cloud Computing Based Simulation Architecture

The scheme of service and cloud computing based distributed simulation platform (SCS-P) is shown in Fig. 2. In the scheme, some principles of cloud communication are embodied [2]:

(1) System development and simulation for a technical field or team is divided into two stages. At first the target component or subsystem shall be designed and the related simulation unit shall be developed. Then the simulation unit is deployed on the SCS-P. Secondly, a simulation flow is developed to link the new developed simulation unit or units of related subsystems. The simulation flow is also deployed on SCS-P. Running the simulation flow, it accesses and calls simulation units with designed logic order, and return the simulation result.

(2) Some simulation units are encapsulated as services, which can be accessed by multiple subsystems. If a simulation unit is related only one or few subsystems, it can be deployed on its simulation environment and be accessed through simulation agent.

(3) All simulation services or units are occupied and controlled by their designers or developers, and their access APIs are published and opened to partner design teams.

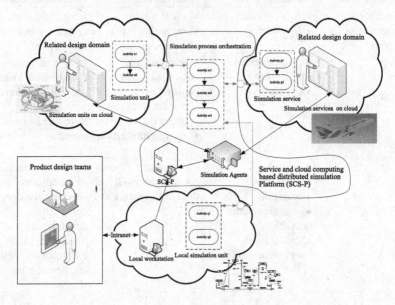

Fig. 2. Simulation mechanism among different design domains and design teams

In order to realize the simulation scheme shown in Fig. 2, some new enabling technologies should be developed:

(1) Simulation unit service encapsulation technology;
(2) Simulation agent technology;
(3) Simulation process modelling and orchestration technology.

As shown in Fig. 3, in order to simulate relative logics of a system, simulation process modelling and deployment is introduced into, which divides simulation system into subsystem simulation units and system intra relationship simulation two parts. The method can simplify simulation frameworks and provide the flexibility of multi-configuration simulation.

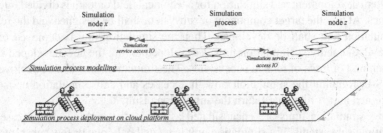

Fig. 3. Simulation process orchestration and deployment

The framework of SCS-P is shown in Fig. 4. Based on service technology and cloud computing architecture, there are seven major sets of applications in this platform, namely Runtime Environment, Execution Component, Simulation Agents, Simulation Agent Management, User Interface, Simulation Integration Tools and Simulation Management Tools [1, 2].

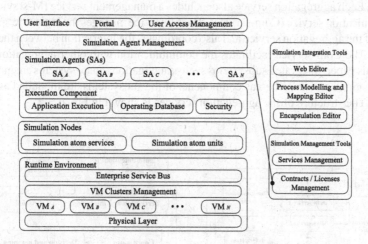

Fig. 4. Framework of service and cloud computing based simulation platform (SCS-P)

The hierarchical structure of cloud computing based simulation platform is shown in Fig. 5. Simulation services can be deployed on ESB of SCS-P. Simulation units can be installed on different VMs and accessed through simulation agents (SAs).

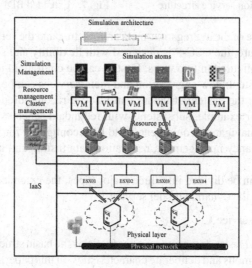

Fig. 5. Hierarchical structure of cloud computing based simulation platform

3   Simulation Unit Service

The SCS-P framework consists of two levels: the aggregation level and the meta-level. The aggregation service is formed by several cooperating or independent meta-services. Meta-services in the same aggregation service share an information environment and a database. Each aggregation service also includes a management service (M-service) and a communication service (Com-service). The M-service manages the logic flow and task control of the aggregation service and also coordinates the interaction between the meta-services. The Com-service facilitates the communication with other aggregation services. In this paper, integrated subsystems such as navigation sensor systems are modelled as aggregation services, whereas components of the subsystems are modelled as meta-services. The structure of the aggregation services is shown in Fig. 6.

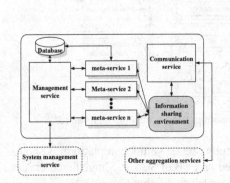

Fig. 6. Aggregation service structure   **Fig. 7.** Extended BDI service structure

Taking advantage of the aggregation-meta architecture and the service management/configuration structure, the CSC-P is designed with flexibility and scalability, and the system can be reconfigured in two ways: First, it can be configured to make functional extensions to the system: new aggregation and meta-services can be implemented into the system. Second, the system structure can also be reconfigured to fulfil different simulation tasks. For example, subsystems with redundant schemes such as the flight control system and navigation equipment could be reconfigured for various functional tests such as redundancy management, navigation data fusion, and fault tolerant flight control.

Meta-services can be divided into three major types: the extended BDI service, the reactive service and the dynamic model service.

(1) Extended BDI service

The BDI (Belief, Desire, Intension) service model is the basic structure for modelling systems with autonomous and deliberate characteristics. In this paper, the basic structure of BDI is extended to improve system flexibility and fast reconfiguration capabilities. The structure of the extended BDI model is outlined in Fig. 7. The service model management and configuration module, along with the coordinator module, function as the core engine for service model management, simulation and operation control functions. They also provide reconfiguration capabilities for the system.

(2) Reactive service

The reactive service acts directly on the changes in the external environment [1]. A reactive service perceives the outer environment and performs actions which effect the environment according to the inner condition - action rules, or changes its own inner knowledge and states. In this paper, components with reactive characteristics such as actuators are modelled as simple reactive services (Fig. 8).

(3) Dynamic model service

The dynamic model service provides storage mechanism for data - based models and dynamic procedures such as aircraft dynamics, actuators and engines. The basic structure is outlined in Fig. 9. The knowledge base stores the data relating to the model. The service model configuration interface manages and has full authority on the knowledge, and it interfaces with the system management aggregation to facilitate model management and reconfiguration functions (e.g. the user may select different aircraft models, or add/remove models). The processing engine performs calculations such as mathematical operations, table lookups and other combined calculations. The aircraft dynamics model, the engine model, the actuators model and the meteorological model are implemented through the dynamic model service structure.

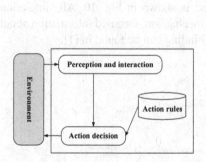

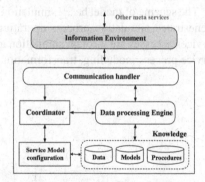

Fig. 8. Reactive service structure   **Fig. 9.** Dynamic model service structure

The communication between aggregation services occurs at regular intervals during the simulation progress. As shown in Fig. 6, each aggregation service executes certain actions independently or reactively using the perceived information from other services and provides output information to the environment. However, communication between meta-services is quite different. Normally, meta-services in the same aggregation act at different simulation paces and usually make use of (or make changes to) the same information and parameters. Therefore, it will be efficient for the meta-services in the same aggregation service to communicate through information sharing. For example, the meta-services inside the flight management service share the flight plan/trajectory buffer (environment). Meta-services which belong to different aggregation services exchange information through the aggregation service first, and then perceive the information through the shared environment. That is because the communication between different meta-services usually changes in accordance to the progress of the simulation (e.g. the flight planning service only interacts with the MCDU service when the pilot modifies the flight plan), and the same information may have different forms in different aggregation services (e.g. the different coordination systems).

4   Simulation Orchestration and Control

Based on Model Driven Architecture (MDA), the simulation orchestration is divided into three levels. The first is simulation process model level, SCS-P provides the simulation process modelling tools to help users use the simulation atom entities to form the simulation process model, the simulation unit entity has function description, data input, control input and data output. The second level is computation and logical model level, in this level, SCS-P will map the process model into computation and logical model, it could be regarded as an instance for this simulation process, the simulation unit entity will be transformed into corresponding service inside SCS-P, which will be connected with corresponding simulation service, the data structure will also be formed and the control mechanism will be constructed. The third level is executive code level, the executive code will be automatically generated according to the computation and logical model, and finally be deployed on the platform.

The scheme of model based simulation services orchestration is shown in Fig. 2. The orchestrated simulation process operating logic is shown in Fig. 10. All simulation services accesses are through simulation agent mechanism. Detailed information about service process modelling, transformation and binding can be found in [1].

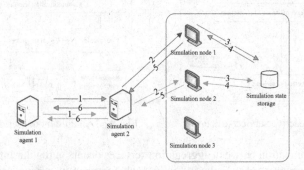

Fig. 10. Simulation service access mechanism

5   Cases Study

In order to validate the effectiveness of the system architecture and algorithms, a prototype of the FMS/Autoflight simulation system was developed and implemented. As show in Fig. 11, Advanced Flight Management System (AFMS)/Autoflight system's

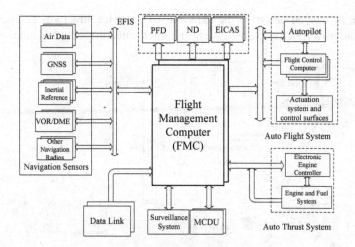

Fig. 11. AFMS/Autoflight system

hardware includes Flight Management System (FMS) computers, navigation sensors, and input/output equipment. It connects with auto flight control system and auto thrust control system. For the airborne com navigation, flight planning, trajectory prediction, performance function, and guidance. AFMS/Autoflight system is a tight coupled complex system developed by multiple developing teams collaboratively. Based on the SCS-P framework, the system is de-constructed as shown in Fig. 12.

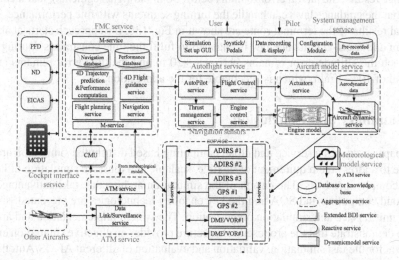

Fig. 12. Multi-service model of AFMS/Autoflight system

The flight management service consists of core functional modules of the FMS which are implemented as meta-services. The flight planning service, 4-D trajectory prediction and performance calculation service, 4-D flight guidance service, and the navigation service are developed based on the extended BDI service structure. The navigation database and performance database are also implemented in the aggregation service.

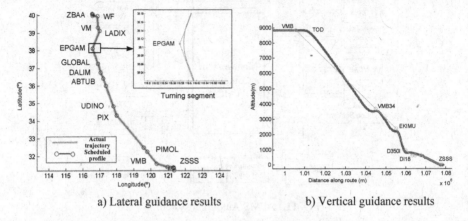

a) Lateral guidance results   b) Vertical guidance results

Fig. 13. Simulation results of the ZBAA-ZSSS route

The fundamental and advanced 4-D-based functionalities of the simulation system were intensively tested using various simulation scenarios based on different actual flight routes. In Fig. 13 typical simulation results of a 4-D route from ZBAA (Beijing Capital Airport) to ZSSS (Shanghai Hongqiao Airport) are depicted. Figure 13a shows the lateral guidance results; the lateral error remains below 50 m (straight segments), and it can be seen that the guidance laws can handle the turning segments with fine performance. The vertical results of the terminal route are shown in Fig. 13b; the approach starts at about 9000 m and the 4-D guidance law is engaged to fulfil the time constraints. During the approach the altitude error remains between ±20 m and the time error remains at an interval of 10 s~1 min, which is acceptable for the application.

6   Summary and Conclusion

This paper proposes a service and cloud computing based distributed simulation architecture to address the requirement of flexible, scalable and reusable simulation of large scare complex products. The design of the simulation architecture takes advantage of the cloud computing and SOA and the key enabling technologies are presented: simulation unit service and simulation orchestration. The system implementation and application demonstrate that the proposed architecture provides an effective simulation environment for the fast simulation, validation and evaluation of different AFMS/Autoflight system designs and functionalities with customized FMS configurations.

Acknowledgements. This work is sponsored by the China High-Tech 863 Program, No. 2001AA415340 and No. 2007AA04Z1A6, the China Natural Science Foundation, No. 61174168, the Aviation Science Foundation of China, No. 20100758002 and 20128058006.

References

1. Li, D.C., Li, Q., Cheng, N., Song, J.Y.: SOA-cloud computing based fast and scalable simulation architecture for advanced flight management system. Adv. Mater. Res. **1016**, 471–477 (2014)
2. Li, Q., Wang, Z.Y., Li, W.H., Li, J., Wang, C., Du, R.Y.: Applications integration in a hybrid cloud computing environment: modelling and platform. Enterp. Inf. Syst. **7**(3), 237–271 (2013)

Smart Manufacturing Standardization: Reference Model and Standards Framework

Qing Li[1(✉)], Hongzhen Jiang[1], Qianlin Tang[1], Yaotang Chen[1],
Jun Li[2], and Jian Zhou[2]

[1] Department of Automation, Tsinghua University,
Beijing 100084, People's Republic of China
liqing@tsinghua.edu.cn
[2] Electronic Technology Information Research Institute, MIIT,
Beijing 100040, People's Republic of China

Abstract. With the progress of world trade and globalization, and the development of information & communication technology (ICT) and industrial technology, manufacturing pattern and technology are now facing a turning point. In order to realize economic transformation, the Chinese government published China Manufacturing 2025 national strategy; German government published Industry 4.0; and American government proposed Re-industrialization and Industrial Internet. All of these mentioned strategies have a key topic: smart manufacturing. In order to present a systematic standard solution for smart manufacturing, standardization organizations of China, Germany and US published standards landscapes or roadmaps. This paper compares these smart manufacturing standardization architectures and methodology, develops a reference model for smart manufacturing standards development and implementation. At the end of the paper, a standards framework is presented.

Keywords: Smart manufacturing, industry 4.0 · Industrial internet · Standardization

1 Introduction

With the progress of world trade and globalization, and the development of information & communication technology (ICT) and industrial technology, manufacturing pattern and technology are facing a turning point. Lots of developed or developing countries published their national strategies to support their economic transformation, which include:

- Integration of Industrialization & Informatization (iI&I) and Manufacturing 2025 of China;
- Industry 4.0 of Germany;
- Re-industrialization and industrial internet of US.

In the past 30 years, the development of China's industrialization has made remarkable achievements, and China industrialization makes a great contribution to the global economic growth. As shown in Fig. 1, since the Chinese industrialization

© Springer International Publishing AG 2017
I. Ciuciu et al. (Eds.): OTM 2016 Workshops, LNCS 10034, pp. 16–25, 2017.
DOI: 10.1007/978-3-319-55961-2_2

process is accompanied with the informatization progress, it is neither feasible nor necessary for China to follow the traditional development pattern (i.e. realizing industrialization first and then informatization). China should grasp tremendous historic opportunity which is brought by the ICT rapid development. Two historical processes (informatization and industrialization) are promoted together and mutually in China.

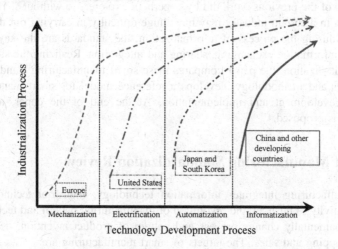

Fig. 1. Industrialization process with technology development process

Faced with the current complicated international and domestic economic situation and trends, the *i*I&I with smart manufacturing is a critical factor related to survival and long-term sustainability of Chinese enterprises. The *i*I&I in Chinese enterprises has its own characteristics. According to China's industrialization and ICT application status and shortcoming, in-depth exploration and practice should be started. In order to support manufacturing industry transformation, standardization is the important part of China's manufacturing technology development strategy, which includes several activities:

- Introducing and translating ISO/IEC standards into Chinese;
- Developing sets of technique standards;
- Developing standard framework for industrial enterprises;
- Develop management architecture and relative management standards.

German manufacturing industry and American manufacturing industry are facing the same transformation progress. In order to realize their national manufacturing development strategies, standardization landscapes were proposed. From this perspective, the significance of the standards is demonstrated.

Standards are the building blocks that provide for repeatable processes and the composition of different technological solutions to achieve a robust end result. With standards, business owners may be able to adopt technologies and innovations more easily. Also, standards raise innovations and can protect them, providing a sustainable environment for the smart manufacturing, which, to be specific, means standards make the goals through improve the reliability of the system, relevance of the market and the security of the investment.

Without the support of standards, the process of implementing ICT can be rough, which may be costly and cause overwhelming waste of manpower and material resources because of those repeat research and survey. Standards allow people to work on the basis of the previous work did by experts or explorer, so without standards, the green hands in a certain industry may have huge difficulty in carrying out their work. Especially, during the process of informatization, the standards are the key of effectiveness of information exchanging, sharing and integration. Realizing the significance of the standardization, the paper compares these smart manufacturing standardization architectures and methodology, develops a reference model for smart manufacturing standards development and implementation. At the end of the paper, a standard framework is proposed.

2   Smart Manufacturing Standardization Review

Smart manufacturing integrates information technology, industrial technology and human creativity to push a rapid revolution of manufacturing pattern and technologies. It will fundamentally change process and pattern of product invention, design, production, shipping and sales. The targets of smart manufacturing are:

- Improving worker safety;
- Protecting the environment;
- Keeping manufacturers competitive in the global marketplace.

Standardization is an important tool to achieve the goal of smart manufacturing. Some standardization organizations develop their roadmaps for smart manufacturing standardization, following are the most remarkable three:

- National Institute of Standards and Technology (NIST) published "Current Standards Landscape for Smart Manufacturing Systems" [1].
- DIN, DKE VDE published "German Standardization Roadmap Industry 4.0" [2].
- Ministry of Industry and Information technology of China (MIIT) and Standardization Administration of China (SAC) published a joint report "National Smart Manufacturing Standards Architecture Construction Guidance" [3].

In order to point out developing trends of smart manufacturing, classifying and positioning all relative standards and describe relationships among standards clusters, the three reports all introduce into reference models.

As shown in Fig. 2(a), based on ARC Advisory Group's collaboration manufacturing management model [4] and ISA95's enterprise – control system integration hierarchical model, NIST describes the smart manufacturing ecosystem. Based on the ecosystem model, NIST's standardization architecture includes 4 dimensions:

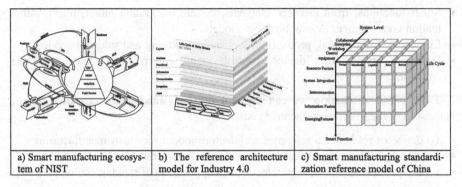

a) Smart manufacturing ecosystem of NIST	b) The reference architecture model for Industry 4.0	c) Smart manufacturing standardization reference model of China

Fig. 2. Smart manufacturing reference architectures

- Product: standards along the product lifecycle from design, process planning, production engineering, manufacturing, use & service, to EOL & recycling.
- Production: standards along the production system lifecycle from design, build, commission, operation & maintenance, to decommission & recycling.
- Business: standards through the supply chain cycle from plan, source, make, deliver to return.
- Manufacturing pyramid: standards aligned to the ISA95 model - enterprise level, manufacturing operations management (MOM) level, supervisory control and data acquisition (SCADA) level, device level and cross levels.

Some current standards related to smart manufacturing are classified and arranged into some standards groups along the four dimensions. NIST's report points out that current standards have not cover all areas of smart manufacturing.

The reference architecture model for Industry 4.0 is shown in Fig. 2(b). There are three dimensions to define the development directions of industry 4.0:

- Layers: from asset, integration, communication, information, functional, to business.
- Life cycle & value stream: from development to maintenance/usage which is defined by IEC 62890.
- Hierarchy levels: from product, field device, control device, station, work centers, enterprise, to connected world defined by ISO/IEC 62264 and IEC 61512.

Standards situation analysis, standard requirements analysis, and standard application analysis are discussed based on the reference model shown in Fig. 2(b).

In order to realize the Chinese Manufacturing 2025 national strategy, the Ministry of Industry and Information technology of China (MIIT) and Standardization Administration of China (SAC) published a joint report "National Smart Manufacturing Standards Architecture Construction Guidance". In the report, the Smart manufacturing standardization reference model of China is shown in Fig. 2(c). It includes three dimensions:

- Smart functions: from resource elements, system integration, interconnect, information convergence, to new business models.
- Life cycle: from design, production, logistics, marketing and sales, to service.
- Hierarchy levels: from device, control, plant, enterprise, to inter enterprise collaboration.

From above discussion we can get that the key standardization global design methodology for smart manufacturing is:

- To define or reference a reference architecture model for smart manufacturing.
- To classify and position standards in multiple dimension systems.
- To analyze current status, requirements, and application of standardization progress.

Although the three reports share some common ideas and similar concepts/elements, it is necessary to develop a general reference model for smart manufacturing standardization:

- A generalized reference model is needed to link the above mentioned reference models together to realize interoperation among these models.
- In the above mentioned reference models, standards are located on every dimension. How to develop and use standards cover two or three dimensions, especially in the NIST report, has not discussed in detail.
- There are different viewpoints for standards development and implementation, how to combine them together is a big challenge.
- For a manufacturing company, it is necessary to accept and apply a standard framework as a whole to support their smart manufacturing program. Therefore, how to describe standards clusters as a system is required.

Based on industrial models and system reference architectures, the paper develops a smart manufacturing standardization reference model and the relative framework.

3   Smart Manufacturing Standardization Reference Model

For a manufacturing enterprise, how to use smart manufacturing technology and management principles to link manufacturing processes together is the core consideration. Based on SIMA reference architecture Part 1 Activity model [5], which divides the ICT application process in an enterprise into Design Product, Engineering Manufacture or Product, Engineer Production System, Produce Products, and Manage Engineering Workflow, the reference model of ICT application along research, development, and manufacturing whole lifecycle is shown in Fig. 3, in which we can see main activities of research, development, and manufacturing, as well as ICT's supporting to these activities.

- For R&D activities, CAD, CAE, and CAPP are involved. CAD, CAE, CAPP and CAM are step by step interconnected and integrated. PDM is implemented to integrate all design applications together.
- For manufacturing activities, from physical layer, MES layer to business layer, multiple layers of the manufacturing pyramid shall be integrated.

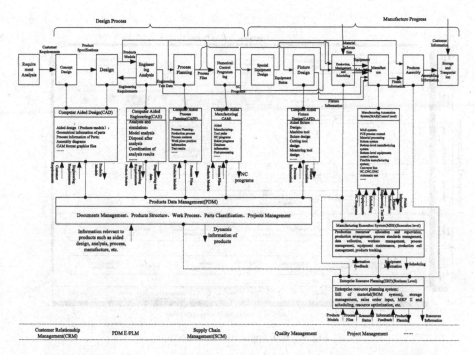

Fig. 3. ICT application relationship along R&D & manufacturing whole lifecycle

- For business operation activities, there are four information systems: enterprise resource planning (ERP), supply chain management (SCM), customer relationship management (CRM), and product lifecycle management (PLM). Some additional information systems, such as BI, are integrated with the four systems.

In order to guide ICT application and integration, it is necessary to analyse and describe relationship among technologies. From the viewpoint of ICT application, ICT application reference architecture model shall consider about requirements of enterprise collaboration and integration, and realize following two kinds of integration:

- From bottom level automation system, through manufacturing excursion system, to decision supporting. All layers of an enterprise shall be integrated, and then the integrated system shall be extended to integrate from suppliers to customers (the whole value chain), and realize inter enterprises collaboration.
- Because informatization relates to multiple enterprise business fields, including research, development, production, service, decision and so forth. ICT application reference architecture model shall consider the whole business/value chains.

Therefore, the analysis dimensions of ICT application architecture and reference model can be defined into two aspects as shown in Fig. 4:

- ICT application layers;
- Life cycle and value stream.

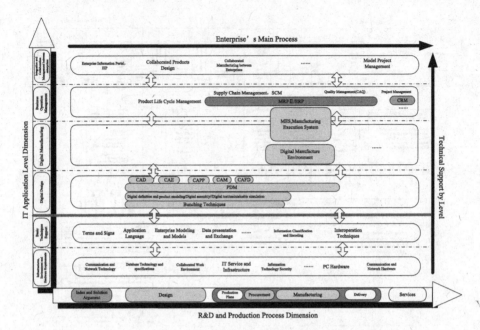

Fig. 4. ICT application architecture

In the Fig. 4, the first dimension relates to ICT application technologies and their functional hierarchical decomposition, which includes smart design technology, manufacturing technology, business operation and management technology, system integration technology, fundamental technology and supporting environment. The second dimension relates to product design and manufacturing whole life cycle, which includes solution argument, design, plan, purchase, production preparation, production, use and maintenance.

According to characteristics of standardization, Fig. 4 shall be adjusted as follows:

- The decomposition of technologies used by business operation and management is not based on current information systems (i.e. ERP, PLM, SCM, CRM and so forth), but based on management fields, which include design management, manufacturing management and business management. Thus can avoid focusing on information system commercial products and keep the relative stability of standardization framework. Application problems of information systems are classified into the combined management.
- Integration technologies are not located among functional technologies. For example, they are not classified as 3C integration, PDM & ERP integration. They are classified as integration interface, interoperability, integration platform and so forth based on the common properties of integration technologies.
- Manufacturing process is divided into production preparation and manufacturing excursion, supported by smart manufacturing environment.

Figure 5 is the resulted ICT application standardization reference model.

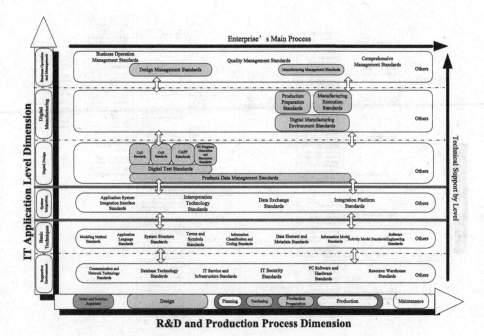

Fig. 5. ICT application standardization reference model

4   Smart Manufacturing Standard Framework

Based on the ICT application standardization reference model, the ICT application standards framework can be derived by methodology below:

- To derive the basic structure elements according to the application domain decomposition of ICT.
- To formulate the basic framework in two dimensions: ICT application layers and Life cycle/value stream.
- To locate the elements technology in the domain, integration technology, basic technology and support environment in the framework, and then determine the basic ICT standards.
- To build relevant standards according to those ICTs.
- To generate the detail branches iteratively.

So the ICT application standards framework can be derived, which is shown in Fig. 6.

- Smart design standards: the group of standards are expanded along the order of design activities, supported by data management standards. The standard framework decomposition does not follow the classification of design subjects.
- Smart production standards: the group of standards are expanded based on working process and technical supporting.

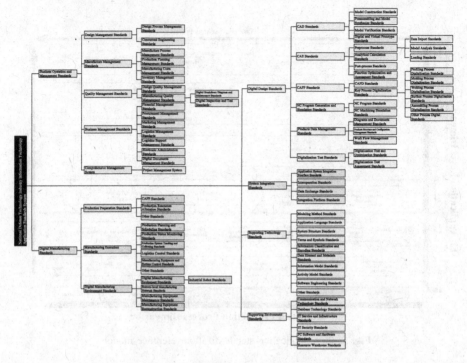

Fig. 6. ICT application standard framework

- Business operation and management standards: the group of standards are focused on management activities for design and production. ERP, SCR, CRM, MES, these commercial applications are not used as standards categories. Their implementation standards are discussed in combined management standard group.
- System integration standards: the group of standards relate to common technologies that integrate systems of different domains. They are classified based on technical types but integration software.
- Fundamental technologies and supporting environment standards: the group of standards includes standards on common supporting technologies, such as infrastructure, database, meta data technology and so forth.

5 Summary and Conclusion

Smart manufacturing is a systematic technology, which relates to ICT, industrial technology and management technology. Smart manufacturing system is a huge scale complex system. Standardization is a powerful tool to push the development and implementation of smart manufacturing technologies.

NIST, DIN, MIIT&SAC published standards landscape, standardization roadmap, or standardization construction guidance for smart manufacturing. Currently existing standards are arranged in relative reference model and reference standardization reference architecture. Based on results of these reports, the paper develops a reference model for smart manufacturing standards development and application. An ICT application standard framework is also developed.

Acknowledgements. This work is sponsored by the China High-Tech 863 Program, No. 2001AA415340 and No. 2007AA04Z1A6, the China Natural Science Foundation, No. 61174168, the Aviation Science Foundation of China, No. 20100758002 and 20128058006.

References

1. Lu, Y., Morris, K.C., Frechette, S.: Current Standards Landscape for Smart Manufacturing Systems. http://dx.doi.org/10.6028/NIST.IR.8107
2. DIN/DKE: German Standardization Roadmap Industry 4.0, Version 2. www.din.de
3. Ministry of Industry and Information technology of China (MIIT) and Standardization Administration of China (SAC). National Smart Manufacturing Standards Architecture Construction Guidance (in Chinese)
4. ARC Advisory Group: Collaborative Manufacturing Management Strategies (2002). ARCweb. com
5. Barkmeyer, E.J., et al.: NISTIR 5939: SIMA Reference Architecture Part 1: Activity Models. U.S. Department of Commerce, Technology Administration, National Institute of Standards and Technology

Integrated Performance Measurement for Optimization Networks in Smart Enterprises

Viktoria A. Hauder[1,2(✉)], Andreas Beham[1,3], and Stefan Wagner[1]

[1] Heuristic and Evolutionary Algorithms Laboratory, School of Informatics, Communications and Media, University of Applied Sciences Upper Austria, Hagenberg Campus, Hagenberg im Mühlkreis, Austria
{viktoria.hauder,andreas.beham,stefan.wagner}@fh-hagenberg.at
[2] Institute for Production and Logistics Management, Johannes Kepler University Linz, Linz, Austria
[3] Institute for Formal Models and Verification, Johannes Kepler University Linz, Linz, Austria

Abstract. Due to the current structural economic transformation towards smart production and logistics, a holistic and interactive connection between involved agents and departments becomes essential. Therefore, also in the field of operations research, an innovative approach of performance measurement is necessary to ensure increasing efficiency in smart enterprises. However, using traditional mathematical optimization methods, the isolated consideration of problem models can lead to high opportunity costs in other departments. In this paper, an integrated approach for measuring the performance of combined logistics optimization problems is presented. The connection of single problems is shown by proposing optimization networks (ON), where isolated problems are solved simultaneously to be able to use synergy effects. A methodology for measuring the results of an ON, called integrated performance measurement system (IPMS), is introduced. It monitors quantitative business goal achievement and ensures an overall increasing efficiency.

Keywords: Smart enterprise · Synergy effects · Production and logistics optimization networks · Integrated performance measurement

1 Introduction

Within the last few years, the term industry 4.0, described as the fourth industrial revolution, has increasingly coined the digital development of enterprises. One core aspect of this economic evolution are smart factories, which are especially characterized by resource efficiency and high adaptability [9]. In a smart factory, all involved systems change information in real-time, generate actions and monitor each others' activities [9]. This economic advancement comes along with a strong competitive environment, in which enterprises need to use possible synergy effects to be able to gain potential savings. By mathematical modeling and optimizing operations, it is possible to obtain quantitative improvements

I. Ciuciu et al. (Eds.): OTM 2016 Workshops, LNCS 10034, pp. 26–35, 2017.
DOI: 10.1007/978-3-319-55961-2_3

for organizations. However, a very good optimization result in one department can lead to very high opportunity costs in other ones, since operating cycles may have to be changed due to a precedent optimization. As in the past the focus of operations research was on the consideration of single problems, new problem models and solution methods are necessary to handle the increasing interconnection of all stakeholders and systems within a smart enterprise.

The approach described in this paper aims to combine interrelated production and logistics processes into one optimization network (ON), where problem models of different units are connected and mastered together. As a result, possible synergy effects can be used and opportunity costs are avoided. This interconnection of several problem models and its simultaneous optimization within a network in contrast to the traditional gradual procedure of optimization is illustrated in Fig. 1. Within an ON, every single optimization problem needs to be examined concerning its holistic integration into the network by measuring its performance. Since different departments are affected, a performance measurement for at least parts or even a whole organization is demanded. Therefore, an integrated performance measurement system (IPMS) for an ON is introduced, where not only single performance indicators but a holistic system for the measurement of an interconnected mathematical optimization is developed. With an IPMS, it is possible to increase company-wide efficiency by monitoring the strategic, predefined achievement of goals of every single problem model and of the whole ON.

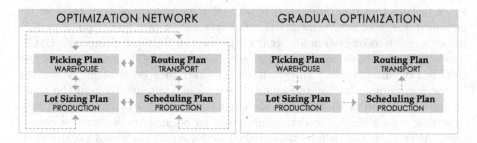

Fig. 1. Optimization networks and gradual optimization.

The article is organized as follows. First, related work concerning mathematical optimization and performance measurement is discussed in Sect. 2. This part is followed by the illustration of an optimization network in Sect. 3. Section 4 contains the development of an IPMS for a smart enterprise. Finally, Sect. 5 provides a conclusion and gives directions for further research.

2 Literature Review

There is a long history of algorithmic approaches concerning the optimization of industrial processes [5]. Examples of such problems include job shop scheduling, storage location assignment and vehicle routing, to name just a few [5]. The integration of different problem formulations is a very young discipline within operations research. Nonetheless it reveals additional optimization potential, as [1,11,12] show in their works. The combination of metaheuristics with mathematical programming, which leads to the development of matheuristics, also shows the possibility of delivering robust and high-quality results for integrated optimization [2,13].

To be able to bring optimization results of decision support systems into conformity with organizational goals, performance measurement is necessary [6,10]. Kotler [8] states that customers' needs and how they can be met more effectively and efficiently than competitors are able to, should always be the center of a company's performance. Neely et al. [10] describe that

- efficient actions are mainly observed as cost-reducing actions, such as financial key figures and
- effectiveness is very often related to the quality of actions, for example product liability or customer satisfaction.

The major goal of performance measurement is to increase performance transparency and as a result, supporting the improvement of effectiveness and efficiency of actions [10]. Within an organization, the performance of the whole company and not only of single departments is essential. Therefore, a PMS which is mostly used as an indicator system and a decision support management system, is required [10]. PMS use a framework which can be defined as a set of metrics that quantifies efficient and effective action and they monitor an organization's goal achievement [10]. One very well-known and popular performance measurement system for organizations is the Balanced Scorecard (BSC), developed and introduced by Kaplan and Norton [6,7]. The main goal of the BSC is a balanced view of an organization's controlling on strategic objectives by measuring quantitative and qualitative goal attainment. To fulfil the goals of assessment and of increasing transparency, they explain that the first step of setting up a PMS is the determination of an organization's strategic objectives. After that, the definition of wished performance goals and performance indicators is necessary. If goals and indicators' results do not correspond, the concerned management has to introduce change to ensure improvement in the achievement of the organization's goals.

3   Optimization Networks in Smart Enterprises

The traditional approach in operations research considers one optimization problem. It is modeled mathematically and solved with a heuristic or an exact algorithm. With the result of the first optimized problem model, another optimization problem can be elaborated, which corresponds to a gradual optimization process within an enterprise. On the contrary, with an optimization network, all existing optimization problems of production and logistics departments are modeled and integrated into one system and solved simultaneously.

Concerning the integration of several problem models into one optimization network, there are scientific contributions on the combination of two or three optimization problems, for example by Fuellerer et al. [3]. However, to the best of the authors' knowledge, there has not been established an optimization network for all major production and logistics optimization problems within an enterprise yet. Therefore, an innovative, conceptual approach for an optimization network for production and logistics is presented.

3.1   Introduction of an Optimization Network

The first step of introducing an ON is the modeling of the optimization problems. Within this process, new models are necessary as the formerly isolated considered problem models have to be connected. After that, new solution methods have to be found, since the interconnection of problem models needs algorithms which can master this new challenge. By connecting all models and implementing them together with the solution algorithms into one digital system, the optimization process can be started. All problems are optimized simultaneously and a data exchange starts between every model until a valid solution is found. The output of the optimization network is an optimized plan for every optimization problem.

In Fig. 2, an illustrative example of an optimization network for the departments warehouse, production and transport is presented. The models represent the problem models which are integrated in the ON. The bidirectional information flows between all problem models show the necessary exchange of data during every optimization run to come to the best possible solution of the optimization process. One could take for example the picking problem of the warehouse and the routing problem of the transport department. By the ongoing exchange of data it could be found out that the best solution for the picking problem as input for the routing problem leads to a routing plan solution which does not bring the best overall solution for the ON. This information is exchanged within the ON and a new optimization run is started. Various solutions of all problem models are tested and the best result for the ON can be found. With this form of modeling and integration of production and logistics optimization problems into one ON, synergy effects between departments can be used and thus, previously undiscovered savings can be generated.

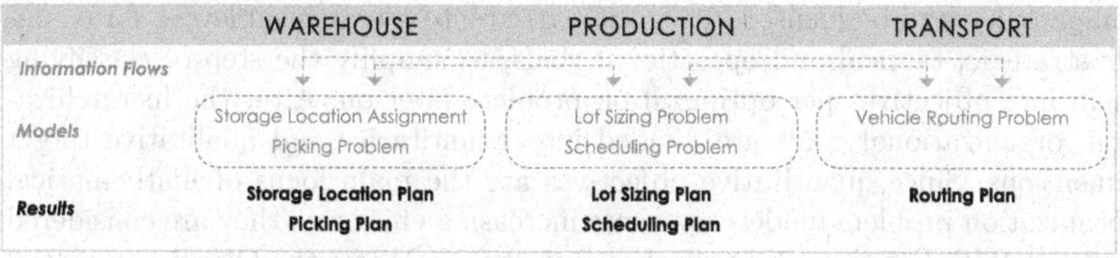

	WAREHOUSE	PRODUCTION	TRANSPORT
Information Flows			
Models	Storage Location Assignment Picking Problem	Lot Sizing Problem Scheduling Problem	Vehicle Routing Problem
Results	Storage Location Plan Picking Plan	Lot Sizing Plan Scheduling Plan	Routing Plan

Fig. 2. Optimization network for warehouse, production and transport.

3.2   Control and Implementation of an Optimization Network

Until now, the described optimization network has not been rolled out but is rather in a conceptional phase. In the current development stage, an orchestration for the whole optimization network has to be designed, since the finding of the overall best solution for the ON and therefore the highest possible efficiency should be guaranteed.

In this context, it should be mentioned that the complexity of a comprehensive optimization network for production and logistics problems and a related monitoring system requires the integration of both systems into one software. Moreover, other related sophisticated questions concerning the development of such a software like the required integration of data have to be considered. Due to the scope of this work, the challenge of data integration has just been mentioned for the sake of completeness but is not further described and discussed.

Concerning the addressed orchestration of an ON, algorithmic strategies for an overall monitoring have already been developed by Beham et al. [1]. However, an utterly new approach for the monitoring of an ON is the integration of a business performance measurement system into an optimization network, which is described in the following Sect. 4.

4   An Integrated Performance Measurement System for an Optimization Network in a Smart Enterprise

As explained in Sect. 2, the monitoring of an organization's goal achievement can be realized by using a performance measurement system, where actions of all departments of an enterprise are controlled and if necessary, improvement activities are introduced. Subsequently, the development of an integrated performance measurement system for an optimization network as a control system for the utilization of synergy effects is presented. Following this, possible control mechanisms of the proposed IPMS are described.

4.1   Development of an Integrated Performance Measurement System

For the introduction of an IPMS, first of all, defined business objectives of the company have to be focused. They are parted into hierarchical levels, for example strategic, tactical and operational goals, to simplify the step of classifying them into objectives per optimization problem later on. After the hierarchization, organizational goals are divided into quantitative and qualitative target dimensions. Since quantitative objectives are the main focus of mathematical optimization problem models to ensure increasing efficiency, they are considered for the IPMS. For the definition of quantitative goals for the ON, it is essential to regard the typical logistics target dimensions high capacity utilization, short processing times, low stock and adherence to schedules [4]. Moreover, resultant goal conflicts, such as the opposed targets of high utilization and low processing times have to be avoided [4]. Of course, for the future advancement of the system, also qualitative objectives have to be incorporated.

After an organization's objectives have been defined, the measurement of goal achievement of the ON has to be developed. For that reason, a framework for an organization-wide performance measurement of an optimization network is designed. All concerned departments of an enterprise and the categories for the measurement of the performance of the optimization problems are considered. Performance indicators are defined per category and department. In the developed framework for the IPMS in Fig. 3, production and logistics departments are divided in three sectors, namely warehouse, production and transport. The chosen performance categories time, utilization ratio, reliability and flexibility especially represent the mentioned logistics target dimensions. With costs, the target dimensions are additionally expressed through financial indicators. Similar categorization approaches can for example be found in [10].

- *Time:* The performance of the optimization network concerning punctual fulfilment of necessary actions and needed time for the performance of a resource (personnel, machines etc.) is shown.
- *Utilization Ratio:* All necessary actions and their effects on workload are presented.
- *Reliability:* Every department has an overall goal which it works for. Taking for example the department production, it should manufacture the required quantity of demanded goods within a demanded time slot. By reliability, the attainment of this overall goal per department is monitored.
- *Flexibility:* How many special orders can be handled beside the daily business, such as getting very short-term orders after a set order deadline.
- *Costs:* The development of costs per department in dependency of the optimization network's result is pointed out.

The methods shown in Fig. 3 which are necessary for the calculation of the indicators are described very generic, since they should be adoptable for enterprises in different markets and sectors. The divisor 'Process Variable' represents

Performance Category	Calculation Methods	WAREHOUSE	PRODUCTION	TRANSPORT
TIME	*Total Needed Time* / *Process Variable*	Average Picking Time	Average Lead Time	Average Transport Time
UTILIZATION RATIO	*Total Used Resources* / *Process Variable*	Resource Utilization Ratio	Average Set Up Processes Resource Utilization Ratio	Resource Utilization Ratio
RELIABILITY	*On-Time Processes* / *Process Variable*	Picking Reliability	Production Unit Reliability	Transport Reliability
FLEXIBILITY	*On-Time Special Processes* / *Process Variable*	Picking Flexibility	Production Flexibility	Transport Flexibility
COSTS	*Process Costs* / *Process Variable*	Picking Costs	Production Costs	Transport Costs

Fig. 3. A performance measurement framework for an optimization network.

a quantity, which can be decided by the company itself. This could be customer orders, pieces, lot sizes or when servicing customers by a vehicle, kilometers. Taking for instance the category 'Time' and the department 'Warehouse', the formula for the indicator 'Average Picking Time' could be 'Total Needed Picking Time per Day/Picked Pieces per Day'. The indicator's outcome would be the average needed picking time per day and per picked piece.

After having finalized the performance measurement framework, the optimization process and its integrated performance measurement can be initiated. The IPMS monitors the validity of the solution of every single problem model and the coherence between the models. The fundamental mechanism of an optimization network with an integrated performance measurement system is illustrated in Fig. 4 and described below in more detail.

Optimization Network: Firstly, the optimization network is started. All problem models are optimized simultaneously. The functions $w(x)$, $p(x)$ and $t(x)$ in Fig. 4 each represent one objective function of an optimization problem which has to be solved.

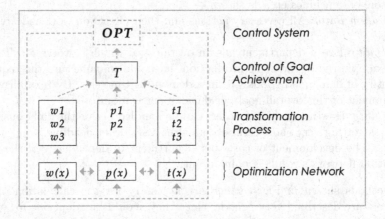

Fig. 4. An integrated performance measurement system for an optimization network.

Transformation Process: Defined quantitative management objectives have to be converted into target values per indicator on the basis of the developed performance measurement framework in Fig. 3. This can be realized by directly getting target value indicators of the management, for example determined picking costs of 0.15 monetary units per piece in the department warehouse. It is also possible to calculate the target values, for instance if the management's objectives contain a maximum total picking costs of 10.000 monetary units and a target throughput volume of 100,000 pieces, the target picking costs would be $10,000/100,000 = 0.1$ monetary units per piece.

As a next step, the results of the single optimization problem models of the ON have to be transformed into the categories of the performance measurement framework, such as time or utilization ratio. In Fig. 4, the concerned categories per problem model are represented by $w1, w2, w3$ and $p1, p2$ and $t1, t2, t3$. On the basis of this transformation, every single indicator is calculated with the defined formulas in Fig. 3.

Control of Goal Achievement: Within T, the performance of the ON is measured, as the calculated performance indicators are compared with the set target values. There have to be rules, which decide whether the comparison is satisfying or a new optimization run has to be initiated. It has to be decided what exactly can be changed within a next optimization run to achieve a new, different result. The design of such rules is discussed in Sect. 4.2, where possible control mechanisms of goal achievement are proposed.

Control System: If a new optimization run is necessary, this information is given from T to OPT. OPT is responsible for the initialization of the new run. After having a new result out of the new optimization run, the whole procedure starts again as described.

4.2 Possible Control Mechanisms

The introduced IPMS is an automated perspective on mathematical optimization and evaluates an ON's result. It initiates a new optimization run if efficiency criteria are not met. Two possible developed control mechanisms for the initialization of a new run are the change of problem data and the change of objective functions.

Control by Change of Problem Data: If the IPMS gets a solution of the ON which does not correspond to the measuring criteria, the problem data as input for the problem models for the next optimization run is changed within a pre-defined, allowed range. This preceding definition has to match management objectives. On the one hand, input data for objective functions can be changed, such as the distance, if it is subject of the minimization of a Vehicle Routing Problem (VRP). The distance could, for example be changed from length to time measurement. On the other hand, also parts of constraints of a problem model can be adopted. For these adoptions, the maximum available capacities have to be considered. An example would be a maximum number of five available vehicles for a VRP. If the belonging capacity constraint is provided with five vehicles for the first optimization run, the number of available vehicles can only be downgraded for the next run.

Control by Change of Objective Functions: All parts of an ON's objective functions are provided with target weights. The target weights are based on management decisions concerning the mentioned target dimensions in Subsect. 4.1. If the IPMS gets a solution of the ON which does not correspond to the predefined measuring criteria, the target weights have to be changed and a new optimization run has to be started. The allowed range within target weights can be modified, also depends on pre-defined decisions of the management. Thereby, an organization's management focus, for example a wished emphasis on high utilization ratio, can be directly implemented in the controlling process.

However, independent of the exact configuration of the control mechanism, it has to be considered how a mechanism reacts, if an already calculated plan which has just been executed is stopped due to stochastic influencing factors such as machine malfunctions. Within the optimization procedure, only the next two or three follow-up actions of the ON's result are shown. As a consequence, the problem of overchallenged staff due to often changing plans cannot arise. For the optimization process itself, such stops are considered within the next run. The optimization is restarted with the new, changed input factors, such as a reduced amount of available machines.

It is noted that beside the introduced IPMS, there is also the possibility of the control by manual problem modeling. The whole ON or parts of all models and algorithms are continually adopted to be able to consider every new environmental impact. However, the effort of a continous manual change of models and solution methods is very high and cost-intensive. Furthermore, production and logistics plans, especially on an operational level, are normally needed within a short period of time, especially when there are last-minute changes, which have to be considered. Therefore, it is in question if manual adoptions of parts of an automated process are quick enough to meet the requirements of the acteurs in a smart enterprise. Additionally, taking a closer look on this control mechanism, it will have to be examined if a complete engagement of all impacts is necessary.

5   Conclusion

In this work, an integrated performance measurement system for a production and logistics optimization network in a smart enterprise has been proposed. Within the network, all production and logistics departments are modeled and the demanded plans are computed. The introduced, automated IPMS is integrated into the ON and at the same time a meta control system. Synergy effects between departments are not only reached by linking optimization problem models but rather by the holistic consideration and implementation of organization-wide objectives.

The proposal has been discussed with an industrial partner as part of a project to achieve the transformation from a traditional, industrial manufacturer to a flexible, smart factory. The first step for the roll-out is the development of individual performance measures and its integration into their ERP system. Next, the ON is modeled and tested concerning its practical feasibility. Afterwards, the IPMS is connected with the ON by integrating both systems into their ERP system. Previous findings do not only show cost-saving effects through used synergies but also that such a system works as an automated management decision support system. Since the industrial partner is a big manufacturer with a lot of interrelated partners, also interoperability modeling developments are arising.

One future challenge will be the harmonization of diverging management objectives of different enterprises to be able to evolve an interoperability optimization network. In general, for future work the different presented control mechanisms of the proposed IPMS will have to be tested and evaluated. Moreover, an essential part will be the modification of the system for totally different economic sectors, where not only the models and algorithms of optimization networks, but also the approach of integrating an IPMS requires a lean, efficient development and modeling structure.

Acknowledgments. The work described in this paper was done within the COMET Project Heuristic Optimization in Production and Logistics (HOPL), #843532 funded by the Austrian Research Promotion Agency (FFG).

References

1. Beham, A., Fechter, J., Kommenda, M., Wagner, S., Winkler, S.M., Affenzeller, M.: Optimization strategies for integrated knapsack and traveling salesman problems. In: Moreno-Díaz, R., Pichler, F., Quesada-Arencibia, A. (eds.) EUROCAST 2015. LNCS, vol. 9520, pp. 359–366. Springer, Heidelberg (2015). doi:10.1007/978-3-319-27340-2_45
2. Doerner, K.F., Schmid, V.: Survey: matheuristics for rich vehicle routing problems. In: Blesa, M.J., Blum, C., Raidl, G., Roli, A., Sampels, M. (eds.) HM 2010. LNCS, vol. 6373, pp. 206–221. Springer, Heidelberg (2010). doi:10.1007/978-3-642-16054-7_15
3. Fuellerer, G., Doerner, K.F., Hartl, R.F., Iori, M.: Metaheuristics for vehicle routing problems with three-dimensional loading constraints. Eur. J. Oper. Res. **201**(3), 751–759 (2010)
4. Gudehus, T., Kotzab, H.: Comprehensive Logistics. Springer, Heidelberg (2012). SpringerLink: Bücher
5. Hillier, F.S.: Introduction to Operations Research. Tata McGraw-Hill Education, New York (2012)
6. Kaplan, R.S., Norton, D.P.: The balanced scorecard: measures that drive performance. Harvard Bus. Rev. **70**(1), 74–79 (1992)
7. Kaplan, R.S., Norton, D.P.: The Balanced Scorecard: Translating Strategy Into Action. Harvard Business Press, Brighton (1996)
8. Kotler, P.: Marketing Management: Analysis, Planning, Implementation, and Control. International Series in Marketing. Prentice Hall (1997). https://books.google.at/books?id=r5duSQAACAAJ
9. MacDougall, W.: Industrie 4.0: Smart Manufacturing for the Future. Germany Trade & Invest (2014)
10. Neely, A.: Business Performance Measurement: Theory and Practice. Cambridge University Press, Cambridge (2002)
11. Polyakovskiy, S., Bonyadi, M.R., Wagner, M., Michalewicz, Z., Neumann, F.: A comprehensive benchmark set and heuristics for the traveling thief problem. In: Proceedings of the 2014 Annual Conference on Genetic and Evolutionary Computation, pp. 477–484. ACM (2014)
12. Raggl, S., Fechter, J., Beham, A.: A dynamic multicommodity network flow problem for logistic networks (2015)
13. Tricoire, F., Doerner, K.F., Hartl, R.F., Iori, M.: Heuristic and exact algorithms for the multi-pile vehicle routing problem. OR Spectrum **33**(4), 931–959 (2011)

Interoperability Standards for Seamless Communication: An Analysis of Domain-Specific Initiatives

Claudia-Melania Chituc[(✉)]

Eindhoven University of Technology, Eindhoven, The Netherlands
C.M.Chituc@tue.nl

Abstract. Achieving seamless interoperability among heterogeneous communication systems and technologies is critical in todays' networked business world, ranging from joint collaborative military operations that need to exchange critical information in real-time, to complex e-business scenarios of organizations from different industry sectors using heterogeneous technologies and communication infrastructures to execute complex inter-organizational business processes. The aim of this article is to present a review of current domain-specific standardization initiatives towards seamless communication, discussing challenges and highlighting directions for further research and development work. This article has two main contributions. First, it provides an up-to-date review of the most relevant domain-specific standardization initiatives aiming at achieving seamless interoperability among communication systems. Second, by comparing these initiatives, a set of recommendations is advanced towards improving further interoperability developments, offering a unique niche for researchers, practitioners and developers to make significant contributions.

Keywords: Interoperability · Domain-specific standardization initiative

1 Introduction

Information and communication technologies (ICTs) are increasingly used by organizations to support and improve their activities and services, and manage their daily operations. As collaborations are more intense in today's networked economy, achieving seamless interoperability among heterogeneous communication systems is crucial. Interoperability, in a broad sense, refers to the use of computer-based tools that facilitate the coordination of work and information flow among heterogeneous and geographically distributed communication systems. According to IEEE [1], interoperability represents the capability of two or more systems or components to exchange information and use it. It emerged from the need to harmonize the operational heterogeneous networked environment, real-time information sharing and the necessity to improve task coordination [2].

Different enterprises from various geographical locations, using heterogeneous ICTs, need to jointly perform complex e-business scenarios relaying on the execution of complex inter-organizational business processes, which require the exchange of

© Springer International Publishing AG 2017
I. Ciuciu et al. (Eds.): OTM 2016 Workshops, LNCS 10034, pp. 36–46, 2017.
DOI: 10.1007/978-3-319-55961-2_4

information in real-time and its correct interpretation by all parties. Similarly, the success of joint collaborative military operations relays on the exchange of critical information in real-time. Different approaches towards seamless interoperability exist, e.g., industry neutral initiatives (such as: ebXML www.ebxml.org or RosettaNet www. rosettanet.org), or domain specific initiatives, such as: HL7 (Health Level Seven www. hl7.org) in the healthcare sector, NATO STANGs for unmanned aerial vehicles [3]. Despite the variety of reference architectures, frameworks, tools, infrastructures and technologies supporting (or claiming to support) seamless interoperability, the scientific community emphasizes this objective is not yet fully achieved and more work needs to be done [3–5].

Different scientific works on interoperability exist. However, most articles focus on e-business interoperability frameworks, e.g., [2, 5–9] and are descriptive in nature. Domain-specific standardization initiatives receive little attention, although numerous advances were made. In order to attain seamless interoperability in today's networked economy, when accurate real-time information exchange is crucial for successful businesses, and spans different organizations from different industries, it is important to understand the specificities of each domain specific approach. Recent works, although aiming to review e-business interoperability frameworks (e.g., [9]), did not actually tackle domain-specific interoperability frameworks. Other works focus on a specific case study (e.g., [10]), or implementations following a certain standard specifications (e.g., [11, 12]). An up-to-date review or analysis of current advances of domain-specific initiatives for seamless communication is not available, although highly relevant. This article addresses this gap.

The objective of this article is to present an up-to-date review of the most relevant domain-specific standardization initiatives aiming at achieving seamless interoperability. In this sense, major interoperability issues are discussed, and the most significant domain specific initiatives are analyzed. Present challenges are identified and possible ways to tackle them are discussed. This article has two main contributions. First, it provides an up-to-date review of the most relevant industry-specific standardization initiatives aiming at achieving seamless interoperability among communication systems. Second, by comparing these initiatives, a set of recommendations is advanced towards improving further interoperability developments, offering a unique niche for researchers, practitioners and developers to make significant contributions.

This article is organized as follows. The following section briefly introduces relevant concepts. Main standardization initiatives are presented next. Section 4 contains a comparative analysis and discussion of the results. The article concludes with a section addressing the need for further research.

2 Background

Interoperability reflects the capability of two or more systems or components to exchange and use (in a heterogeneous network) the information that was exchanged [13]. In the military domain, interoperability refers to the ability of different military organizations to conduct joint operations, allowing forces, units or systems to operate together [14]. Interoperability solutions enable ICT systems to facilitate information exchange and promote service compatibility between systems [15, 16].

Research challenges for future interoperable enterprise systems are discussed in [5], concerning: context awareness, semantic interoperability, cyber-physical oriented enterprise systems, cloud based systems, new organizational forms, new business models, and interoperability assessment. Barriers towards seamless interoperability were divided in three categories in [17]: conceptual, technological, and organizational barriers. For the (e-)business domain, the main requirements for interoperability were grouped in [6]: technical requirements (e.g., standards, implementation guidelines profiles), business (e.g., business agreements, working methods) and policy (e.g., compliance and governance). Interoperability needs to be addressed at several distinct levels [9], e.g., technical, syntactic, semantic and organizational [17, 18]. According to [2], four main views on interoperability need to be addressed: technical (e.g., messaging infrastructure), business/economic aspects (e.g., economic performance assessment), information (e.g., information sharing and retrieval), semantic aspects (e.g., common dictionary or sets of business documents). To address these interoperability challenges and requirements, different e-business initiatives were developed, either industry-neutral (such as: ebXML or RosettaNet), or industry-specific, e.g., papiNet (www.papinet.org) targeting the paper and forest products industry. Non-commercial initiatives were also created towards attaining seamless interoperability in a specific domain, e.g., NATO STANAG 4586 [3] defines standard message formats and data protocols, provides a common interface between the unmanned aerial vehicles and ground stations. The gap analysis on inter-enterprise interoperability presented in [2] illustrated the diversity of initiatives, such as: B2B industry-specific and industry-neutral solutions, standards for automatic exchange of model information (e.g., Process Specification Language-PSL [19]). Standard gaps were referred in [2]: standards supporting cross-industry interoperability, standards acceptance, harmonization of terms and concepts for inter- and cross-industry communication, interface standards for inter-enterprise communication. Although interoperability standards are highly used in industry, an up-to-date analysis of the recent advances of domain-specific interoperability initiatives is not available. The topic of seamless interoperability is broadly studied by scientists and practitioners. However, the review performed revealed that existing studies extensively focus on enterprise framework initiatives (e.g., [9], INTEROP project, ATHENA project, www.athena-ip.org), and little focus is on domain-specific standardization initiatives. This research gap is a focal point of this article. The main standardization initiatives discussed most extensively in the literature and supported by standardization organizations are briefly presented next.

3   Review of the Standardization Initiatives

3.1   Standards and Standardization Initiatives

Different initiatives were created to carry out planned activities (e.g., in accordance with specific rules developed by the members of a community) towards the development and promotion of standards that serve a specific goal (or a set of goals), as referred next.

The Organization for Advancement of Structured Information Standards (OASIS, www.oasis-open.org) is a non-profit consortium advancing the development, convergence and adoption of open standards, such as: Universal Business Language (UBL[1]), Universal Description, Discovery and Integration (UDDI[2]), ebXML BPSS, ebXML CPPA, ebXML messaging service.

The *United Nations Centre for Trade Facilitation and Electronic Business (UN/CEFACT* http://www.unece.org/cefact.html) was established as a subsidiary inter-governmental body of the UNECE Committee on Trade, serving as a focal point for trade facilitation recommendations and e-business standards, covering commercial and government business processes.

The *World Wide Web Consortium* (W3C, www.w3.org) is an international community supporting the development of Web standards, e.g., for Web design and applications, XML technology, Web services.

NATO standardization agreements (known as STANAG) target unmanned aerial vehicles (UAV). STANAG 4586 [3] defines standard message formats and data protocols, provides a common interface between the UAVs and ground stations. On-going NATO standardization projects were summarized in [20]: network standards, Internet standards, Internetworking standards, data link standards, data standards, flight operation standards, and operation standards.

Numerous B2B standards have been developed, e.g., catalog systems standards, such as: Electronic Catalog XML (ecX, www.ecx-xml.org), Open Catalog Protocol (OCP, www.martsoft.com/ocp), process standards, such as BPEL4WS (Business Process Execution Language for Web Services). The Electronic Data Interchange (EDI) standards continue to be noticed in e-business, although numerous XML-based e-business frameworks have been standardized.

3.2 Reference Models and Architectures

The Service Oriented Architecture (SOA) was defined by OASIS as a paradigm for organizing distributed capabilities, providing the means to reorganize applications interacting services. Several approaches to attain interoperability following the SOA specifications exist, e.g., SOA interoperability in heterogeneous tactical networks is discussed in [21], and an implementation in the healthcare sector is presented in [22].

The LISI Reference Model [23] was developed to provide the US Department of Defense with a maturity model and process to determine joint interoperability needs, assessing the information systems' ability to meet those needs, and selecting pragmatic solutions and a transition path for achieving higher states of capability and interoperability. It also provides a common vocabulary, ensuring semantic interoperability.

---

[1] http://docs.oasis-open.org/ubl/os-UBL-2.1/.

[2] http://www.uddi.org/pubs/uddi_v3.htm.

3.3 Frameworks

E-business frameworks represent a standard for information sharing within and between companies, tackling business and technical issues, e.g., business documents, business processes and messaging, reflecting on what, when and how to share information [7]. According to [8], the purpose of e-business frameworks is to support interoperability. Different interoperability frameworks exist, e.g., industry neutral (such as: *ebXML*, *RosettaNet*), and domain-specific (e.g., papiNET, Chem eStandards, HL7). Nine relevant industry-specific initiatives are discussed next.

papiNet is an international paper and forest industry e-business initiative. It is a set of standard e-business documents which facilitate the flow of information among parties engaged in buying, selling and distribution of paper and forest products.

Chem eStandards (www.cidx.org) have become the *de facto* standards for transacting business electronically in the chemical industry, comprising business process guidelines, message, envelope and security specifications. Towards intensifying cross-industry trading, CIDX works with other standardization bodies (e.g., RosettaNet).

Petroleum Industry Data Exchange (PIDX, www.pidx.org) standardizes business processes supporting the exchange of data between trading partners in the oil and gas business. The PIDX standards encompass XML schemas, business process guidelines, implementation specifications, industry code lists, the data dictionary and the Petroleum Industry Glossary. Initially focusing on EDI, it moved in the 1990's to XML standards. It comprises 14 business documents and business processes.

TexWeave (Standardization and Interoperability in the Textile Supply Chain Integrated Networks, www.tex-weave.org) is a standardization initiative targeting the textile/clothing sector, based on standardized XML e-documents. It comprises business models for fabric and clothing supplying, XML templates for document exchange, and a common dictionary. eBiz[3] is an initiative pursuing the use and interoperability of digital communication across the fashion supply chain. The eBiz reference architecture released in 2013 defines specifications on business models, business processes, data models, product identification and classification, communication protocols.

The *Logistics Interoperability Model*[4] (LIM) aims at establishing business processes interoperability for transport and warehousing. It describes the high level business processes and transactions that occur in these processes, covering the following business functions: procurement, planning, warehousing, transport, financial settlement.

HL7 (Health Level Seven International www.hl7.org) is a not-for-profit ANSI-accredited standards developing organization aiming at providing a comprehensive framework and related standards for the exchange, integration, sharing and retrieval of electronic health information that supports clinical practice and the management, delivery and evaluation of health services. HL7 v3 aims at supporting all healthcare workflows. Different from v2, it follows HDF methodology. The HL7 Reference Information Model (RIM) expresses the data content required in a specific clinical or

---

[3] http://www.ebiz-tcf.eu/index.php/ebiz/interoperability-in-e-business.

[4] http://www.gs1.org/docs/tl/LIM_Foundation_Report.pdf.

administrative context, tackling the semantics for the HL7 XML-based messages. The HL7 Development Framework v3 (HDF) documents the messaging layer, the processes, rules and artefacts. It can be used as a basis for semantic interoperability. HL7 v3 also includes a formalism for vocabulary support.

For the financial world, different initiatives exist, such as: *SWIFT MT* standard, *TWIST, FIX. SWIFT*[5] was funded in 1973 with the vision of creating shared worldwide financial messaging service and a common language for international financial messaging. The SWIFT Standards group maintains several message standards. The SWIFT MT standard, for example, is used for international payments, cash management, trade finance and treasury business. SWIFT Standards, under contract to ISO, also maintains two open messaging standards: ISO 15022 - used for securities settlement and asset servicing, and ISO 20022 targeting financial industry processes. Four complementary messaging services are offered over SWIFTNet messaging platform: FIN, InterAct, FileAct and WebAccess. *FIN* and *InterAct* enable the exchange of messages on a message-per-message basis and support the exchange of proprietary formats. *InterAct* offers additional options, such as: store-and-forward messaging, real-time messaging, real-time query-and-response options. *FileAct* enables files transfer (e.g., large batches of messages, such as bulk payment files, very large reports, operational data). The Financial Information eXchange[6] Protocol (firstly released in 1995) facilitates the communication of trade information. It provides messaging specifications, supporting post-trade and straight-through processing, from indications of interest to allocations and confirmations. FIX v4.4 added detailed support for fixed income instruments, futures and options, and post-trade allocations.

The collaboration framework for the Joint Automotive Data Model (JADA, www. aiag.org) started in 1999, supported by AIAG, JAMA/JAPIA and Odette, focusing on the supply chain management transactions, aiming at harmonizing the use of EDIFACT messages. The JADM business processes range from forecast to payment, e.g., deliver forecast and instruction, dispatch/shipment notification, receiving notification, invoicing processing, and remittance advice. The description of BP models is compliant with UMM, and the semantics (data model) is mapped to the syntax (EDIFACT), producing the EDIFACT Implementation Guideline.

AgXML (http://www.agxml.org/) represents an organization of grain and processing companies and related entities focusing to identify, develop and implement e-business standards and guidelines to grain, oilseed and renewable-fuel companies. It focuses on specific BPs, XML-based schema definition supporting data requirements, integration of XML-based messaging. AGRIS Application profile was created to enhance the description, exchange and retrieval of agriculture data. AGROVOC is a vocabulary covering areas in agriculture, forestry, fisheries, food and related domains.

---

[5] https://www.swift.com/standards.

[6] http://www.fixtradingcommunity.org.

4   Comparative Analysis

This section presents a comparative analysis of 7 relevant domain-specific initiatives: HL7, SWIFT, Chem eStandards, papiNet, AgXML, PIDX, TexWeave. This analysis was mainly performed based on frameworks specifications, and the analysis of scientific articles and technical reports. Table 1 provides an overview of the main

Table 1. An overview of relevant domain-specific initiatives

Initiative	Website	Start	Targeted domain	Aim	Promoters/supporting bodies	Status	Main elements
HL7	www.hl7.org	1987	Healthcare	To provide a comprehensive framework and standards for the exchange, integration, sharing and retrieval of e-health information to support clinical practice and the management, delivery and evaluation of health services	More than 1600 members from over 50 countries	V3	Messaging, HDF, RIM v2.41, vocabulary
SWIFT	https://www.swift.com/standards	1973	Financial sector	To create a shared worldwide financial messaging service and a common language for international financial messaging			Messaging service (and messaging standards ISO 15022 and ISO 20022), common dictionary, proprietary message formats
Chem eStandards	www.cidx.org	1985	Chemical industry	To help companies in this industry adopt common communication principles, which reduces the overall cost of XML-based integration projects and enables realizing e-business gains	Chemical Industry Data Exchange (CIDX)	CIDX documents v.6.2.1	ChemXML message specifications v4.0; specification of business transactions, data dictionary
papiNet	www.papinet.org	2000	Paper and forest products industry	To provide a set of standard electronic documents that facilitate the flow of information among parties engaged in buying, selling and distributing paper and forest products	papiNet Europe, papiNet NA	V2R31/v2R40	Data dictionary, eDocuments, complete set of XML designs and definitions on forest, paper and printing attributes
AgXML	www.agxml.org	2000	Grain processing sector	To develop standards for efficient and effective communication throughout the entire agribusiness supply chain	Grain and processing companies, and related entities	AgXML v2	Dictionary, messaging, business processes
PIDX	www.pidx.org	1986	Oil and gas	To achieve petroleum industry and enterprise-wide integration of business processes through seamless e-business communication	American Petroleum Institute, Shell, Total, ChevronTexaco, etc.	PIDX v1.61	Business documents, business processes, data dictionary and glossary
TexWeave	www.tex-weave.org	2005	Textile industry	To provide the textile/clothing sector with a framework of for interoperability based on standardized XML-based e-document exchange, and foster its adoption in the real business communities	EURATEX	RA2.0	XML templates

characteristics, illustrating the promoting organizations, aim of the initiative, and the main elements of each framework, following the approach in [2]. Most initiatives focus on messaging and e-documents/message specifications. In this way, it is ensured the transmission of messages, though the messaging service, and information interoperability. The semantic interoperability is assured by the domain specific dictionaries, vocabulary and glossary, e.g., as in the case of HL7, SWIFT, Chem eStandards, papiNet, PIDX. Only AgXML and PIDX provide business process specifications.

Four interoperability dimensions are advanced in [2]: technical, information, semantic, business. The technical interoperability concerns issues related to e-communication, e.g., interfaces, ICT platforms, security standards, messaging service. Business interoperability concerns economic performance assessment, goals and strategy alignment. The knowledge interoperability refers to information representation and management. Semantic interoperability assures that the information exchanged by heterogeneous distributed systems is meaningful and all the communicating parts interpret it in the same way. As information-intensive dimensions, semantic and knowledge aspects are referred together next.

Table 2 illustrates the coverage of technical, semantic/knowledge and business interoperability dimensions. Five of the frameworks analyzed provide a messaging service. Semantic interoperability is ensured by a domain-specific dictionary/ vocabulary, and all the initiatives analyzed address it. None of the initiatives tackles business interoperability. This emphasizes the extensive focus on technical aspects.

Table 2. Mapping to interoperability dimensions

Framework/Initiative	Interoperability		
	Technical	Semantic/Knowledge	Business
HL7	✓	✓	–
SWIFT	✓	✓	–
Chem eStandards	✓	✓	–
papiNet	✓	✓	–
AgXML	✓	✓	–
PIDX	–	✓	–

5 Discussion, Conclusions and Future Research Directions

Industry-specific initiatives towards seamless interoperability were initiated more than 30 years ago. Certain vertical standards already have a high recognition (e.g., papiNet), while in other sectors the maturity level is below moderate, e.g., the UAD domain [20]. Accordingly, until the maturity level of the operational side of the UAV domain reaches above the moderate level, the use of UAVs and benefit from this technology will be limited. Another example is from the logistics sector. Although an approach targeting the logistics sector exists, it seems it did not gain much acceptance. This can be explained by the fact that different industry initiatives already incorporate specifications for transactions, business processes or e-documents for the logistics-related activities (e.g., papiNet, Chem eStandards, RosettaNet).

Table 3 provides an overview of the main advantages and drawback of the analyzed initiatives towards seamless interoperability. An extensive focus is currently on technical-related aspects (e.g., messaging service, message format/specifications), and business interoperability aspects are neglected. Semantic interoperability is ensured for all the frameworks analyzed. While several industry-specific frameworks bring promising solutions towards achieving seamless interoperability (e.g., papiNet), many initiatives did not mature, requiring further developments (e.g., AgXML). The big challenge, however, will be achieving cross-industry seamless interoperability. As it is not realistic to consider possible the merge of all standards and general acceptance, it is important to ensure a certain level of compliance between different standardization initiatives towards attaining seamless interoperability between communication systems built following the specifications of these standards.

Table 3. Strengths and weaknesses towards seamless interoperability: an overview

Initiative	Strengths	Weaknesses
HL7	Support from numerous bodies	Heterogeneity of regulations hindering the implementation of software tools
SWIFT	Messaging standards ISO15022 & 20022	Diversity of initiatives in this sector
Chem eStandards	Clear message specifications that ease the implementation of specific solutions	A large number of business transaction models are required
papiNet	Recognition and support from many organizations	Lack of automation to set collaboration agreements
AgXML	Dictionary ensuring semantic interoperability	Existence of different initiatives

While some initiatives compete with each other (e.g., SWIFT and FIX), other complement each other. For example, CIDX uses for packaging RNIF 1.1. Thus, the CIDX document exchanges are always asynchronous. CIDX does not use RosettaNet PIPs, but Chem eStandards message specification, without defining business processes for transactions. Chem eStandards leverage the transport, envelope and security aspects of RosettaNet Implementation Framework (RNIF) version 1.1, and Chem eStandards define the XML for specific transactions.

The industry-specific initiatives analyzed represent a step forward towards seamless interoperability. However, many challenges need to be further explored, e.g., scalability issues, gathering and maintaining the semantic content in domain communities, economic performance assessment, legal, security and privacy implications. These directions require urgent attention. Although a variety of reference architectures, frameworks, tools, infrastructures and technologies supporting (or claiming to support) seamless interoperability exist, the scientific community emphasizes this objective is not yet fully achieved and more work needs to be done [3–5].

Looking ahead, big challenges will be related to IoT interoperability (e.g., harmonization of solutions for the management of personal health devices, interoperability of big data sets), and seamless interoperability in a multi-cloud environment.

References

1. IEEE Standard Computer Dictionary: A Compilation of IEEE Standard Computer Glossaries, Institute of Electrical and Electronics Engineers, NY (1990)
2. Chituc, C.-M., Toscano, C., et al.: Interoperability in collaborative networks: independent and industry-specific initiatives - the case of the footwear industry. Comput. Ind. **59**, 741–757 (2008)
3. NATO STANAG (North Atlantic Treaty Organization Standardization Agreement) 4586
4. Pollock, J.T.: The biggest issue: interoperability vs. integration. eAI J. October issue, 48–52 (2001)
5. Panetto, H., Zdravkonic, M., Jardim-Goncalves, R., Romero, D., Cecil, J., Mezgar, I.: New perspectives for the future interoperable systems. Comput. Ind. **79**, 47–63 (2016)
6. Li, H.: XML and industrial standards for electronic commerce. Knowl. Inf. Syst. **2**(4), 487–497 (2000)
7. Nurmilaakso, J.M., Kotinurmi, P.: A review of XML-based supply-chain integration. Prod. Plann. Control **15**, 608–621 (2004)
8. Nurmilaakso, J.M., Kotinurmi, P., Laesvuori, H.: XML-based e-business frameworks and standardization. Comput. Stand. Interfaces **28**, 585–599 (2006)
9. Rezaei, R., Kian Chiew, T., Pack Lee, S.: A review of e-business interoperability frameworks. J. Syst. Softw. **93**, 199–216 (2014)
10. Wasala, A., Buckley, J., Schaler, R., Exton, C.: An empirical framework for evaluating interoperability of data exchange standards based on their actual usage: a case study on XLIFF. Comput. Stand. Interfaces **42**, 157–170 (2015)
11. Barron-Gonzalez, H.G., Martinez-Espronceda, M., Tiago, J.D., Led, S., Serrano, L.: Lessons learned from the implementation of remote control for the interoperability standard ISO/IEEE 11073-20601 in a standard weighing scale. Comput. Methods Progr. Biomed. **123**, 81–93 (2016)
12. Zhang, Y.-F., Tian, Y., Zhou, T.-S., Araki, K., Li, J.-S.: Integrating HL7 RIM and ontology for unified knowledge and data representation in clinical decision support systems. Comput. Methods Progr. Biomed. **123**, 94–108 (2016)
13. Bretfielder, K., Messina, D.: IEEE 100: The Authoritative Dictionary of IEEE Standards Terms, vol. 879. Standards Information Network IEEE Press, New York (2000)
14. NATO: Backgrounder interoperability for joint operations, July 2006. http://www.nato.int/nato_static/assets/pdf/pdf_publications/20120116_interoperability-en.pdf
15. Jardim-Goncalves, R., Grilo, A., Agostinho, C., Lampathaki, F., Charalabidis, Y.: Systematisation of interoperability body of knowledge: the foundation for Enterprise Interoperability as a science. Enterp. Inf. Syst. **7**, 7–32 (2013)
16. Mattiello-Francisco, F., Martins, E., Cavalli, A.R., Yano, E.T.: InRob: an approach for testing interoperability and robustness of real-time embedded software. J. Syst. Softw. **85**, 3–15 (2012)
17. Chen, D.: Enterprise interoperability framework. In: Proceedings of Enterprise Modelling and Ontologies for Interoperability, EMOI-Interop (2006)

18. Munk, S.: An analysis of basic interoperability related terms, system of interoperability types. Acad. Appl. Res. Mil. Sci. **1**, 117–131 (2002)
19. Pouchard, L.C., Cutting-Decelle, A.F., Michel, J.J., Gruninger, M.: ISO 18629 PSL: a standardized language for specifying and exchanging information. IFAC Proc. Volumes **38**(1), 37–45 (2005)
20. Demir, K.A., Cicibas, H., Arica, N.: Unmanned aerial vehicle domain: areas of research. Defence Sci. J. **65**(4), 319–329 (2015)
21. Bloebaum, H., Lund, K.: CoNSIS: demonstration of SOA interoperability in heterogeneous tactical networks. In: Proceedings of MCC Conference, pp. 1–7 (2012)
22. Batra, U., Sachdeva, S., Mukherjee, S.: Implementing healthcare interoperability utilizing SOA and data interchange agent. Health Policy Technol. **4**(3), 241–255 (2015)
23. C4ISR: Architecture Working Group (AWG), Levels of Information Systems Interoperability (LISI), 30 March 1998

Using Formal Measures to Improve Maturity Model Assessment for Conceptual Interoperability

Gabriel S.S. Leal[1,2,3(✉)], Wided Guédria[3], Hervé Panetto[1,2],
Erik Proper[3], and Mario Lezoche[1,2]

[1] CNRS, CRAN UMR 7039, Vandœuvre-lès-Nancy, France
{gabriel.da-silva-serapiao-leal,herve.panetto,
mario.lezoche}@univ-lorraine.fr,gabriel.leal@list.lu
[2] Université de Lorraine, CRAN UMR 7039, Boulevard des Aiguillettes, B.P. 70239,
54506 Vandœuvre-lès-Nancy, France
[3] ITIS, TSS, Luxembourg Institute of Science and Technology (LIST),
5, avenue des Hauts-Fourneaux, 4362 Esch-sur-Alzette, Luxembourg
{wided.guedria,erik.proper}@list.lu

Abstract. To handle challenges such as globalization, new technologies and fast-changing environments, enterprises are progressively collaborating with others and becoming part of a Networked. In this context, Enterprise Interoperability (EI) is a crucial requirement that needs to be respected by enterprises when starting a collaborative relationship. As soon as this requirement is not achieved, EI becomes a problem that must be solved. To avoid these problems and consequently, take corrective actions on time, enterprises need to predict and solve potential problems before they occur. The Maturity Model for Enterprise Interoperability (MMEI) was proposed to assess the interoperability potential of an enterprise as well as to help enterprises evaluating the suitability of partners in an interoperability context. However, this method has some inconveniences such as the lack of formal definitions specifying the boundaries between each maturity level. Hence the objective of this paper is to formalize the MMEI maturity levels boundaries by defining formal measures. Finally, a case study is proposed to validate the defined measures.

Keywords: Networked Enterprise · Maturity Model · Enterprise interoperability assessment · Conceptual interoperability · Formal measures

1 Introduction

With the current fast changing environment, enterprises are progressively collaborating with each other and participating to a Networked Enterprise (NE) [1], to face challenges such as globalisation, new technologies, financial crisis, new markets, etc. Considering this NE context, we argue that one of the difficulties enterprises may face is the development of Enterprise Interoperability (EI) [2, 3] among their Collaborative Enterprise Systems (CESs) [4]. EI is a crucial requirement having to be verified by enterprises when starting a relationship with others to attain shared goals [1, 5]. As soon as this requirement is not achieved, interoperability becomes a problem that must be solved

© Springer International Publishing AG 2017
I. Ciuciu et al. (Eds.): OTM 2016 Workshops, LNCS 10034, pp. 47–56, 2017.
DOI: 10.1007/978-3-319-55961-2_5

[1, 6]. To deal with this kind of problem, accurate evaluations can be performed to have a clear view of strengths and weaknesses of the considered NE regarding interoperability, at an early stage [1]. Some surveys and comparisons [4, 7–9] have been performed to evaluate existing interoperability assessment methods. Among these evaluation methods, the Maturity Model for Enterprise Interoperability (MMEI) [10, 11] proposes five maturity levels, describing the stages through which systems should evolve to reach higher completeness in the realisation of a given objective. It covers the three main interoperability aspects which are: Conceptual, Technical and Organizational interoperability [3]. MMEI was mainly conceived to assess the potentiality of an enterprise (or a system) to be interoperable with a possible future partner whose identity is not known at the moment of evaluation. Although the MMEI maturity levels are well structured, their definitions are based on qualitative measures i.e. the levels are subjective and the evaluation depends on the expertise of the assessors. This kind of measure has some inconveniences such as the lack of formal definitions specifying the boundaries between each maturity level and requires a very high level of expertise to apply these models in an industrial context [12]. A possibility raised by [4] to formalise the boundaries between each maturity level, is the use of quantitative measures (numeric values characterising the interoperations between CESs). Indeed, quantitative methods such as [13–16] are capable of formalising and quantifying interoperability between known systems. However, they are not prepared and/or they do not have coherent value scales to be used with maturity models. Hence, the objective of this paper is to improve the MMEI interoperability evaluation by formalising its maturity levels boundaries. This will allow quantifying and qualifying the degree of interoperability between heterogeneous enterprises that need to participate in a NE. In this paper, we will focus only on the conceptual interoperability aspect. The technical and organisational aspects are out of the scope and will be investigated in future work. The formalisation of the MMEI conceptual maturity levels will be done by defining formal measures based on the quantitative methods. It will allow us to establish the transition between each maturity level by specifying thresholds (numeric values) for levels' boundaries. The proposed improvement is essential and will serve as one more step towards proposing a new approach for assessing enterprise interoperability within a NE, using both qualitative and quantitative measures. The rest of the paper is organised as follow – Sect. 2 presents the relevant related work. It is followed by Sect. 3 where the formal measures are proposed and the levels' boundaries are established. Section 4 illustrates a real case study based on an active NE in the field of marketing and communication in Luxembourg. The conclusion and future work are given in Sect. 5.

2   Related Work

This section gives an overview of the Networked Enterprise Meta-Model (NEMO) [1], highlighting the core concepts of NE and interoperability, as well as, relationships between them. The different classifications and properties of enterprise interoperability assessment methods are also presented. Furthermore, the MMEI and its five maturity levels, as well as some formal measures proposed to assess the conceptual interoperability aspect, are brought forward.

2.1 Networked Enterprise and Enterprise Interoperability

NEMO [1] aims at providing a common understanding of the NE and interoperability concepts, based on a systemic approach. It defines a NE as: *"a system composed of at least two autonomous systems (enterprises) that collaborate during a period of time to reach a shared objective"*. According to [17, 18] enterprise systems are all sub-systems of an enterprise (e.g. Information systems, decisional systems, physical systems, etc.). Taking into account this view, [4] adopt the term Collaborative Enterprise System (CES) in order to represent the enterprise systems that collaborate with systems from other enterprises within the NE. Considering these perspectives, NEMO describes two views of interoperability: as a *requirement* that needs to be met when there is a need for at least two CESs to work together and as a *problem* when this requirement is not fulfilled. To describe the interoperability concepts within a NE, NEMO is based on the interoperability dimensions [1, 3]. Here, we present the three most important concepts that will be considered in the metrics proposition in Sect. 3. The first one is the *interoperability concerns* representing the areas concerned by interoperability in an enterprise (business, process, service and data). The second, is *conceptual interoperability aspect* dealing with knowledge and information sharing among systems. Finally, the *conceptual barriers* concerning with the syntactic and semantic incompatibilities of information to be exchanged between systems. This kind of barrier can be related to enterprise models and the capacity of knowledge and semantic representation. More details about interoperability dimensions and other concepts can be found on [1, 3].

2.2 Enterprise Interoperability Assessment

In order to support enterprises to better interoperate with their partners within a NE, the interoperability between their CESs requires being assessed and continuously improved. According to [4, 10] the interoperability assessment methods can be classified based on the criteria depicted on Table 1.

Table 1. Interoperability assessment methods classification

Criteria		Classification		
Method properties	Structure	Levelling		Non-levelling
	Used measure	Qualitative		Quantitative
	Used approach	White box		Black box
	Type of interop. assessment	Known partner		Unknown partner
Interop. aspects		Conceptual	Technical	Organisational

It is worth noting that interoperability is a non-bidirectional property [13]. It means that: Given two entities A and B and measuring their interoperability level $I(x,y)$ it is structurally coherent to find $I(A, B) \neq I(B, A)$. This structural property doesn't impact the evaluated methods because of its internal feature but it explains the behavioural aspects of the approached property concepts [4]. The following sections present the MMEI (a qualitative method) and quantitative methods.

2.3 Maturity Model for Enterprise Interoperability (MMEI)

MMEI has two primary purposes: (1) Define a common framework for assessing and measuring potential interoperability maturity, providing information for how far along an enterprise is regarding targeted maturity levels. (2) Provide information about 'best practices' that allow enterprises to improve their interoperability potential [10]. MMEI is a levelling method using qualitative measures and following a white box approach. It is mainly used when interoperation partners are unknown. MMEI defines five enterprise interoperability maturity levels: Unprepared, Defined, Aligned, Organized and Adaptive. Each maturity level is an instantiation of the main elements of an interoperability aspect with an evolution of the elements regarding the evolution of the level. When considering the conceptual interoperability aspects, these elements are: data models, service models, process models, business models, enterprise visions, strategies, objectives, policies, etc. Aligned to the enterprise maturity levels, MMEI identify five conceptual maturity levels that are: Incomplete, Modelled, Adhered, Mapped and Accommodate [19].

However, MMEI cannot guarantee that two enterprises having the same maturity levels can interoperate without problems. According to [11], a possibility to an enterprise to verify if a partner is compatible or not, is to assess their potential interoperability individually, using the MMEI model and then compare the obtained results to identify their differences. For example, if two enterprises have the conceptual maturity level 2, it means that both are using enterprise modelling standards, but if the used standards are incompatible, the interoperability between the two enterprises will be very difficult.

2.4 Quantitative Methods for Interoperability Assessment

Quantitative methods emphasize objective measurements and the statistical, mathematical, or numerical analysis of data collected through polls, questionnaires, and surveys, or by manipulating pre-existing statistical data using computational techniques [20]. Considering the enterprise interoperability domain, we identified the following methods dealing with the interoperability assessment: Based on a mathematical formalisation of the semantic relationship, Yahia et al. [13] proposed two measures, the maximal potential and the minimum effective interoperability. The i-score [14] intend to measure interoperability of complex networks using operational thread as its foundation and provides a single number measure of how well the systems interoperate along the thread. Barut et al. [15] propose a single 2-tuple index that encompasses both the depth of the information exchanged and used within the network as well as the richness and the amount of the information exchanged and used. The compatibility matrix [16] provides a matrix with 24 interoperability areas where the value "1" is attributed when an incompatibility is found. The degree of compatibility is given by the sum of incompatibilities found, where "0" means higher compatibility and "24" poorest compatibility between the considered systems.

3 Improving MMEI with Formal Measures

In this section, our objective is to deal with the lack of formal definitions specifying the boundaries between each conceptual maturity level. First, we present the selected quantitative methods that will be used as basis to formulate the formal measures as well as the identified links between MMEI and those methods. Furthermore, the formal measures and the maturity levels' boundaries are presented.

3.1 Linking MMEI and the Selected Quantitative Methods

Among the identified methods in Sect. 2.4, we chose the approach proposed by Yahia et al. [13] because it deals especially with the conceptual interoperability aspect and uses numeric values to characterize the interoperability. Moreover, as is the case for the MMEI, the selected approach uses a white box approach (where systems' inputs-outputs as well as their elements and structures are known). This facilitates the identification of problems in specific parts of a system. MMEI and the selected approach [13], consider that interoperability is mainly concerned by interactions between systems. When dealing with the conceptual interoperability assessment, the **Conceptual Models** are the objects of evaluation. These models are composed by Semantic blocks that represent independent piece of knowledge containing their own minimal semantics. A Semantic Block is composed by Concepts which can be "Lexical" or "Non-Lexical" concepts [21]. Figure 1 shows the links between MMEI concepts and the meta-model of semantic block structure [21] used by Yahia et al. [13] to determine their proposed measures. The specific MMEI elements are coloured in grey and the meta-model elements are coloured in white. The "Conceptual Model" is coloured in black as it's an element used from both approaches.

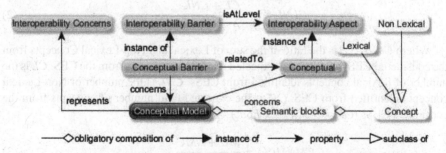

Fig. 1. Linking concepts from MMEI and Yahia et al. [13] approach.

Considering the studied measures to assess the conceptual interoperability, Yahia et al. [13] provides two indexes: (1) the potential interoperability index (ν), which represents the maximal number of semantic relationships existing into the considered network. (2) The effective interoperability index (ε) which verifies the number of mandatory concepts that are instantiated. Here, a set of *mandatory concept (MC)* represents all the necessary and sufficient elements which make the conceptual model semantically coherent and understandable. On the contrary, a *non-mandatory concepts (NMC)* correspond to the non-mandatory roles and are only enriching the semantics of the CESs conceptual models. It is worth noting that our proposition has some limitations. For instance, as models from different enterprises can been made by different experts with various modelling experiences, we cannot ensure that the used languages are compatible. Hence, we can only apply the formal measures when enterprises are using the same modelling standard.

3.2 Defining Maturity Levels' Boundaries

Considering the five conceptual maturity levels and the indexes defined by [13], we define the boundaries of each level based on a set of equations. These will be used to improve the step 4 (Assessment) of the MMEI methodology [10]. Before that, we present the linguistic value' ranges and notations that we adopt to characterize the achievement of a maturity level. This is based on [10] and [22] notations. The four defined variables and their related scales are: "Not Achieved (NA) ($0 \leq x \leq 15$)", "Partially Achieved (PA) ($15 < x \leq 50$)", "Largely Achieved (LA) ($50 < x \leq 85$)", "Fully Achieved (FA) ($85 < x \leq 100$). Based on that, we define the following equations:

$$CA(\%) = \frac{CESc + CESa}{CESc^e + CESa^e} \tag{1}$$

Where *CA(%)* is the ratio of the number of CESs' concepts and attributes identified and modelled over the total expected number of CESs' concepts and attributes. *CESc* is the number of modelled concepts from the concerned CES. *CESa* is the number of modelled attributes from CES. *CESc^e* is the expected total number of modelled concepts from CES. *CESa^e* is the total expected number of modelled attributes from CES.

$$CLNL(\%) = \frac{CL + CNL}{CT^e} \tag{2}$$

Where *CLNL (%)* is the ratio of the sum of Lexical and Non-Lexical Concepts from the considered CES over the total expected number of concepts from the CES. *CL* is the number of Lexical concepts identified from CESs. *CNL* is the number of Non-Lexical concepts identified from CES. *CT^e* is the expected total number of concepts from the considered CESs ($CT^e = CESc^e + CESa^e$).

$$CMNM(\%) = \frac{MC + NMC}{CT^e} \tag{3}$$

Where *CMNM (%)* is the ratio of the sum of MC and NMC from both considered CESs over the total expected number of concepts from the considered CESs. The following equations are the same from Yahia et al. [13]. They represent the maximal potential interoperability (how many semantic relationships can be established within the considered network) and minimal effectiveness interoperability (the interoperability's quality).

$$\text{Maximal potential} = \left(v_{1 \to 2} = \frac{\left| R_C^2 \right|}{\left| R_{Cexpected}^2 \right|}, \varepsilon_{1 \to 2} = \frac{\left| R_C^{2e} \right|}{\left| R_C^2 \right|} \right) \tag{4}$$

$$\text{Minimal effectiveness} = \left(v_{1 \to 2}^e = \frac{\left| R_C^{2e} \right|}{\left| R_{Cexpected}^2 \right|}, \varepsilon_{1 \to 2}^e = 100\% \right) \tag{5}$$

Where, $\left| R_C^2 \right|$ is the set of the retrieved semantic relationships. $\left| R_C^{2e} \right|$ is a subset of $\left| R_C^2 \right|$ that contains only MC. $\left| R_{Cexpected}^2 \right|$ represents the set of the expected semantic relationships needed to ensure a full semantic interoperation. Further, Table 2 describes the levels' boundaries and what need to be done to reach each one of them.

Table 2. Conceptual maturity levels and their boundaries.

Level – Boundaries description	Metric
Level 1 – Modelled: In order to reach this maturity level, the considered conceptual models need to be modelled. This is achieved by modelling the concepts and attributes from the concerned CES and achieving $CA = FA$	(1)
Level 2 – Adhered: The conceptual model needs to be fully modelled to achieve this level of maturity. The goal is reached using the standards and if needed translate them using the Fact-oriented modelling. This is achieved by identifying and modelling the lexical and non-lexical concepts and their attributes from the considered CES i.e. $CLNL = FA$ and the entire mandatory and non-mandatory concepts and their attributes from CES i.e. $CMNM = FA$	(2), (3)
Level 3 - Mapped. This level represents the capability to perform Meta modelling for multiple model mappings. Identifying and classifying all semantic relationships from the considered semantic blocks within the conceptual models tackle this issue. All concepts from the CESs must be identified and have all their potential semantics relationships recognized as well. This can be verified if the Maximal Potential Interoperability (MPI) is achieved i.e. $(v) = (\varepsilon) = FA$	(4)
Level 4 - Accommodated. In order to reach this maturity level, business, process, service and data models must be adaptive: They might be capable to dynamically adjust and accommodate 'on the fly'. This can be verified if $(\varepsilon^e) = 100\%$ and $(v) = (\varepsilon) = (v^e) = FA$. It is worth noting that when (v) and (ε) are equal to 100%, the CES1 is fully interoperable to CES2	(4), (5)

4   Case Study

This section illustrates the evaluation of the proposed metrics using a real case study. The objective is to present the improvements brought to MMEI by implementing the formal measures and to prove that the metrics cover the lack of levels' boundaries formalization. This case study is based on an active NE in the field of marketing and communication in Luxembourg which brings together five independent companies linked by their capital structure or by joint venture agreement. For security reasons, the names of the network and their members are kept confidential. Hence, we use *"The Network"* to address the NE in question and the two considered members in this particular case are addressed as *"EntA"* and *"EntB"*. Following the MMEI methodology assessment [10, 11], the first step is to define the assessment scope which is to evaluate the interoperability between *EntA* and *EntB*, considering the collaborative process responsible for planning future collaborative tasks. The information used to define the scenario was gathered through interviews and analysis of provided documents by the different enterprises from *The Network*. The selected interviewees are members of the board of directors of each considered enterprise. Based on the gathered information, we have first applied the MMEI criteria assessment in each concerned enterprises individually and we have crossed the obtained results from each one of them in order to identify which potential incompatibilities may appear when the interoperation starts. One of the main points in this case study is that according to the gathered information, the collaborative process responsible for planning future collaborative tasks is not modelled. This process was introduced when the new responsible was chosen (the *EntB* Account Director). This leads to work on the tacit knowledge [21]. In the specific case study the knowledge is trapped in employees mind. The assessors, working to structure and to understand the level of knowledge possessed, realised that despite the process was not modelled in both enterprises, most employees knows what need to be done i.e. which steps they need to take to realize the process. Table 3 shows some of the obtained results for each enterprise, considering the first MMEI maturity level (Modelled).

Table 3. Simplified view of MMEI raiting."NA" stands for Not Achieved, "PA" for Partially Achieved, "LA" for Largely Achieved and "FA" for Fully Achieved.

Level	Activities to evaluate	EntA				EntB			
		NA	PA	LA	FA	NA	PA	LA	FA
1	Process models are explicitly defined and documented (objective evaluation)	X				X			
1	Process models are explicitly defined and documented (assessors perception)			X				X	

Even though the process are not modelled in both enterprises, the assessors considered that both enterprises largely achieved the level 1. The assessment was based on the tacit knowledge presented by the interviewees and their perception considering the day-of-day from employees. However, the linguistic values assigned to those criteria are subjective, as it depends of the expertise and considerations of the assessors. Another inconvenience related to the dependence of the assessor's expertise, is that results may vary from among assessors. Using the same gathered information, we use the proposed measures, in the assessment step, to verify if the concepts and attributes from the processes conceptual models are really identified. The obtained results are the following: $CA_{EntA} = 0\%$ (NA) and $CA_{EntB} = 0\%$ (NA). The assessment takes in count mainly the available conceptual models from both enterprises. *EntB* has some data models that are used as basis to gather the needed information in order to plan the weekly tasks but the process's activities are not modelled nor documented. *EntA* does not have any available conceptual model concerning this kind of process. Having this numeric values, allow assessor to identify what need to be done to achieve a given maturity level. For example, in this case study, *EntA* and *EntB* need to model the entire process. A possible solution could be both enterprises realize the process modelling together.

5   Conclusion and Future Work

In this paper, we have proposed an improvement of the Maturity Model for Enterprise Interoperability by defining formal measures to identify the maturity levels boundaries. It has been asserted that despite being well structured, the boundaries of MMEI maturity levels lack formalization. Although, it is clear which requirements are needed to reach a given maturity level, the assessment depends on subjective criteria. Formal measures have been identified as a possibility to fulfil this gap. Furthermore, a brief analysis considering the MMEI conceptual aspect and quantitative methods was done. Based on the related work, we proposed to improve the MMEI conceptual interoperability assessment by establishing formal measures in order to define each maturity level boundaries. A real case study of an active NE in Luxembourg has been studied to validate the proposed approaches, by illustrating the interoperability evaluation between two enterprises. As future work, we intend to improve MMEI technical and organisational aspects, by applying quantitative evaluation methods. Furthermore, we intend to develop an Interoperability Assessment Approach for Networked Enterprise context. This approach will be part of a Framework for the Networked Enterprise Interoperability that will serve as basis to the development of a decision-support system for preventing and solving interoperability problems in the NE context.

Acknowledgements. This work has been conducted in the context of the PLATINE project (PLAnning Transformation Interoperability in Networked Enterprises), financed by the national fund of research of the Grand Duchy of Luxembourg (FNR), under the grant C14/IS/8329172.

References

1. Leal, G., Guédria, W., Panetto, H., Proper, E.: Towards a meta-model for networked enterprise. In: Schmidt, R., Guédria, W., Bider, I., Guerreiro, S. (eds.) BPMDS/EMMSAD -2016. LNBIP, vol. 248, pp. 417–431. Springer, Heidelberg (2016). doi:10.1007/978-3-319-39429-9_26
2. Institute of Electrical and Electronics Engineers. IEEE standard computer dictionary: a compilation of IEEE standard computer glossaries (1990)
3. ISO: Advanced automation technologies and their applications—Part 1: Framework for enterprise interoperability, International Organization for Standardization, ISO 11354, ISO/TC 184/SC 5 (2011)

4. Leal, G., Guédria, W., Panetto, H., Lezoche, M. Towards a comparative analysis of interoperability assessment approaches for collaborative enterprise systems. In: 2016 ISPE International Conference on Transdisciplinary Engineering Proceedings, Brazil (2016)
5. Mallek, S., Daclin, N., Chapurlat, V.: The application of interoperability requirement specification and verification to collaborative processes. Comput. Ind. **63**(7), 643–658 (2012)
6. Naudet, Y., Latour, T., Guedria, W., Chen, D.: Towards a systemic formalisation of interoperability. Comput. Ind. **61**(2), 176–185 (2010). Towards a systemic formalisation of interoperability
7. Ford, T., Interoperability Measurement. Dissertation, Air Force Institute of Technology, Wright-Patterson AFB, OH (2008)
8. Panetto, H.: Towards a classification framework for interoperability of enterprise applications. Int. J. Comput. Integr. Manuf. **20**(8), 727–740 (2007). Taylor & Francis: STM, Behavioural Science and Public Health Titles
9. Guédria, W., Naudet, Y., Chen, D.: Interoperability maturity models – survey and comparison –. In: Meersman, R., Tari, Z., Herrero, P. (eds.) OTM 2008. LNCS, vol. 5333, pp. 273–282. Springer, Heidelberg (2008). doi:10.1007/978-3-540-88875-8_48
10. Guedria, W., Naudet, Y., Chen, D.: Maturity model for enterprise interoperability. Enterp. Inf. Syst. **9**(1), 1–18 (2015)
11. Guédria, W., Naudet, Y., Chen, D.: Maturity model as decision support for enterprise interoperability. In: Meersman, R., Dillon, T., Herrero, P. (eds.) OTM 2011. LNCS, vol. 7046, pp. 604–608. Springer, Heidelberg (2011). doi:10.1007/978-3-642-25126-9_73
12. Panetto, H., Zdravković, M., Jardim-Goncalves, R., Romero, D., Cecil, J.: New perspectives for the future interoperable enterprise systems. Comput. Ind. **79**, 47–63 (2016). Elsevier
13. Yahia, E., Aubry, A., Panetto, H.: Formal measures for semantic interoperability assessment in cooperative enterprise information systems. Comput. Ind. **63**(5), 443–457 (2012)
14. Ford, T., Colombi, J., Graham, J., Jacques, D. The interoperability score. In: Proceedings of the 5th Annual Conference on Systems Engineering Research, Hoboken, NJ (2007)
15. Barut, M., Faisst, W., Kanet, J.J.: Measuring supply chain coupling: an information system perspective. Eur. J. Purchasing Supply Manage. **8**(3), 161–171 (2002)
16. ATHENA Integrated Project. Guidelines and best practices for applying the ATHENA Interoperability framework to support SME participation in digital ecosystems, ATHENA deliverable DA8.2, January 2007
17. Chen, D., Vallespir, B., Doumeingts, G.: GRAI integrated methodology and its mapping onto generic enterprise reference architecture and methodology. Comput. Ind. **33**, 387–394 (1997)
18. Guédria, W., Naudet, Y.: Extending the ontology of enterprise interoperability (OoEI) using enterprise-as-system concepts. In: Mertins, K., Bénaben, F., Poler, R., Bourrières, J.-P. (eds.) Enterprise Interoperability VI. PIC, vol. 7, pp. 393–403. Springer, Heidelberg (2014). doi: 10.1007/978-3-319-04948-9_33
19. Guédria, W., Chen, D., Naudet, Y.: A maturity model for enterprise interoperability. In: Meersman, R., Herrero, P., Dillon, T. (eds.) OTM 2009. LNCS, vol. 5872, pp. 216–225. Springer, Heidelberg (2009). doi:10.1007/978-3-642-05290-3_32
20. Babbie, E.: The Practice of Social Research, 13th edn. Wadsworth Publishing, Belmont (2012)
21. Lezoche, M., Yahia, E., Aubry, A., Panetto, H., Zdravkovic, M.: Conceptualising and structuring semantics in cooperative enterprise information systems models. Comput. Ind. **63**(8), 775–787 (2012). Elsevier
22. Rout, T.P., El Emam, K., Fusani, M., Goldenson, D., Jung, H.W.: SPICE in retrospect: developing a standard for process assessment. J. Syst. Softw. **80**(9), 1483–1493 (2007)

An Integrated Collaborative Approach for Micro Devices Assembly

J. Cecil[✉] and Sadiq Albuhamood

Center for Cyber Physical Systems, Computer Science, Oklahoma State University,
Stillwater, USA
j.cecil@okstate.com

Abstract. This paper presents an integrated collaborative approach for Micro Devices Assembly (MDA). The cyber and physical components of such an approach is described in this paper along with a discussion of their design and implementation. The cyber modules focus on assembly planning and 3D Virtual Reality (VR) based simulation activities. The physical components use the outcomes of the cyber modules to perform physical assembly for target MDA activities. A discussion of an Insertion Algorithm is also provided for generating near optimal assembly sequence of micro devices.

Keywords: Micro devices assembly · Collaborative manufacturing · Assembly planning algorithm · Insertion algorithm · Virtual reality · Simulation

1 Introduction

Collaborative manufacturing approaches hold the potential to facilitate agile principles where changing customer requirements can be studied virtually prior to physical manufacturing. In the advanced manufacturing field, such integrated collaborative approaches provides a basis where both cyber and physical tools and resources can be used in an integrated manner. Collaborations among cyber physical components in advanced manufacturing will greatly benefit the field as many advanced manufacturing depends on collaboration between cyber (software) and physical (hardware) modules to produce the desired products. VR based simulation analysis plays an important part in evaluating an assembly plan from cross functional perspectives. A well planned collaborative framework can provide an effective basis for integration among cyber and physical resources. The manufacturing domain of interest discussed in this paper involves Micro Devices Assembly (MDA). MDA refers to the manual, semi-automated and automated assembly of micron-sized parts in the scale of 10^{-6} m. MDA is an emerging field from advanced manufacturing which involve assembling micron sized devices, sensors and objects. Manufacturing designs that involve assembly of micro sizes have complex features and variety of materials cannot be manufactured using the micro-electro mechanical system (MEMS) technologies [4, 11]; in such situations, MDA assembly techniques are needed. As its difficult to directly assemble micro devices physically, the

© Springer International Publishing AG 2017
I. Ciuciu et al. (Eds.): OTM 2016 Workshops, LNCS 10034, pp. 57–64, 2017.
DOI: 10.1007/978-3-319-55961-2_6

use of simulation approaches to study assembly plans and alternatives becomes necessary. Given this context, the need to develop integrated collaborative approaches assumes significance.

2   Literature Review

As this paper deals with the emerging field of MDA, a brief discussion of relevant research is provided. In [5], a comprehensive review of micro gripping technologies and approaches is provided. Several research efforts have focused on various elements of MDA research including study of gripping forces, using innovative materials [1–3] and automating the process of assembly [4–20]. The use of VR based approaches has been explored by various researchers [15, 17, 25]. Cassier et al. [15] proposed a hybrid approach involving the use of VR based simulation and machine vision based servoing techniques assembly. Probst et al. [17] presented a VR system which enabled users to view the work cell in different angles and helped accomplish micro assembly operations without collisions. Our review of literature indicates a need to develop more extensive collaborative approaches for the field of micro assembly. There is a need to develop algorithm based assembly planning and sequencing approaches. The role of simulation needs to be explored in greater detailed especially the use of semi and fully immersive VR environments. Past research work has focused on non-immersive VR based simulators in MDA assembly contexts. Semi-immersive environments (while more expensive) hold the potential of providing a more intuitive user friendly 3D environment where various assembly plans and physical layouts can be modified interactively. Our research addresses these issues by developing an integrated collaborative approach for micro devices assembly.

3   Overview of the Collaborative Architecture and Approach

The collaborative architecture consists of the following components: Assembly Generation Module, VR based Assembly analysis Environment (VRAE), Physical Work cells and Collaboration Manager. The Assembly generation module and VRAE can be viewed as the cyber modules and the Physical work cells are the physical components. Figure 1 shows the key components of this architecture which is used to support the integrated approach for micro devices assembly.

The Assembly Generation Module takes an input of customer requirements, location of parts and feeders. It outputs candidate assembly sequence (using a modified Insertion Algorithm based approach) as well as provides feedback to the Collaboration Manager.

VRAE takes candidate assembly sequence as an input for determining the feasibility of the assembly sequences and plans. If the proposed or candidate assembly plan (which includes the sequence and the 3D path plan) are analyzed to be feasible, the VRAE outputs this feasible assembly sequence which is then communicated to the Collaboration Manager for subsequent activities; users can also propose their own assembly plans and

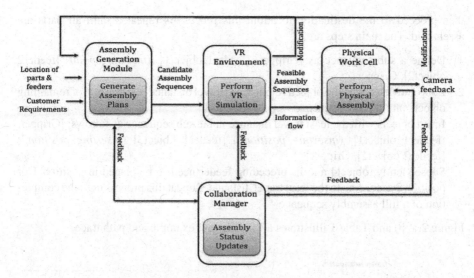

Fig. 1. The components of the collaborative approach

compare it with the automated generation plan and select the one most feasible. If collisions are detected or other problems identified, these are communicated as feedback to the Collaboration Manager and modifications to the Assembly Generation Module.

The Physical assembly modules receives the feasible assembly sequences, which is used as the basis to complete the physical assembly tasks. During assembly, monitoring cameras provide feedback to the Collaboration Manager of the work in progress as the assembly progresses.

A Collaboration Manager (software) maintains overall control of the various interactions among the three modules discussed using the feedback data. Detailed discussions of the various modules of the collaborative approach is in the subsections.

3.1 Assembly Generation Module

The objective of the assembly plan generator is to enable identifying feasible assembly sequences or plans. Our long term goal is for manufacturing and engineering partners to share a diverse set of such planning modules which can be used to generate assembly plans. For example, when considering a collaborative enterprise, several partners can share their individual assembly planning modules which can be placed on a Cloud. While such a cloud based approach is not the focus of discussion in this paper, this is the long term context for collaboration among the various software modules. In our planning module, our approach is based on the Insertion Algorithm (IA). During assembly, the gripper picks up a micro part or object from a feeder and then places it in the designated assembly destination or location; a complete feasible plan is a sequence in which each objects is picked up from a feeder and then placed in the destination. The objective function is to minimize the travel distance of the assembly robot in completing these tasks; the gripper has to travel to a given feeder's location, pick up the target object and then proceed to the destination location; this process is repeated until all parts are assembled. The main steps are:

1. Define a sub sequence as [Gripper, [feeder1 object1], (*inserting point*) [feeder2 object2], Gripper]
2. Loop and determine the objective function (travel distance) of insertion of remaining objects into the sub sequence.
3. Insert objects with the least travel distance in the sub sequence as follows: [Gripper, [feeder1 object1], (*inserting position1*) [feeder1 object3] (*inserting position2*) [feeder2 object2], Gripper]
4. Subsequently, object4 and its preceding feeder need to be placed in position 1 or position 2 according to the least travel distance. Repeat this process until the completion of a full assembly sequence

Figure 2(a, b) and Table 1 illustrates a MDA layout example and path trace.

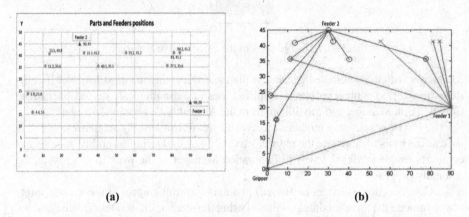

(a) (b)

Fig. 2. (a) Layout of parts and feeders and (b) trace of assembly path

Table 1. Assembly sequence (left and right tables)

X	Y	Index	X	Y	Index
0	0	Home	30	45	F2
90	20	F1	77.5	35.6	10
81	41.2	9	90	20	F1
90	20	F1	11.2	35.6	4
84.2	41.2	8	30	45	F2
90	20	F1	32.33	41.2	5
55.2	41.2	7	30	45	F2
90	20	F1	13.5	40.8	3
1.8	23.8	1	30	45	F2
30	45	F2	4.4	16	2
40.1	35.4	6	0	0	Home

3.2   The Virtual Reality Based Assembly Analysis Environment (VRAE)

In general, virtual environments have been used in research and educational context in the field of manufacturing as well as other domains [14, 21–24]. The collaborative approach uses the VRAE to simulate and study proposed assembly plans for a given target of micro devices. The VRAE was implemented using the Unity 3D game engine, C# and JavaScript. The VRAE takes an input of candidate assembly sequence and simulate assembly of the parts. Simulations analysis is carried out to determine the feasibility of the candidate assembly sequence. The assembly plan can be proposed, studied and modified using this virtual environment. After the validation and analysis of assembly plan, the most feasible can be identified by users. Subsequently, VRAE provides the Collaboration Manager with updates and submits the selected assembly sequence and path plan to the physical work cell component in the integrated approach. Modifications to a candidate plan are also possible at this stage of the approach and they are communicated to the Collaboration Manager and other modules. We have developed both non immersive and semi immersive environments for the VRAE. Figure 3 shows a view of the non-immersive VRAE and Fig. 5 shows a semi immersive environment built. Camera trackers and sensors (see Fig. 5) enable the semi immersive environment to track the position of the user who can navigate within this VRAE using a controller.

Fig. 3.   The non-immersive VRAE

3.3   Physical Resources and Work Cells

The work cells represent the physical components in this collaborative approach. The feasible assembly sequence obtained from VRAE acts as an input for the physical work cell to assemble a set of micro devices. Several work cells are available to accomplish assembling micro devices and parts. The first work cell (Work cell 1) has 4 degrees of freedom (DOF); X, Y, Z movements for the assembly plate and linear movement for the gripper mounted on a micro positioner. The second work cell (Work cell 2, Fig. 4) is equipped with an assembly plate which has a rotational DOF and two linear DOF; the gripper is mounted on a tool holding support which can move vertically. Two cameras mounted on the work cells provide the needed feedback to the Collaboration Manager.

Fig. 4. Work cell 2

Fig. 5. A user interacting with the semi-immersive VRAE environment

3.4   Collaboration Manager and Feedback

The collaborative manager receives feedback from the various cyber and physical components as the process underlying this approach progresses (from assembly planning, to VR based simulation and subsequently final physical assembly and camera based monitoring). The feedback from the cameras is an important part of this cyber physical approach which is communicated to the collaboration manager and used to ensure better control and integration of various activities. A state chart is used to monitor and keep track of the various activities as they progress (when a cyber or physical task is initiated, in progress or completed, their status is updated by the Collaboration Manager and communicated to other modules).

4   Examples and Discussion

We have assembled a variety of micro-meso scale parts using the approach outlined in this paper. The assembly tasks involved manipulation of meso/micro part designs where some of the target parts may be in the meso scale while others are in the micro scale range. Meso scale refers to including part sizes greater than 1 mm, with accuracies greater than 25 μm. The first example is shown in (Fig. 6a) shows a gripper placing a target gear in its location. The second example (Fig. 6b) involved assembling millimeter sized gears and pins. The third example in (Fig. 6c) is more complex and involves assembly of micro pins, rocker, and other objects on a gold mesh.

Fig. 6. (a), (b), (c). Views of micro and meso scale parts being assembled

5 Conclusion

In this paper, we discussed the design and implementation of a collaborative approach for the emerging field of MDA. The main focus of discussion includes cyber modules (for assembly planning, VR based simulation) which work in collaboration with physical assembly components to accomplish micro assembly tasks. The Physical work cells can be used to assemble micro devices (after the assembly alternatives have been studied virtually). A Collaboration Manager is used to coordinate the overall task activities. Research is continuing on exploring a Next Generation Internet framework which will allow the cyber resources to be hosted on a cloud which can be accessed from different locations.

Acknowledgments. This material is based upon work supported by the National Science Foundation (Grant Numbers 0423907, 0965153, 1256431, 1257803, 1359297, 1447237 and 1547156), Sandia National Laboratories and Los Alamos National Lab.

References

1. Saeedi, E., Abbasi, S., Böhringer, K.F., Parviz, B.A.: Molten-alloy driven self-assembly for nano and micro scale system integration. Fluid Dyn. Mater. Process. **2**(4), 221–246 (2007)
2. Rivero, R., Shet, S., Booty, M., Fiory, A., Ravindra, N.: Modeling of magnetic-field-assisted assembly of semiconductor devices. J. Electron. Mater. **37**, 374–378 (2008)
3. Shetye, S., Eskinazi, I., Arnold, D.: Magnetic self-assembly of millimeter-scale components with angular orientation. J. Microelectromech. Syst. **19**, 599–609 (2010)
4. Greminger, M.A., Yang, G., Nelson, B.J.: Sensing nanonewton level forces by visually tracking structural deformations. In: Proceedings of IEEE International Conference on Robotics and Automation, ICRA 2002, vol. 2, pp. 1943–1948. IEEE (2002)
5. Cecil, J., Kumar, M.B.R., Lu, Y., Basallali, V.: A review of micro-devices assembly techniques and technology. Int. J. Adv. Manuf. Technol. **83**, 1–13 (2015)

6. Gunda, R., Cecil, J., Calyam, P., Kak, S.: Information centric frameworks for micro assembly. In: Meersman, R., Dillon, T., Herrero, P. (eds.) OTM 2011. LNCS, vol. 7046, pp. 93–101. Springer, Heidelberg (2011). doi:10.1007/978-3-642-25126-9_17

7. Van Brussel, H., Peirs, J., Reynaerts, D., Delchambre, A., Reinhart, G., Roth, N., Weck, M., Zussman, E.: Assembly of microsystems. CIRP Ann.-Manuf. Technol. 49(2), 451–472 (2000)

8. Chu, H.K., Mills, J.K., Cleghorn, W.L.: Parallel microassembly with a robotic manipulation system. J. Micromech. Microeng. 20(12), 125027 (2010)

9. Das, A.N., Murthy, R., Popa, D.O., Stephanou, H.E.: A multiscale assembly and packaging system for manufacturing of complex micro-nano devices. IEEE Trans. Autom. Sci. Eng. 9(1), 160–170 (2012)

10. Jain, R.K., Majumder, S., Ghosh, B., Saha, S.: Design and manufacturing of mobile micro manipulation system with a compliant piezoelectric actuator based micro gripper. J. Manuf. Syst. 35, 76–91 (2015)

11. Gorman, J.J., Dagalakis, N.G.: Force control of linear motor stages for micro assembly. In: Proceedings of IMECE 2003, Washington DC, pp. 615–623 (2003). New Reference

12. Thompson, J.A,, Fearing, R.S.: Automating microassembly with ortho-tweezers and force sensing. In: IROS 2001, Maui, HI, 29 October–3 November, pp. 1327–1334 (2001)

13. Rizzi, A.A., Gowdy, J., Hollis, R.L.: Distributed coordination in modular precision assembly systems. Int. J. Robot. Res. 20(10), 819–838 (2001)

14. Alex, J., Vikramaditya, B., Nelson, B.J.: A virtual reality teleoperator interface for assembly of hybrid MEMS prototypes. In: Proceedings of DETC, vol. 98, no. 1998, pp. 13–16, September 1998

15. Ferreira, A., Cassier, C., Hirai, S.: Automatic microassembly system assisted by vision servoing and virtual reality. IEEE/ASME Trans. Mechatron. 9(2), 321–333 (2004)

16. Cassie, C., Ferreira, A., Hirai, S.: Combination of vision servoing techniques and VRbased simulation for semi-autonomous microassembly workstation. In: Proceedings of 2002 IEEE: International Conference on Robotics and Automation, pp. 1501–1506 (2002)

17. Probst, M., Hürzeler, C., Borer, R., Nelson, B.J.: Virtual reality for microassembly. Project report, Institute of Robotics and Intelligent Systems, ETH Zurich, Switzerland (2007)

18. Dembele, S., Tamadazte, B., Le Fort-Piat, N., Marchand, E.: CAD model-based tracking and 3D visual-based control for MEMS microassembly. Int. J. Robot. Res. 29(11), 1416–1434 (2010)

19. Popa, D., Kang, B., Sin, J., Zou, J.: Reconfigurable micro-assembly system for photonics applications. In: Proceedings of the IEEE International Conference on Robotics and Automation, Washington, DC, pp. 1495–1502 (2002)

20. Hollis, R., Gowdy, J.: Miniature factories for precision assembly. In: Proceedings of International Workshop on Micro-Factories, Tsukuba, Japan, pp. 1–6, December 1998. (Hériban, D., Gauthier, M., September 2008)

21. Zyda, M.: From visual simulation to virtual reality to games. IEEE Comput. Soc. 38(9), 25–32 (2005)

22. De Sa, A.G., Zachmann, G.: Virtual reality as a tool for verification of assembly and maintenance processes. Comput. Graph. 23(3), 389–403 (1999)

23. Gallagher, A.G., Cates, C.U.: Virtual reality for the operating room and cardiac catheterisation laboratory. Lancet 364(9444), 1538–1540 (2004)

24. Stapleton, C., Huges, C., Moshell, M., Micikevicius, P., Altman, M.: Applying mixed reality to enterainment. IEEE Comput. 35(12), 122–124 (2002)

25. Lu, Y., Cecil, J.: An Internet of Things (IoT)-based collaborative framework for advanced manufacturing. Int. J. Adv. Manuf. Technol. 84(5), 1141–1152 (2016)

Designing an Ontology for Agent-Based Planning and Control Tasks in Semiconductor Supply Chains

Raphael Herding and Lars Mönch[✉]

Chair of Enterprise-Wide Software Systems, University of Hagen,
Universitätsstraße 1, 58097 Hagen, Germany
{Raphael.Herding,Lars.Moench}@fernuni-hagen.de

Abstract. In this paper, we describe how we ensure interoperability of software agents that support planning and control decisions in semiconductor supply chains by means of a domain- and task-specific ontology. The sheer size of the facilities and the supply chains in the semiconductor domain, the permanent appearance of uncertainty, and the rapid technological changes lead to an industrial environment that gives rise to applying software agents for next-generation enterprise information systems. The S^2CMAS prototype is a hierarchically organized agent-based system that allows for decisions ranging from long-term capacity planning for the entire network to detailed scheduling decisions for single wafer fabrication facilities (wafer fabs). The ontology for the S^2CMAS system is designed based on a domain analysis. The usage of the proposed ontology is illustrated by an example.

Keywords: Semiconductor supply chains · Enterprise interoperability · Agent-based decision support · Ontology design

1 Introduction

Planning and control of semiconductor supply chains is an important research and development topic that receives a lot of attention in the last decade [1]. Integrated circuits (ICs) are the main outcome of such supply chains. Their production is carried out in four main stages, namely, wafer fabrication, sort or probe, assembly, and final test. The wafer fabrication and sort stages are called frontend, while the assembly and final test stages are abbreviated by backend. Wafer fabrication is the most important stage among the four stages. Here, the ICs are manufactured on wafers, thin discs made from silicon. Lots, the moving entities in wafer fabs, have a cycle time of several weeks, including up to 600 process steps that are performed on up to 400 machines [11]. A single lot may contain up to 50 wafers. The machines in wafer fabs are very expensive. Therefore, capacity is often scarce in semiconductor supply chains. Reentrant process flows occur, i.e., the same machine group is visited up to 50 times by the same lot in wafer fabs. Disturbances caused by machine breakdowns are typical. Forecasts are rarely accurate because of the rapid pace of change in the semiconductor market. In addition, many products have only a very short life cycle. A typical semiconductor supply chain contains dozens of wafer fabs and related assembly and test (A/T) facilities for the backend

© Springer International Publishing AG 2017
I. Ciuciu et al. (Eds.): OTM 2016 Workshops, LNCS 10034, pp. 65–75, 2017.
DOI: 10.1007/978-3-319-55961-2_7

operations. The corresponding supply chain-wide planning and control tasks are challenging [1, 2] because of the long lead times and the high demand uncertainty.

It is well-known that semiconductor supply chains place Enterprise Resource Planning (ERP) and Advanced Planning and Scheduling (APS) software under major stress [12]. Because of the sheer size of semiconductor supply chains, their highly distributed nature, and the frequent changes semiconductor supply chains are an ideal environment to apply software agent-based planning and control systems (cf. [10, 11]). Proposals for distributed planning and control systems for the semiconductor supply chain domain only rarely exist in the literature. We are only aware of [17] where important steps towards a distributed planning and control system for semiconductor supply chains are described, however, it seems that a prototype does not exist, and [6] where the multi-agent system (MAS) prototype S^2CMAS for planning and control tasks in semiconductor supply chains is sketched. The S^2CMAS prototype is based on the idea to allow for a distributed hierarchical planning and control approach. Decision-making agents are supported by staff agents in course of their decision making. Staff agents encapsulate domain-specific planning and control algorithms. In addition to staff agents, web services are deployed in some situations to provide planning and control functionality. Discrete-event simulation can be used to assess the performance of the S^2CMAS prototype in a rolling horizon setting. Therefore, simulation models of semiconductor supply chains are used. The S^2CMAS prototype is implemented using the C# and C++ programming languages by extending the FABMAS prototype [10]. However, ingredients for a rich communication between the different agents are not provided for the S^2CMAS prototype in [6]. In the present paper, we will close this gap by discussing the design of an ontology that allows ensuring interoperability of the agents in S^2CMAS. Our effort aligns with [3], where it is stated that the standardization of communication protocols in the manufacturing domain is important for the success of the Industry 4.0 vision.

The paper is organized as follows. The problem is stated in Sect. 2. This includes a discussion of related work. The design of the ontology is described in Sect. 3. The proposed ontology is applied in Sect. 4. Some conclusions and future research directions are provided in Sect. 5.

2   Problem Setting

2.1   Planning and Control Problems for Semiconductor Supply Chains

We start by describing the major planning and control elements of semiconductor supply chains. Note that we can only sketch the overall approach due to space limitations. We will present a more detailed view only for elements that are important for the understanding of the present paper. The overall planning and control functionality can be summarized as follows:

1. **Demand Planning:** Forecasts of different granularity are computed based on historical data and customer order information.

2. **Network Planning:** The structure of the semiconductor supply chain, i.e. which wafer fabs and A/T facilities have to be opened or closed, is determined. Demand scenarios for a long horizon, i.e. for several years, are taken into account. In addition to production-related decisions, i.e., which quantity of which product family should be produced in which period, capacity expansion decisions, for instance, purchasing new machines or do outsourcing for single nodes of the supply chain are made.

3. **Capacity planning:** Taking the results of demand and network planning into account, capacity planning decides which quantities, i.e. which volume, of which product family should be released in which period into the network of wafer fabs. Moreover, outsourcing decisions are made too.

4. **Master Planning:** It is decided by this functionality which quantities have to be produced in which wafer fab or A/T facility. Volume information of capacity planning is used as input. Outsourcing decisions are made.

5. **Operational Production Planning**: Based on the results of master planning, order release decisions are made for single wafer fabs and A/T facilities.

6. **Inventory Planning:** Safety stocks are calculated based on demand and lead time characterizations. These decisions form the input for master planning and production planning decisions.

7. **Available to Promise (ATP) and Order Management:** An order promising system calculates delivery dates based on customer requests. After this offer is accepted by the customer, supply is reserved. First, availability of the requested product through ATP is checked. When the customer order cannot be assigned to ATP, master planning is used to allocate the order to a new plan. Additional planning activities are required to match fab lots to customer orders, i.e. lot-to-order matching or pegging.

Note that we are not interested in discussing detailed operations in a single wafer fab or A/T facility because this is already carried out in [10, 11]. The main characteristics

Table 1. Characteristics of the different P/C tasks in semiconductor supply chains

P/C task	Scope	Horizon	Period length	Uncertainty
Demand planning	Network	Long to short	Months to weeks	Large
Network planning	Network	Long	Quarters to months	Large
Capacity planning	Network	Medium	Month to weeks	Moderate
Master planning	Network	Medium	Weeks	Moderate
Operational production planning (order release planning)	Single node	Short	Weeks to days	Moderate
Inventory planning	Network/single node	Medium to short	Months to weeks	Moderate
ATP and order management	Network	Short	Weeks to days	Moderate

of the different planning and control (P/C) tasks are summarized in Table 1. Note that we see the distributed hierarchical structure of the planning and control system from Table 1.

2.2 Related Work and Problem Statement

Ontologies for supply chain management are reviewed in [5, 14]. A specific ontology for a supply chain that deals with electronics products is proposed in [20]. A conceptual framework for supply chain modeling based on the Supply Chain Operations Reference (SCOR) model is presented in [7]. However, the framework is rather generic. Therefore, it can hardly be applied to model semiconductor supply chains.

The ISA 95 standard [16] is not appropriate for the planning and control tasks in semiconductor supply chains since supply chain issues are not considered. Ontologies for supply chain planning, so called task ontologies, are surveyed in [15]. It seems that no widely accepted ontology is available for supply chain planning tasks. However, ontologies for representing plans [4] and planning tasks [13] are described in the literature. These ontologies can be used as a starting point for the S^2CMAS ontology.

Ontologies are rarely presented for semiconductor manufacturing. We are only aware of [17] where a distributed planning and control system for semiconductor supply chains is discussed. A corresponding ontology is outlined. However, only a fairly simple planning logic is described that concentrates on order management. In [8, 9], ontologies are provided that are used in the FABMAS prototype, a MAS for scheduling lots in a single wafer fab [10].

However, we have to design an ontology for planning and control tasks in an entire semiconductor supply chain in the present paper. This ontology should include the FABMAS ontology. It should allow for a rich communication of the various software agents in the S^2CMAS prototype. Especially the communication between decision-making and staff agents has to be supported by the proposed S^2CMAS ontology.

3   Ontology for Planning and Control in Semiconductor Supply Chains

An ontology is a specification of the different concepts and their abstractions that exists for a specific domain for the purpose of reuse. In the present paper, we present an ontology that supports planning and control activities in semiconductor supply chains. Therefore, it is a hybrid between a domain and a task ontology. The ontology has to support the communication of software agents in the S^2CMAS prototype and more general in agent-based planning and control systems for semiconductor supply chains. Therefore, it is an important ingredient to support interoperability. The following activities have to be supported by the ontology to be designed:

1. Start of various planning activities either by staff agents or by web services in a rolling horizon manner. Staff agents support decision-making agents in course of their decision making by encapsulating planning algorithms [6].

2. Gather and prepare information that is required to populate planning models with data.
3. Exchange of information that is required for computing different types of plans.
4. Transfer of various plans back to the corresponding decision-making agents.
5. Communication of exceptions such as infeasible plans or cancelation of customer orders.
6. Development of demand scenarios to support what-if planning functionality.
7. Support of control and monitoring activities.

We start by presenting a UML class diagram in Fig. 1 that models the data needed for planning and control tasks in semiconductor supply chains. We use the data model as a starting point to derive concepts for semiconductor supply chains. Note that some of the concepts are already exist in general-purpose ontologies such as the Enterprise Ontology [19]. However, various extensions and refinements are necessary for the semiconductor supply chain domain. These extensions, for instance with respect to product structure and demand, will be described in more detail when we discuss below the corresponding concepts.

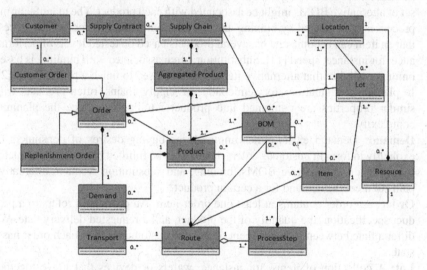

Fig. 1. Data model for semiconductor supply chains

We derive the following important concepts for semiconductor supply chains based on the data model:

1. **Item:** Items are raw material, semi-finished, or finished products that can be find in the different locations of a supply chain. Items appear as wafers, untested devises, devices, modules, and cards in semiconductor supply chains [2]. Wafers are diced. The result of these step are devices. Then the devices are bonded to a substrate and packaged to obtain modules. Cards are made from tested and assembled modules. Each item belongs to a location.

2. **Location:** Items are consumed, manufactured, or stored in a location. In semiconductor supply chains, we differentiate between production sites, i.e. wafer fabs and sort facilities and A/T facilities, and storage locations [2]. Die banks are storage locations that decouple the frontend from the backend. Distribution centers are the second type of storage location in semiconductor supply chains. They are located between customers and A/T facilities. Outsourcing options for frontend operations are provided by silicon foundries and for backend operations by subcontractors. Silicon foundries and subcontractors are considered as specific (aggregated) locations for planning purposes.

3. **Bill of Material (BOM):** It relates a set of items that are consumed to a set of items that are manufactured. Alternative BOMs/locations complicate the manufacturing process in semiconductor supply chains [2].

4. **Route:** A route is used to describe how items are processed or transported. In the first situation, routes are called process flows. They are formed by a set of process steps that are necessary to manufacture an item. In the latter situation, a route is a set of transportation steps to model the material flow from one location to another.

5. **Product:** A product is a good that fulfills a prescribed set of requirements [19]. A set of alternative BOMs might be associated with each product. The manufacturing process is complicated by binning and substitution. Binning refers to the process that an item can become one of several products based on tested levels of performance, for instance, speed [11]. Substitution, often associated with binning, is based on the possibility that alternative items might be used to finish a process step [2]. In planning formulations for semiconductor supply chains, often products with similar properties are combined into product families to reduce the planning complexity.

6. **Demand:** Demand exists either implicitly as buying desires of consumers or explicitly in form of customer orders that have to be fulfilled by the semiconductor supply chain. Alternative BOMs, binning, and substitution result in alternative paths to meet the demand for a certain product.

7. **Order:** An order contains at least one order item. An order item refers to a product specification, the quantity of the product, and a requested delivery date. We differentiate between replenishment orders and customer orders. Each order has a state.

8. **Lot:** A collection of items, for instance, wafers or devices that move together through a production site is called a lot [11]. Lots have to be matched to orders. A lot has a state.

9. **Resource:** An entity that enables the execution of activities is called a resource [19]. Each resource has a capacity. The capacity constrains the number of activities that can be executed by the resource in a given period. Various aggregated resource types exist.

10. **Cost:** Cost is an entity that represents the temporal, fiscal, or monetary dimension, attribute, or characteristic of an activity [18]. In semiconductor supply chain planning approaches, Work in Process (WIP) costs, inventory holding costs, and backlog costs occur in objective functions.

11. **Plan:** An activity is something done over a specific time interval [19]. Generally, a plan is an activity specification with an intended purpose. Planning is an activity with the purpose to determine a plan [13]. Planning is associated with goals [4], in our situation represented by objective functions to be optimized. Planning in supply chains is associated with a planning horizon. The planning horizon is formed by periods of a specific length. We differentiate, for instance, between network, capacity, master, and order release planning in semiconductor supply chains (see Table 1). The different planning activities result in different plans. A plan that is a results of capacity planning contains information with respect to which quantity of a product family should be released (or completed) in which period. In addition, it contains information with respect to necessary capacity expansions, for instance, which new machines have to be purchased in which period. A master plan determines which quantity resulting from confirmed orders and from forecasted demand should be completed in which location in which period of the planning horizon [11]. Moreover, outsourcing decisions have to be represented in master plans.

12. **Customer:** A customer requires a product by means of orders.

Next, we derive important domain- and task-related predicates. Domain-related predicates on the one hand are facts concerning a given semiconductor supply chain. On the other hand, predicates related to tasks describe how the goals of the planning and control process are fulfilled. Due to space limitations, only some predicates are exemplified in Table 2.

Table 2. Examples for predicates in the S^2CMAS ontology

Predicate	Scope	Description
VALID_WAFER_FAB	D	Determines whether a given wafer fab is able to produce a certain product or not
VALID_SUBCON-TRACTOR	D	Determines whether a given subcontractor can be used for manufacturing a certain product or not
VALID_DC	D	Determines whether a given distribution center (DC) is allowed for a make-to-stock product or not
MASTER_PLAN_FEASIBLE	T	Determines whether a given master plan is feasible or not
MASTER_PLAN_AVAILABLE	T	Determines whether a given master plan is available for order release planning or not
ORDER_COMPLETED	T	Determines whether a given order is completed or not
ALTERNATIVE_BOM_AVAILABLE	T	Determines whether alternative BOMs are available or not, in the latter case, a simplified master planning formulation can be used

Here, the D symbol in the scope column indicates that the predicate is domain-related whereas the T symbol refers to task-related predicates.

Agent activities have to be specified to ensure that the S^2CMAS prototype is able to meet its design goals. In the majority of situations, agent activities are used by decision-making agents to inform the corresponding staff agents about initiating specific planning and control activities. Again, only some examples for agent activities are shown in Table 3.

Table 3. Examples for agent activities in the S^2CMAS ontology

Activity	Description
INITIATE_MASTER_PLANNING	Initiates master planning activities through the master planning agent, a decision-making agent in S^2CMAS
CALCULATE_MASTER_PLAN	Asks the mid-term network-wide planning agent, a staff agent belonging to the master planning agent, to compute a master plan
START_ORDER_RE-LEASE_PLANNING	Initiates order release planning through the order release agent, a decision-making agent in S^2CMAS

4   Application of the Proposed Ontology

We apply the ontology to model the interaction between the master planning agent and the corresponding staff agent, the mid-term network-wide planning agent [6]. The master planning agent asks the mid-term network-wide planning agent to start master planning activities. Therefore, the master planning agent makes decisions with respect to the maximum amount of computing time, the length of the planning horizon, the lengths of the planning periods, and the cost settings in the objective function of the master planning formulation.

When the mid-term network-wide planning agent knows this information, this agent is able to gather the remaining data to make master planning decisions. In addition, based on the allowed computing time, an appropriate master planning approach is selected by the staff agent. Finally, the master planning agent asks the mid-term network-wide planning agent to calculate a master plan. A more detailed model of the interaction between master planning agent, mid-term network-wide planning agent, and order release planning agents is depicted in Fig. 2 by means of a Specification and Description Language (SDL) diagram. Note that failure situations are not modeled in Fig. 2.

Concepts, agent activities, and predicates of the S^2CMAS ontology are used in the discussed scenario. The master planning agent first initiates the calculation of a master plan. Therefore, a message with the following content is sent to the staff agent:

(CALCULATE_MASTER_PLAN)(NOT(TIME_REACHED:MAX_TIME)).

If the mid-term network-wide planning agent agrees to the request, the master planning agent sends a message with the following content:

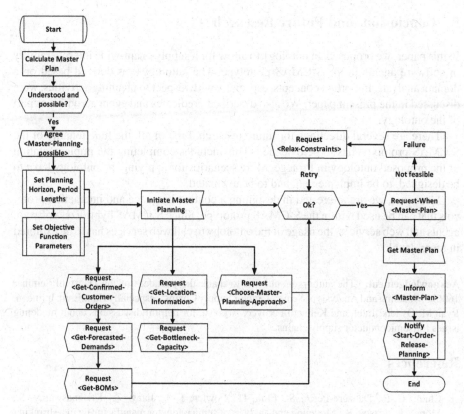

Fig. 2. SDL diagram for the discussed scenario

(INITIATE_MASTER_PLANNING
: PLANNING_HORIZON
: PERIOD_LENGTH
:OBJECTIVE_FUNCTION_PARAMETERS)
((NOT(TIME_REACHED:MAX_TIME)).

Here, the agent activity INITIATE_MASTER_PLANNING is refined by a more detailed description including, for instance, the concept identifiers PLAN-NING_HORIZON and PERIOD_LENGTH from the ontology.

After receiving this message, the mid-term network-wide planning agent starts collecting the planning-related data, for instance, confirmed orders, forecasted demand, and WIP and inventory and backlog levels. The mid-term network-wide planning agent also chooses the algorithm used for master planning. In a next step, the master planning agent asks for the calculated master plan. The staff agent sends the master plan to the master planning agent. Predicates of the ontology are used to communicate the success or failure of agent activities. Due to space limitation, we do not present the details.

5   Conclusions and Future Research

In this paper, we proposed an ontology to allow for a supply chain-wide interoperability of software agents in the S^2CMAS prototype. The ontology was derived based on a domain analysis. Important concepts, especially with respect to planning activities, were discussed in the present paper. We also described predicates and agent activities as part of the ontology.

There are several directions for future research. First of all, the functionality of the S^2CMAS prototype has to be extended. This includes completing the implementation of the proposed ontology in Protégé. More scenarios for applying the ontology have to be designed, to be implemented, and to be evaluated.

Moreover, we are interested in designing a content language and interaction protocols that can be used within the S^2CMAS prototype. Since S^2CMAS hybridizes software agents and web services, the usage of the ontology to call web services has to be explored in more detail.

Acknowledgement. The authors would like to thank the attendees of the Dagstuhl Seminar 16062 "Modeling and Analysis of Semiconductor Supply Chains", especially Hans Ehm, Infineon, Irvan M. Ovacik, Intel, and Kenneth Fordyce, Arkieva, for helpful discussions about modeling issues for semiconductor supply chains.

References

1. Chien, C.-F., Dauzère-Pérès, S., Ehm, H., Fowler, J.W., Jiang, Z., Krishnaswamy, S., Mönch, L., Uzsoy, R.: Modeling and analysis of semiconductor manufacturing in a shrinking world: challenges and successes. Eur. J. Ind. Eng. **5**(3), 254–271 (2011)
2. Degbotse, A., Denton, B.T., Fordyce, K., Milne, R.J., Orzell, R., Wang, C.-T.: IBM blends heuristics and optimization to plan its semiconductor supply chain. Interfaces **43**(2), 130–141 (2013)
3. DKI/DKE Roadmap: German Standardization Roadmap Industry 4.0, Version 2 (2016). http://www.din.de/blob/65354/f5252239daa596d8c4d1f24b40e4486d/roadmap-i4-0-e-data. pdf. Accessed 16 July 2016
4. Gil, Y., Blythe, J.: PLANET: a sharable and reusable ontology for representing plans. In: Proceedings of the AAAI - Workshop on Representational Issues for Real-World Planning Systems, pp. 28–33 (2000)
5. Grubic, T., Fan, I.-S.: Supply chain ontology: review, analysis and synthesis. Comput. Ind. **61**, 776–786 (2010)
6. Herding, R., Mönch, L.: S^2CMAS: an agent-based system for planning and control in semiconductor supply chains. In: Klusch, M., Unland, R., Shehory, O., Pokahr, A., Ahrndt, S. (eds.) MATES 2016. LNCS (LNAI), vol. 9872, pp. 115–130. Springer, Heidelberg (2016). doi: 10.1007/978-3-319-45889-2_9
7. Jain, S.: A conceptual framework for supply chain modelling and simulation. Int. J. Process Model. **2**(3/4), 164–174 (2006)

8. Mönch, L., Stehli, M.: An ontology for production control of semiconductor manufacturing processes. In: Schillo, M., Klusch, M., Müller, J., Tianfield, H. (eds.) MATES 2003. LNCS (LNAI), vol. 2831, pp. 156–167. Springer, Heidelberg (2003). doi:10.1007/978-3-540-39869-1_14

9. Mönch, L., Zimmermann, J.: An ontology to support adaptive agents for complex manufacturing systems. Proc. COMPSAC **2008**, 531–536 (2008)

10. Mönch, L., Stehli, M., Zimmermann, J., Habenicht, I.: The FABMAS multi-agent-system prototype for production control of waferfabs: design, implementation, and performance assessment. Prod. Plan. Control **17**(7), 701–716 (2006)

11. Mönch, L., Fowler, J.W., Mason, S.J.: Production Planning and Control for Semiconductor Wafer Fabrication Facilities: Modeling, Analysis, and Systems. Springer, New York (2013)

12. Ovacik, I.M.: Advanced planning and scheduling systems: the quest to leverage ERP for better planning. In: Kempf, K., Keskinocak, P., Uzsoy, R. (eds.) Planning Production and Inventories in the Extended Enterprise: A State of the Art Handbook, chap. 3, vol. 1, pp. 33–43. Springer, New York (2011)

13. Rajpathak, D., Motta, E.: An ontological formalization of the planning task. In: Proceedings International Conference on Formal Ontology in Information Systems (2004)

14. Scheuermann, A., Leukel, J.: Supply chain management ontology from an ontology engineering perspective. Comput. Ind. **65**, 913–923 (2014)

15. Scheuermann, A., Leukel, J.: Task ontology for supply chain planning: a literature review. Int. J. Comput. Integr. Manuf. **27**(8), 719–732 (2014)

16. Scholten, B.: The Road to Integration: A Guide to Applying the ISA-95 Standard in Manufacturing. ISA, Research Triangle Park (2007)

17. Soares, A.L., Azevedo, A.L., De Sousa, J.P.: Distributed planning and control systems for the virtual enterprise: organizational requirements and development life-cycle. J. Intell. Manuf. **11**, 253–270 (2000)

18. Tham, K.D., Fox, M.S., Gruninger, M.: Cost ontology for enterprise modelling. In: Proceedings Third Workshop on Enabling Technologies: Infrastructure for Collaborative Enterprises, pp. 197–210 (1994)

19. Uschold, M., King, M., Moralee, S., Zorgios, Y.: The enterprise ontology. Knowl. Eng. Rev. **13**(1), 32–89 (1998)

20. Yan, Y., Yang, D., Jiang, Z., Tong, L.: Ontology-based semantic models for supply chain management. J. Adv. Manuf. Technol. **37**, 1250–1260 (2008)

Big Data Harmonization for Intelligent Mobility: A Dynamic Toll-Charging Scenario

Paulo Figueiras[1]([⊠]), Guilherme Guerreiro[1], Ruben Costa[1],
Luka Bradesko[2], Nenad Stojanovic[3], and Ricardo Jardim-Gonçalves[1]

[1] CTS, UNINOVA, Dep. de Eng.ª Eletrotécnica, Faculdade de Ciências
e Tecnologia, Universidade Nova de Lisboa, 2829-516 Caparica, Portugal
{paf, rddc, rg}@uninova.pt,
g.guerreiro@campus.fct.unl.pt
[2] Institut Jozef Stefan, Ljubljana, Slovenia
luka.bradesko@ijs.si
[3] Nissatech Innovation Centre, Niš, Serbia
nenad.stojanovic@nissatech.com

Abstract. The need for interoperability in mobility data is more crucial than ever. Due to a panoply of data sources, from traffic sensors to GPS data, mobility data is increasingly more complex in terms of volume, heterogeneity, availability and quality. To turn such complex data into shareable, meaningful data, interoperability approaches must be implemented, namely through the use of standards. The presented work, aims at developing an approach for transforming and harmonize, traffic related data acquired from highway sensor network, supported by an ITS reference data model (DATEX-II). CRISP-DM methodology is addressed here, as a methodology for guiding the developments of the proposed approach. The main challenge is to cope with a scalable big data- platform for traffic-related data collection, supporting an innovative dynamic toll-charging model in a real-world scenario. This work is supported by a European Commission-funded project, named OPTIMUM, and presents some preliminary results from data harmonization processes developed.

Keywords: Intelligent Transportation Systems · Interoperability · DATEX II · Data fusion · Big data

1 Introduction

Particularly in the last few years data is created in quantities never seen before. From the sensors on our smartphones to sensors in roads connected to the Internet, all of these have contributed for the exponential increase in data availability. Nowadays, especially in the Transportation sector, large volumes of data are collected from a panoply of sources, each of which with its own differences in terms of granularity, format, frequency and type. The correct storage, usage and sharing of such an amount of mobility-related data may change

© Springer International Publishing AG 2017
I. Ciuciu et al. (Eds.): OTM 2016 Workshops, LNCS 10034, pp. 76–86, 2017.
DOI: 10.1007/978-3-319-55961-2_8

the way people live, move and interact. Intelligent Transportation Systems (ITS) refers to the integration of information and communication technologies with transport infrastructure to improve economic performance, safety, mobility and environmental sustainability for the benefit of all citizens [1].

Such challenges are related with data availability, since sensors sometimes go offline and do not collect data for particular periods of time, data quality, in the sense that sometimes data lacks some important features that define crucial mobility aspects, data size, because it is difficult to store such huge amounts of data and data variety, since data coming from different providers is not harmonized and linked within the same types, formats, etc. In order to cope with such challenges, data needs to be gathered, cleaned, transformed and stored efficiently so as to extract value from data. The Extract-Transform-Load (ETL) concept represents the process in which data is loaded from a source to a unified data repository.

ETL software houses have been extending their solutions to provide big data extraction, transformation and loading between big data platforms and traditional data management platforms - "Big ETL" [2, 3], because, with the exponential growth of data collected, the challenges presented before are going towards Big Data challenges, better known as the four original V's of Big Data – Velocity, Volume, Variety and Veracity of data [4]).

The work presented here proposes and evaluates a Big ETL-based approach for the efficient transformation and harmonization of large volumes of raw traffic-related data, which will be able to (i) deal with data quality, (ii) manage data interoperability through the use of already existing data standards under the ITS domain and (iii) provide a robust and scalable storage system, even for big data. The chosen methodology to implement Big ETL was CRISP-DM (Cross Industry Standard Process for Data Mining) [5, 6]. CRISP-DM was adopted here mainly because it is considered very complete.

The approach presented here is being developed under the H2020 R&D OPTIMUM project [7]. The OPTIMUM project establishes largely scalable architecture for the management and processing of multisource big data, which enables the continuous monitoring of transportation system needs while facilitating proactive decisions and actions in a semi-automated way, introducing and promoting interoperability, adaptability and dynamicity.

This paper is structured as follows: Sect. 2 details some aspects of the DATEX II standard and refers to some works on the field of traffic interoperability using DATEX II; Sect. 3 presents the application scenario in which the presented work was developed; Sect. 4 encompasses CRISP-DM's Data Understanding procedures; Sect. 5 presents the processes adopted for CRISP-DM Data Preparation step; Sect. 6 has the concluding remarks and paves the way for future work.

2 Background and Related Work

In order to manage the interoperability of several heterogeneous data sources, this work adopts an ITS standard-based data model. The DATEX-II [8] standard was first published at the end of 2006 and acknowledged in 2011 by the European Technical

Specification Institute (ETSI) [9], for modelling and exchanging ITS related information, being a European standard for ITS data exchange ever since. DATEX II is maintained by the EasyWay project [10] and supported by the European Commission.

Endeavors on how to use DATEX II so as to make ITS and Mobility-related frameworks interoperable are not new. In [11], a Cooperative ITS framework is devised in order to manage and optimize a Traffic Light Assistant. In this context, DATEX II is used as the messaging and communication means, being at the same time the interoperability provider, but also the messenger between road operators, users and infrastructure. In [12] authors present a scalable Big Data multimodal framework able to manage both public and private road transport, by using DATEX II and other standards to represent data. In [13], a V2V (vehicle to vehicle), V2I (vehicle to infrastructure) and I2I (infrastructure to infrastructure) communication architecture is presented and DATEX II is innovatively used as the I2I messaging format. Finally, [14] presents the Norwegian case of a ITS framework for the Norwegian Public Roads Administration, in which several standards are used, such as DATEX II, while custom formats which would then be new local standards or extensions to the existing ones would be developed. Figure 1 shows a conceptual view on the DATEX II standard. Areas highlighted in light blue are covered within the pilot.

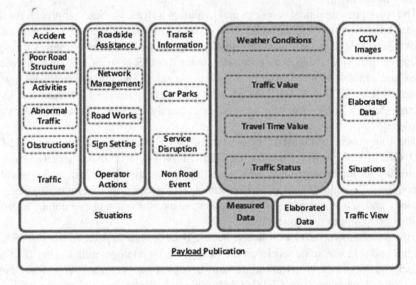

Fig. 1. The scope of DATEX II

There are four main design principles involved in the creation of DATEX II: separation of concerns, in terms of their application domains, a rich domain model, which allows a comprehensive and well defined modelling of data, extensibility, allowing specific extensions depending on country or area, and data exchange.

DATEX II supports and informs many ITS applications, in particular when cross-border trips are concerned. DATEX II provides the platform and technical specification for harmonized and standardized data modelling and data exchange in ITS applications. For the sake of the work presented, the most important section is measured data, which provides a way of describing traffic sensor data. In the case of measured data, data sets are normally derived from direct inputs from outstations or equipment at specific measurement sites (e.g. loop detection sites or weather stations) which are received on a regular (normally frequent) basis.

3   Application Scenario

The application scenario involves the development of a dynamic (toll) charging model, aiming to induce behavioral changes in drivers by transferring heavy traffic from the urban and national roads into highways. Such dynamic charging model will combine historical and real-time data collected, in order to calculate highways tolls pricing with x hours advance time. This way, the logistic companies could plan their routes according to the variation of the tolls. It will also establish a table of tolls prices for periods of the day and the week, and measure the different impacts in traffic, accidents, revenues, maintenance costs, CO_2 emissions and noise levels in the highways versus national roads.

The testing pilot will be implemented in the North of Portugal, on six highways and their alternatives. In this context, data acquired during the pilot's execution are mainly provided by two partners: Infraestruturas de Portugal (IP), a road infrastructure operator, for road network data, and Luis Simões (LS), a big logistics operator, for floating-car data. In the next sub-section, two different sensor-based data sources used on the dynamic toll-charging pilot, and provided by IP, are presented: road counters and toll sensors.

The first sensor-based data source is road counters. A road counter, or traffic counter is a device, often electronic in nature, used to count, classify, and/or measure the speed of vehicular traffic passing along a given roadway. The device is usually deployed in near proximity to the roadway and uses an on-road medium, such as pneumatic road tubes laid across the roadway, or piezo-electric sensors embedded in the roadway to detect the passing vehicles [15]. The second sensor-based source is toll sensors. Regarding toll sensors, electronic toll collection systems rely on four major components: automated vehicle identification, automated vehicle classification, transaction processing, and violation enforcement. Toll sensors preform the first two.

3.1   Collected Data

The road infrastructure operator has many vehicle-counting sensors throughout their road network. For the purpose of the pilot, which covers only a portion of Portugal's highways, focusing on the northern part of Portugal, IP has selected about 270 active sensors (135 in each road direction) from which to extract vehicle passages, road occupancy and average speeds. Apart from these counters, IP also agreed on delivering toll counts collected from their toll sensors. Counter data is delivered in two main ways: by Secure FTP, in CSV or XLSX formats and via SQL dumps. All sensor readings have a sample rate of five minutes.

Also, IP has access to toll counters' data, which are provided by the different concession holders. In the pilot's area, there are two main concession holders: Via-Livre, which holds highway A28, and Ascendi, which is the concessionaire for A4, A25, A29 and A41. These highways have a total number of 66 toll sensors (33 for each bearing), from which 8 are from ViaLivre and the rest from Ascendi. Both concession holders deliver their data through SFTP, in CSV files.

4   Data Understanding

As it was already mentioned, this step focuses on data collection, checking quality and exploring data to get insights to form hypotheses for hidden information. Data was thoroughly studied in order to check its veracity and availability. Reports about data quality and data availability were developed in order to assess the quality level of the data sources.

4.1   Road Counters

Available counter data spans from January 1st, 2014 at 00:00 to July 2016, 23:55 (still collecting), and it has a sample rate of five minutes, which means 12 readings per hour. Per year, the number of readings for one counter is 105120 readings. Multiplying by the total number of sensors we get the number of total readings per year, 28382400.

Of course some counters have time spans with no data, due to inactivity or malfunctioning periods. Data quality tests were made on sensor data, in order to check the overall quality of the readings. A sample of the data availability test is shown in Fig. 2.

The sensors are organized in pairs, each for a specific direction of the highway. It is visible the time spans of inactivity for each sensor, represented by the white spaces. Figure 2 represents a sample of 50 counters for the year of 2014 in the horizontal axis, while the vertical axis corresponds to the total timespan of the collected data. From this test, a quality factor was introduced, η_{sensor}^{year}, which represents the percentage of data completeness for a sensor per year:

$$\eta_{sensor}^{year} = \frac{\#\ of\ stored\ readings\ per\ year}{\#\ of\ expected\ readings\ per\ year} * 100 \tag{1}$$

For instance, regarding the sensor with ID A20_0+650_CT3683_C, corresponding to the 7th column of Fig. 2, for the year 2014, the quality factor is:

$$\eta^{2014}_{A20\_0+650\_CT3683\_C} = \frac{103.206}{105.120} * 100 = 98,1792\%\ \ \ \ \ \ \ \ (2)$$

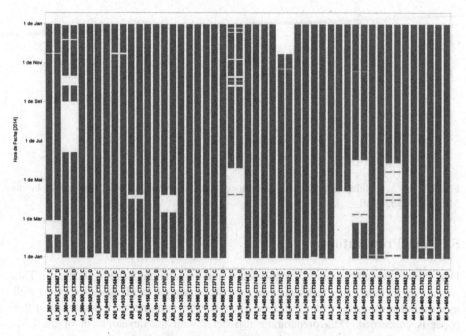

Fig. 2. Data availability test sample

4.2 Toll Sensors

Available toll sensor data from ViaLivre spans from October 15th, 2010 at 00:00 to July 2016, 23:55 (still collecting), and it has a sample rate of five minutes, which means 12 readings per hour. Available toll sensor data from Ascendi spans from January 1st, 2014 at 00:00 to July 2016, 23:55 (still collecting), and it has a sample rate of five minutes, which means 12 readings per hour. Per year, the number of readings is the same as in the case of counters, 6937920.

Of course some toll sensors have time spans with no data, due to inactivity or malfunctioning periods. Data quality and availability tests were made on sensor data, in order to check the overall quality of the readings. A sample of the data availability tests is shown in Fig. 3.

The figure represents the number of readings per hour for a sensor in A28 (vertical axis), during the data span covered for 2010 (horizontal axis). In a generic case, there are 12 readings per hour (one reading per 5 min), but there are flaws in the data, due to toll sensor malfunctioning.

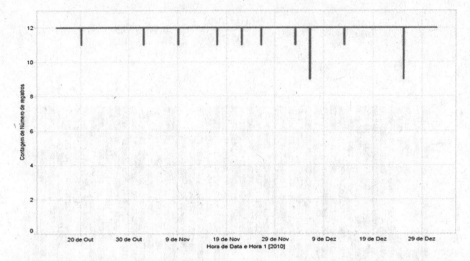

Fig. 3. Data availability test for a A28 toll sensor's readings per hour, from 15th of October to 31st December, 2010

5 Data Preparation

Data Preparation corresponds to the selection and preparation of the final data set. This phase may include many tasks, such as records, tables and attributes selection as well as cleaning and transformation of data. This step is where the work addressed in this paper is concerned. Data preparation also deals with the development of the ETL architecture. For the data preparation step, an architecture and tools to extract, transform and store efficiently (ETL stage) all the data previously described are proposed. Such proposed architecture addresses the following technical requirements: (i) deal with raw data in many formats and sizes; (ii) assure data quality; (iii) efficient big data transformation and storage; (iv) address interoperability at the data level, enabling the development of additional added-value services for highways users; (v) and a robust and efficient distributed storage system, that is scalable enough in order to process data from additional traffic sensors.

To address the previous technical requirements, the main tools and standards used for developing the proposed architecture were (i) Apache Spark, used for large-scale data processing, which includes the tasks of data cleaning and transformation; (ii) DATEX-II, as data reference model which the data is stored; (iii) MongoDB, as a NoSQL approach, for storing and managing the traffic data. Figure 4 depicts the conceptual architecture, where the data sources may arrive in different means (local or server documents, web services using SOAP or REST), and in different formats (txt, CSV, XLS, XML, JSON) and with all kinds of sizes. Spark is responsible for the data preparation step, which entails data harmonization and cleaning processes.

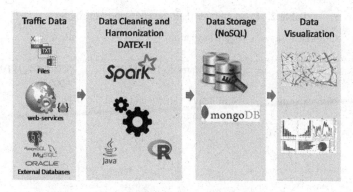

Fig. 4. Data preparation approach

5.1 Road Counters

Road counters' data was provided with the fields shown in Table 1. Each field was analyzed in order to get the corresponding standard field. In the case of non-existing standard fields, the original data field will not be transformed to DATEX II.

Table 1. Road counters' data fields and standard correspondence

Data source	Field name	Standard field
Road counters	Identifier	datex:SiteMeasurements(measurementSiteReference)
	Category A	N.A.
	Category B	N.A.
	Category C	N.A.
	Category D	N.A.
	Date	datex:DateTimeValue(dateTime)
	Light	N.A.
	Heavy	N.A.
	Occupancy	datex:TrafficConcentration (occupancy)
	Speed	datex:TrafficSpeed(averageVehicleSpeed)
	Volume	datex:TrafficFlow(vehicleFlowValue)

For road counters, several transformation steps had to be made, in order to harmonize the data. Dates were standardized to comply with DATEX II standard and the total number of vehicles was calculated from the data in order to fill in the total number of vehicles field of the standard (Table 2). Figure 5 shows the final format, stored into MongoDB.

Table 2. Road counter data transformation examples

Original field	Original data	Transformation	Result
Date	"2014-01-01 00:00:00"	Change dates to ISO 8601	"2014-01-01T00:00:00 +000"
Total vehicles	Non existing	Sum heavy vehicle and light vehicle counts	N.A.

```
 1 {
 2    "_id" : ObjectId("56ab5c569f6ed594781cc00f"),
 3    "concession_name" : "EP Grande Porto (ex AEDL)",
 4    "road_name" : "A1",
 5    "road_type" : "highway",
 6    "sensor_type" : "counter",
 7    "km_point" : 297.0,
 8    "sensor_id_ip" : "A1_297+975_CT3687_C",
 9    "sensor_id_holder" : NumberInt(-1),
10    "section" : "Santo Ovideo - Coimbrões (A44) ",
11    "state" : "Ativo",
12    "concession_holder" : "IP",
13    "bearing" : "c",
14    "location" : {
15       "type" : "Point",
16       "coordinates" : [
17          -8.607517,
18          41.11034
19       ]
20    }
21 }
```

```
 1 {
 2    "_id" : ObjectId("56ab5ce39f6ed594781cc171"),
 3    "sensor_id" : ObjectId("56ab5c569f6ed594781cc153"),
 4    "a_vehicles" : NumberInt(0),
 5    "b_vehicles" : NumberInt(2088),
 6    "c_vehicles" : NumberInt(48),
 7    "d_vehicles" : NumberInt(0),
 8    "date_time" : ISODate("2014-01-02T09:15:00.000+0000"),
 9    "total_vehicles" : NumberInt(2136),
10    "light_vehicles" : NumberInt(2088),
11    "heavy_vehicles" : NumberInt(48),
12    "occupancy" : NumberInt(12),
13    "average_speed" : NumberInt(76),
14    "volume" : NumberInt(178)
15 }
```

Fig. 5. Final data format for road counter data (right) and metadata (left)

5.2   Toll Sensors

In the case of toll sensors, there is no direct way of describing the data through DATEX II. A possible solution would be to create an extension to the standard, in order to encompass toll classes and vehicle classes. The collected and harmonized sensor metadata and data in MongoDB format is shown in Fig. 6.

```
 1 {
 2    "_id" : ObjectId("56ab5c569f6ed594781cc081"),
 3    "concession_name" : "Costa Prata",
 4    "road_name" : "A25",
 5    "road_type" : "highway",
 6    "sensor_type" : "toll",
 7    "km_point" : 12.93,
 8    "sensor_id_ip" : "-1",
 9    "sensor_id_holder" : NumberInt(2509),
10    "section" : "Aveiro",
11    "state" : "Ativo",
12    "concession_holder" : "Ascendi",
13    "bearing" : "c",
14    "location" : {
15       "type" : "Point",
16       "coordinates" : [
17          -8.611389,
18          40.64592
19       ]
20    }
21 }
```

```
 1 {
 2    "_id" : ObjectId("57015e7c60a5dee6439d5122"),
 3    "sensor_id" : ObjectId("56ab5c569f6ed594781cc081"),
 4    "date_time" : ISODate("2015-01-01T22:45:00.000+0000"),
 5    "class_1_vehicles" : NumberInt(5),
 6    "class_2_vehicles" : NumberInt(0),
 7    "class_3_vehicles" : NumberInt(0),
 8    "class_4_vehicles" : NumberInt(0),
 9    "class_5_vehicles" : NumberInt(0),
10    "light_vehicles" : NumberInt(5),
11    "heavy_vehicles" : NumberInt(0),
12    "total_vehicles" : NumberInt(5)
13 }
```

Fig. 6. Final data format for Toll Sensor data (right) and metadata (left)

Hence, the data model for storing harmonized data, and linked to the possible DATEX II classes and enumerations, is developed. There are also some future work objectives on this on-going work, which are presented in the following section.

6 Conclusions and Future Work

This paper presents a big mobility-related data harmonization and transformation architecture for ITS, addressing an application scenario on dynamic toll charging. The approach proposed here offers a big data-driven solution, which will lead to seamless transportation services for the movement of people and goods, through the use of DATEX II data exchange standard. This work has to take into account the real-time nature of sensor data, which makes it crucial to have a scalable and performance-based solution. Hence, the application scenario is also of extreme importance, due to the already built road infrastructure, and the quality of the data extracted from the sensors scattered throughout the network. Although this document focus on the efforts made to harmonize traffic sensor data, it is necessary to say that other data sources are being applied to this solution, such as traffic event, weather and floating car data, among others.

The work presented in this document is part of an on-going work, but some intermediate results may be acquired. Still, there is much work to be done: The authors plan to develop DATEX II-based adaptors for input/output of data; some extensions to the standard may be needed, for instance, to include toll and vehicle classes; another objective is to apply some prediction and CEP algorithms in order to catch events from sensor data, preferably in real-time; finally, due to the time-consuming task of the Data Understanding step, the authors decided to develop a Web-based user interface in order to better find insights in traffic sensor data. This Web interface will, in the future, encompass data visualization techniques together with the results of CEP and prediction, and possibly more data that can be linked with traffic sensor data.

References

1. European Commission: Intelligent Transport Systems. Directorate-General for Research Transport, Brussels (2010)
2. Bala, M., Boussaid, O., Alimazighi, Z.: Big-ETL: extracting-transforming-loading approach for big data. In: International Conference on Parallel and Distributed Processing Techniques and Applications (PDPTA), Las Vegas, USA (2015)
3. Caserta, J., Cordo, E.: Big ETL: The Next 'Big' Thing, 9 February 2015. http://data-informed.com/big-etl-next-big-thing/
4. IBM: The Four V's of Big Data. IBM (2013). http://www.ibmbigdatahub.com/infographic/four-vs-big-data
5. Azevedo, A., Santos, M.F.: KDD, SEMMA and CRISP-DM: a parallel overview. In: IADIS European Conference Data Mining, pp. 182–185 (2008)
6. Shafique, U., Qaiser, H.: A comparative study of data mining process models (KDD, CRISP-DM and SEMMA). Int. J. Innov. Sci. Res. 12(1), 217–222 (2014)

7. OPTIMUM Consortium: OPTIMUM Project, 1 October 2015. http://optimumproject.eu/. Accessed 20 April 2016
8. EIP/EIP+Project: Datex EasyWay (2014). http://www.datex2.eu/
9. European Telecommunications Standards Institute (2015). http://www.etsi.org/
10. Easyway: DATEX II –The standard for ITS on European Roads (2011). http://www.datex2.eu/
11. Freudenstein, J., Cornwell, I.: Tailoring a reference model for C-ITS architectures and using a DATEX II profile to communicate traffic signal information. In: Transport Research Arena, Paris, France (2014)
12. Duperet, A., Damas, C., Scemama, G.: Public authorities support for a large scale data infrastructure for mobility (LaSDIM). In: 22nd ITS World Congress, Bordeaux, France (2015)
13. Besnier, J., Ta, V.-B., Ehrlich, J., Simon, L.: SCORE@F project: a new usage of DATEX II in cooperative systems. In: Transport Research Arena, Paris, France (2014)
14. Westerheim, H., Supporting overall interoperability in the transport sector by menas of a framework: the case for the ITS station. In: Norsk konferanse for organisasjoners bruk av IT, vol. 22, no. 1 (2014)
15. Middleton, D., Parker, R., Longmire, R.: Investigation of vehicle detectir performance and ATMS interface. Texas Transportation Institute, College Station, TX, USA (2007)

Selective Redundancy in Network-as-a-Service: Differentiated QoS in Multi-tenant Clouds

Pradeeban Kathiravelu[(✉)] and Luís Veiga

INESC-ID Lisboa/Instituto Superior Técnico,
Universidade de Lisboa, Lisbon, Portugal
{pradeeban.kathiravelu,luis.veiga}@tecnico.ulisboa.pt

Abstract. Data centers consist of various users with multiple roles and differentiated levels of access. Tenant execution flows can be of different priorities based on the role of the tenant and the nature of the process. Traditionally enterprise network optimizations are made at each specific layer, from the physical layer to the application layer. However, a cross-layer optimization of cloud networks would utilize the data available to each of the layers in a more efficient manner.

This paper proposes an approach and architecture for differentiated quality of service (QoS). By employing a selective redundancy in a controlled manner, end-to-end delivery is guaranteed for priority tenant application flows despite congestion. The architecture, in a higher level, focuses on exploiting the global knowledge of the underlying network readily available to the Software-Defined Networking (SDN) controller to cater the requirements of the tenant applications. QoS is guaranteed to the critical tenant flows in multi-tenant clouds by cross-layer enhancements across the network and application layers.

Keywords: Software-Defined Networking (SDN) · Network-as-a-Service (NaaS)

1 Introduction

Multi-tenant clouds consist of applications that are of varying priority. The priority and differentiated levels of delivery time are either mandated by the service level agreements (SLA), or are perceived by the tenant themselves on their own application processes. It is argued that redundancy can be used more pervasively, in order to reduce latency in critical network flows and applications [1].

How to efficiently and effectively leverage redundancy in the priority subflows for better QoS, is a crucial and interesting research question in mission critical applications. Redundancy is often exploited at higher levels across the network stack for reliable networks. However, leveraging redundancy of flows at a lower network level is made possible with the advancement in network traffic monitoring [2], SDN [3], and middleboxes [4]. Software and hardware middleboxes offer additional capabilities to the network than merely forwarding or routing the packets of the network flows. SLA-aware data center networks should be

© Springer International Publishing AG 2017
I. Ciuciu et al. (Eds.): OTM 2016 Workshops, LNCS 10034, pp. 87–97, 2017.
DOI: 10.1007/978-3-319-55961-2_9

designed by exploiting the functionality offered by the middleboxes with minimally replicated resources, overhead, and redundancy to ensure timely delivery of priority content.

Figure 1 depicts application and network views of a cloud deployment. In the level of application layer, the system can be seen as tenant applications and application processes. Applications can be of various priorities - some of them more critical and time-sensitive than the others. Information on priorities can be forwarded to the underlying network as policies along with the control flow by extending and leveraging the SDN controller.

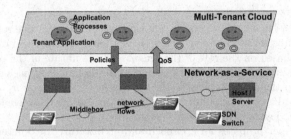

Fig. 1. Application and network views of a cloud deployment

Thus end-to-end delivery is guaranteed for (i) the applications spanning across multiple hosts traditionally with remote executions, and (ii) the tenants involving data communication between distributed systems or systems hosted in multiple computers. Moreover, an integrated management is offered across the multiple layers. NaaS consists of switches, servers hosting the tenant applications, and the middleboxes in the network level, where data flows across the distributed tenant processes are seen as mere packets and flows. The flow packets can effectively be handled at the transport and network layers to ensure a differentiated QoS to the tenants.

While the cloud providers focus on SLA guarantees to the users, the cross-layer optimizations remain still mostly underutilized. SDN and middleboxes should be leveraged to offer a tenant-aware NaaS and cloud deployment. Software middleboxes can be used in parallel with the SDN controller to translate the tenant policies and requirements into network flow rules. This paper presents *SMART*, a novel cross-layer architecture that leverages adaptive redundancy in the flows of NaaS for a differentiated QoS for multi-tenant cloud applications, processes, and sub-processes. *SMART* redundancy at the NaaS ensures that critical application flows are delivered on time, increasing the usability of the cloud deployment for mission-critical systems.

Flows that are identified to have priority over the others are defined as priority flows, and tagged so by *SMART* from the higher levels. Tags are read and interpreted at the intermediate nodes as policies, and exploited in detecting potential network congestion, SLA violation, or delays in routing the priority flows. An intermediate node is typically a switch in the network path of a flow.

Tags define thresholds and soft-thresholds. Thresholds consist of properties such as maximum permissible time for flow completion and other user-defined QoS parameters at the origin node, where a fraction of the threshold is defined as its respective soft-threshold. The controller is notified when a soft-threshold is met. Subsequently the packets from a subflow of the flow are diverted in an alternative route to the destination, or the subflow is cloned and routed in an alternative route along with the original flow. *SMART* opens an interesting research question on how network-level enhancements can be beneficial for the application requirements, and attempts to answer it by benchmarking against the traditional network routing in the cloud and data centers.

In the upcoming sections, we will further analyse the proposed *SMART* approach of differentiated redundancy. Section 2 discusses the design, solution architecture, and the prototype implementation of *SMART*. Preliminary evaluations on *SMART* are discussed in Sect. 3. Section 4 briefly discusses the related work, and compares them with the *SMART* approach. Section 5 closes the paper discussing the current state of the research and further future work.

2 *SMART* Redundancy Approach for QoS

SMART is a software middlebox architecture that enforces a set of enhancements over existing network flow routing algorithms. *SMART* exploits the monitoring capabilities offered by SDN, while extending the complimentary features provided by middleboxes to include the information on SLA parameters, in the form of tags attached to the packets of priority flows. FlowTags [5] software middlebox is extended to tag the flows with minimal overhead, as no other existing SDN-based approach enables per-flow custom policy enforcement in a network with presence of software and hardware middleboxes. Packets of the priority flows are tagged at the origin node by the distributed *SMART* software middlebox architecture consisting of FlowTagger deployed on the nodes, and the tags are read at the nodes en route destination, by the FlowTagger. Priority flows can be all the flows of a given user, all the flows originating at a given node, or a set of flows following a policy defined by the tenant at the application layer.

SMART architecture includes the soft-thresholds or soft limits as well as the thresholds as SLA parameters. Upon encountering a soft limit, based on the policy and the length and the priority level of the flow, either the flow is replicated and rerouted from its origin to the destination in an alternative route, or it is cloned or diverted from a breakpoint node partially, to mitigate the potential SLA violation by certain malfunctioning or congested nodes in the initial route. With a little redundancy, *SMART* attempts to meet the deadlines of the priority flows.

2.1 Software Architecture and Design

Figure 2 depicts the higher level deployment architecture of *SMART*. OpenDaylight [6] is extended and used as the base SDN controller, physically distributed across a cluster of computers, with a logically centralized view. FlowTags is extended and adapted as a software middlebox inside each node of the data plane as well as a FlowTags controller. The *SMART* middlebox consisting of the FlowTagger resides inside the nodes that are the origins of the flows. FlowTagger reads and writes tags to the packets. Tags include current time stamp to track the time consumed in routing so far which can be used to estimate other optional information such as estimated monetary cost and energy consumption.

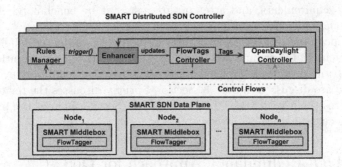

Fig. 2. *SMART* deployment architecture

FlowTags controller parses the tags from the packets forwarded to the controller, and also to control and invoke the FlowTagger to tag the packets of the flows originating from a node. Policies, thresholds, and business rules are read and stored into the *SMART* controller from the configuration files, as defined in the network by system administrators or the users, and managed by the rules manager. Rules manager gets and parses the rules from the tags, and triggers the *SMART Enhancer* according to the defined policies. *SMART Enhancer* consists of the enhancement algorithms that would wrap the base routing algorithms to enhance them. FlowTags controller, *Enhancer*, and the rules manager are designed as extensions to OpenDaylight SDN controller.

Along with the other rules set by the SDN controller, the custom user-defined tags in the packets read from FlowTagger are interpreted as policies, which the packets should respect. Upon the violation of the policies in any of the nodes, first packet of the violating flow is sent to the *SMART* controller and triggers it. Then controller sets a breakpoint in the flow on the packet that triggered the controller and the location node of the packet when the violation occurred. The breakpoint node or packet can also be chosen algorithmically from the application layer.

2.2 *SMART* Enhancement Approaches

SMART offers 3 alternative approaches: (1) divert, (2) clone, and (3) replicate, based on the priority level of the flow, to provide an SLA-aware data center network. Algorithmic improvements handle these cases based on the nature of the flow and the defined policies. Table 1 presents the potential overhead for the priority flows in completion time and bandwidth usage. Time overhead is measured as a potential delay that may happen in the flow delivery compared to the original flow. Here n refers to the number of times the packets are cloned, diverted, or replicated. $SMART$ aims at enabling the exploration of a tradeoff between additional overhead and increased flow reliability in a fine-grained way, rather than a full replication of flows.

Table 1. Time and bandwidth overhead

Approach with n number of diverts/clones of priority flow packets	Duplicate packets as a function of n	Potential time overhead
$Divert(n)$	$(n-1) * (0, 100]\%$	Possible
$Clone(n)$	$n * (0, 100)\%$	No/negligible
$Replicate(n)$	$n * 100\%$	No/negligible

1. Flow Diverting Approach: In the diverting approach, subflows of a few selected priority flows are routed in an alternative path to the destination, when an SLA violation is expected due to a congested node or link in the original route. The subflow is diverted in a single or multiple alternative routes except the original route. Choosing multiple routes in the divert approach will be useful for higher priority flows, when there is no certain alternative route that can be considered the best alternative. As the chosen routes may be longer or suboptimal than the original route, and as there is a need to reconstruct the flow, there is a potential time overhead or delay. Divert approach does not have duplicate packets if the subflow is diverted in just one alternative direction. However, diverting to multiple alternative directions will have duplicate packets similar to the following two approaches.

2. Flow Cloning Approach: The cloning approach clones the subflow to a single or multiple alternative routes. The cloning approach is employed for higher priority flows, where flows are cloned partially, instead of merely diverted. The original flow is left to continue in its route, while subflows are cloned and routed in an alternative route towards the destination. The updated rule in the breakpoint ensures sending the packets in the original route as well as an alternative route. As the original flow is left to continue in its original route unmodified, clone approach does not have a time overhead, yet there is bandwidth overhead.

3. Flow Replicating Approach: In the cloning and diverting approaches, the controller clones or diverts the packets that follow the breakpoint packet respectively, by changing the routing rules for the packets of the priority flows in the breakpoint node. Alternatively, the entire violating flow can be replicated from the origin to destination in a single or multiple alternative routes. Flow cloning and replicating are further enhancements to flow diverting, as the original route could end up being the better choice, if the congested links or nodes recover during the transmission. Similar to the cloning approach, the replicating approach does not have a time overhead as well. Replicating entire flows imposes however 100% of duplicate packets till the routing is complete. This can be considered a special case of the cloning approach that the entire flow is cloned, instead of a subflow starting from a breakpoint. The replicating approach can also be extended to later drop the original flow, as in the divert approach. However, while reducing the duplicate packets, this may introduce a time overhead.

The 3 approaches can be used in conjunction in an adaptive manner, than defining them statically to be mutually exclusive. In an adaptive execution of the cloning approach, once the clone procedure is invoked in a path on a flow for violation of soft limits, all the subsequent flows in the same path will be just replicated. The replicate action may continue till a status change occurs and/or till the controller finds the offending links or nodes in the path to have recovered. This minimizes the overhead of branching and merging the flows, while also minimizing the inherent overhead of using replicate approach as the sole enhancement approach.

Clone Destination Selection: When a congestion is encountered, the exact destination is decided based on the characteristics of the congestion. Flows are recomposed at either the destination of the original flow, or the next node following the congestion. A data center network may host mission critical systems and applications in a distributed manner. While delivery time may be guaranteed at higher levels such as the application layer, the network layer can be utilized in ensuring an end-to-end delivery in a timely manner for packets of critical flows.

In a large data center with a few nodes identified to be contributing to the congestion, the cloned or diverted subflow can be routed towards the node that immediately follows the congested link or node, to avoid routing in a suboptimal path when the congestion affects just one or a few of the nodes in the original route. This also minimizes redundant packets by early recomposing of the original flow. If there are no such nodes or links identified to be contributing to the congestion, the cloned or diverted subflow is routed towards the original destination in an alternative route.

2.3 Analysis of Performance Enhancements

Equation 1 presents the potential enhancement in a network flow transfer with $SMART$. It considers the overheads and time taken for various actions in transmitting and receiving the network flows.

$$T_{enh} = T^o - \{T_{det} + T_{update} + T_{dest} + T'\} > \epsilon > 0. \tag{1}$$

Here, T_{enh} - $SMART$ enhancement in flow completion time.
T^o - Estimated flow completion time (FCT), if the flow continues in the original (and currently congested) path.
T_{det} - Time taken to detect and report soft-threshold violation to the controller.

T_{update} - Time taken to update the flow table rules in switches.
T_{dest} - Time overhead at destination to recompose the flow.
T' - Minimum FCT with the cloned/diverted subflow in an alternative path.

For long running flows, T_{det} and T_{update} can be ignored as the controller is fast enough to detect and update the policy violations in milliseconds. Similarly, T_{dest} is estimated to be in the scale of milliseconds. For flows that take less than 1 s to complete routing, subflows of the violating flow as well as the following priority flows in the same route are cloned at the breakpoint, if they enhance the flow completion time of priority flows by a positive value when the soft threshold is met. Otherwise, instead of cloning the violating flow, all the subsequent priority flows are replicated at the origin and routed towards the destination in an alternative route. This is expected to avoid the potential overheads in short or mice flows.

Hence, an adaptive approach is chosen to offer the best of both worlds. While the first few flows may have violated the SLA, the following priority flows will abide to the SLA. Replicating the priority flows at the origin also avoids the potential overhead $SMART$ may impose by cloning in breakpoint for shorter mission-critical flows. The flow completion time of the subflow following the breakpoint to the destination can be considered a double integral of a time function as in Eq. 2.

$$T = \int_{bn}^{fn} \int_{bp}^{fp} t(p,n) \, dp \, dn \qquad (2)$$

Here, bn and fn refer to the breakpoint node and final/destination node, where bp and fp refer to the breakpoint packet and the final packet in the flow. The time function depends on the number of packets and nodes in the routing path, which is integrated for the packets from bp to fp and nodes from bn to fn.

2.4   Prototype Implementation

A prototype of $SMART$ has been implemented leveraging the OpenDaylight controller, while exploiting simulation and emulation environments to provide the network. Nodes consisting of hosts and switches along with middleboxes including the $SMART$ software middlebox are emulated. A distributed controller environment is created with an Infinispan [7] cache over a distributed network cluster. An elastic in-memory cluster architecture proposed in our previous work has been extended for the distributed adaptive execution of the controller [8].

Network flow routing algorithms that are commonly used in data center and cloud networks, such as the shortest path algorithm are implemented as the base algorithms. $SMART$ algorithmic improvements were then applied on top of these base algorithms. As OpenDaylight follows the OSGi (Open Service Gateway Initiative) [9] specification and offers a componentized modular architecture deployed on top of Apache Karaf OSGi container, the controller extensions are developed as independent OSGi bundles and deployed alongside with the controller core bundles. FlowTags controller is developed as a middlebox controller, to function alongside the SDN controller along with its other $SMART$ extensions.

Upon a soft-threshold is met, as identified by the tags in the flows, the flows are cloned/diverted in an alternative path towards the destination. The flows are recomposed once all the packets of the flow have reached the clone destination. While FlowTags controller helps as an input source in reading the tags and retrieving the information for *SMART* actions, rules manager offers the input for the control actions on how they should be enforced. As the core of *SMART*, *Enhancer* enforces the *SMART* enhancement approaches on the priority flows.

3   Evaluation

SMART enhancements were evaluated for their efficiency in enhancing SLA-awareness to applications through selective redundancy. Prototype implementation of *SMART* enhancements was benchmarked against the base algorithms commonly used, to assess SLA fulfilment regarding priority flows. *SDNSim* [10] SDN simulator was used to simulate the system. Experiments were carried out on multiple routing scenarios with the different *SMART* approaches, to evaluate the QoS and efficiency.

A data center network was modelled with 1024 nodes and shortest path as the base routing algorithm, and flows were routed between the chosen origin and destination nodes. Network congestion was modelled dynamically, along the path of the flows. Congestion was uniformly randomized by hitting a few uplinks of nodes concurrently, or routing overwhelming amount of flows through the same nodes and links, hence making them slower to respond or route.

The experiment was modelled with up to 100,000 of short flows each consuming less than 1 s to complete its routing. A few non-priority elephant flows were added to the experiment occasionally. The routing process was repeated with *SMART* enhancements applied over the base routing algorithm, where the subflows of the priority flows were cloned. SLA was defined as the maximum permitted flow completion time for the priority flows.

Figure 3 shows the time taken for a flow to route using shortest path as the base routing algorithm, as well as with the *SMART* clone enhancements.

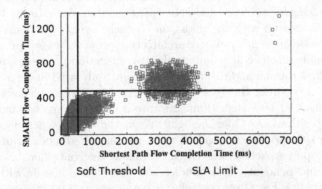

Fig. 3. *SMART* clone enhancements with shortest-path

Thick and solid filled blocks in the diagrams indicate clustered outcomes for the pairs of base flow completion time vs *SMART* enhanced flow completion times, where thin and white blocks indicate single or less repeating pairs of observed values. An immediate overhead of around 100 milliseconds caused by *SMART* was observed during the congestion. Yet *SMART* offered a speed up of up to 500% in the presence of congestion.

SMART was configured to replicate the following flows at the origin when a flow of the same path reported a violation and was cloned. Figure 4 indicates the time taken for *SMART* configured with this adaptive behaviour, indicating there was no SLA violation with *SMART* enhancements. This indicates that with the differentiated level of redundancy, *SMART* offers a differentiated QoS to various flows in the multi-tenant cloud and data center environments.

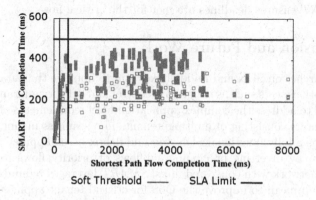

Fig. 4. *SMART* adaptive clone/replicate with shortest-path

4   Related Work

While hosts in the data center networks are connected through multiple paths, TCP limits the connection of a flow to a single path. Multipath TCP (MPTCP) is a transport protocol that uses the available multiple paths between the nodes concurrently to route the flows across the nodes. MPTCP is proposed and implemented as an enhancement to TCP to improve the performance, bandwidth utilization, and congestion control through a distributed load balancing [11]. MPTCP uses subflows in data transmitting, leveraging the multiple paths between the nodes in a network, and reconstructs the data flows in the destination in the original order [12]. FastPass leverages a centralized arbiter to find the ideal time to determine when the packets should be transmitted and through which path [13].

Dynamically rerouting the network flows to optimize the bandwidth consumption has been proposed in the previous work [14]. QJump [15] is a Linux Traffic Control module that allows critical latency-sensitive applications to jump the queues in the presence of packets of lower priority, focusing a shorter flow completion time. Hence, QJump and *SMART* focus on SLA for the higher priority flows through bypassing the traditional network routing, though *SMART* leverages redundancy in an adaptive manner in addition to 'jumping the queues'.

ProgNET [16] leverages WS-Agreement and SDN for SLA-aware cloud networks. Though data center networks are efficiently orchestrated and scaled with SDN, SLAs cannot be promised without dedicated and replicated resources. pFabric ensures deadlines are met for the flows that have deadline constraints, while still minimizing flow completion time for all the flows [17]. The existing work that leverages MPTCP or flowlets do not use redundant subflows for a reliable transfer of flows, or prioritize the flows based on user preferences to satisfy SLAs. In addition to addressing these research gaps, *SMART* further proposes an extended SDN and middleboxes based architecture for resending or cloning the subflows, if a flow has not reached the destination within the stipulated time. Hence, *SMART* ensures deadlines are met for the critical flows.

5   Conclusion and Future Work

Current researches on SDN and middleboxes aim to improve the data centers in various network aspects such as congestion control and delivery guarantees. However, they fail to address the complex application-level requirements of the enterprise data centers consisting of multiple tenants in a seamless manner. *SMART* is developed as a fully functional SDN and middlebox-based approach for multi-tenant clouds, by diverting or cloning subflows of priority flows for a timely delivery in a network with congested links. *SMART* leverages redundancy in the NaaS flows as a mean to improve the QoS for critical tenant applications.

Acknowledgements. This work was supported by national funds through Fundação para a Ciência e a Tecnologia with reference UID/CEC/50021/2013 and a PhD grant offered by the Erasmus Mundus Joint Doctorate in Distributed Computing (EMJD-DC).

References

1. Vulimiri, A., Godfrey, P.B., Mittal, R., Sherry, J., Ratnasamy, S., Shenker, S.: Low latency via redundancy. In: Proceedings of the Ninth ACM Conference on Emerging Networking Experiments and Technologies, pp. 283–294. ACM (2013)
2. Bauer, B.: Network traffic monitoring, US Patent App. 10/236,402 (2002)
3. Nadeau, T.D., Gray, K.: SDN: Software Defined Networks. O'Reilly Media, Inc., Sebastopol (2013)
4. Walfish, M., Stribling, J., Krohn, M.N., Balakrishnan, H., Morris, R., Shenker, S.: Middleboxes no longer considered harmful. In: OSDI, vol. 4, p. 15 (2004)
5. Fayazbakhsh, S.K., Chiang, L., Sekar, V., Yu, M., Mogul, J.C.: Enforcing network-wide policies in the presence of dynamic middlebox actions using FlowTags. In: Proceedings of the USENIX NSDI (2014)
6. Medved, J., Varga, R., Tkacik, A., Gray, K.: Opendaylight: towards a model-driven SDN controller architecture. In: 2014 IEEE 15th International Symposium on a World of Wireless, Mobile and Multimedia Networks, pp. 1–6. IEEE (2014)

7. Marchioni, F.: Infinispan Data Grid Platform. Packt Publishing, Birmingham (2012)
8. Kathiravelu, P., Veiga, L.: An adaptive distributed simulator for cloud and mapreduce algorithms and architectures. In: 2014 IEEE/ACM 7th International Conference on Utility and Cloud Computing (UCC), pp. 79–88. IEEE (2014)
9. Gu, T., Pung, H.K., Zhang, D.Q.: Toward an OSGI-based infrastructure for context-aware applications. IEEE Pervasive Comput. **3**(4), 66–74 (2004)
10. Kathiravelu, P., Veiga, L.: Software-defined simulations for continuous development of cloud and data center networks. In: Debruyne, C., et al. (eds.) OTM 2016. LNCS, vol. 10033, pp. 3–23. Springer, Cham (2016)
11. Raiciu, C., Barre, S., Pluntke, C., Greenhalgh, A., Wischik, D., Handley, M.: Improving datacenter performance and robustness with multipath TCP. ACM SIGCOMM Comput. Commun. Rev. **41**(4), 266–277 (2011)
12. Ford, A., Raiciu, C., Handley, M., Bonaventure, O.: TCP extensions for multipath operation with multiple addresses. Technical report (2013)
13. Perry, J., Ousterhout, A., Balakrishnan, H., Shah, D., Fugal, H.: Fastpass: a centralized zero-queue datacenter network. In: Proceedings of the 2014 ACM Conference on SIGCOMM, pp. 307–318. ACM (2014)
14. Al-Fares, M., Radhakrishnan, S., Raghavan, B., Huang, N., Vahdat, A.: Hedera: dynamic flow scheduling for data center networks. In: NSDI, vol. 10, p. 19 (2010)
15. Grosvenor, M.P., Schwarzkopf, M., Gog, I., Watson, R.N., Moore, A.W., Hand, S., Crowcroft, J.: Queues don't matter when you can jump them! In: Proceedings of the NSDI (2015)
16. Stanik, A., Koerner, M., Lymberopoulos, L.: SLA-driven federated cloud networking: quality of service for cloud-based software defined networks. Procedia Comput. Sci. **34**, 655–660 (2014)
17. Alizadeh, M., Yang, S., Sharif, M., Katti, S., McKeown, N., Prabhakar, B., Shenker, S.: pFabric: minimal near-optimal datacenter transport. ACM SIGCOMM Comput. Commun. Rev. **43**(4), 435–446 (2013)

Program Synthesis for Configuring Collaborative Solutions in Feature Models

Lina Ochoa and Oscar González-Rojas[✉]

Systems and Cómputing Engineering Department, School of Engineering,
Universidad de los Andes, Bogotá, Colombia
{lm.ochoa750,o-gonza1}@uniandes.edu.co

Abstract. We create a program synthesis for searching optimal configurations in collaborative decision-making models. At the specification level, existing approaches do not consider both individual and business constraints to configure products in a cooperative manner. Usually, the combination of independent specifications is manually implemented into low level platforms, which limits the management of constraint-intensive decision processes. Our proposed model-driven collaboration system analyses multiple domain and preference models to help selecting goal-driven technological solutions. First, we extend an existing domain-specific language to specify multi-objective and constraint-based business rules. Next, we created model transformations to generate a program that can be executed into two different constraint-based platforms, which combine heterogeneous and highly expressive models. We apply our approach to find a goal-driven enterprise information system solution. The program synthesis analyzed in average 697 constraints across multiple specifications to avoid inconsistencies in manual configurations.

Keywords: Enterprise interoperability · Domain modeling · Collaborative product configuration · Program synthesis · Constraint programming

1 Introduction

Feature modeling is a variability modeling technique used for representing common and variable characteristics of a given concept [5]. This technique allows representing a complete system family or Software Product Line (SPL).

Current approaches to configure SPL products [8,14,15] address a multi-stakeholder configuration environment. However, business constraints (*e.g.* optimization over product attributes) are tangled and scattered within implementations with a low level of abstraction such as Constraint Programming (CP) [8,9,13,15], Evolutionary Algorithms (EA) [4,6,7], and boolean satisfiability problems [14]. The manual implementation of these programs generates static solutions which increase the complexity to specify and evolve both independent stakeholders' products and business constraints. Thus, dynamic implementations are required to support the continuous change of expressiveness and size in these specifications, according to changing business needs (Sect. 2).

© Springer International Publishing AG 2017
I. Ciuciu et al. (Eds.): OTM 2016 Workshops, LNCS 10034, pp. 98–108, 2017.
DOI: 10.1007/978-3-319-55961-2_10

We developed a collaborative program synthesis to solve these issues. First, the program synthesis takes the following domain specifications as inputs: (i) a SPL feature model; (ii) stakeholders' points-of-view represented as feature model configurations; and (iii) business constraints identified as solution constraints, which are specified with the CoCo Domain-specific Language (DSL) [11]. Second, we extended CoCo with new solution constraints (*i.e.* selection state, finite domain, and multi-variable optimization) to increase the expressiveness available for decision-makers at the specification level. Third, we defined the implementation semantics of interoperable domain specifications in terms of a Constraint Satisfaction Problem (CSP). The combination of heterogeneous and highly expressive models into a single implementation semantics allows the identification of optimal configurations that conform to both individual and business constraints. Fourth, we created model transformations that automatically translate domain specifications into two different constraint-based platforms (*i.e.* Choco and JaCoP) to validate the implementation semantics' flexibility. Our model-driven collaboration system entails the evolution of both program synthesis and implementation platforms (Sect. 3).

We applied this approach to a telecommunications company to select an optimal configuration for an Enterprise Information System (EIS) investment. We evaluated the effectiveness of configuring products manually and with our program synthesis for a set of given solution constraints (Sect. 4). The program synthesis enhanced the search process by analyzing a large amount of constraints. We conclude by discussing related work (Sect. 5) and future work (Sect. 6).

2 Background and Motivation

2.1 Core Concepts

Common and variable characteristics of a given concept are represented as features in a tree structure known as feature model [5]. The edges between features are known as tree constraints. There are four different types: *mandatory* where the child feature has to be included in all SPL products; *optional* where the child feature may be included; *or* where at least one feature from the or-group should be selected; and *alternative* where at most one feature from the alternative-group should be selected [5]. Additionally, a feature model considers cross-tree constraints between connected or non-connected features, which are represented as consistent logical formulas where propositions represent features.

A feature model can be extended with numeric or descriptive feature attributes related to different attribute types (*e.g.* costs) [11]. A *configuration* is an instance of a feature model representing the features' state (*i.e.* selected or deselected). A configuration specifies a product or group of products in a SPL.

Program synthesis is "the process for transforming high level models into executables" [1]. The focus of our approach is on transforming domain specifications (*i.e.* feature models, feature attributes, configurations, and solution constraints) into an executable CSP program that allows searching for optimal product configurations.

2.2 Open Issues for Optimal Configurations: A Running Example

In 2009, a telecommunication company decided to support the marketing and sales processes with IT. However, they spent a lot of resources studying the project alternatives to arrive to an agreement. We used an extended feature model to represent IT investment alternatives relevant to the company. Figure 1 shows a subset of this model by illustrating feature attributes, tree constraints, and cross-tree constraints. The complete extended feature model contains 12 decision types (*e.g.* Business Drivers, target EIS), and 125 decision options which are leaf children of the feature model.

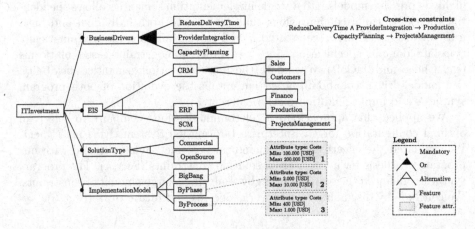

Fig. 1. Extract of the IT investment feature model extended with attributes.

In Fig. 1, the *mandatory* relationship associated with the *IT investment* feature forces the selection of the *EIS* feature in all product configurations. The *alternative* relationship associated to the *EIS* feature implies that at most one of the following systems should be selected: Customer Relationship Management (*CRM*), Enterprise Relationship Planning (*ERP*), or Supply Chain Management (*SCM*). In addition, *CRM* handles an *or* relationship between *sales* and *customers* modules, which means that at least one of those features should be selected if *CRM* is selected. The first cross-tree constraint states that if both the *Reduce Delivery Time* and *Provider Integration* business drivers are selected, then the ERP *production* module should also be selected. In this context, the following is a valid stakeholder configuration: $SE_1 = \{ITInvestment, BusinessDrivers, ReduceDeliveryTime, ProviderIntegration, EIS, SCM, SolutionType, Commercial, ImplementationModel, BigBang\}$. The three feature attributes associated with the *Implementation Model* decision options represent money in *USD*. These attributes are specified with a *Costs* attribute type, and with minimum and maximum values to restrict their domain. In the running example we defined four different attribute types: *costs*, needed *human resources*, employed *time*, and related *risks*. All of these types are specified as *integers*.

The company aims to consider independent decisions of the involved stakeholders, thus disagreements can arise between stakeholders' configurations. The SE_1 presents inconsistencies and different solutions with another stakeholder configuration: $SE_2 = \{ITInvestment, BusinessDrivers, ProviderIntegration, ReduceDeliveryTime, EIS, CRM, Sales, SolutionType, Commercial, ImplementationModel, ByPhase\}$. For instance, both stakeholders prefer a different implementation model (*i.e.* Big Bang, By Phases). Both features are exclusive, thus a solution that considers conciliation rules is needed in order to search a good decision alternative that complies with the company needs. Therefore, the company defines a set of requirements or solution constraints: minimize *costs*, minimize risks, and force CRM selection.

The following problems were identified when configuring products considering individual and business constraints in multi-stakeholders environments.

- P1. *Low expressive solution constraints.* Some approaches [10,15] propose the optimization of a cost function to search desired configurations without considering further solution constraints that change over time (*e.g.* limits over attribute types), and the independent knowledge of involved people. The combination of crosscutting specifications (individual configurations and multiple solution constraints), with a concrete implementation semantics independent of specific platforms, is required to increase their expressiveness.
- P2. *Static implementations.* Current solutions for searching optimal SPL configurations rely on manually implemented program abstractions [4,6,10]. Thus, solution constraints are difficult to incorporate, isolate, and evolve when the organization requires it since they are entangled and scattered in the program. This results in an inflexible, complex, and time consuming task. A dynamic implementation of domain specifications is required.

3   A Program Synthesis for Searching Optimal Solutions

The created constraint-based program synthesis considers all the required information for deriving a domain-specific program: a SPL feature model, a set of stakeholders' configurations, and solution constraints (*cf.* motivating scenario in Sect. 2.2). Then, these specifications are transformed into a CSP implementation to search optimal configurations according to business needs.

3.1   Specification of Solution Constraints: CoCo in a Nutshell

The existing DSL named CoCo [11] allows extending feature models with attribute types (*e.g.* costs), feature attributes, and hard limit and one-variable solution constraints. Both constraint types have their corresponding specification and implementation into a CSP model. This level of abstraction eases the evolution, maintenance, and incorporation of solution constraints (*cf.* P1 in Sect. 2.2).

We extended the expressiveness of CoCo to support the specification of new solution constraints (*cf.* motivating scenario in Sect. 2.2): (*i*) *multi-variable optimization* constraints where the organization defines more than one optimization function over a set of attribute types; (*ii*) *finite domain* constraints where the organization assigns a set of well-defined integer values to the domain of a feature attribute related to a specific feature; and (*iii*) *selection state* constraints where *mandatory* and *forbidden* options are allowed. The *mandatory* option forces the selection of a feature, while the *forbidden* option prohibits it. This type is different from a mandatory tree constraint, because it defines a temporary rule that does not affect the entire feature model, but just one configuration scenario.

Listing 3.1 illustrates the specification of an attribute type, feature attributes, and solution constraints described in the motivating scenario. Only the three constraints defined by the company are executed at the end of the DSL.

```
1  Attribute_Types {                                 1  Solution_Constraints {
2    Costs { int minValue;                           2
3      int maxValue; string unitMeasure;}}           3    optimization R1 : minimize Costs;
4                                                     4    optimization R2 : minimize Risks;
5  Feature_Attributes {                              5    hardLimit R3 : Costs lt 500000;
6    Costs c1 = {100000, 200000, USD};               6    selectionState R4 : CRM mandatory;
7    Costs c2 = {2000, 10000, USD};}                 7    finiteDomain R5: BigBang assigns
8                                                     8    Costs = {100000, 150000};
9  Features {                                         9
10   feature BigBang attributes = {c1};              10   execute R1, R2, R4;
11   feature ByPhase attributes = {c2};}             11 }
```

Listing 3.1. Extract of the CoCo DSL specification for the motivating scenario.

3.2   Implementation Semantics of Domain Specifications

The aforementioned specifications are integrated into a *composed feature model* which is translated into a CSP program. We selected CSP since it respects all given constraints obtaining valid products, contrary to other methods like EA where there is a need to minimize the number of violated constraints. CSP also manages arithmetic, boolean, and optimization functions, which support a further expressiveness of solution constraints.

Features, feature attributes, and tree constraints are mapped in the CSP according to Benavides et al. [3] proposal. Features and feature attributes are expressed as boolean and integer variables respectively. Tree constraints are defined with the equality operation, as well as a combination of boolean operators (*i.e.* AND, OR, NOT, implication, double implication). Cross-tree constraints (*i.e. requires* and *excludes*) are defined with implications over feature values [11]. Optimization and hard limit constraints employ arithmetic constraints over integer values and optimization solving functions [11]. The implementation semantics for new solution constraints is described as follows.

In the case of *finite domain constraints* we modified the domain related to a feature attribute variable. Then, for a finite domain of integers $D_{i:fd}$ assigned to a variable V_i, where $i \in \mathbb{Z}$ and $1 \leq i \leq |V|$, V is the complete set of the CSP variables, then we define $D_i = D_{i:fd}$. Similarly, when defining a *selection state mandatory* option over a feature we assigned it a domain of $D_i = \{1\}$.

Multi-variable optimization constraints employ the CSP global constraint *sum*. This constraint adds all feature attribute variables related to an specific attribute type obtaining the expression $\sum_{i=1}^{n} fa_i$ where $fa_i \in V$, $0 < n < |V|$, and $1 \leq i \leq n$. We defined a set of objective functions *obj* to maximize or minimize the sum of specific attribute type at, therefore $obj(at) = \sum_{i=1}^{n} fa_i$. We employ a search in the Pareto front of the search space for this optimization.

3.3 Program Synthesis Implementation

The *composed feature model* was translated into two particular CSP implementations (*i.e.* Choco and JaCoP) to instantiate the implementation semantics[1]. Both solvers were selected to evaluate the compliance of target implementations in terms of highly expressive and crosscutting specifications (*cf.* P2 in Sect. 2.2).

Feature models and configurations where represented with FeatureIDE. Feature attributes and solution constraints were specified with CoCo DSL [11]. The homogenization and composition of all specifications was modeled in an XMI instance of an Eclipse Modeling Framework (EMF) Ecore metamodel [12]. We employed Xtext to specify text-to-model transformations (T2M) (*i.e.* CoCo grammar). We used the Epsilon Transformation Language (ETL) for implementing two model-to-model transformations (M2M); 281 LOC were used for transforming FeatureIDE models into our own schema, and 182 LOC for including the CoCo specification into the new generated model. We used the Epsilon Generation Language (EGL) for implementing one model-to-text transformations (M2T) for mapping the complete decision scenario into a CSP (*i.e.* 940 LOCs).

4 Assessment

We present the evaluations performed to assess the effectiveness when configuring a suitable SPL product in our collaborative constraint-based program synthesis. We validated the following hypotheses: the use of the program synthesis improves the coverage and time for searching optimal configurations.

4.1 Subjects and Design

The experiment counted with nine IT professionals with mature knowledge in the field. We randomly arranged them into three groups in order to simulate five decision-making scenarios to characterize the program synthesis in terms of coverage and configuration time. Coverage is related to the amount of constraints that are analyzed across domain specifications to fulfill the solution constraints. Table 1 illustrates the solution constraints that were defined by a person who participated in the actual IT investment project.

Each scenario is considered a run and it counts with an independent SPL composed by four decision types and 42 features from the original feature model.

---

[1] Both encodings can be found at: https://github.com/CoCoResearch/CSPMappings.

Table 1. Configuration scenarios setup.

Run	Features	Solution constraint types	Constraints
1	42	(3) Minimize risks AND minimize costs AND maximize human resources	655–745
2	42	(2) Minimize risks AND mandatory selection of a business driver	678–798
3	42	(3) Minimize costs AND limit risks values between 4 and 15.5 AND mandatory selection of a business driver	741–781
4	43	(4) Minimize costs AND assign a finite domain to three feature attributes	726–806
5	41	(5) Maximize time AND assign a finite domain to two feature attributes AND mandatory selection of two different business drivers	776–840

The decision types correspond to the *business drivers* and the *EIS* decision types presented in the motivating scenario, and two randomly selected branches that differ in all runs. This was done in order to maintain the same complexity between the five experimental models. For each run, each stakeholder analyzed solution constraints and they specified them through CoCo DSL. Afterwards, each stakeholder created a configuration by deciding over the four decision types. We considered one qualitative independent variable with two levels that refers to the product configuration approach. First, the team had a meeting to define a final configuration that satisfied individual and solution constraints (manual approach). Second, we used the program synthesis to generate the domain and solution constraint specifications into both solvers (semi-automated approach).

4.2   Results

Two of the three teams presented inconsistent and invalid configurations in different runs that did not aligned to the *feature model* constraints. Nonetheless, *stakeholders' independent decisions* were completely considered in a meeting discussion that resulted in unanimous selected configurations. In the case of *solution constraints*, team participants considered the associated feature attributes without a rigorous mathematical analysis. Conversely, with our approach all of the searched configurations presented a valid and consistent state in all experimental runs by evaluating all the defined *feature model* and *solution* constraints. Additionally, they aligned to *stakeholders' individual configurations*, proposing solutions over the search space defined by the previously selected features.

Figure 2 shows the average coverage and configuration time of all teams per configuration scenario. Bars labeled C describe the number of evaluated constraints. Bars labeled M show the manual configuration time, whereas bars labeled SA show the time by using our program synthesis. The time is grouped in the different phases of the configuration process: the configuration of individual

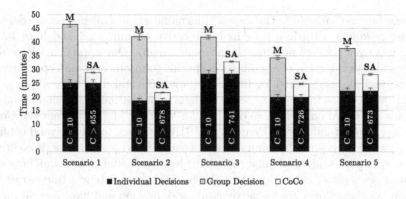

Fig. 2. Configuration time per scenario and approach.

decisions (*cf. Individual Decisions* series), the conciliation performed by teams (*cf. Group Decision* series), the specification of solution constraints with CoCo DSL (*cf. CoCo* series), and the execution time of CSP solvers (*cf. Solver* series).

Coverage Results. All manual specifications considered the 10 tree constraints related to feature model of the configuration scenario. Cross-tree constraints were not considered by teams. In contrast, the number of evaluated constraints oscillated between 655 and 741 in the semi-automated approach. Therefore, the semi-automated approach entails more accurate business-specific solutions.

Configuration Time Results. All teams presented a positive percentage of improvement with the semi-automated product configuration. They employed between 21.37% and at most 48.53% less time in the configuration process (32.1% in average). Nevertheless, the difference between approaches varies in all configuration scenarios. The average sample standard deviation of the manual approach runs was of 4.64 statistical points, while the semi-automated approach had 4.28 statistical points for the same metric. The execution time of the program synthesis was neglected since both solvers found a solution in tens or hundreds of milliseconds for all scenarios.

5 Related Work

Current approaches [3,9,13] that use CSP for automating the configuration of products consider a single-stakeholder approach. Benavides et al. [3] translate extended and cardinality-based feature models within two different Java CSP solvers. Despite their capabilities for optimizing one or multiple variables where a filter operation can be previously applied, this approach is missing a mechanism to allow stakeholders to define their preferences and business objectives. Our approach complements this approach by defining the encoding of cross-tree and solution constraints. Liang [9] presents a CSP implementation of the Clafer [2] language for one-variable optimization. Siegmund et al. [13] present a tool for deriving products according to a multi-objective optimization and hard limit constraints over a set of non-functional requirements. Our approach allows the crosscutting specification of organization-specific solution constraints to increase their expressiveness required for integrating multiple stakeholders.

CSP approaches for deriving valid configurations in multi-stakeholder environments are based on structural constraints. White et al. [15] present the Configuration Understanding and Remedy (CURE) approach to solve invalid configurations while proposing the minimum set of features to be selected or deselected. Junker [8] present QuickXplain, a tool that identifies conflicts in a configuration and proposes a set of relaxations in order to restore consistency. In contrast to these approaches, CoCo allows the dynamic specification and implementation of structural and business-oriented constraints.

Other approaches can be used to derive optimal configurations in a multi-stakeholder environment. Machado et al. [10] use Search-Based Software Engineering (SBSE) to derive optimal configurations based on customer budget and other non-functional requirements. This approach requires a manual definition of benefits for features, and the objective functions are predefined by the system implementation. White et al. [16] select a configuration based in resources' constraints with the Filtered Cartesian Flattening algorithm which is based on the Multi-dimensional Multiple-choice Knapsack Problem (MMKP). This approach performs a minimization of the number of features to modify without considering additional business concerns. Even though these approaches consider more complex constraints than CoCo in the configuration search, they are missing the expressiveness given by CoCo in the specification domain.

EA approaches [4,6,7] for searching optimal products for a single-stakeholder environment. Although these approaches improve scalability, they do not warranty the nonexistence of inconsistencies in derived configurations. Moreover, optimization objectives are predefined in the low level implementation. CoCo allows the definition of solution constraints at a high level of abstraction, and it warranties the execution of all business defined constraints. The comparison between Pareto and non-Pareto algorithms presented in [7] is planned to be incorporated in CoCo. Stein et al. [14] explore product configuration as a boolean satisfability problem. They define soft and hard constraints by multiple stakeholders, while employing social choice theory with a SAT-based solution that considers different configuration strategies. Nonetheless, objective functions and resolution criteria are predefined by each solution. Global business rules that consider arithmetic capabilities are not supported as they are done in CoCo.

6   Conclusions and Future Work

We presented a collaborative constraint-based program synthesis for configuring optimal products aligned to a set of individual and solution constraints. Through a series of model transformations from domain models we generate a CSP implementation with any of Choco or JaCoP solvers, obtaining a platform independent solution. Afterwards, the CSP implementation is executed in order to obtain a set of optimal products that consider the specified business concerns.

We evaluated the effectiveness of the proposed constraint-based program synthesis by analyzing the number of constraints considered against a manual approach, and the configuration time in a multi-stakeholder environment. Our semi-automated approach evaluated 98.6% more domain constraints to avoid inconsistencies that arise in the manual approach. This entails more accurate business-specific solutions. The average configuration time was reduced in almost 32% and all suggested configurations were consistent to all defined specifications.

Further research is required to exploit our configuration approach. First, we already modeled and captured the business criteria (*e.g.* costs, time, risks) associated with the actual investment performed by the telecommunication company. A comparison with the business criteria identified by the program synthesis is the first activity planned as future work. Second, the performance of resources and latency among CSP implementations must be tested. Third, the expressiveness of the integrated model specification should be increased to support the configuration of solutions that are dependent on multiple feature models. Finally, new resolution techniques related to CSP solvers and other type of approaches such as EA and integer logic programming could be considered to support the implementation of highly expressive and scalable specifications.

References

1. Batory, D.: Program refactoring, program synthesis, and model-driven development. In: Krishnamurthi, S., Odersky, M. (eds.) CC 2007. LNCS, vol. 4420, pp. 156–171. Springer, Heidelberg (2007). doi:10.1007/978-3-540-71229-9_11
2. Bąk, K., Diskin, Z., Antkiewicz, M., Czarnecki, K., Wąsowski, A.: Clafer: unifying class and feature modeling. Softw. Syst. Model. **15**, 811–845 (2016)
3. Benavides, D., Trinidad, P., Ruiz-Cortés, A.: Automated reasoning on feature models. In: Pastor, O., Falcão e Cunha, J. (eds.) CAiSE 2005. LNCS, vol. 3520, pp. 491–503. Springer, Heidelberg (2005). doi:10.1007/11431855_34
4. Colanzi, T.E., Vergilio, S.R.: Applying search based optimization to software product line architectures: lessons learned. In: Fraser, G., Teixeira de Souza, J. (eds.) SSBSE 2012. LNCS, vol. 7515, pp. 259–266. Springer, Heidelberg (2012). doi:10.1007/978-3-642-33119-0_19
5. Czarnecki, K., Eisenecker, U.W.: Generative Programming: Methods, Tools, and Applications. Addison-Wesley, New York (2000)
6. Henard, C., Papadakis, M., Harman, M., Le Traon, Y.: Combining multi-objective search and constraint solving for configuring large software product lines. In: 37th International Conference on Software Engineering, pp. 517–528. IEEE Press (2015)
7. Hierons, R.M., Li, M., Liu, X., Segura, S., Zheng, W.: SIP: optimal product selection from feature models using many-objective evolutionary optimization. ACM Trans. Softw. Eng. Methodol. **25**, 17:1–17:39 (2016)
8. Junker, U.: QUICKXPLAIN: preferred explanations and relaxations for over-constrained problems. In: 19th National Conference on Artifical Intelligence, pp. 167–172. AAAI Press, Menlo Park (2004)
9. Liang, J.: Solving Clafer models with Choco. University of Waterloo, Technical report (2012)

10. Machado, L., Pereira, J., Garcia, L., Figueiredo, E.: SPLConfig: product configuration in software product line. In: Brazilian Conference on Software: Theory and Practice - Tools Session, pp. 85–92 (2014)
11. Ochoa, L., González-Rojas, O., Thüm, T.: Using decision rules for solving conflicts in extended feature models. In: 8th ACM SIGPLAN International Conference on Software Language Engineering, pp. 149–160. ACM, New York (2015)
12. Ochoa, L., González-Rojas, O., Verano, M., Castro, H.: Searching for optimal configurations within large-scale models: a cloud computing domain. In: Link, S., Trujillo, J.C. (eds.) ER 2016. LNCS, vol. 9975, pp. 65–75. Springer, Cham (2016). doi:10.1007/978-3-319-47717-6_6
13. Siegmund, N., Rosenmüller, M., Kuhlemann, M., Kästner, C., Apel, S., Saake, G.: SPL conqueror: toward optimization of non-functional properties in software product lines. Softw. Qual. J. **20**, 487–517 (2012)
14. Stein, J., Nunes, I., Cirilo, E.: Preference-based feature model configuration with multiple stakeholders. In: 18th International Software Product Line Conference, pp. 132–141. ACM, New York (2014)
15. White, J., Benavides, D., Schmidt, D., Trinidad, P., Dougherty, B., Ruiz-Cortes, A.: Automated diagnosis of feature model configurations. J. Syst. Softw. **83**, 1094–1107 (2010)
16. White, J., Dougherty, B., Schmidt, D.C.: Selecting highly optimal architectural feature sets with filtered cartesian flattening. J. Syst. Softw. **82**, 1268–1284 (2009)

Fact Based Modeling (FBM) 2016

FBM 2016 PC Co-chairs' Message

The FBM 2016 workshop gives insight into the professional application of Fact Based Modeling in government and business practice. Our main theme for this workshop was versatility in conceptual modeling. For FBM 2016, 7 high quality papers were selected for presentation. We congratulate the authors of these contributions.

For regulation based services we can design and test out a FBM protocol on how to produce the complete and IT-independent specifications for regulation based services. One paper at this workshop is dedicated to the extended insights into the overall architecture starting with the laws, the government and ministerial decrees and the service organization policies. Another paper will present the current insights into the language to specify the durable services.

UML is by far the most widely used language in modeling. Two papers describe how certain aspects of UML relate to FBM functionality to shed more light on the semantics in UML and Object-Orientation. It makes a case for using a modeling protocol when using an object-oriented modeling language.

Another paper reports about the experience with designing a rule configurator for the designers of bank products to play with rules in a safe environment such that simulations can be performed before launching a product.

The subject of Data Warehousing is described from a FBM point of view based on the application of over 10 years of FBM to Data Warehousing in government practice.

The subject of Open EDI and the associated Cloud Architecture is described with FBM.

An open discussion was held at the end of the workshop on how to set the focus for FBM 2017.

October 2016

Robert Meersman
Peter Bollen
Hans Mulder
Maurice Nijssen

Comparative Analysis of Open-edi and Cloud Computing Architectures Using Fact Based Modeling

Baba Piprani[⊠]

MetaGlobal Systems, Ottawa, Canada
babap@attglobal.net

Abstract. With the ever-changing dynamic Information and Communications Technology environment and the new shared deployment options for computing, a paradigm shift is occurring that enables ubiquitous and convenient computing on a pay-as-you-go basis in Cloud Computing. Access on demand is becoming available to networks of scalable, elastic, self-serviceable, configurable physical and virtual resources. In a companion pre-cloud-era focused IT and business front, there exists a parallel universe in the implementation of Open Electronic Data Interchange (Open-edi) services and processes based on agreed upon business scenarios between parties for the realization of interoperability and location transparency in context-specific implementations. This paper analyzes the on-going ISO work on Cloud Computing Interoperability and Portability and the existing Open-edi ISO standards, and offers a concept comparison using Fact Based Modeling (FBM) methodology.

Keywords: Cloud Computing · Interoperability · Portability · Reference architecture · Open-edi · Electronic Data Interchange · edi · ISO · Fact Based Modeling · FBM

1 Introduction and Background

Information and Communications Technology (ICT) is being transformed to a model based on cloud services that are commoditized and delivered in a standardized manner. In a cloud service-based model, users access services based on their requirements without regard to where the services are hosted or how they are delivered.

Several computing paradigms have promised to deliver this computing vision, of which the latest is known as Cloud Computing. The term "Cloud" denotes a computing infrastructure from which businesses and users are able to access applications from anywhere in the world, on-demand. Thus, the ICT world is rapidly evolving to develop software for millions to consume as a service, rather than to run on individual computers. Cloud computing represents a paradigm shift that redefines the relationship between buyers and sellers of IT-related products and services [1]. One influential organization that has influenced some early work in this area has been the US NIST [9, 10].

© Springer International Publishing AG 2017
I. Ciuciu et al. (Eds.): OTM 2016 Workshops, LNCS 10034, pp. 111–121, 2017.
DOI: 10.1007/978-3-319-55961-2_11

With multiple Cloud Computing initiatives on the horizon, ISO, in conjunction with ITU in 2011, initiated a project on ISO standard for Cloud Computing vocabulary and a Cloud Computing reference architecture. The two groups have successfully completed their collaborative work on developing a common set of standards/ recommendations for Cloud Computing vocabulary [2] and reference architecture [3]. Current work in cloud computing is focused on aspects concerning Cloud Service Level Agreements [7], Cloud Computing Interoperability and Portability [11], and Cloud Computing data and its Flow [12]. The new cloud computing work is essentially focused on items like agreed upon service levels and expected standard service level measurements, standardized definitions and common understanding of interoperability and portability, and, related flows of data - between cloud services, cloud service customers and cloud service users and their devices.

Emanating from the pre-cloud and even pre-internet era, the Open-edi ISO (and ANSI, EDIFACT, ebXML) standard also addresses services and interoperability through electronic data interchange via computer-to-computer exchange of business documents between business parties (read: Open-edi parties) using a standard electronic format.

Considering that both of these technologies address distributed platforms and services, interchange of information, parties etc., it is important that we understand the differences between the Cloud Computing and Open-edi architectures, and that there exists a harmonious set of interfaces and common points of overlap. Without this harmonization we would be back at "square one" facing a plethora of incompatible and duplicated standards. More importantly, it is our responsibility that we bring to the attention of the concerned ISO standards bodies any common overlap in semantics or architectures and expose any redundancies or déjà vu of revisiting the same feature or functionality albeit in sheep's clothing!

On a more personal note, this author is also the liaison officer between the two ISO committees involved in the production of the Cloud Computing work, and the Open-edi work. Perhaps this paper should have been re-titled: 'Helsinki Principle Analysis of Open-edi and Cloud Computing Architectures using Fact Based Modeling'. Recall the Helsinki Principle from ISO TR9007 [6]:

> "Note: These utterances are to be interpreted (recursively) as international English utterances: Any meaningful exchange of utterances depends upon the prior existence of an agreed set of semantic and syntactic rules. The recipients of the utterances must use only these rules to interpret the received utterances, if it is to mean the same as that which was meant by the utterer."

This paper examines the basic concepts that have been developed for both Cloud Computing and Open-edi, and illustrates how Fact Based Modeling (FBM) provides a useful means to compare and contrast these initiatives using formal semantic modelling techniques, hopefully leading to a more cohesive and consistent direction for the next generation of ICT.

NOTE: The contents of this paper are intended to be illustrative and should not be considered as an authoritative description of the referenced ISO standards.

In this paper, we have used the FBM notation and methodology as a description technique to define semantic models abstracted from the Cloud Computing and

Open-edi standards, or, being progressed towards standardization. FBM is a methodology for modeling the semantics of a subject area.

FBM is based on logic and controlled natural language, whereby the resulting fact based model captures the semantics of the domain of interest by means of fact types, together with the associated concept definitions and the integrity, [8].

The roots of FBM go back to the 1970s. NIAM, a FBM notation style, was one of the candidate methodologies used for developing conceptual schemas as defined in ISO TR9007:1987 Concepts and Terminology for the Conceptual Schema and the Information Base. Subsequently, several developments have taken place in parallel, resulting in several fact based modeling "dialects", including NIAM, ORM2, Cog-NIAM, DOGMA and FCO-IM. The notation used in this paper is ORM2 notation.

A simplistic description of usage and reading the ORM2 notation follows. The subject area is seen as consisting of semantic objects (representing objects in the real world model) that can be described using natural language sentences—consisting of an object, predicate and possible one or more objects, each connected with a predicate-object pair. A real world object is represented by an object type denoted by a circle, also known as an entity type. Object types may have subtypes denoted by arrows from the subtype to supertype (e.g. object type Role has subtype Sub-role). Object types are involved in fact type sentence descriptions that can be binary, or n-ary (ternary, quaternary etc.), as depicted by rectangle boxes, each box representing a role that the object type plays in that sentence. Integrity rules are then associated with the fact types like mandatory (shown as a dark dot on the object type connector), and also a horizontal bar on top of a role of a fact type denoting a restriction on the occurrence of the set of role populations. The ORM2 notation contains several other rules that can be graphically depicted but are out of scope for our discussions. An example of a fact type reading from Fig. 2 is: A Party (in the cloud computing paradigm schema) shall be assigned to one or more Role(s). A Role may be assigned to one or more Parties.

2   Cloud Computing Concepts

Figure 1 depicts the main Cloud Computing concepts using FBM, along with examples, as defined in the ISO draft document [2]. The concepts are defined in terms of the cloud services that are available to cloud service customers and the cloud deployment models that describe how the computing infrastructure that delivers these services can be provided and shared by users.

It is interesting to note that the Cloud Computing vocabulary and concepts were developed prior to an agreed upon architecture. The architecture itself takes its basis from the approach used in the ISO Open Distributed Reference Model [4] by utilizing the user view and functional view.

The cloud paradigm is composed of key characteristics, roles and activities, service capabilities and service categories, deployment models, and cross cutting aspects as shown. The concept relationships generally appear in the cloud computing reference architecture.

Tables 1 and 2 are the relevant definitions pertaining to the cloud computing models shown.

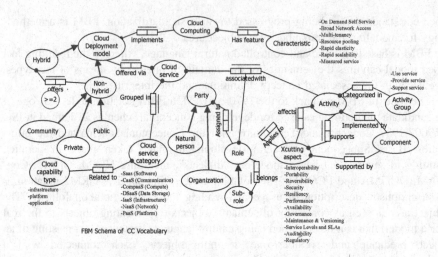

Fig. 1. Basic Cloud Computing concepts from ISO 17788

Table 1. Definitions of concepts used in Cloud Computing

Concept	Definition	Examples
Party	Entities that play one or more roles (and sub-roles)	Natural person, or an organization
Role	Sets of activities	Cloud service customer Cloud service provider Cloud service partner
Subrole	A subset of the activities associated with a role	Sub-roles for a partner role are: service integrator, auditor, and cloud broker
Activity	A logical functional element of a cloud service	Using services, providing services, and supporting services
Component	An implementation of an activity.	
Cross-cutting aspect	Behaviors or capabilities that need to be implemented and coordinated across roles	Interoperability, portability, reversibility, security, privacy, governance, etc.
Cloud Computing	paradigm for enabling network access to a scalable and elastic pool of shareable physical or virtual resources with on-demand self-service provisioning and administration	
Cloud characteristic	Basic user-oriented features of a Cloud Computing environment	On-demand self-service, Broad network access, Multi-tenancy, Resource pooling, Rapid elasticity and scalability, Measured service

Table 2. Definitions of concepts used in Cloud Computing-continued

Concept	Definition	Examples
Cloud service	One or more capabilities offered via cloud computing invoked using a declared interface	Natural person, or an organization
Cloud service category	group of cloud services that possess some qualities in common with each other	Infrastructure as a service, Platform as a service, Software as a service, Network as a service, Data storage as a service, Compute as a service, Communication as a service
Capability	A quality of being able to perform a given activity	
Cloud capability type	Classification of the functionality, based on the type of resources used Cloud capability types follow the principle of separation of concerns, i.e. they have minimal functionality overlap between each other	Infrastructure capabilities, Platform capabilities, Application capabilities
Cloud deployment model	The way in which cloud computing can be organized based on control of physical or virtual resources and how those resources are shared	Community cloud, Public cloud, or Private cloud
Hybrid cloud	A cloud deployment model that includes at least two different deployment models	Interoperability, Portability, Reversibility, Security, Privacy, Governance, etc.

3   Cloud Computing Reference Architecture

A Fact Based Model for the Cloud Computing Reference Architecture (CCRA) is shown in Fig. 2.

As noted earlier, the CCRA takes as its basis the ODP reference model but focuses only on the user and functional views. The CCRA does not address the implementation and deployment views. The user view is the ecosystem (or system context) including the parties, the roles, the sub-roles and the activities. The functional view is the distribution of functions necessary for the support of cloud activities.

The Fact Based Models in this paper represent the distillation and transforms as interpreted from the Open-edi text [6, 7] and the CCRA text [3]. The purpose of the FBM grammar diagrams is being able to compare them using a formal methodology to represent the involved semantics represented by facts, relationships and constraints as opposed to comparing syntax based text paragraphs.

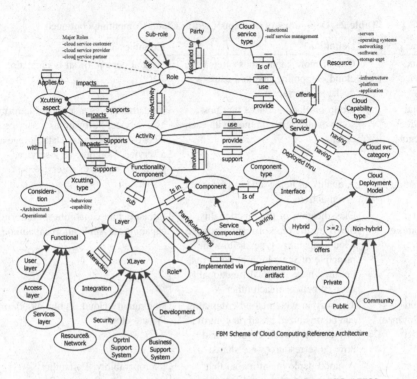

Fig. 2. Cloud Computing reference architecture model from ISO 17789

4   Open-edi Concepts

The Open-edi ISO standard was published in 1997 in the pre-Internet era. Open-edi addresses interoperability through exchange of business documents between business partners or trading partners—the most common form being invoices, purchase orders, ship notices etc., essentially concerning financial content. Open-edi is not the exchange of personal use items or emails etc. but is a computer-to-computer exchange of information that is in a standard agreed upon format.

Figure 3 represents the FBM model of the Open-edi reference model, exhibiting the main perspectives of Business Operational View and Functional Service View.

Figure 4 portrays the main concepts of the BOV as to how it addresses and defines business semantics and uses the concept of an Information Bundle.

Figure 5 discusses Open-edi scenarios, the establishing of profiles and functional capabilities for the BOV.

Figure 6 portrays the Open-edi scenarios, characteristics and measures relating to Roles, Information Bundles, and Scenario Attributes.

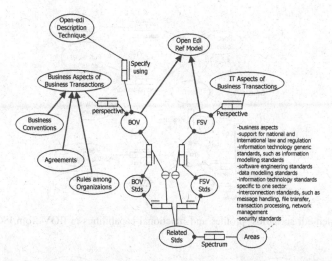

Fig. 3. Open-edi reference model and basic concepts from ISO 14662

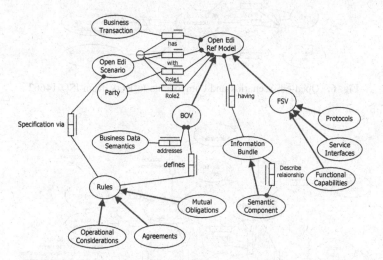

Fig. 4. Open-edi business operational view and functional service view from ISO 14662

5 Open-edi Functional Concepts and Capabilities

Figure 7 addresses the Functional Service View that provides the perspective of business transactions limited to those information technology interoperability aspects of IT Systems needed to support the execution of Open-edi transactions. A word of caution: the FSV also discusses functional capabilities in the IT context that is not the same as BOV functional capabilities (Table 3).

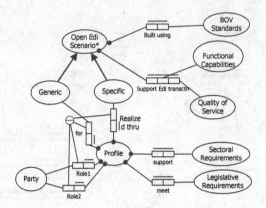

Fig. 5. Open-edi scenarios, profiles and functional capabilities in BOV from ISO 14662

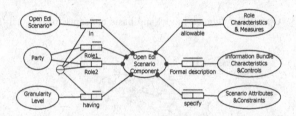

Fig. 6. Open-edi scenarios and components in BOV from ISO 14662

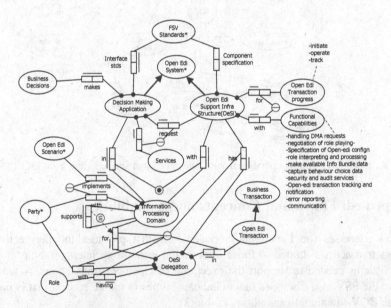

Fig. 7. Open-edi functional concepts and capabilities in FSV from ISO 14662

Table 3. Definitions of concepts used in Open-edi [5]

Concept	Definition
Business Operational View (BOV)	Perspective of business transactions limited to those aspects regarding the making of business decisions and commitments among Persons, which are needed for the description of a business transaction
Decision Making Application (DMA)	Model of that part of an Open-edi system which makes decisions corresponding to the role(s) that the Open-edi Party plays as well as the originating, receiving and managing data values contained in the instantiated Information Bundles, and which is not required to be visible to the other Open-edi Party(ies)
Decision Making Application Interface (DMA Interface)	Set of requirements that permit a Decision Making Application to interact with the Open-edi Support Infrastructure
Functional Service View (FSV)	Perspective of business transactions limited to those information technology interoperability aspects of Information Technology Systems needed to support the execution of Open-edi transactions
Information Bundle (IB)	Formal description of the semantics of the recorded information to be exchanged by Open-edi Parties playing roles in an Open-edi scenario
Information Processing Domain (IPD)	Information Technology System which includes at least either a Decision Making Application and/or one of the components of an Open-edi Support Infrastructure (or both), and acts/executes on behalf of an Open-edi Party (either directly or under a delegated authority)
Open-edi	Electronic data interchange among multiple autonomous Persons to accomplish an explicit shared business goal according to Open-edi standards
Open-edi Party (OeP)	Person that participates in Open-edi, i.e. as the entity within an Open-edi Party that carries the legal responsibility for making commitment(s) NOTE 1 Synonyms for "legal person" include "artificial person", "body corporate", etc., depending on the terminology used in competent jurisdictions
Open-edi scenario (OeS)	Formal specification of a class of business transactions having the same business goal
Open-edi Support Infrastructure (OeSI)	Model of the set of functional capabilities for OpenEdi systems which, when taken together with the Decision Making Applications, allows Open-edi Parties to participate in Open-edi transactions
Open-edi system	Information Technology System which enables an Open-edi Party to participate in Open-edi transactions
Open-edi transaction	Business transaction that is in compliance with an Open-edi scenario
Role	Specification which models an external intended behaviour (as allowed within a scenario) of an Open-edi Party
Semantic Component (SC)	Unit of recorded information unambiguously defined in the context of the business goal of the business transaction NOTE An SC can be atomic or composed of other SCs
Semantic Component (SC)	Unit of recorded information unambiguously defined in the context of the business goal of the business transaction

6   Cloud Computing and Open-edi Analysis

By transforming each of the Open-edi and Cloud Computing concepts, terminology and architectures using Fact Based Modeling, we are able to distill the salient object types, relationships and some of the business rules to enable a comparative analysis of the two architectures.

It immediately becomes apparent that, cloud computing uses the term 'cloud service' so as to not be confused with a 'service' in Open-edi. Both the architectures address interoperability

Cloud Computing uses ODP views whereas Open-edi focuses on BOV and FSV with layers implied in each view in the Annex description [5].

Cloud computing is defined as a paradigm for enabling network access to a scalable and elastic pool of shareable physical or virtual resources with self-service provisioning and administration on-demand. ISO/IEC 17788 and ISO/IEC 17789 provide a starting point for understanding of different types of interoperability and portability and leading to definition of facets, and relationships with activities and roles, and capabilities types.

Open-edi addresses a focused interchange of Business-to-Business limited set of Open-edi transactions based on established scenarios.

Both standards involve Party and Roles—albeit in a different sense. Roles in Open-edi are Buyer and Seller, whereas in Cloud Computing the role includes other actors.

Both standards use controls and measures—Cloud Computing calls these as Service Level Agreements, whereas Open-edi declares these as Open-edi scenario components.

These are just a few examples of items that appear not to be not in sync between the two sets of standards. Cloud Computing has distinctly identified the various roles of the various providers, brokers, auditors and users of the cloud services and has a wide platform of seamless expandability across platforms, software, infrastructure etc. Open-edi includes protocols and limited bi-directional roles of buyer and seller.

Cloud Computing stays away from the physical implementation and deployment area, whereas Open-edi includes the FSV as addressing the physical aspects of interchange.

The purpose of this paper was to enable further analysis to be conduced to determine overlaps, or areas of duplication, including lessons learnt etc. It is planned to present the contents of this paper to the respective ISO committees to assist them.

It is clear that there needs to be an accord between the Cloud Computing standards group and the Open-edi standards group.

7   Conclusions

In this paper we have demonstrated the use of Fact Based Modeling to facilitate a comparative analysis of the emerging ISO vocabulary and reference architecture standards for Cloud Computing and Open-edi architectures. As a result, we have identified a number of areas where the concepts in the vocabulary and architecture documents appear to be misaligned. We have also identified a number of areas where

Cloud Computing and Open-edi are using similar concepts, typically in ways that are not readily compared.

Fact Based Modeling appears to provide significant assistance both in the development of consistent architectures based on sound concepts and also in the analysis and comparison of different architectures.

Further effort to analyze the models in more detail would provide valuable insight into the complex relationships between Cloud Computing and Open-edi.

References

1. ISO/IEC JTC1 SC38 N430 JTC1 SC38 Study Group on Cloud Computing Report – Final Version, 30 September 2011
2. ISO/IEC 17788 Information technology – Cloud computing – Overview and vocabulary
3. ISO/IEC 17789 Information technology – Cloud computing – Reference Architecture
4. ISO/IEC 10746-1:1998, Information technology – Open distributed processing – Reference Model: Overview
5. ISO/IEC 14462:2010, Information technology – OpenEdi reference model
6. van Greutheuysen, J. (ed.): Technical report on concepts and terminology for the conceptual schema and the information base. ISO Technical report ISO IEC TR9007:1987, International Standards Organization, Geneva (1987)
7. ISO/IEC 19086-1: Information technology – Cloud computing – Service level agreement (SLA) framework
8. Nijssen, G.M., Halpin, T.A.: Conceptual Schema and Relational Database Design. Prentice Hall, Victoria (1989)
9. NIST Special Publication 500-292, The NIST Cloud Computing reference Architecture, September 2011
10. NIST Special Publication 800-145, The NIST Definition of Cloud Computing, September 2011
11. ISO/IEC 2CD 19941 Information technology – Cloud computing – Interoperability and Portability
12. ISO/IEC DIS 19944 Information technology – Cloud computing – Cloud services and devices: data flow, data categories and data use

An FBM Grammar of Dimensional Modelling

Baba Piprani[✉]

MetaGlobal Systems, Ottawa, Canada
babap@attglobal.net

Abstract. This paper abstracts the modelling approaches and techniques used in modelling Dimensional Models in a BI data warehousing environment using FBM grammar to enable analysis and harmonization and assist information architects to bridge FBM concepts in Dimensional Modelling. The resulting FBM model allows us to distill the concepts, relationships and business rules, and in particular, create a graphic supported grammar to enable analysis and recognize the strengths and weakness of dimensional modelling.

Keywords: Dimensional modelling · Data warehousing · BI · Business Intelligence · Reporting · Metamodel · Fact based modeling · FBM · ORM

1 Introduction and Background

There are several interpretations of data warehousing—from the simplest avatar of basic reporting requirements at one end, to the other end of the spectrum of multi-source integrated database, analysis and reporting requirement. The data modelling approaches to be used for the data warehouses appropriately vary in terms of simple data marts driven by basic constructs of de-normalized table forms or data marts driven by dimensional models [1] through to the establishment of top-down/bottom-up attribute based data models like Entity Relationship Models transcribed to RDBMSs.

Different data modelling approaches are practised for modelling data warehouses vs. operational databases—with particular emphasis on history, temporal, query optimized vs. transaction optimized, capability to recognize multiple aliases of the same business attribute across multiple business functional areas etc.

There are at least many popular data warehousing approaches in North America—that of top down (Inmon) [2] and bottom up (Kimball) [3], and to a much lesser extent the data vault model—hybrid between the normalized model and dimensional model. Both the Inmon and Kimball approaches have the usual pros and cons, and both are relatively widely used—albeit with adopted variations. The Inmon approach promotes an integrated normalized data model accompanied by denormalized data marts. The Kimball approach envisions the entire data warehouse based on a dimensional model—consisting of Facts and Dimensions in an architecture that may prove to be a challenge to integrate multitude of source databases. Unfortunately, there is not much formal documentation available to describe the dimensional data modelling rules per se, except of series of notes, question and answers, tips etc. This author found it frustrating that

© Springer International Publishing AG 2017
I. Ciuciu et al. (Eds.): OTM 2016 Workshops, LNCS 10034, pp. 122–129, 2017.
DOI: 10.1007/978-3-319-55961-2_12

the lack of formal material left data warehouse practitioners needing to invent ad-hoc rules. What little is available to support the explanation of formal concepts of dimensional modelling is rather 'fluid' and contains much terminology like 'may', 'should', 'recommended', etc. and, is essentially lacking in delivery of some formal ruleset—as compared to formal constructs available for ER, Relational, FBM, UML etc. Perhaps it is the nature of the beast in dimensional modelling that it is really performance focused, severely de-normalized, opening up large chasms for enabling easy corruption of data if due diligence is not followed in the Extract Transform Loading (ETL) of the datasets in the data warehouse. A hybrid advanced generation data warehouse approach using a data quality firewall approach as described in [4, 5] which essentially has the 'best of' concepts from both the above approaches—with a heavy emphasis on automating data quality and integrity checking—incorporating a flexible architecture with audit controls that is suitable for large data warehouses.

If one examines Gartner's observations, the success rate for data warehouse implementations remains flat-topped at near 50% since 2004 [6, 7] and, in fact getting worse. Sure, any coded application can be made to work—'courtesy of bubble-gum and chicken wire with spaghetti coding, akin to a Saturday afternoon dart throwing exercise to get at the target', to directly quote one of my major clients.

It is not the intent of this paper to tout one data warehousing school of thought with another—and start yet another data modelling religious war. One can look up several write-ups on this comparison, like [8] (http://www.computerweekly.com/tip/Inmon-vs-Kimball-Which-approach-is-suitable-for-your-data-warehouse), and other references.

Whatever approach is chosen, the basic process of data modelling essentially consists of abstracting business requirements and objectives, and formalizing them into some formal or semi-formal like notation, i.e. requirements gathering, abstraction, modelling, validation and so on.

In this paper, we have used the Fact Based Modelling (FBM) notation and methodology as a description technique to define a non-exhaustive abstracted version of grammar for dimensional modelling. FBM is a methodology for modeling the semantics of a subject area.

FBM is based on logic and controlled natural language, whereby the resulting fact based model captures the semantics of the domain of interest by means of fact types, together with the associated concept definitions and the integrity rules [9].

The roots of FBM go back to the 1970s [10]. NIAM, a FBM notation style, was one of the candidate methodologies used for developing conceptual schemas as defined in ISO TR9007:1987 Concepts and Terminology for the Conceptual Schema and the Information Base. Subsequently, several developments have taken place in parallel, resulting in several fact based modeling "dialects", including NIAM, ORM2, Cog-NIAM, DOGMA and FCO-IM. The notation used in this paper is ORM2 notation.

A simplistic description of usage and reading the ORM2 notation follows. The subject area is seen as consisting of semantic objects (representing objects in the real world model) that can be described using natural language sentences—consisting of an object, predicate and possible one or more objects, each connected with a predicate-object pair. A real world object is represented by an object type, denoted by a circle, also known as an entity type. Object types may have subtypes denoted by arrows from the subtype to supertype (e.g. object type Role has subtype Sub-role). Object types are involved in fact type sentence descriptions that can be binary, or n-ary (ternary, quaternary etc.), as depicted by rectangle boxes, each box representing a role that the object type plays in that sentence. Integrity rules are then associated with the fact types like mandatory (shown as a dark dot on the object type connector), and also a horizontal bar on top of a role of a fact type denoting a restriction on the occurrence of the set of role populations. The ORM2 notation contains several other rules that can be graphically depicted but are out of scope for our discussions.

2 Dimensional Modelling Grammar—Facts and Dimensions

Figure 1 depicts the foundational pillars of a dimensional model as representing end user output requirements for querying, analysis, reporting, dashboarding, and cubes. The base concepts of the dimensional model are in terms of Fact tables and Dimensional tables. A Fact table corresponds to a physical observable event, which is a subtype of a Business Intelligence (BI) event. A BI event has a subtype Measurable event, which is supported by one or more measures. Fact tables enable collecting numeric facts or measures of the measurable event.

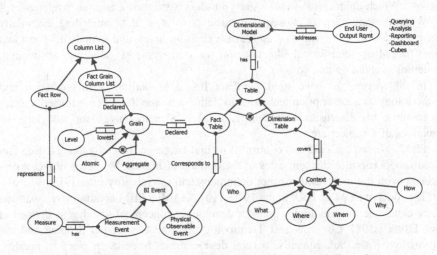

Fig. 1. Basic dimensional modelling concepts—facts and dimensions

Fact tables have Dimension tables defining the nouns involved with the facts, e.g. date, location, product, etc. A dimension table involves setting one of the contexts of the fact being collected, like Who, What, Where, When, Why, and How.

Facts tables have a declared grain. A Fact table must only have one grain—the grain essentially drives what a single fact table row represents. A Fact concerns exactly one event, and a fact table contains facts that all concern the same event type. An FBM comparison would be to group the FBM facts around the focus Entity type, i.e. representing the grain. Each grain would result in a separate fact table—akin to grouping the FBM roles involved with uniqueness constraints emanating from the same entity type.

When the grain represents the fact measures at the lowest level of granularity, we are able to arrive at aggregate or coarser levels of granularity, e.g. sales totals by cities instead of the lowest level of the grain being the individual store. The identification of the grain is useful in establishing data quality controls during the ETL operation, by establishing integrity constraints on incoming data based on this grain—which many projects ignore and inadvertently slip into the cyclical rectifying and pulling out duplicate rows of the grain.

Again, it is not the intent of this paper to define or explain dimensional modelling—please refer to books or other published material. The intent here is to portray the grammar of dimensional modelling using an FBM schema so as to be able to grasp and graphically understand many of the concepts of dimensional modelling, along with some basic formal rules of what is permissible. What is being provided is a summary form of an 'FBM reading' of the fact types represented along with some associated rules.

3   Dimensional Modelling Grammar—Fact Attribute Characteristics

A Dimensional Modelling Grammar involving Fact Attribute Characteristics is shown in Fig. 2.

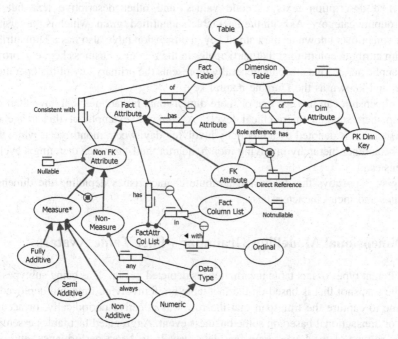

Fig. 2. Basic dimensional modelling concepts—fact attribute characteristics

A dimensional table is made up of dimension attributes, one of which is the PK primary key (read surrogate key) of the dimension table, that has no meaning except to act as a fact table foreign key attribute involved in a join link to the dimension table. The same dimension table can also be referenced from the same fact table, but either via another role playing attribute (e.g. start date, stop date). However, some projects at this point may choose to establish another SQL-view table instead. Much of the material is not clear in the sense that a 'view' is to be used to establish an additional attribute's role in a 'logical' sense vs. actually creating an 'SQL-view' in the data model, and thus proliferating duplicated SQL-view tables and cluttering the data model. Dimension attributes need to contain values and are not nullable.

A Fact Attribute of a Fact table may be an FK attribute referencing a Dimension table's dimension key, or, a non-FK attribute which is possibly nullable. A non-FK attribute is either a measure or a non-measure. A measure can be fully additive that can apply to any dimension, semi additive that can apply to only some dimensions, or non-additive like a ratio. Measures are always numeric.

4   Dimensional Modelling Grammar—Dimension Attribute Characteristics

As noted earlier, a Dimension attribute is not nullable. A Dimension attribute is subject to grouping or non-grouping in terms of BI context, e.g. a report being grouped by location or product commodity type. Grouping attributes generally correspond to operational systems reference table codes or dates or indicator flags, whereas many text fields like description texts of code values, and other descriptive text fall into non-grouping category. As with the Fact table's identified 'grain' which is the business key or sometimes known as the natural key, a dimension table also has a Dim attribute or a dim attribute column list that participates in the role of a business key, e.g. product id, or applicant id. This attribute generally represents the primary key of the operational system and known as the Durable natural key.

A dimension can involve one or more dimensional hierarchies that have their own path up their separate hierarchical levels. A common example of this is the date dimension that is denoted by a hierarchy involving day, week, month year, while there could be another hierarchy involving month, quarter, half-year etc., denoting a cycle of sorts instead.

Figure 3 portrays the dimension attribute characteristics depicting the dimension attributes and their characteristics.

5   Dimensional Modelling Grammar—Fact Table Avatars

The different types of fact table incarnations is depicted in Fig. 4, as being subtypes like periodic snapshot that is based on the fact table grain involving time and deployed via datetime to capture the timespan that the row was effective periodically, or accumulating or transactional based on some business event. Aggregated fact tables essentially contain rollups of the lower grain fact data, usually to boost performance, and often

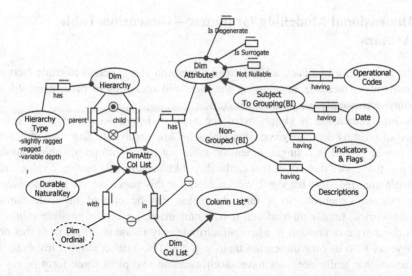

Fig. 3. Basic dimensional modelling concepts—dimension attribute characteristics

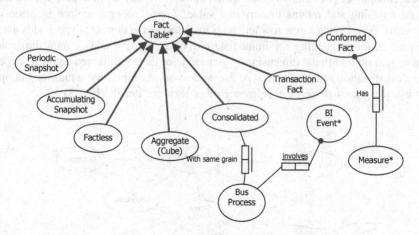

Fig. 4. Basic dimensional modelling concepts—fact table avatars

built as cube involving multiple dimensions that enable cross-dimension processing. The term confirmed fact is used to denote for example the same dimension occurs in separate fact tables. This is where data warehouse governance has to play the part in ensuring the usage of this fact is consistent across the multiple fact tables, having the same meaning and semantics.

6   Dimensional Modelling Grammar—Dimension Table Avatars

Similar to a Conformed Fact, a Conformed dimension also is across multiple facts and is consistent in meaning in allowing the facts and measures to be categorized and described consistently across multiple facts.

A Junk dimension is simply what the name indicates—a grab bag collection. Instead of creating separate dimension tables for low cardinality flags and indicators, these can be placed in a single dimension table—at times with permissible combinations e.g. two codes that are of low cardinality, like male/female having 2 values, and, married/unmarried, also having 2 values. Note for this paper we are not considering other modern variances. So a Junk dimension can be created for male-married, male-unmarried, female-married and female-unmarried, i.e. all the possible values.

A degenerate dimension is where an attribute may reside in a Fact table that does not have a FK to its own dimension table, e.g. could be a ticket number involved in a transaction that really does not have much meaning except as some form of textual reference that is placed in a fact.

The issue of time is incorporated in the subtype Slowly changing dimension to handle changes in dimension values, which consists of 8 other subtypes, Type 0 does not do anything and retains the original value, Type 1 does a replace in place via overwrite, Type 2 adds a new row and flags the latest as the current, Type 3 adds a new alternate attribute retaining the immediate old value, Type 4 adds a mini dimension used to spin off additional dimensions—generally for large partitioned datasets, Type 5 uses a combination of type 1 and type 5… and so on. As this is not a tutorial, but only portrays the grammar, one can reference other texts for details (Fig. 5).

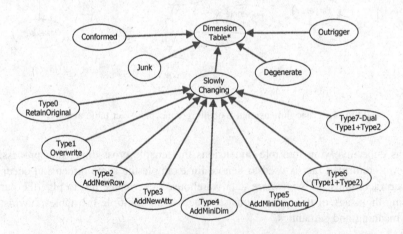

Fig. 5. Basic dimensional modelling concepts—dimension table avatars

7 Conclusions

In this paper we have demonstrated the use of Fact Based Modeling to facilitate a grammar of Dimensional modelling. As a result, we are able to graphically and formally view the various constructs and characteristics involved. This also enables us to identify areas of strengths and weaknesses in terms of ensuring smooth running of Data Warehouse operations—in particular the question on data quality and auditing. We have also identified a number of areas where FBM analysis and concepts can be used to make Dimensional models more rigorous and consistent, typically in ways that are not readily compared without the use of FBM.

Fact Based Modeling appears to provide significant assistance both in the development of consistent grammar based on sound concepts and also in the analysis and comparison of different model architectures.

Further effort to analyze the models in more detail would provide valuable insight into the complex relationships between Dimensional Modelling and other approaches.

References

1. Ballard, C., Herreman, D., Schau, D., Bell, R., Kim, E., Valencic, A.: Data Modelling Techniques for Data Warehousing. IBM, Rayleigh (1998)
2. Inmon, W.H.: Building the Data Warehouse, 4th edn. Wiley, Hoboken (2005)
3. Kimball, R., Ross, M.: The Data Waraehouse Toolkit, 3rd edn. Wiley, Hoboken (2013)
4. Piprani, B.: Using ORM-based models as a foundation for a data quality firewall in an advanced generation data warehouse. In: Meersman, R., Tari, Z., Herrero, P. (eds.) OTM 2006. LNCS, vol. 4278, pp. 1148–1159. Springer, Heidelberg (2006). doi:10.1007/11915072_18
5. Piprani, B.: Using ORM-based models as a foundation for a data quality firewall in an advanced generation data warehouse (extended edition). In: Spaccapietra, S., Pan, J.Z., Thiran, P., Halpin, T., Staab, S., Svatek, V., Shvaiko, P., Roddick, J. (eds.) Journal on Data Semantics. Springer, Heidelberg (2008)
6. Gartner Group Report. Gartner Press Release, Gartner Website – Media relations (2005). http://www.gartner.com/press_releases/pr2005.html
7. Standish Group International, Inc.: Chaos Chronicles and Standish Group Report (2003). http://www.standishgroup.com/sample_research/index.php
8. Nijssen, G.M., Halpin, T.A.: Conceptual Schema and Relational Database Design. Prentice Hall, Victoria (1989)
9. ISO TR9007, Concepts and terminology for the Conceptual Schema and the Information Base. ISO Technical report (1987)
10. Nijssen, G.M.: A Framework for Discussion in ISO/TC97/SC5/WG3, 78.09/01 (1978)

The Application of UML Association End Multiplicities for Conceptual Modeling

Peter Bollen[(⊠)]

Department of Organization and Strategy, School of Business and Economics,
University of Maastricht, P.O. Box 616, 6200 MD Maastricht, The Netherlands
p.bollen@maastrichtuniversity.nl

Abstract. In this paper we will present the results of research into the semantics of association end multiplicities (AEMs) in the Unified Modeling Language (UML). In this paper we will give a precise definition of the AEM concept in UML based upon the various definition 'fragments' we have encountered in the UML literature and we will give explicit rules for the application of the AEM for the conceptual modeling of an application subject area.

1 Introduction

The unified modeling language (UML) is the de-facto standard for conceptualizing and specifying business- and software systems [3, p. 64]. The models used for the specification of the information perspective for an application subject area in the UML are *class diagrams*. In this paper we will focus on the *association* fact-encoding construct. An *association* has at least two *association ends* [9, p. 9–67]. If an association has *two* association ends we will call this association a *binary* association. In case an association has *3 or more* association ends it is called a *N-ary* association. In most UML publications the example *class diagrams* only contain 'binary' associations. Nevertheless, in the UML language reference manual [6, p. 352] the reason for applying the N-ary association modeling construct is given: *"Generally, N-ary associations are useful only when all the values are needed to uniquely determine a link. An N-ary association will almost always be implemented as a class whose attributes include pointers to the participant objects. The advantage of modeling it as an association is the constraint that there can be no duplicate links within an association."* This interpretation excludes the application of the association in those cases in which N-1 association ends determine association end N. For those cases the application of the *association class* fact encoding construct is recommended. Many, if not most of the semantic relationships that we encounter in business applications at least have an arity of 3, e.g. *<employee> works for <department> since <date>*. It is essential that a modeling language can express N-ary (N > 2) relationships. The way in which these conceptual relationships are often modeled in UML lead to serious modeling drawbacks. If the association class is used for the encoding of a N-ary relationship in which N-1 association ends determine association end N, an 'artificial' or 'non-domain related' class has to be introduced in many applications.

I. Ciuciu et al. (Eds.): OTM 2016 Workshops, LNCS 10034, pp. 130–142, 2017.
DOI: 10.1007/978-3-319-55961-2_13

The *constraint* encoding construct in UML that must be used in combination with the *association* construct is the *association end multiplicity (AEM)*. In the official UML documentation the following definition fragment for the *AEM* concept can be found: *"Multiplicity: when placed on a target end, specifies the number of target instances that may be associated with a single source instance across the given association"* [7, p. 2–23]. This definition is phrased in terms of the number of instances that *may* exist but it does not tell us that a multiplicity can be used to specify the number of instances that *must* participate in a (binary) association. This leads us to the *first* research question in this paper:

Research Question 1:
*How is the number of target instances that **must** be associated with a single source instance across the given association represented in UML using the AEM?*

Most definition fragments in the official original UML publications apply to *AEMs* for binary associations. A definition fragment that contains an interpretation for association end multiplicities in N-ary associations is the following: *"Multiplicity for N-ary associations may be specified but is less obvious than binary multiplicity. The multiplicity of a role represents the potential number of instance tuples in the association when the other N-1 values are fixed"* [8]. Some researchers advocate to replace this 'less obvious' *AEM* by a textual constraint or OCL constraint [4, p. 92-93]: *"... Indeed, using only a small set of features can reduce the complexity of a design and facilitate communication....how to translate n-ary associations with cardinality restrictions..... The UML subset we use employs general n-ary associations with additional constraints formulated in OCL"*. In an effective diagramming language the *semantics* of diagramming conventions should therefore be made explicit. In order to make the semantics of the AEM for N-ary associations in UML explicit we need a precise definition for the AEM concept. This has resulted in the *second* research question:

Research Question 2:
What is the precise definition of the AEM in UML for N-ary associations?

In Sect. 2 we will give an analysis of the commonly found interpretations of the *AEMs* in binary associations in the UML literature. In Sect. 3 the definition fragments for the *AEMs* in N-ary associations are analyzed and we will provide the answer to research question 2. In Sect. 4 we will give a procedure in which *AEMs* (based upon the precise definition of AEM that is given in Sect. 3) can be derived. Finally, in Sect. 5 conclusions will be drawn.

2 Interpretation of Multiplicities in Binary Associations in UML

The application of multiplicities for conceptual modeling can be divided into two groups. The first group specifies how many times an object instance (combination) *may* exist in the information base at *any* point in time. This type of restriction is normally modeled as the association multiplicity (in case only one type of multiplicity has to be specified for an association end) or the *upper (or maximum)* multiplicity. The second group of multiplicities specifies whether an instance (combination) *must* participate in a relationship at *every* point in time. This type of restriction is **not** always specified in multiplicities (for example in many dialects of the ER or EER models), but if it is specified it is normally called the *lower (or minimum)* multiplicity (or *participation* constraint [5, p. 249, 3, p. 57]. On page 67 of [2], the following definition fragment can be found:

> *"When you state a multiplicity at one end of an association, you are specifying, that for each object of the class at the opposite end, there must be that many objects at the near end. You can show a multiplicity of exactly one (1), zero or one (0..1), many (0..*) or one or more (1..*)."*

In UML the *AEM* for a binary association is defined in terms of the 'opposite' association end. The origin of this 'opposite' perspective is in the mathematical interpretation in which a binary association is considered a relation *R* defined on two domains (for example *A* and *B* in Fig. 1). From Fig. 1 we conclude that the following instances of domain (class) *A* exist: *A1, A2* and *A3* plus instances *B1, B2* and *B3* of domain (class) *B*. Furthermore, we conclude that following value pairs for the relation (association) *R* exist: *(A1, B1); (A1, B2)* and *(A2, B3)*. Finally we see that instance *A3* of domain A can exist without participating in the relation *R*. AEMs encode the mathematical restrictions that apply in terms of the relation. In the example of Fig. 1, a lower multiplicity of *0* and a upper multiplicity of * for the association end to which object class B is attached means that for each value of domain A *multiple* values from domain B *can* exist or *no* value at all. If the multiplicity defined on the association end B is *1..1* it can be interpreted as the restriction of the relation *R* to a *function*. If in addition there exists a maximum multiplicity of *1* for association end *A* then the function R is an *injection*. In Fig. 2 it is summarized how the *upper* AEM of the target association end specifies what the *maximum* number of instances is of the class that is connected to the target association end, which *may* be connected to *one* instance of the object class that is connected to the source association end. The *lower* AEM of the target association end specifies what the *minimum* number of instances is of the class that is connected to the target association end that *must* be connected to one instance of the object class that is connected to the source association end.

In Fig. 3 an example of a binary association and an accompanying significant *object diagram* is given. In the object diagram in the lower part of Fig. 3 we see that

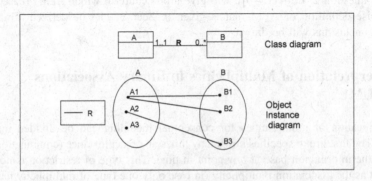

Fig. 1. Class diagram and instances

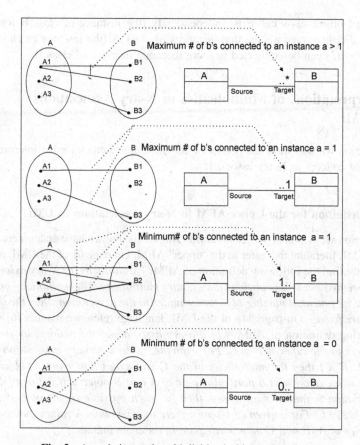

Fig. 2. Association end multiplicities in binary associations

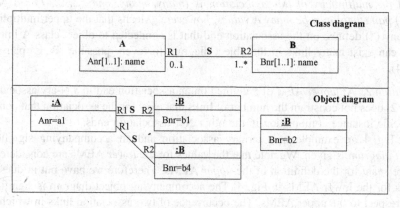

Fig. 3. Class diagram and example object diagram

instances of object class can exist independently (the instance of class B for which bnr = *b2*). Furthermore, we see that instances of class A (the instance of class A for which anr = *a1*) can be connected to more than one instance of class B.

3 Interpretations of Multiplicities in N-ary Associations in UML

In this section we will show the results of our literature research for the interpretations of the *AEM* concept in N-ary associations.

3.1 A Definition for the Upper AEM in N-ary Associations in UML

In this section we will analyze the definition fragments that we have encountered in the original UML literature that refer to the 'upper' AEM. On page 61 of the UML notation guide [8] we find the following definition of AEM: *"Multiplicity for N-ary associations may be specified but is less obvious than binary multiplicity. The multiplicity on a role represents the potential number of instance tuples in the association when the other N-1 values are fixed."* On page 348 of the UML language reference manual [6] we find the following definition of AEM: *"In a n-ary association, the multiplicity is defined with respect to the other n-1 ends. For example, given a ternary association among classes (A, B, C) then the multiplicity of the C end states how many C objects may appear in association with a particular pair of A and B objects. If the multiplicity of this association is (many, many, one), then for each possible (A, B) pair, there is a unique value of C. For a given (B,C) pair, there may be many A values, however, and many values of A, B and C may participate in the association."*

Definition 1. An *upper AEM* of *1* defined on an association end in a N-ary association (N > 2) constrains the number of links that exist for the association that contain a specific instance combination in the other N-1 association ends to 1.

"If the multiplicity of this association is (many, many, one)........... For a given (B, C) pair, there may be many A values, however." Means that the upper multiplicity of many (*) defined on the association end that is connected to object class A implies there can exist many links in the object diagram for every possible (B, C) pair (see Fig. 4).

Definition 2. An *upper AEM* of * defined on an association end in a N-ary association (N > 2) does not constrain the number of links that exist for the association that contain a specific instance combination in the other N-1 association ends.

In Fig. 4 an example of a ternary association and an accompanying significant *object diagram* is given. We note that the values for the *lower* AEMs are considered to be irrelevant for the definition of the *upper* AEMs. Therefore we have put in question marks for the lower AEMs in Fig. 4. The accompanying object diagram is significant with respect to the upper AEMs. The occurrence of two association links in which the instance a1 of class A plays role R3 and instance c1 of class C plays role R5 implies the upper AEM of * defined on association end R4. The absence of two association links in

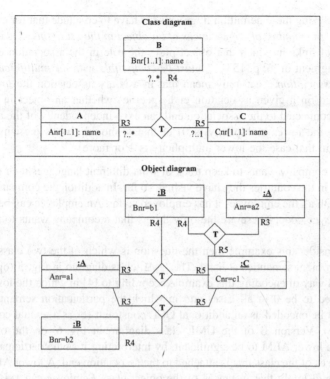

Fig. 4. Class diagram and significant object diagram for upper AEMs

which the combination of instances for class A in role R3 and instances of class B in role R4 have the same value implies an upper AEM of 1 for association end R5. The occurence of two association links in which the instances for class C in role R5 and instances for class B in role R4 are identical implies an upper AEM of * for association end R3.

3.2 A Definition for the Lower AEM in N-ary Associations

In [6, p. 153], the following references to association end multiplicity can be found: *"Each association end specifies properties that apply to the participation of the corresponding objects, such as how many times a single object may appear in links in the association (multiplicity)." "The number of appearances of an object in the set of links must be compatible with the multiplicity on each end of the association."*[1]

---

[1] Although in version 2 2.5 of the OMG modelling language, the following definition fragment can be found: *"A lower multiplicity for an end of an n-ary Association of 1 (or more) implies that one link (or more) must exist for every possible combination of values for the other ends."* [10: p. 198], this is a trivial definition in terms of the existence of a value for a given role in a fact type for any fact instance.

After analyzing these definition fragments we have to conclude that for every N-ary association: *"the number of appearances of an object in the set of links"* is identical to the number of links in which that object plays the role in the association end. In the definition fragment in [6, p. 153]: *"..must be compatible with the multiplicity on each end of the association."* can only mean that in a N-ary association the *lower* multiplicity defined on a given association end, specifies whether an object in the object class that is connected to the association end can exist independently of the association (in that case the lower multiplicity is 0) or that it should always participate in this association (in that case the lower multiplicity is 1 or more).

Example. A company wants to keep track of what different languages their employees have spoken in the countries they have visited, so far. In addition the company wants to keep a list with all the employees it has employed so far. An employee can be identified by the employee code. These are the only things that a company wants to record.

If we consider this example then the question is which of the two class diagrams reflect the problem semantics at hand. The UML class diagram in Fig. 5 (option A) is the proposed way of encoding this example according to [4] in which the lower AEMs are considered to be 0 in all cases and in which the participation semantics in this example will be encoded as an additional OCL constraint (or as a textual constraint in our example). Version B of the UML class diagram in Fig. 6, on the other hand, considers the lower AEM to be significant, by interpreting it as the participation status of the instances of the class that is attached to the association end. A lower AEM of 0 in this case would imply that instances of the object class *Employee* can exist independently of the association *language spoken abroad*. A lower AEM of 1 implies that every instance of object class *Country* and every instance of object Class Language must participate in the association *language spoken abroad*.

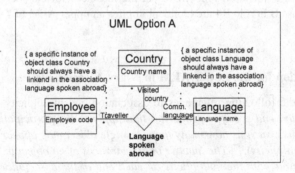

Fig. 5. UML class diagram option A

In Fig. 7 we have given a general example of a ternary association in a UML class diagram together with a significant accompanying object diagram. The general example in Fig. 7 is the extension of the general example from Fig. 4 in which we have added the lower AEMs, thereby extending the significant object diagram by adding instance

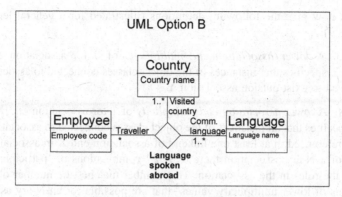

Fig. 6. UML class diagram option B

b3 of class B that is not involved in association T, implying that the lower AEM for association end R4 is 0. Furthermore we have added instance c2 of object class c to the significant object diagram, this implies that the lower AEM for association end R5 is 0.

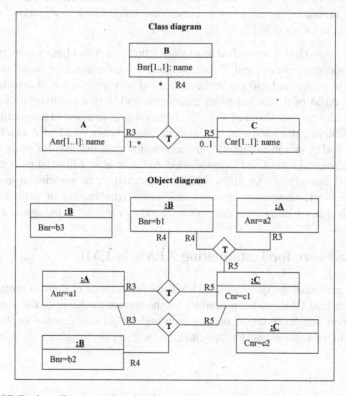

Fig. 7. UML class diagram and a significant object diagram for upper and lower AEM's

We can now give the following definitions (illustrated for a general ternary fact type in Fig. 7).

Definition 3. A *lower association end multiplicity* of 0 for association end X in association Y specifies that instances of the object classes connected to association end X are allowed to exist outside association Y.

Definition 4. A *lower association end multiplicity* of 1 for association end X in association Y specifies that all instances of the object classes connected to association end X have to be referenced in at least one linkend of association end X in association Y.

In case of a N-ary association there exist 2^N combinations of 'participation' constraints for the roles in the association. This number matches the number of different combinations of lower multiplicity values[2] that are possible for an N-ary association. This means that in principle we can use the *lower* association end multiplicity for encoding the 'participation' constraints for the classes in every role in a N-ary association.

3.3   A Single Definition for the Association End Multiplicity in UML

In this section we will integrate Definitions 1, 2, 3 and 4 into Definition 5 that contains the explicit semantics for *all* possible conditions under which *association end multiplicities* have to be specified in UML.

Definition 5. An AEM *x..y* attached to an association end A in a binary association that contains association ends A and B specifies that at least *x* instances *must* and at most *y* instances in association end A *may* be associated with an instance of association end B. A lower AEM of *0* attached to an association end A in a meaningful N-ary association specifies that an object of the object class that is attached to association end A can exist without participating in that association. A lower AEM of *1* attached to an association end A in a meaningful N-ary association specifies that for every object of the object class that is attached to association end A at least *1* linkend *must* contain (a reference to) that object. An upper AEM *..y* attached to an association end A in a meaningful N-ary association specifies that every combination of instances in the remaining N-1 association ends can appear at most in *y* links of the association.

4   A Procedure for Instantiating AEMs in UML

In order to guarantee the quality of the UML model in terms of domain semantics, we propose to extend UML with a procedure for the precise modeling of the semantics of an application area in terms of participation and uniqueness constraints that can be mapped onto association end multiplicities.

---

[2] In case we restrict the allowed values for the lower multiplicity to {0,1}.

Rule 1.
IF   all values in an association are needed to uniquely determine a link
THEN   assign the value * to the upper AEM for all association ends in the association.

Rule 2.
IF   N-1 values in an association are needed to uniquely determine a link
THEN   assign the value 1 to the upper AEM for the remaining association end in the association.

Rule 3.
IF   an instance of an object class that is connected to an association end of an association is allowed to exist outside that association
THEN IF the association is a binary
      THEN assign a lower multiplicity of 0 to the opposite association end
      ELSE assign a lower multiplicity of 0 to the association end
ELSE IF the association is a binary
      THEN assign a lower multiplicity of 1 to the opposite association end
      ELSE assign a lower multiplicity of 1 to the association end

Rule 4.
IF   after rules 1 or 2 and 3 have been applied still one or more upper AEMs have not been defined
THEN   assign the value * to each upper AEM that has not yet been defined.

Once an integrated class diagram is created for an application area we will be able to determine whether instances of object classes can exist independently of any association. If instances of an object class need to participate in at least one of the associations in which the object class is involved, a *global participation constraint* needs to be added [1]. We have illustrated this in Fig. 8 in which we have extended the class diagram with a second association in which object classes C and D participate. Because the lower association end multiplicity on the 'far' end of object class C of this binary association is *0*, instances of object class C are not required to participate in association U. Because the lower association end multiplicity on the 'source' end of object class C of the ternary association T is *0*, instances of object class C are not required to participate in association T. The significant object diagram in the lower part of Fig. 8, however, tells us that instances of class C can **not** exist independently. Therefore, a global textual participation constraint: *{every instance of object class C should participate in assoçiation T or association U}* has been added to the UML class diagram in Fig. 8. We can now give the following rule for the derivation of global participation constraints in UML.

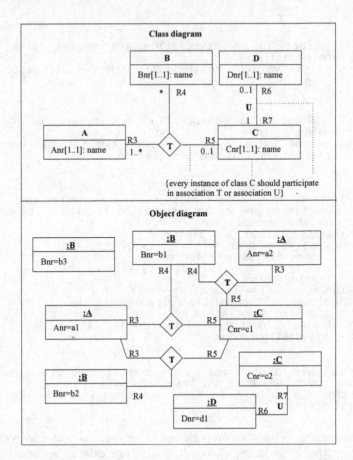

Fig. 8. UML class diagram and a corresponding object diagram for upper and lower AEM' and global participation constraints

Rule 5.
```
IF instances of an object class (X) are not allowed to
   exist independent from at least one  association
   (A1,..An)
THEN IF no mandatory participation in one or more
         specific associations is defined
      THEN add the following global participation constraint:
           {every  instance  of    object  class  X  should
           participate  in  association  A1  or  or  A2…  or
           association An}
```

The procedure for deriving the association end multiplicities and participation constraints in a complete UML data structure class diagram is the following:

Procedure derive AEMs.
```
BEGIN
WHILE still associations left
        DO take next association
            Apply <Rule 1, Rule 2>
        WHILE still association ends let in association
                DO take next association end in association
                    Apply <Rule 3>
        ENDWHILE
            Apply <Rule 4>
ENDWHILE
WHILE still classes left
        Do take next class
        Apply <Rule 5>
ENDWHILE
END
```

5 Conclusion

In this paper we have carefully studied the concept of *association end multiplicity* in the UML literature. We have constructed a precise definition for the association end construct for conceptual modeling out of several definition 'fragments' that were found in the literature. The main conclusion with regard to these definition fragments is that they are *not symmetrical* from the point of view of the *lower* multiplicity. For binary associations the lower multiplicity is defined in terms of the *opposite* association end whereas in N-ary associations the lower multiplicity is defined in terms of the association end to which it is attached. In UML the association end multiplicities for a binary association have a set-theoretical foundation that cannot be generalized in a consistent way to N-ary associations. We have also illustrated that if instances of an object class are not allowed to exist independently, under some conditions on the UML class diagram, additional global participation constraints have to be added. In this paper we have defined the conceptual semantics of the AEM in such a way that for most application models the lower AEM will become a significant modeling option. Only in the rare case that only global participation is required for an object class, we will have to add a textual (global participation) constraint. We have given transformation rules in Sect. 4 that enable us to unambiguously derive a specific configuration of *association end multiplicities* and *global participation* constraints in an application UML class diagram.

References

1. Bollen, P.: Using object-role modeling for capturing user requirements expressed as UML class diagrams. In: Proceedings 6th World Conference on Systemics, Cybernetics and Informatics, Orlando, Florida (2002)

2. Booch, G., Rumbaugh, J., Jacobson, I.: The Unified Modeling Language User Guide. Addison-Wesley, Boston (1999)
3. Elmasri, R., Navathe, S.: Fundamentals of Database Systems, 3rd edn. Addison-Wesley, Boston (2000)
4. Gogolla, M., Richters, M.: Transformation rules for UML class diagrams. In: Bézivin, J., Muller, P.-A. (eds.) UML 1998. LNCS, vol. 1618, pp. 92–106. Springer, Heidelberg (1999). doi:10.1007/978-3-540-48480-6_8
5. Liddle, S., Embley, D., Woodfield, S.: Cardinality constraints in semantic data models. Data Knowl. Eng. **11**, 235–270 (1993)
6. Rumbaugh, J., Jacobson, I., Booch, G.: The Unified Modeling Language Reference Manual. Addison-Wesley, Boston (1999)
7. UML semantics version 1.3 (1999). http://www.rational.com/uml/resources/documentation/index.jtmpl
8. UML notation guide version 1.3 (1999). http://www.rational.com/uml/resources/documentation/index.jtmpl
9. UML modeling language 2.0 proposal (2002)
10. OMG Unified Modeling Language, version 2.5 (2015)

The Need for a OO Modeling Methodology

Peter Bollen[✉]

Maastricht University, Maastricht, The Netherlands
p.bollen@maastrichtuniversity.nl

Abstract. In this paper we discuss the pitfalls in the OO-paradigm for its application in conceptual analysis and subsequently its application in IS design. It is argued that there should exist a modeling procedure or methodology that guides the business domain analyst and the application designer on how to apply the OO modeling constructs in the different stages of the IS development life cycle.

1 Introduction

In this paper we will focus on the basic modeling concepts in object-orientation (OO) or object technology (OT). We note that the object-oriented modeling concepts have their roots in programming: object-oriented programming [1], and object-oriented software construction [2]. The OO-paradigm, however, has been applied intensively during the last three decades for information systems analysis and design: object-oriented modeling and design [3], object-oriented systems design (OOD) [4], object-oriented information engineering; analysis, design and implementation [5]. In this article we will, firstly, focus on the definition of 'building blocks' from the OO-paradigm and the essential properties of the OO-paradigm. Secondly we will show how these building blocks can be put together using the essential properties of the OO paradigm. Finally, we will show that the application of the OO building blocks in a conceptual OO model can result in conceptual models that do not reflect the application domain semantics at all times.

2 Basic Building Blocks in the OO-Paradigm

2.1 Objects

The foundation of the object-oriented paradigm is the object. The question arises: what is an object. In the OO paradigm, objects are considered to be software objects that represent real-world objects or concepts. Real-world objects or concepts have a state and (in some cases) behavior.

The real-world object *car* has a *state* (license plate number, color, number of doors, speed) and it can perform behavior (accelerating, braking). The state of a 'real-life' object or entity is represented in the OO-paradigm by means of data values for the variables defined on the conceptual object that represents the 'real-life' entity or object. The state of a specific real world object *car* can be represented by the following values:

I. Ciuciu et al. (Eds.): OTM 2016 Workshops, LNCS 10034, pp. 143–154, 2017.
DOI: 10.1007/978-3-319-55961-2_14

licenseplate number *45-UI-56*, the color *yellow*, the number of doors is *4*, the speed is *45* miles/h. With this, we can now give the following preliminary definition of an object:

Definition 1. A (conceptual) object is a representation of an entity, thing or concept in the real world. The relevant properties of such a real world entity, thing or concept (or state) are represented as values of the variables of the (conceptual) object.

2.2   Methods

In addition to its state, an object has behavior. For example, a car can accelerate or it can brake. The behavior of the car results in a new state (or properties). Accelerating the car will lead to a change in its state from 45 miles/h to 60 miles/h. The behavior of a car is a complex technical and physical process that can be represented as a method that calculates the new speed [V(t + Δt)] as function of the old speed [V(t)] and the amount of acceleration [A]: V(t + Δt) = V(t) + (A*Δt). We note that the representation of the physics of real-life velocity and acceleration is applicable to every car or every vehicle. The description for the method Accelerate (Acceleration, NewTime) as illustrated in Fig. 1 can be given as follows:

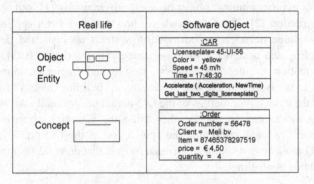

Fig. 1. Objects with variables, data values and methods

ON execute Accelerate(Accelaration, NewTime)
    IF (time exists AND Speed exists)
        *THEN Speed:=speed + acceleration *(NewTime-Time)*
            Time:=NewTime
      ENDIF
  END

The method *accelerate* uses the object's state variables *speed* and *time* plus the method arguments *acceleration* and *newtime* to create new values for the object's state variables *speed* and *time*. The execution of methods will not always have an effect on the state of an object. For example, the method that determines the last two digits of a car's license plate number:

```
ON get_last_two_digits_licenseplate
        IF  Licensplatenumber exists
        THEN help:=trunc last 2 digits (Licensplate)
                Show help
        ENDIF
END
```

Definition 2. A method is a representation of (parts of) the behavior of a real world entity, thing or concept. A method may have an effect on one or more variable values of the object. An object can have one or more methods that represent the behavior of the entity, thing or concept.

According to the OO paradigm, the entity or thing that has to be represented as the object; and the properties of the entity or thing that has to represented as an object (licenseplate, color, speed) and the behavior that can be executed by these entities or things is encapsulated in the object itself.

Some properties will be enclosed in the object itself (in the form of data values of object variables), others (the ones that are not considered to be properties of the object itself) will be modeled as a relation or link in which different objects can be involved.

2.3   The Object Class

In the Fusion method, the following definition of object class is given: *"A class is an abstraction that represents the idea or general notion of a set of similar objects."* [6: p. 14]. In [7] a class is defined as: *" ... a template or descriptor representing a set of models (more often called methods) packaged around an internal structure that will hold the state of each object belonging to the class. This structure is the set of internal variables."* [7: p. 147]. In the UML semantics version 1.3 [8] a(n) (object) class is defined as follows: *"A description of a set of objects that share the same attributes, operations, method, relationships and semantics."* We will now give the following definition of object class:

Definition 3. An object class is a template for objects that provide the same information services and that may encapsulate data values for the same variables.

2.4   Relationships or Associations in the OO-Paradigm

In the OO-literature a relationship (or association) is defined for binary associations [9]. In such a binary relationship world, an association instance or link involves two different objects. For example, the link *Person Barry Brown owns car 45-hu-34* can be implemented as a data value for the variable owns of object *Person Barry Brown*. In order to be able to encode the symmetry in the relationship there needs to be an inverse association instance: *Car 45-hu-34 is owned by person Barry Brown*, that is encoded as a data value for the variable *is owned by* of object *Car 45-hu-34*. In such a binary world, the implementation of a binary association instance or binary link will be as data values for 'link' variables of the objects (see Fig. 2).

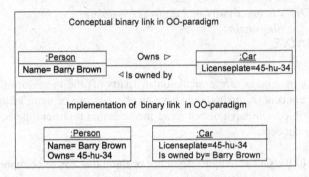

Fig. 2. Implementation binary link in the OO paradigm

Other authors [3, 6] consider also ternary or higher order (N > 2) relations or association links that enable OO modelers to conceptualize these higher order relations in an application domain. Internally the OO-paradigm needs to encode links as objects having data values for the object variables that refer to the different 'roles' played by the objects.

In Fig. 3 we have given an example of a ternary link and the implementation in the OO paradigm of such a ternary link using a link object. In the upper part of Fig. 3 a ternary link is given in which we have used a synthesis of the notation conventions from the OO modeling languages OMT [3] and UML [8]. The ternary link ...*married*... *in*.... has three 'roles' or 'slots': *Groom, Bride* and *Marriage Year*. These 'roles' or

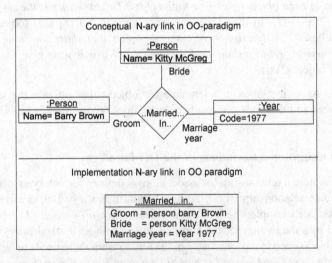

Fig. 3. Implementation N-ary link in the OO paradigm

'slots' are respectively connected to the object instances: *person Barry Brown, person Kitty McGreg* and *Year 1977*. We can conclude that if we want to apply the modeling concepts in the OO paradigm in conceptual models to encode semantic associations between objects of degree 3 or higher, it will be in the format of non-semantic objects, i.e. objects that do not represent application domain concepts [10: p. 27] but that represent an association. The objects that are involved in such an association are represented as 'pointer' values for the variables in that object.

3   How the Building Blocks in the OO Paradigm Work Together

3.1   Encapsulation

Encapsulation provides protection for the values of the state variables for an object because it restricts selection, insertion, deletion to/of values of state variables to (predefined) methods defined on the object instance (see Fig. 4). For example, if no *select* method is defined for a given object's variable it will not be possible to know the value of a data variable for the object. Furthermore, if no insert method is defined for an object variable, it will not be possible to assign a data value to that object variable.

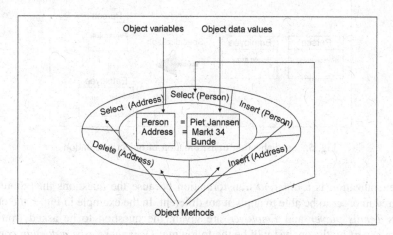

Fig. 4. Encapsulation of object variable data values by methods

In the example in Fig. 4 the object has the variables *person* and *address* and the methods to insert the data values for Person and Address: *insert(person), insert(address)*. Furthermore, the object has methods for selecting current data value the object's variable address: *select(address),* and selecting the current data value for the object's variable person: select(person). In addition, this example object has a method that can delete the current data value for the address variable: *delete(address)*. We can consider encapsulation as the 'hiding' of implementation details of the object's behavior from the user of the information service [1: p. 52].

3.2   Generalization/Specialization

The concept(s) of specialization and generalization can be considered as cornerstones for the 'inheritance' concept that will be discussed in the next section. The reason that we need specialization or generalization is that some application domain concepts or intensions have either the same, overlapping or including extensions (for example *Employee* and *Person*) and/or they share the same properties (*Tennis player* and *Employee*). These characteristics serve as a trigger to look for additional domain intensions that were not uttered initially by the user(s). Specialization and generalization are semantic transformations that require explicit domain knowledge. In case of specialization the following question should be asked: *Is every employee a person?* It is essential that the 'subtype' by its nature is also an instance of the 'supertype' which means that there exists the same naming convention for instances of the subtype and instances of the supertype(s).

We will now illustrate the concept of specialization in the object-oriented paradigm in Fig. 5. The result of this transformation is expressed using the 'is-a' relationship between object classes that is denoted by a solid line. The 'upper' class is called the superclass and the 'lower' class is called the subclass.

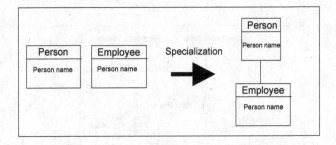

Fig. 5. Specialization transformation in object orientation

Generalization is a *different* transformation because the questions that should be answered in order to be able to apply it are different. In the example in Fig. 6 the object classes *Tennis player* and *Employee* are given, the question to be asked from the domain expert by the analyst will be the following: *Does there exist a domain concept that refers to a set of 'real-life' domain things or concepts that is exactly the union of Tennis player and Employee?*

In addition a second question should be posed when the answer of the first question is yes: *Does there exist a naming convention for the generalized concept?* We will note that the naming convention for the generalization is in general not implied by the naming conventions for the subtypes. This means that theoretically it is possible to define a generalized concept that does *not* have a generalized naming convention. In the example in Fig. 6, the user tells the analyst that there exists a concept *Person* that precisely refers to the union of the concepts *Tennis player* and *Employee*. The

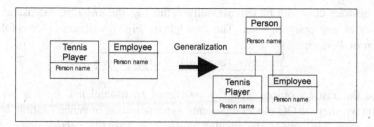

Fig. 6. Generalization transformation in object orientation.

intensions *Employee* and *Tennis Player* have the same naming convention namely the person name name class. There does also exist a naming convention for the generalized concept person.

The user tells the analyst that the *Person Name* is a good naming convention for the generalized concept *Person*. We can now create a proper 'generalization' for the example on the left-hand side of Fig. 7.

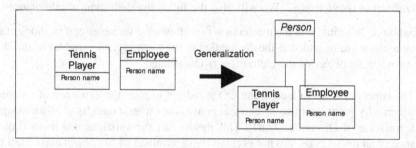

Fig. 7. Generalization transformation using abstract class construct

The OO paradigm uses the same 'is-a' relationship for denoting specialization and generalization. In the OO-paradigm: *"Generalization and specialization are two different viewpoints of the same relationship, viewed from the superclass or from the subclasses. The word generalization derives from the fact that the superclass generalizes the subclasses. Specialization refers to the fact that the subclasses refine or specialize the superclass."* [3: p. 42]. The concept that is used in the OO paradigm for modeling generalizations is the abstract class concept in combination with the 'is-a' relationship.

Definition 4. An abstract class is an object class that does not have instances.

We will denote an abstract class by showing the class name of the generalized class in italics. The abstract class concept should be used in the OO paradigm in the following way. If the 'superclass' is a generalized concept (of two or more concepts that are modeled as 'sub classes') then we will model such a 'super class' as an abstract object class. In Fig. 7 the generalization transformation in OO is shown using the abstract class construct.

The abstract class can be extensionally defined as the *union* of extensions of the subclasses at any point in time. The example in Fig. 7 will lead to the following definition of *Person*:

Person:= Tennis player ∪ Employee

Since the abstract object class *Person* cannot be instantiated, there is no longer confusion whether the OO model represents a specialization or generalization. In Fig. 6 we have explicitly shown the naming convention variable *person name*, for the superclass *Person* as well as for the subclasses *Tennis player* and *Employee*. In the next section we will show how variables and methods can be generalized by applying the concept of inheritance.

3.3   Inheritance

The most significant concept in the object-oriented paradigm is the concept of inheritance. Rumbaugh et al. [3: p. 42] give the following description of inheritance: *"... inheritance refers to the mechanism of sharing attributes and operations using the generalization relationship."* We will give the following definition of inheritance:

Definition 5. Inheritance is the mechanism that allows the variables and methods of the ancestor classes to be added to the declaration of the methods and variables of the child classes when an object of the child class is instantiated.

The concept of inheritance in the OO paradigm implies the existence of an object class hierarchy (of at least two levels) that consists of (at least one) 'is-a' relationship(s) for a Universe of Discourse (UoD). This means that the variables and method of an instance of an object class, are not exclusively determined by the object class itself but also by the position of that object class within a class hierarchy. We will now illustrate the concept of 'inheritance' by an example in which we start with a class diagram that consists of a set of independent object classes (Fig. 8). In the 'specialized' example in Fig. 9 the object class *Vehicle* is the superclass of the object classes *Land Vehicle* and *Sea Vehicle*. The object class *Land Vehicle* is the superclass of the object classes *Car* and *Autobus*. Finally, the object class *Sea Vehicle* is the superclass of the object class *Boat*. In the object-oriented paradigm a subclass inherits all variables and methods of its superclass and the ancestors of its superclass. Moreover, subclasses can have variables and methods that are specific for that subclass. We note that the specialization transformation is allowed in this UoD because each vehicle within the union of all vehicles can be identified by its vehicle code. In the specialized example in Fig. 9 the inheritance transformation has not been applied yet.

Applying inheritance to this example will result in the object-class hierarchy in Fig. 10 in which the variables and methods are assigned onto the appropriate object class (level) in the hierarchy. The root of the object class hierarchy in Fig. 10 consists of the object class *Vehicle*. This object class contains those variables and methods that are shared by every object class in the hierarchy: *vehicle code, maximum speed, passenger capacity* and *insert max. Speed()*. The object class *Land vehicle* is defined as a

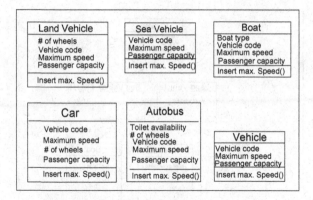

Fig. 8. Object model with independent object classes

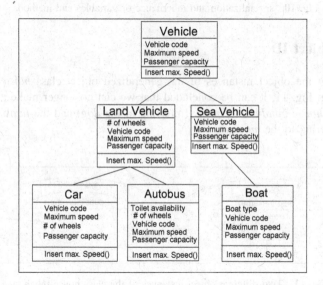

Fig. 9. Specializations in example

subclass of the object class *Vehicle*. Therefore, it inherits all the variables and methods from the class *Vehicle* plus it extends this set of variables and methods by an additional variable: *# of wheels*. This means that the subclasses of *Land Vehicle*: *Car* and *Autobus* will inherit all variables and methods of their ancestor classes: *Land Vehicle* and *Vehicle*. Furthermore, the object class *Autobus* is extended by the class variable: *toilet availability*.

Definition 6. An object is instantiated from a non-abstract object class, thereby, the object inherits all variables and methods of the non-abstract object class from which it is instantiated plus all variables and methods defined on all ancestor classes of the object class from which it is instantiated.

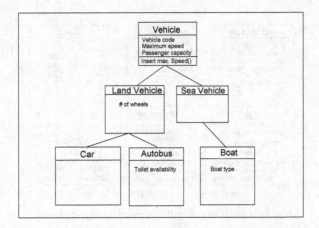

Fig. 10. specialization and inheritance of variables and methods

4   The Object ID

If we look at the object instances of the generalized object class *house inhabitant* example from Fig. 11, it can be concluded that we can no longer make a distinction between the *house inhabitant Tommy* (referring to the *dog*) and the *house inhabitant Tommy* (referring to the *human*).

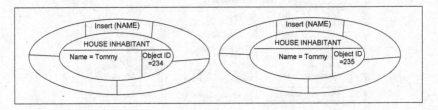

Fig. 11. Two different object instances of the class house inhabitant

To overcome this side-effect of generalization inheritance the OO paradigm contains the concept of 'global' unique object ID's to identify objects within a specific application system which makes it possible to make a precise distinction between two objects that have the same state and behavior. The existence of these object IDs allows us to refer to the house inhabitant with object ID 234 having the name Tommy and the house inhabitant with object ID 235 having the name Tommy as two different objects (see Fig. 11).

In addition to the declaration of the object's class, the declaration of the variables and methods that an object inherits, the OO paradigm states that each object instance has a 'unique' identity [3: p. 24, 11: p. 20, 12: p. 144] *"Object identifiers must uniquely identify as many objects as may ever coexist in the system at any one time"* [1: p. 54].

Every time a new object is instantiated, a new object ID is assigned to the object (see Fig. 12). How these object IDs are determined is not specified explicitly in the OO-paradigm We should think of this assignment process in terms of an object counter that is incremented every time a new object is created.

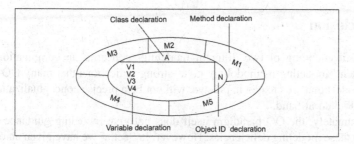

Fig. 12. Object ID declaration

We will now give the definition of object ID:

Definition 7. The object ID is a name class the elements of which can be used for identifying an object within the union of all objects in a system.

5   The Need for a Modeling Procedure

Because the naming conventions in an application domain normally are 'locally' unique and known to the application users, it is generally impossible to enforce users in the application domain to use 'abstract' object IDs to represent domain-based naming conventions. The best way of encoding a user-based identifier for the concepts that are modeled as object classes is to encode such an identifier as a class variable. In case variables and methods are defined in an abstract object class, these variables and methods serve only one purpose: that they can be inherited by at least one non-abstract subclass or by a non-abstract descendant of such a subclass in the class hierarchy. These generalizations are only created to have an efficient OO model that promotes code re-use by defining a variable or method as 'high' as possible in the object class hierarchy [3: p. 41, 13: p. 43]. It is this distinction between the application of OO concepts for domain analysis versus application design [14] that should be embedded in a procedure. This procedure firstly guides a domain analyst on how to apply OO modeling concepts in the domain analysis process. Subsequently, such a procedure should contain guidelines on how to map such a OOA-model onto an efficient OOD model. A simple outline of an example of such a procedure is the following:

Step 1. Identify the concepts or entities in the application domain
Step 2. Map these concepts or entities onto object classes
Step 3. Assign the appropriate name variables to these object classes
Step 4. Show specialization relationships in the OOA model.
Step 5. Show generalizations that exist in the application domain.

Step 6. Add associations between object classes that reflect the semantic relationships in the application domain.

Step 7. Create a OOD model out of the OOA model by pushing methods and variables as 'high as possible' in the class-hierarchy.

6 Conclusion

The implicit encoding of two different modeling 'concerns' in combination with a 'non-existent' modeling methodology gives strong indications that many OO-analysis (OOA) models that are created in practice will not be a precise conceptualization of the problem domain at hand.

Unfortunately, the OO paradigm itself does not give modeling guidance that will overcome these modeling deficiencies. However, in Sect. 5 we have given an outline of an example of a procedure that specifies how conceptual OOA models can be created and how they should be transformed into 'efficient' OOD models.

References

1. Cox, B.J.: Object-Oriented Programming. Addison-Wesley, Boston (1986)
2. Meyer, B.: Object-Oriented Software Construction. Prentice Hall, Upper Saddle River (1988)
3. Rumbaugh, J., Blaha, M., Premeriani, W., Eddy, F., Lorensen, W.: Object-Oriented Modeling and Design. Prentice-hall, Upper Saddle River (1991)
4. Yourdon, E.: Object-Oriented Systems Design: An Integrated Approach. Prentice-hall, Upper Saddle River (1994)
5. Montgomery, S.: Object-Oriented Information Engineering: Analysis, Design and Implementation. Academic press limited, Cambridge (1994)
6. Coleman, D., Patrick, A., Bodoff, S., Dollin, C., Gilchrist, H., Hayes, F., Jeremaes, P.: Object-Oriented Development: The Fusion Method. Prentice-Hall, Upper Saddle River (1994)
7. Page-Jones, M.: Comparing techniques by means of encapsulation and connascence. Commun. ACM 35(9), 147–151 (1992)
8. OMG, UML Specification v. 1.3 final draft (1999)
9. Booch, G.: Object-Oriented Analysis And Design With Applications, 2nd edn. Benjamin-Cummings, San Francisco (1994)
10. Tkach, D., Puttick, R.: Object Technology in Application Development. The Benjamin-Cummings publishing company, San Francisco (1994)
11. Brown, A.W.: Object-Oriented Databases: Their Applications To Software Engineering. McGraw-Hill, New York (1991)
12. Khoshafian, S.: Insight into object-oriented databases. Inf. Softw. Technol. 32(4), 274–289 (1990)
13. Korson, T., McGregor, J.: Understanding object-oriented: a unifying paradigm. Commun. ACM 33(9), 41–60 (1990)
14. Monarchi, D.E., Puhr, I.: A research typology for object-oriented analysis and design. Commun. ACM 35(9), 35–47 (1992)

The Rule Configurator

A Tool to Execute a Model and Play with the Rules

Inge Lemmens[✉] and Jean-Paul Koster

CogNIAM Finance, Amsterdam, The Netherlands
{inge.lemmens,jean.paul.koster}@cogniamfinance.com

Abstract. To implement a customer-oriented approach for financing products, a financial organization has developed a conceptual model for it. The model identifies the basic components of a financing products and the relationships between these components. Instantiation of this conceptual model leads to specific products.

The conceptual model is defined as generic as possible. It describes the playfield within which the products can be offered to customers, but it does not describe all the rules that apply as that is something to discover and to manipulate over time. For the latter, a rule configurator is under development that will provide the means to define and tailor the rules that apply before implementing them in the conceptual model as well as the final application. This rule configurator thereby provides end users the means to play with the conceptual model without having to learn a specific representation and the means to update a conceptual model in a for them intuitive manner.

Keywords: Conceptual model · Tailoring rules · Simulation of scenarios · Hierarchy

1 Introduction

Due to changing customer expectations and the rise of new competitors, a financial organization has decided to improve its financing chain through which credit products are provided to customers. Therefore, it started an improvement program aimed to achieve the following two goals with respect to the financing chain:

1. To define a client-oriented approach on financing, and
2. To rationalize and standardize and thus reduce the cost of the IT-landscape and credit processes.

To achieve these goals, and in particular the first goal, the organization has chosen for a solution-driven (customer originated) approach instead of a product-driven approach. In particular, instead of developing a set of predefined products that can be sold to customers, a conceptual model has been developed that identifies the basic components of a financing product and the relationships between these components. Instantiation of this conceptual model provides a specific product that fulfils the customer's objectives.

© Springer International Publishing AG 2017
I. Ciuciu et al. (Eds.): OTM 2016 Workshops, LNCS 10034, pp. 155–163, 2017.
DOI: 10.1007/978-3-319-55961-2_15

The developed conceptual model, called the *product model,* is the driver for the development of the software solution chosen to support the front-office in the quotation process as it provides the means to identify any allowed combination of values for the identified fact types.

In essence, the product model defines a product as being a set of values of fact types that are grouped in 11 main components. Each component describes a dimension of a product, like the collateral, the interest, or the facts associated with the limit of a financing product. The components are related to each other, and can even be conditional towards each other based on e.g. legislative rules or internal policies. For example, when a limit exceeds a certain amount, the collateral component becomes obligatory (i.e. the customer has to provide collateral) while in other cases it is optional.

1.1   Defining the Concrete Instances – Limiting the Allowed Choices

The defined conceptual model is developed as *generic* as possible. As described by the product model team, the product model describes exactly the *playfield* within which the products can be offered to the customers. It specifies the outer lines of the playfield, but does not specify the exact rules of the game, as that is something to discover and to adjust over time.

Concrete, this means that the product model team has chosen to implement in the product model only those constraints that are, as they call it, *"physically impossible to break".* For example, a financing product without a limit cannot exist, as such the constraint specifying that each financing product has at least one limit, is a constraint that is implemented in the conceptual model. As an analogy, a constraint specifying that it is impossible for a person to be at two locations at the same time, is considered to be a "physically impossible to break constraint".

These type of constraints are directly implemented in the conceptual model. All other constraints are not implemented in the conceptual model as integrity constraints but are implemented in such a manner that they can be easily configured by the end-users.

In particular, we distinguish between:

1. Constraints that express a dependency between two or more variables, and
2. "Conditional constraints" which are constraints that apply only when a specific condition is fulfilled.

2   Making Constraints Configurable

In the product model, a lot of dependencies between variables of different fact types exist. For example, a limit of type A cannot be combined with a guarantee of type B. To handle these type of dependencies (these type of constraints), fact types are introduced, which we call in the product model the *relation fact types*. These fact types are only introduced to specify that a combination of values or variables (i.e. a relation) is, or is not allowed.

Figure 1 provides an example of a relation fact type that specifies that a combination of values is allowed and thus can be used in the population of other fact types. In particular, the fact type "Country – currency allowed relation" specifies which combination of values are allowed for country and currency. Only those combination of values are allowed in the fact type "Loan", through implementation of a subset constraint (as indicated by the "red" color of the not-allowed population in the fact type loan).

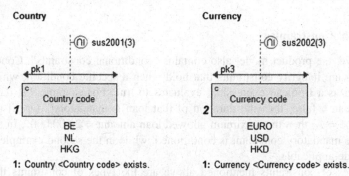

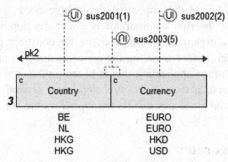

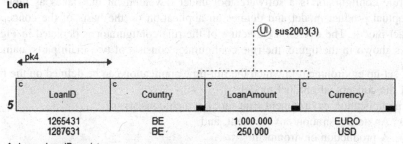

Fig. 1. Defining relation tables. (Color figure online)

Note, relation fact types can only be developed for variables that have a range of values. That is, we cannot define a relation fact type between a variable like loan amount and another value, because of the (almost) infinite number of potential values for loan amount and thus also the (almost) infinite number of combinations. Therefore, relation fact types are only defined between variables of so-called domain fact types, which are fact types that are marked as such in the conceptual model. In the example of Fig. 1, the fact type diagrams "Country" and "Currency" represent such domain fact types.

2.1 Conditional Constraints

Besides the above, the product model also contains "conditional constraints". Conditional constraints are integrity constraints that hold when a specific condition, which can be expressed as a Boolean expression, evaluates to true. For example: "If daily revocable of a loan = false, then the duration of that loan is mandatory". Or "if the credit facility type = A, then the maximum allowed loan amount = 2.500.000". In the first example, the mandatory constraint is conditioned, while in the second example, a value rule is made applicable.

The two types of constraints mentioned above are the types of constraints that *define the rules of the game*. These rules need to be defined, they can change over time as experience is obtained, and the impact of the change needs to be insightful. To support these objectives, the rule configurator is under development. With the rule configurator, the financial organization aims to define the constraints, see the impact on the behavior of the model, **before** updating the conceptual model and before realizing the changes in the front office application that is based on the conceptual model. That is, the rule configurator acts as the *training and simulation ground*, the area where the game can be exercised and strategies can be tested, before the real game takes place.

3 The Rule Configurator

The rule configurator is a software tool under development that takes as input the conceptual product model and defines an application on the basis of the conceptual product model. The overall architecture of the rule configurator is depicted in Fig. 2.

As shown in the figure, the rule configurator consists of two main parts, namely:

1. A set-up environment in which the run-time application can be defined on the basis of the conceptual product model,
2. An application environment (run-time), which consists of:
   (a) An administration environment, and
   (b) A production environment.

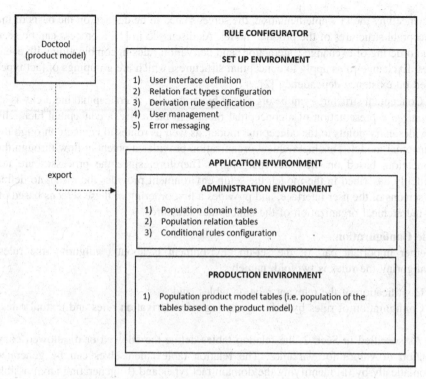

Fig. 2. Overall architecture of the rule configurator.

3.1 Set-up Environment

To come to an application that can be used in the simulation, the rule configurator takes as input the conceptual model. This input is the basis for the set-up environment which contains functionality for:

1. Composing user interfaces,
2. Specifying which relation tables are of relevance and need to be monitored in the production environment,
3. Specifying the logic of the derivation rule in the target language,
4. User management, and
5. Error messaging.

Composing the User Interface

The main functionality of the set-up environment consists of the means for the user to define the user interface for the run-time application associated with the conceptual model. That is, in the set-up environment, it is possible to define screens, to place variables associated with the product model on the screens, and order the screens to come to a natural flow through the application. For the latter, we would normally take as input the process models associated with the conceptual model [1]. However, since the product model team has decided not to develop a process model in order not to be influenced by the IT implementation, the screens need to be defined on the basis of the conceptual structures of the product model. As discussed in [1], a process can be seen as an ordering of exchange (interaction) and derivation rules in combination with event rules. Exchange rules apply to conceptual structures, which are groupings of fact types based on existence dependency [2].

Conceptual structures can be organized hierarchically. A conceptual hierarchy is an *organized re*presentation of a conceptual model. In particular, a conceptual hierarchy provides entry points to the conceptual model, as well as routes to navigate through the conceptual model. This hierarchical organization provides a potential flow through the application, based on the rules that apply. Therefore, since the processes are not explicitly described in the model, the setup environment provides the means to define the screens of the user interface, and provides a first ordering of these screens based on the hierarchical organization of the conceptual structures.

Rule Configuration

Another important part of the set-up environment is about configuring the rules. Configuring the rules is twofold, namely:

1. Identification of the relevant relation tables, and
2. Configuration of rules by defining the logic for derivation rules and textual rules.

As specified in Sect. 2, the relation tables define the allowed or disallowed combination of values for variables. The relation tables themselves can be generated automatically by (a) identifying the domain fact types and (b) generating any possible combination of variables of different domain fact types twice, namely once for providing the means to specify the allowed combinations, and once for providing the means to specify the disallowed combinations. Not all generated relation tables are of relevance for the run-time application, as such in the set-up environment, the functionality is provided to identify the relevant relation tables for the run-time application. These relation tables will, in the run-time application, be part of the administration environment.

Besides identifying the relevant relation tables, the set-up environments also will provide the means to specify the program code for those constraints that cannot (yet) be automatically generated. In particular, the program code for derivation rules and textual constraints can be specified in the set-up environment, such that these will be checked in the run-time application.

User Management and Error Message Definition

Another aspect of the set-up environment is the means provided to define users, user groups and their permissions on the application. This is in particular of relevance for defining who is allowed to manipulate the values of the domain tables and relation tables in the administration area of the run-time application, as well as the specification of the conditional requirement. Manipulation of this information has an effect on the behavior of the application in the production environment and thus can only be performed by explicitly authorized users.

Error message definition is the part of the set-up environment in which the error specification of the constraints can be tailored. That is, for each constraint identified, a user-friendly message can provided which will be shown in the run-time application when the constraint is violated.

3.2   The Application Environment

Once the application is completely set-up in the set-up environment, it can be executed in the application environment. This application environment, which corresponds to the run-time environment, consists of two parts, namely:

1. The administration environment, and
2. The production environment.

The Administration Environment

The administration environment contains the domain tables, relation tables and conditional constraints of the product model, which together define the *rules of the game*. That is, they form together with the "physically impossible to break constraints" the rules that govern the product model.

Due to the fact that the rules that apply are changing over time, as the products and their definitions change over time, the administration environment provides the means to populate the domain tables and relation tables as well as the means to define the conditional constraints. For the latter, the administration environment foresees an expression editor with which compound Boolean expressions can be constructed as antecedents of the conditions and attached to the constraints that are the consequences of the conditions.

Since the configuration of these types of rules impact the run-time application, the administration environment has restricted access, as defined in the user management module of the set-up environment.

The Population Environment

The final part of the rule configurator is the population environment. This environment forms the run-time application, as it provides the means for the end-user to populate the product model with concrete facts. The visualization of the product model in the population environment is based on the screens as defined in the set-up environment, while the behavior of the application is steered by the rules as defined in the administration environment.

4   Usage of the Rule Configurator

The financial organization aims to use the rule configurator for three purposes, which steer the development process of the rule configurator. The three purposes are:

1. Demonstration of the product model,
2. Definition of the applicable product assortment, and
3. Simulation.

4.1 Demonstration of the Product Model

In a first phase of the project, the product model was documented in Microsoft® Word. This resulted in a document of almost 400 pages, containing the concepts, their definitions, the fact types and the relation tables. Although this document contains all the required information and has been accepted as valuable for the organization, there was still a lack of understanding of the product model by relevant stakeholders. To overcome this, the idea of a "model demonstrator" came about. This demonstrator is the first functionality that will be provided by the rule configurator. It will be possible to demonstrate the working of the product model, especially the dependencies of variables (selection of a value of a variable leads to unavailability of certain values of another variable), as well as the reasons for unavailability of the values.

In this functionality, the administration environment of the rule configurator is prefilled by import of the population from the product model as specified in Doctool.

4.2 Definition of the Applicable Product Assortment

The second important functionality is to provide the means to define the product assortment. This implies that the population of the product model in the application environment must be saved, marked as eligible product, and reported upon. For the latter, an export to HTML, XML and Microsoft® Word is a minimum requirement. Additionally, it will be checked whether the result can be exported in a format that can be imported in the front-office application that is used in the quotation process. The success of this export functionality is highly dependent on whether the front-office application has correctly implemented the product model.

Also required is an important functionality with which a previously defined assortment can be loaded in the application. This is in particular of relevance when the product model has changed and the effect of the change is to be visualized in the previously defined product assortment.

4.3 Simulation

The last identified functionality is the simulation functionality. This functionality goes beyond the previously defined functionalities by implementing the administration environment in the rule configurator. By implementing this, the user can populate the relation tables and define the conditional constraints. In further development, the possibility to add constraints like value constraints, mandatory constraints, exclusion constraints,... is considered. In doing so, the rule configurator can be seen as a true simulator that can be used to identify the rules by the end user before implementing these in the conceptual model.

5 Conclusions

In this paper, we introduced the need of a financial organization for a rule configurator that aids them in the tailoring of a conceptual model for financial products. This rule configurator takes as input a conceptual model developed in Doctool and provides the means to demonstrate the model as well as the means to configure the constraints that apply and as such to simulate the working of the model.

One of the main reasons for developing the rule configurator is to provide the means to demonstrate the working of the conceptual model to important stakeholders like management, business end users, as well as IT *before* implementation.

As the organization has changed its approach to product development from a product-oriented approach to a customer-oriented approach, it has a need for rationalizing the existing product assortment and defining the new situation and associated assortment. Therefore, the rule configurator will provide the means to identify population as specific products and provide this information to the front office system used in the quotation process. This way, the end users have insight in the product assortment, the potential conflicts between the different products before realization in the front office system used in the quotation process.

The final, and most challenging, reason to develop the rule configurator is to have the means to configure the constraints that apply to the conceptual model. This is achieved by implementing relation tables and conditional constraints which can be tailored in the application.

References

1. Lemmens, I.: Integrating modelling disciplines at conceptual semantic level. In: Ciuciu, I., Panetto, H., Debruyne, C., Aubry, A., Bollen, P., Valencia-García, R., Mishra, A., Fensel, A., Ferri, F. (eds.) OTM 2015. LNCS, vol. 9416, pp. 188–196. Springer, Heidelberg (2015). doi:10.1007/978-3-319-26138-6_22
2. Lemmens, I., Sgaramella, F., Valera, S.: Development of tooling to support fact-oriented modeling at ESA. In: Meersman, R., Herrero, P., Dillon, T. (eds.) OTM 2009. LNCS, vol. 5872, pp. 714–722. Springer, Heidelberg (2009). doi:10.1007/978-3-642-05290-3_87
3. Nijssen, G.M.: A Framework for Discussion in ISO/TC97/SC5/WG3 and comments on 78.04/01 and 78.05/03 (1978)
4. ISO, ISO/TC97/SC5/WWG3 - TR9007 Information Processing Systems - Concepts and Terminology for the Conceptual Schema and the Information Base (1987)

A Durable Architecture as a Foundation for Regulation Based Services

Jos Rozendaal[1] and Sjir Nijssen[2(✉)]

[1] Independent Consultant, Roosendaal, The Netherlands
jos.rozendaal@gmail.com
[2] PNA Group, Heerlen, The Netherlands
sjir.nijssen@pna-group.com

Abstract. In 2012 a co-creation has been established in The Netherlands involving government service providers, academia and innovative businesses to develop a durable architecture for services that are based on laws, decrees or regulations and the specification of a formal language to specify the formal requirements for regulation based services. The authors have been involved in the deliberations how to develop a durable architecture that can be used as a practical guideline in the various discussions how to improve the specification, the design, the production and delivery of regulation based services. It has been observed that the vast majority of these regulation based services are information-intensive and require a substantial IT effort. As regulations change fairly often, it is a requirement to reduce the traditional procedural complexity and introduce a more manageable declarative approach.

Keywords: Durable architecture · Verbalizable Architecture · Regulation based services · Legal Services · Fact based modeling (FBM)

1 Introduction

Since the establishment of the co-creation The Blue Chamber in 2012 by two large government services, the Dutch Customs and Tax Administration and the Immigration and naturalization Service, the University of Amsterdam and PNA, quite some time has been invested in developing a durable architecture. Intermediate results have been reported in [5–7]. At FBM 2015 the papers [2, 4, 10] reported progress. One major goal of the durable architecture is to provide enough precision such that the architecture can serve at any level of discussion with the various stakeholders. It can be extended when needed as its basis contains all the necessary elements.

The primary purpose of The Blue Chamber is to develop and test a protocol how to produce the durable, tested and conceptual (= IT independent) specifications for the regulation based services, using an engineering approach.

The authors have come to the conclusion that regulation based services represent more than half of all IT based services. They ask attention to the fact that banks and insurance companies and many other industries like pharma and aviation have to deal with many new large regulations, hence it is not only the government services.

© Springer International Publishing AG 2017
I. Ciuciu et al. (Eds.): OTM 2016 Workshops, LNCS 10034, pp. 164–173, 2017.
DOI: 10.1007/978-3-319-55961-2_16

It would be interesting to investigate that regulation based services would be the best representative to develop and test requirements engineering. This is a research topic outside the scope of this paper.

Of course as said before "Legislation is the basis for all public services. Legislation is the union of laws, government decrees, ministerial decrees and several other regulations, including court decisions." [7] The Legislation describes, traditionally speaking which rights and duties are applicable for a specific citizen or company and under which circumstances or conditions. One of the greatest challenges of requirements engineers for regulation based services is to specify in an engineering way which services the law makers intended in the laws and associated decrees. Hence what does a piece of text in a regulation mean in a practical scenario, is the most relevant question for such services. Of course, it helps if the DNA of regulations as building blocks for the associated services is explicitly used.

In the previous 10 months the durable architecture under development has stabilized and tested in various situations as a foundation to be used by many stakeholders.

In Sect. 2 we describe the key characteristics of the durable architecture. We see that we have come to the conclusion that a productive architecture needs to have 4 co-operating actor groups,

1. The actor group writing the laws, decrees and service policies,
2. The actor group that writes the durable and formal specifications for the regulation based services,
3. The actor group that transforms the durable specifications for regulation based services into formal software specifications for regulation based services and
4. The actor group consisting of the service providers and the citizens or companies receiving the service.

The Blue Chamber has decided to accept the laws, decrees and service policies as a given, just like a biologist accepts the living ecosystem.

The Blue Chamber has adopted the way of working in the sciences for the field of regulation based services and undertook to detect the underlying legal DNA, or deep structure, as far as it is relevant for the associated services. This is used in the specification of the services. This DNA makes it further possible to consider specifications for regulation based services as a scalable knowledge base.

The Blue Chamber has decided to focus on the development of a protocol how to produce durable, tested, formal and conceptual specifications, completely independent of a certain IT.

The Blue Chamber will also investigate the field from durable service specifications to software specifications for the regulation based services.

The Blue Chamber will also offer its insights to the people that specify the laws, decrees and service policies, but only after it has been demonstrated beyond any doubt that this approach has produced sufficient practically relevant results.

In Sect. 3 we describe why the Blue Chamber has decided to give priority 1 to the development of a protocol how to produce the durable specifications for regulation based services.

In Sect. 4 we propose that the actor group that writes the laws, decrees and service policies could be better represented as two sub groups. Why? The laws and decrees are made by politicians and they have in their own opinion more important things to do than to worry about formal languages. The service policies are produced by the service providers. It may be expected that there is more inclination to use innovative techniques to formulate the service policies, once the value in practice of the approach of The Blue Chamber has been sufficiently demonstrated. Hence we propose an extension to the previous durable architecture of Sect. 2 for the situation that it is essential to consider the world of the laws and decrees makers from the world of the people determining the additional service rules.

In Sect. 5 we will briefly discuss the legality principle, the understandability principle and the ISO TR9007 [11] principles in relation to the durable architecture.

In Sect. 6 we present conclusions and suggestions for further work.

2 The Durable Architecture with 4 Actor Groups

As has been stated in an earlier paper: "In the spring of 2013 The Blue Chamber published its first report regarding regulation based services in The Netherlands. Reference [7] contains the essence in English of the original Dutch version. It was concluded that the current situation is far from ideal." In the first report of The Blue Chamber we read: "In legislation rights and obligations are defined: among citizens, citizens towards the government and vice versa. Legislation contains concepts, rules and conditions that directly affect the actions of citizens, businesses and government organizations. These concepts, rules and conditions form the basis for the services and processes of public implementing bodies. For the following reasons, it is important to be able to distill concepts, rules and conditions from the legislation in an unambiguous and repeatable manner:

A. It promotes legal certainty for citizens and prevents unnecessary disputes and proceedings in court.
B. It enhances the transparency of government. The government can show that what they are doing is in accordance with the democratically established legislation. This includes providing insight into the rules that give the authorities a margin of discretion to do justice in special cases.
C. It simplifies implementation of legislation in services and processes. Thus, orders from politics and public demands can be accommodated more rapidly.
D. It improves an implementing body's capacity to, as part of ex ante feasibility tests, to provide feedback on proposed changes in legislation. This contributes positively to the effectiveness and efficiency of the implementation.
E. It provides insight into the coherence of the complex of legislation. Consequently, generic and specific elements in processes and services can more easily be distinguished. This offers possibilities for reuse, not only within an organization, but also between organizations.

In short, the added value of a repeatable approach to the organization of the implementation of legislation comes from the ability to transform legislation into legitimate services for citizens and companies that they experience as meaningful and to perform this in a truthful, efficient, multidisciplinary and timely fashion." [7].

The major challenge was identified as the proper specification of the durable and formal conceptual specification for the regulation based services. In the development of this piece of knowledge we could built upon the work of Corbin [3] and Hohfeld [8]. In many government organized services this means that we have to distinguish between the regulations determined by parliament, government and ministers and the service policies determined by the directorate of the government service provider. The Blue Chamber used also elements provided in [1, 9, 12–14].

Hence we see in Fig. 1 the actor group 1, consisting of the parliament, the government and the ministers that write the laws, the government decrees or the ministerial decrees respectively as well as the directorate of the service organization that specifies the service policies. Between the laws and decrees there are delegations possible; the author of the law can delegate to the government a well specified part (to be included in a government decree), with the option to further delegate it to the ministerial level (ministerial decree); in a government decree a delegation can be given to the authors of the associated ministerial decrees.

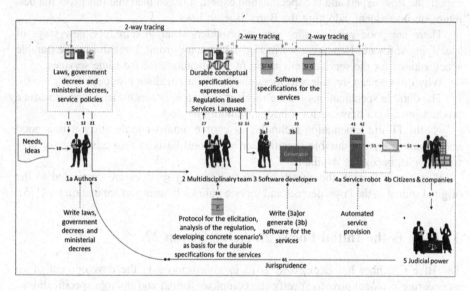

Fig. 1. Durable architecture for regulation based services

For practical purposes a citizen or a company can consider the union of the law, government decree, ministerial decree and the service policy as one regulation. The major difference is in the speed with which a law or decree can be updated to changing circumstances.

We furthermore see that actor group 2, a multidisciplinary team, takes as input the union of the law, government and ministerial decrees and service policies and produces the durable service specifications, fully independent of IT and including a representative set of test cases. Actor group 2 consists of a multidisciplinary team, a service expert, a legal expert and a conceptual specification expert being at the same time an expert in the DNA, or deep structure patterns of regulations.

It became gradually clear in recent years that the critical step in the entire process chain was the lack of durable specifications for the services. In many current implementations of services one goes directly from the laws, decrees and service policies to a specific software implementation language. One of the negative aspects of such an approach is that the service provider is locked into a specific IT.

From procedural complexity to manageable simplicity in declarative mode.

For many decades specifications for regulation based services were produced with a kind of procedural language. For reasonably large service offerings this is difficult to manage and very difficult when changes become a constant stream. There is now a movement underway to minimize the procedural part and use more declarative techniques.

When are durable specifications considered complete?

One of the essential parts of the complete specifications is the representative set of cases, test cases or scenarios. By using as early as possible in the process that produces the durable specifications the test cases, in a language understandable to the service expert, the legal expert and the specification expert, it is assumed that this gives the best return on investment, adopting the Barry Boehm law.

There are good reasons why service providers want to introduce new ways of specifying software. Hence we see in Fig. 1 that actor group 3 transforms the durable specifications for the services into software specifications for the same services.

Why do we need durable specifications as an intermediate product?

The durable specifications for the services is a strongly recommended intermediate product just like a drawing for a bridge, building or road.

As the IT implementation technologies evolve almost continuously it is a good investment to have a durable specification as a solid basis to take advantage of new technologies becoming available.

Please note that all the specifications and running services are connected to the original source in the laws, decrees and service policies by using an annotation tool [15].

3   Why Is the Initial Focus on Actor Group 2?

The Blue Chamber has decided in 2012 to give priority to the development of an engineering protocol how to specify the complete, formal and durable specifications.

Why was this priority 1?

The people that write the laws, government decrees and ministerial decrees have shown little interest to listen to the experts that they hold mainly responsible for the enormous time and budget blows in many of the large government services projects. Hence do not start with the people that have more important things to do than worry about formal languages.

In theory The Blue Chamber could have selected to put priority 1 to the work of actor group 3, the software developers. But the input to this group would not be complete when they would take the laws, government and ministerial decrees and service policies as input. There are seldom test cases included in the regulations. And why do, with the maximum of efficiency, what should not be done at all? Hence invest in high quality and tested requirements.

The first actor group consists of law makers, government and ministers. When they observe desired or presumed or identified needs, they start a new law which is followed by associated decrees, or start to modify an existing law and associated decrees. The government service organizations can also modify or introduce a new operational policy. Judges are a special group of actors. Their decisions can have an effect on the service execution with regard to similar cases (jurisprudence). It is the combination of the work of these actors that determines the effective regulation (Fig. 2).

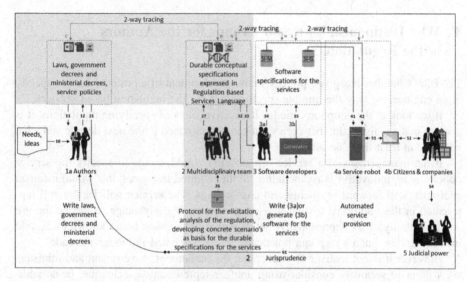

Fig. 2. Durable architecture, focus on multidisciplinary team

Regulations are produced to provide services for the citizens and companies, or have them perform certain duties. These services are information-intensive and often heavily supported by IT. The traditional textual representation of law performs a good job in creating legal security, along with all the legal authorities. However, a textual representation lacks the necessary "hooks" and explicitly depicted relations between these "hooks" to be used as support for the formal specification of services.

What is needed is a complete specification that takes the (new) laws, decrees and service policies as input and produces a well-tested and by the various stakeholders agreed and therefore accepted specification of the interaction between the government service providers and the citizens or enterprises. This is a multidisciplinary effort [2] and in principle independent of IT or in case of human processes, the specific implementation of these human processes such that new IT technologies and other organizational structures can be based on the durable specifications or model.

Actor group 2 also provides the two-way references between the durable model or specifications and the regulations. The group consists of legal experts, service experts and specification experts. A two-way reference is needed for impact analysis [15]. Often this is also referred to as annotation services.

Actor group 3 consists of the software service builders. At the current state of affairs, the majority of services are heavily based on IT services. The builders can use the specifications depicted in the durable model in the same way as a builder of a large office block uses the blue prints of the architect. We have already seen cases in which this building process has been automated, creating IT services directly from specifications.

Actor group 4a provides the automated services and actor group 4b consists of the citizens or companies that receive the services of the government service provider.

4   Why Distinguish Two Sub Groups for the Authors of the Regulations?

The Blue Chamber has given priority to the development of a protocol how to specify in an engineering way the durable specifications for the regulation based services.

If we look at the adoption time for innovative ways of specifying regulations, it is good to make a distinction between what can be innovated in the next decade and what will take at least three decades.

If the management of a service organization would decide to specify the service policies in an innovative way, including all the required test cases, this would mean an enormous step forward in quality and cost savings. The service policies are still represented in the traditional textual way. However the big advantage would be the use and availability of the representative set of scenarios or cases, better known as ex-ante in legal circles. Such a step can practically be implemented in the next decade.

However it is not realistic to expect that the parliament, government and ministers are willing to seriously consider using another representation technique, or an additional representation technique in the next 30 years. Why not?

Some service organizations are currently implementing part of these recommendations.

We believe that it is necessary to first introduce in secondary school a subject "the fundamentals of regulation, regulation specification and service modeling", in a science based way. When this has been going for 20 years one may expect that enough people enter parliament and governments to make a reasonable chance to introduce an additional scalable representation for all laws and decrees.

The two subgroups of actor group 1 are presented in the architecture of Fig. 3.

We furthermore see that actor group 1b takes the union of the laws, government and ministerial decrees as input and adds the service policies where necessary. We want to remark that this addition is not always present.

One of the requirements for which the law makers are not willing to compromise, is that the services provided should be fully based on the regulation and faithfully represents the intended semantics in cases. This is referred to as the legality principle. Only services that are described in the laws, regulations and policies are legally permitted.

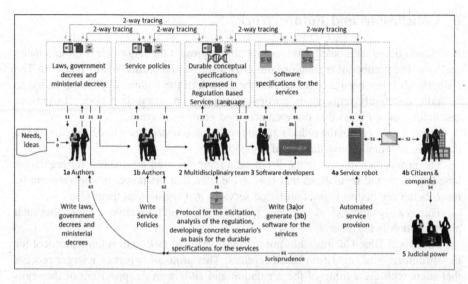

Fig. 3. Durable architecture, actor group 1 decomposed in 2 groups

Hence that means that the durable model must include a two-way link between the services and the (textual) representation of the legislation, and represent the full semantics as intended in the legislation (regulation level) to apply to all the foreseen cases (scenario level).

5 The Legality Principle and the ISO TR9007 Principles

It is expected that the members of parliament and government will have as a non-negotiable requirement that the regulation based services satisfy the legality principle. That means that all services are based on approved laws and decrees and that the services provide all that was intended in the laws and decrees and nothing more, at least not in substance.

Hence that means that the language for durable specifications for regulation based services need to have the representation power as intended for services in the laws and decrees.

There is furthermore the principle of understandability. All the members of the multidisciplinary team producing the durable specification have to be able to read and understand these specifications.

The Blue Chamber furthermore has adopted the ISO TR9007 principles: the Helsinki principle, the Conceptualization principle and the 100% principle.

6 Conclusions and Future Work

Regulation based automated services probably represent the largest class of automated services. The number of regulations has grown substantially after World War 2. In The Netherlands it has been recognized that the growth of the volume of regulations has to be more effectively reduced; in particular it has been stated as a policy to remove conflicting sets of rules that drive citizens and companies crazy.

The question is: can the reduction and the required consistency be obtained with the current representation mechanism of regulations?

The provisional answer is no. We need a representation mechanism for regulation based services and regulations that is scalable such that the power of software can be much better applied to regulation based services and regulations themselves.

This is a gigantic task as not many people in the legal field are convinced that such an innovation is necessary.

The Dutch Blue Chamber has put its priority on the task to develop a protocol for the specification of regulation based *services*. This protocol is part of a larger process that starts with the writing of the regulation and ends with the provision of the regulation based services. There is a substantial feedback loop filled by the courts and jurisprudence.

In this paper we have described the architecture of the Blue Chamber. We use this architecture in the various stakeholder groups.

The Blue Chamber has adopted a major principle of the sciences. It uses the so-called knowledge microscope principle to find out what the elements of the legal DNA, or deep structure for services is. That means that the regulation based service and its associated cases, or scenarios are the primary object of study. Once the legal DNA for services is properly described, it is clear which concepts are needed in a durable model. It is fair to say that facts and rules play a primary role in the regulation based services field.

There is at the time of writing no single ISO, OMG, Open Group or W3C standard modeling language that has the representational power required by the legality principle.

The question may be asked: is it possible to specify a combination of various standards that would satisfy the legality principle? The Blue Chamber is investigating this proposal. It is good to remark that the sciences have gone through similar stages in the last few centuries.

We have described a durable architecture that results in a durable model for services based on legislation. An architecture that can be understood by all stakeholders. The architecture is based on the same principles as the sciences, namely accept the regulations for services as natural phenomena and produce a practical model to work with.

Acknowledgements. The authors gratefully acknowledges the many discussions in the co-creation the Blue Chamber and the Open Afternoons.

References

1. Bouwman, H., van Houtum, H., Janssen, M., Versteeg, G.: Business architectures in the public sector: experiences from practice. Commun. Assoc. Inf. Syst. **29**, 411–426 (2011). Article 23
2. Brattinga, M., Nijssen, S.: A sustainable architecture for durable modeling of laws and regulations and main concepts of the durable model. In: Ciuciu, I., Panetto, H., Debruyne, C., Aubry, A., Bollen, P., Valencia-García, R., Mishra, A., Fensel, A., Ferri, F. (eds.) OTM 2015. LNCS, vol. 9416, pp. 254–265. Springer, Heidelberg (2015). doi:10. 1007/978-3-319-26138-6_29
3. Corbin, A.: Jural relations and their classification. Yale Law Sch. **30**(3), 226–238 (1921)
4. Dulfer, D., Nijssen, S., Lokin, M.: Developing and maintaining durable specifications for law or regulation based services. In: Ciuciu, I., Panetto, H., Debruyne, C., Aubry, A., Bollen, P., Valencia-García, R., Mishra, A., Fensel, A., Ferri, F. (eds.) OTM 2015. LNCS, vol. 9416, pp. 169–177. Springer, Heidelberg (2015). doi:10.1007/978-3-319-26138-6_20
5. Van Engers, T.M., Nijssen, S.: Bridging social reality with rules. Paper Presented at IRIS 2014, Das Internationale Rechtsinformatik Symposion, Salzburg, Austria, 21 February 2014
6. Van Engers, T., Nijssen, S.: Connecting people: semantic-conceptual modeling for laws and regulations. In: Janssen, M., Scholl, H.J., Wimmer, M.A., Bannister, F. (eds.) EGOV 2014. LNCS, vol. 8653, pp. 133–146. Springer, Heidelberg (2014). doi:10.1007/978-3-662-44426-9_11
7. Van Engers, T.M., van, Nijssen, S.: From legislation towards service development – an approach to agile implementation of legislation. Paper Presented at EGOVIS 2014 in München, 1–5 September and Included in the Proceedings (2014)
8. Hohfeld, W.N.: Fundamental Legal Conceptions as Applied in Judicial Reasoning (2010). Ed. by Cook, W.W. ISBN-13: 978-1-58477-162-3
9. Lemmens, I., Pleijsant, J.M., Arntz, R.: Using fact-based modelling to develop a common language. In: Ciuciu, I., Panetto, H., Debruyne, C., Aubry, A., Bollen, P., Valencia-García, R., Mishra, A., Fensel, A., Ferri, F. (eds.) OTM 2015. LNCS, vol. 9416, pp. 197–205. Springer, Heidelberg (2015). doi:10.1007/978-3-319-26138-6_23
10. Lokin, M., Nijssen, S., Lemmens, I.: CogniLex: a legal domain specific fact based modeling protocol. In: Ciuciu, I., Panetto, H., Debruyne, C., Aubry, A., Bollen, P., Valencia-García, R., Mishra, A., Fensel, A., Ferri, F. (eds.) OTM 2015. LNCS, vol. 9416, pp. 235–244. Springer, Heidelberg (2015). doi:10.1007/978-3-319-26138-6_27
11. ISO TR9007: Concepts and Terminology for the Conceptual Schema and the Information Base, ISO Technical report (1987)
12. Nijssen, G.M.: A Framework for Discussion in ISO/TC97/SC5/WG3, 78.09/01 (1978)
13. Nijssen, S., Valera, S.: An Architecture Ecosystem for the Whole Systems Perspective, Including System Dynamics, Based on Logic & Set Theory and Controlled Natural Languages, Working paper for the OMG Architecture Ecosystem SIG (2012)
14. Rozendaal, J.: Industrial experience with fact based modeling at a large bank. In: Meersman, R., Tari, Z., Herrero, P. (eds.) OTM 2007. LNCS, vol. 4805, pp. 678–687. Springer, Heidelberg (2007). doi:10.1007/978-3-540-76888-3_90
15. Straatsma, P., Dulfer, D.: Wendbare Wetsuitvoering. In: DREAM 2014, The Netherlands (2014)

A Proposal for a Regulations Based Services Language

Jos Rozendaal[1] and Sjir Nijssen[2(✉)]

[1] Independent Consultant, Driehuis, The Netherlands
jos.rozendaal@gmail.com
[2] PNA, Heerlen, The Netherlands
sjir.nijssen@pna-group.com

Abstract. This paper describes the current state of the development of a formal Regulations Based Services Language that is understandable to various stakeholders, including legal experts, service experts and specification experts. This research and development work is the result of a co-creation that in 2012 has been established in The Netherlands involving government service providers, academia and innovative businesses to develop a durable architecture for services that are based on regulations. The authors have been involved in try outs of parts of the Regulations Based Services Language. The Regulations Based Services Language is primarily intended to be used as the language to express the durable specifications for the regulation based services. One of the requirements of the Regulations Based Services Language is use a declarative approach wherever possible. This Regulations Based Services Language is meant as a formal Controlled Natural Language (CNL).

Keywords: Regulations Based Services Language · Formal Controlled Natural Language · Structured Dutch for regulation based services · Fact based modeling (FBM)

1 Introduction

In 2012 the co-creation The Blue Chamber was established by two large government services, the Dutch Customs and Tax Administration and the Immigration and Naturalization Service, the University of Amsterdam and PNA. The initial focus was on the development of a durable architecture. The results until summer 2015 have been reported in [1, 2, 4, 9]. One major goal of the durable architecture is to provide enough precision such that the architecture can serve at any level of discussion with the various stakeholders. It can be extended when needed as its basis contains all the necessary elements.

The primary purpose of The Blue Chamber is to develop and test a protocol how to produce the durable, tested and conceptual (hence independent of IT) specifications for the regulation based services, using an engineering approach.

This specification needs to satisfy the legality principle (the services must provide what the politicians intended in the laws and decrees), hence the Regulations Based Services Language must be a powerful language.

© Springer International Publishing AG 2017
I. Ciuciu et al. (Eds.): OTM 2016 Workshops, LNCS 10034, pp. 174–182, 2017.
DOI: 10.1007/978-3-319-55961-2_17

The language must be understandable to all stakeholders such that everybody can read the formal specifications for the regulation based services. Please note that not everybody has to be able to formulate the specifications in the Regulations Based Services Language.

The Regulations Based Services Language is widely applicable. Regulation based services represent more than half of all IT based services. Banks and insurance companies and many other industries like pharma and aviation have to deal with many large external regulations, hence it is not only the government services.

In Sect. 2 we describe shortly the architecture such that we have the precise position of the Regulations Based Services Language in the broader context.

In Sect. 3 we describe the key requirements for the Regulations Based Services Language.

In Sect. 4 we present the various sublanguages and discuss how they relate to each other. After long deliberations and try-outs it was decided to have the durable specifications produced in a multidisciplinary team, consisting of a legal expert, a service expert and a specification expert.

In Sect. 5 we present conclusions and suggestions for further work.

2   The Durable Architecture of Regulation Based Services

The Blue Chamber has spent quite some time to arrive at a durable architecture as presented in Fig. 1. Although the architecture looks like a graphic, it is essentially a diagrammatic representation of a small number of facts.

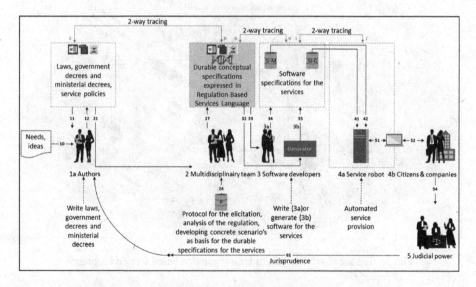

Fig. 1. Durable architecture with focus on the durable specifications

The actor group Multidisciplinary team consults via flow 21 the laws, government decrees, ministerial decrees and service policies and produces via flow 27 the durable, formal and tested conceptual specifications for the services using the protocol for the elicitation, analysis of the regulation via flow 26, developing a representative set of concrete scenario's as basis for the durable specifications for the services.

The actor group Software developers consults via flow 33 the durable conceptual specifications for the services and produces via flow 34 the formal software specifications for the services.

The actor group Authors produces the laws, government decrees, ministerial decrees and service policies via flow 12.

Please note that the actor group Authors has no formal document to consult, nor a protocol. The actor group Software developers has no known protocol. The multidisciplinary group has a legally formal but in the logical language sense informal input and uses a protocol, how to develop the durable and formal conceptual specifications for the regulation based services.

3   Key Requirements for the Regulations Based Services Language

In the previous section we have described the position of the durable specifications in the durable architecture. The durable specifications are expressed in the Regulations Based Services Language, a formal Controlled Natural Language (CNL).

In Fig. 2 we see that the Regulations Based Services Language contains a set of related sublanguages [7]. We will now briefly describe each of the sublanguages.

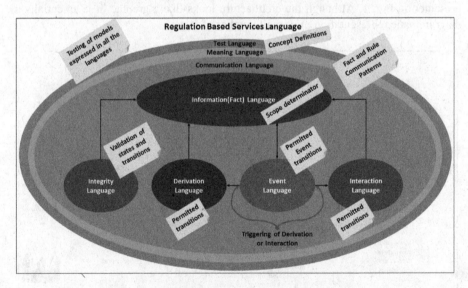

Fig. 2.   The set of sub Languages for a regulation based service language

Test Language
Probably new is the fact that the Test Language includes all the other sublanguages. Why is this the case? We propose a Test Language that can be used to test expressions

in every sublanguage. This is needed to be able to use the ex-ante to the fullest extent possible.

Meaning Language

A Meaning Language is used to express structured concept definitions [3].

The function of the structured concept definitions is to describe every term that may be used in a communication language, information (fact) language or in integrity, derivation, interaction or event language needed in a specification of a service.

A structured concept definition may use other terms that have a concept definition, but circular definitions are to be avoided, except with recursion and in a so-called all-at-once basket of concept definitions. Thus, the set of structured concept definitions has a well-defined order, in which all structured concept definitions only use words that have been defined previously and words supposed to be already known to the reader. The latter is community or context sensitive. It is a major practical challenge to describe how different but partly overlapping concepts in various communities that have to cooperate, relate to each other.

The first structured concept definitions in Meaning Language in the list are those that use only terms that in the given community in a certain context can be assumed to be already known. This Meaning Language gives an answer to the following question: What is a/an/the <Concept> or what are we talking about in a certain community in a certain context? In short: What is it?

Communication Language

Communication Language facilitates among other things the communication about the contents of the fact population needed in the service, but also about the rules expressed in the integrity, derivation, interaction and event languages. This Communication Language gives an answer to the following question: how do we communicate about facts, integrity rules, derivation rules, interaction rules and event rules?

Information (Fact) Language

The function of the Information Language is to act like a conceptual data structure and to make it possible to exchange or record data or declarative facts. An example of a fact type is: Of a country the capital is recorded. A second example: Of a country is recorded which languages are spoken. The recorded or communicated data can be perceived as the variable parts of otherwise equal facts. This perception is expressed in patterns called Fact Communication Patterns and Rule Communication Patterns as part of the Communication Language. This language gives an answer to the following question: Which facts are within scope of a certain system?

Integrity Language

The function of the Integrity Language is to restrict the communication of facts to only those that are considered useful. E.g.: A country has exactly one capital and a city is capital of at most one country. Examples of structural units from this sub language are the sub set, the disjunction and the unique member rule. This language gives an answer to the following question: Which restrictions apply to guarantee the integrity of the populations and transitions of the facts needed for the service?

Derivation Language
The function of a Derivation Language is to derive new facts from facts existing in the layer of facts. E.g., if we know for persons in which country they were born, a derivation rule can produce facts which state how many persons were born in a country. This language gives an answer to the following question: How are certain facts established in the service using existing facts?

Interaction Languages
The function of an Interaction Language is to make known facts about the outside world into the system or remove facts from the fact base. This language gives an answer to the following question: How is the contents of the fact population in the service altered?

Event Language
The function of an Event Language is to notify when a certain derivation rule or inter-action rule used in a service needs to get started. This language gives an answer to the following question: When are the facts established or altered?

The legality principle and the ISO TR9007 principles [5, 6].

It is expected that the members of parliament and government will have as a non-negotiable requirement that the regulation based services satisfy the legality principle. That means that all services are based on approved laws and decrees and that the services provide all that was intended in the laws and decrees and nothing more, at least not in substance. Screen colors are usually outside the scope!

Hence that means that the language for durable specifications for regulation based services need to have the representation power as intended in the laws and decrees.

There is furthermore the principle of understandability. All the members of the multidisciplinary team producing the durable specification have to be able to read and understand these specifications.

The Blue Chamber furthermore has adopted the ISO TR9007 principles: the Helsinki principle, the Conceptualization principle and the 100% principle.

4   The Sublanguages Related

The sub languages are briefly described in Sect. 3. In this section we focus on the relations or connections between the different sublanguages. Of course it is important to use the relevant context, for instance the Act flexible work in the Netherlands.

The metaphor of an integrated printed circuit board (Fig. 3) is used to further explain these connections.

The connection points (the round orange circles with a number and/or code) 1a–1f represent that the meaning of the concepts used in the different sublanguages must be defined in the Meaning language, unless assumed to be known. The switch on connection point 1a says that there is a concept used in a concept definition that is assumed to be sufficiently unknown and has to be clarified in the Meaning Language.

If we look at the Communication Language we see that it includes all sublanguages except Test and Meaning language, for all the other sublanguages it would be necessary to express them in the Communication Language. Why? Because we want Structured

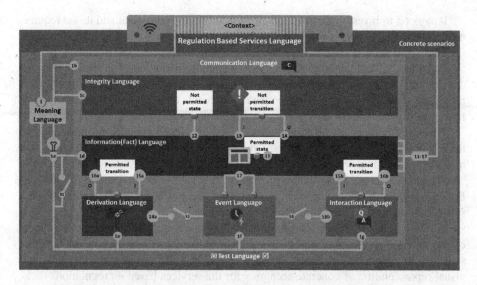

Fig. 3. Printed circuit board to illustrate the sub languages and their connection

Dutch as a formal and understandable specification language for regulation based services (or the corresponding meaning in English) as input for the Software developers, human or generation mechanism.

Connection point 11–17, let it be beyond any doubt, the printed circuit board is fed with concrete examples also referred to as scenarios or cases, which will be systematically used and extended during the multidisciplinary analysis. They are expressed in the Test Language and submitted to a kind of prototype executor.

Connection point 11 are the permitted states or situations in a concrete scenario we need to analyze in the multidisciplinary team.

Connection point 12 contains the not permitted states or situations in a concrete scenario to determine the integrity rules to be expressed in the Integrity Language to guarantee the integrity of the fact populations.

Connection point 13 with the arrow to connection point 14 tells us that we would analyze the not permitted transitions to guarantee the integrity of the transitions of the fact populations needed for the service.

Connection point 15a with the arrow to connection point 16a represents the permitted transitions for the Derivation Language, for the Interaction Language you see the connection points 15b and 16b with the arrow. 15 represents the input and 16 represents the output of one of the types of processes clarified in the Derivation Language respectively the Interaction language.

We use at last, to complete the durable specifications the permitted event transitions expressed in connection point 17, the trigger and 18a, the Derivation rule to be started or 18b the interaction rule to be started.

This protocol is based on the CogNIAM protocol for fact based modelling (FBM).

How will the Regulations Based Services Language help in the clarification?

It pays off to invest more time and effort in supplying consistent and tested requirements and specifications to developers resulting in a decrease in misunderstandings, irritations and delays, and costly corrections later in the process [8].

By using the Regulations Based Services Language in combination with an iterative development approach in a multidisciplinary team, it is possible to achieve fairly short timelines, without having to compromise requirements quality (so no postponement of functionalities to next releases in order to realize timelines).

The visual variant of the Regulations Based Services Language is rather easy to understand for different stakeholders, who are glad they are equipped to explain in a much better way that what they want IT to develop.

We have observed in a number of projects that the application of the Regulations Based Services Language results in a substantial decrease in misunderstandings and a substantial increase in communication productivity.

In Fig. 4 we present the multidisciplinary team consisting of a service expert, a legal expert and a specification expert. They have learned to communicate in concrete scenarios in a Regulations Based Services Language. This is a combined textual and visual representation of concrete scenarios for the services based on regulations (acts, decrees, and so on). The specification expert is the author of the concrete scenarios in that language. The specification expert presents these scenarios to the other experts who will discuss the concrete scenarios to decide whether the scenario is right or that something must be changed. When there is a decision about the concrete scenario by the combination of the service expert and the legal expert, the specifications expert can start representing it in the Regulations Based Services Language. We must say that there will be a 2-way tracing between the concrete scenarios and the durable conceptual specifications for the services expressed in the Regulations Based Services Language. Please note that this 2-way tracing is between concrete scenarios and the domain specific model expressed in the Regulations Based Services Language. See for the other 2-way traces Fig. 1, the durable architecture.

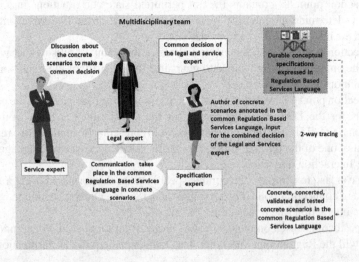

Fig. 4. The multidisciplinary team in action

5   Conclusions and Future Work

Regulation based automated services probably represent the largest class of services. The number of regulations has grown substantially after World War 2. In The Netherlands it has been recognized that the growth of the volume of regulations has to be more effectively reduced; in particular it has been stated as a policy to remove conflicting sets of rules that drive citizens and companies crazy.

The question is: can the reduction and the required consistency be obtained with the current representation mechanism of regulations?

The provisional answer is no. We need a representation mechanism for regulation based services and regulations that is scalable such that the power of software can be much better applied to regulation based services and regulations themselves.

This is a gigantic task as not many people in the legal field are convinced that such an innovation is necessary.

The Dutch Blue Chamber has put its priority on the task to develop a protocol for the specification of regulation based services. This protocol is part of a larger process that starts with the writing of the regulation and ends with the provision of the regulation based services. There is a substantial feedback loop filled by the courts and jurisprudence.

In this paper we have described the Regulations Based Services Language, a visual and textual specification language. We expect that this Regulations Based Services Language will help the implementing bodies can offer their services to citizens and companies more quickly than is currently the case, but particularly less expensive. Currently we are working on software to support this Regulations Based Services Language.

We use this architecture in the various stakeholder groups.

The Blue Chamber has adopted a major principle of the sciences. It uses the so-called knowledge microscope principle to find out what the elements of the legal DNA for services is. That means that the regulation based service and its associated cases, or scenarios are the primary object of study. Once the legal DNA for services is properly described, it is clear which concepts are needed in a durable model. It is fair to say that facts and rules play a primary role in the regulation based services field.

There is at the time of writing no single ISO, OMG, Open Group or W3C standard modeling language that has the representational power required by the legality principle. OWL fails the legality principle, the understandability principle and the two ISO 9007 principles, called Conceptual and 100%. For the combination of UML and OCL the same holds.

The question may be asked: is it possible to specify a combination of various standards enhanced with some glue that would satisfy the legality principle? The Blue Chamber is investigating this proposal.

Acknowledgements. The authors gratefully acknowledges the many discussions in the co-creation the Blue Chamber and the Open Afternoons.

We thank the reviewers for excellent suggestions. One reviewer makes the following statement: "While the paper addresses an interesting issue and shows us that a set of inter-related languages would be needed to serve as a formal specification for legal regulations, it lacks exactly the concrete scenarios and examples the authors argue need to be included to fully grasp the meaning."

We thank this reviewer as it is the trigger for two points.

The primary aim of the authors is to develop a language to express the specifications for regulation based *services*. That is a formal language and the resulting specifications need to satisfy the legality principle, also be legally formal. However the language under investigation here in NOT meant to replace the textual language in which currently a regulation is expressed and those expressions (laws, decrees, treaties) are currently not fully formal in the sense of logic. We believe that one first need to accept the regulations as they are now and with that as input (using human intelligence) and a formal language and fully independent of IT, specify the requirements for the regulation based services, of course satisfying all the regulations. And maybe thereafter, and that could be decades in the future is the expectation of the authors, would it be possible to start the introduction in practice to gradually introduce formal languages in the regulation specification processes.

The authors agree with one of the reviewers that "the concrete scenarios and examples need to be included [in the durable specifications for the regulation based services (added by the authors)] to fully grasp the meaning"; however the size of the concrete scenarios and the examples is many pages and a paper for the FBM workshop is limited to 10 pages. The authors intend to publish these scenarios and examples.

References

1. Brattinga, M., Nijssen, S.: A sustainable architecture for durable modeling of laws and regulations and main concepts of the durable model. In: Ciuciu, I., et al. (eds.) OTM 2015. LNCS, vol. 9416, pp. 254–265. Springer, Heidelberg (2015). doi:10.1007/978-3-319-26138-6_29
2. Dulfer, D., Nijssen, S., Lokin, M.: Developing and maintaining durable specifications for law or regulation based services. In: Ciuciu, I., et al. (eds.) OTM 2015. LNCS, vol. 9416, pp. 169–177. Springer, Heidelberg (2015). doi:10.1007/978-3-319-26138-6_20
3. Lemmens, I., Pleijsant, J.M., Arntz, R.: Using fact-based modelling to develop a common language. In: Ciuciu, I., et al. (eds.) OTM 2015. LNCS, vol. 9416, pp. 197–205. Springer, Heidelberg (2015). doi:10.1007/978-3-319-26138-6_23
4. Lokin, M., Nijssen, S., Lemmens, I.: CogniLex. In: Ciuciu, I., et al. (eds.) OTM 2015. LNCS, vol. 9416, pp. 235–244. Springer, Heidelberg (2015). doi:10.1007/978-3-319-26138-6_27
5. ISO TR9007: Concepts and terminology for the conceptual schema and the information base. ISO Technical report (1987)
6. Nijssen, G.M.: A framework for discussion. In: ISO/TC97/SC5/WG3, 78.09/01 (1978)
7. Nijssen, S., Valera, S.: An architecture ecosystem for the whole systems perspective, including system dynamics, based on logic and set theory and controlled natural languages. In: Working Paper for the OMG Architecture Ecosystem SIG (2012)
8. Rozendaal, J.: Industrial experience with fact based modeling at a large bank. In: Meersman, R., Tari, Z., Herrero, P. (eds.) OTM 2007. LNCS, vol. 4805, pp. 678–687. Springer, Heidelberg (2007). doi:10.1007/978-3-540-76888-3_90
9. Straatsma, P., Diederik, D.: Wendbare Wetsuitvoering. In: DREAM 2014, The Netherlands (2014)

Industry Case Studies Program
(ICSP) 2016

ICSP 2016 PC Chair Message

Cloud computing, service-oriented architecture, business process modelling, enterprise architecture, enterprise integration, semantic interoperability—what is an enterprise systems administrator to do with the constant stream of industry hype surrounding him, constantly bathing him with (apparently) new ideas and new "technologies"? It is nearly impossible, and the academic literature does not help solving the problem, with hyped "technologies" catching on in the academic world just as easily as the industrial world. The most unfortunate thing is that these technologies are actually useful, and the press hype only hides that value. What the enterprise information manager really cares about is integrated, interoperable infrastructures, industrial IoT, that support interoperable information systems, so he can deliver valuable information to management in time to make correct decisions about the use and delivery of enterprise resources, whether those are raw materials for manufacturing, people to carry out key business processes, or the management of shipping choices for correct delivery to customers.

The OTM conference series have established itself as a major international forum for exchanging ideas and results on scientific research for practitioners in fields such as computer supported cooperative work, middleware, Internet/Web data management, electronic commerce, workflow management, knowledge flow, agent technologies and software architectures, Cyber Physical Systems and IoT, to name a few. The recent popularity and interest in service-oriented architectures & domains require capabilities for on-demand composition of services. These emerging technologies represent a significant need for highly interoperable systems.

As a part of OnTheMove 2016, the Industry Case Studies Program on "Industry Applications and Standard initiatives for Cooperative Information Systems - The future for the Cyber Physical Systems", supported by OMG, IIC (Industrial Internet Consortium), IFAC TC 5.3 "Enterprise Integration and Networking", the SIG INTEROP Grande-Région, and the Greek Interoperability Centre on "Interoperability" emphasized Research/Industry cooperation on these future trends. The focus of the program is on a discussion of ideas where research areas address interoperable information systems and infrastructure. Four short papers have been presented, focusing on industry leaders, standardization initiatives, European and international projects consortiums and discussing how projects within their organizations addressed software, systems and architecture interoperability. Each paper has been reviewed by an international Programme Committee composed of representatives of Academia, Industry and Standardisation initiatives. We thank them for their dedication and interest.

We hope that you find this industry-focused part of the program valuable as feedback from industry practitioners, and we thank the authors for the time and effort taken to contribute to the program.

October 2016   Hervé Panetto

Big Data Concept to Address Performance Aware Infrastructure Monitoring Challenge for Hybrid Cloud

Prabal Mahanta[✉] and Himanshu Pandey

SAP Labs India Pvt Ltd, Bangalore 560076, Karnataka, India
{p.mahanta, h.pandey}@sap.com

Abstract. There has been increasing complexity of cloud infrastructure to sustain the growth of enterprise applications and so as the need to constantly monitor loads and resource utilization. Numerous sophisticated techniques are applied to achieve a unified observation but disparate environments, sources and policies restrain the objective to be achieved using a standard methodology. The paper tries to present a model for standardizing the monitoring platform for applications which are highly environment aware and are restraint by governance using a novel algorithmic approach. The models tries to instrument APIs to monitor single to multitude of parameters to cover the transactions across geography. The model also covers a timeline for evolving big data analytic methods for application performance monitoring systems for environment based applications covering the high data rates and computation requirements. The concept of Data Lake brings a unique dimension to the model and resource utilization and performance metrics for varied workloads and also configuration complexities.

Keywords: Monitoring · Hybrid-Cloud · Big-data

1 Introduction and Challenges

One of the aspect of monitoring is to process and present the data for the user in a centralized way to provide the bigger picture. The problem identified here is the speed of processing the data. This problem can be extended to the design of the tools. Currently there are set of tools which are able to index large amount of data but a single tool cannot suffice operations to get a clear view of the health of applications as well as datacenters [1].

Any cloud provide would want to analyze their logs to see the current scenario of their data centers for taking preventive measures, another aspect is to predict any loss of operation due to certain data center elements. In this case the major challenge is the size of the data so indexing, aggregating and operating on data size of petabytes would require a redesign of the concept.

Often in operations, the clarity of data to be analyzed may be seasonal or historical but both variations would require different priorities as per speed/accuracy or patterns.

© Springer International Publishing AG 2017
I. Ciuciu et al. (Eds.): OTM 2016 Workshops, LNCS 10034, pp. 185–189, 2017.
DOI: 10.1007/978-3-319-55961-2_18

The issue of logs would also extend to the hierarchy level that operations would require for their activity which cannot be limited to finding service errors [2].

Various tools like Elasticsearch, Logstash and Kibana serve this purpose. While Elasticsearch [3] is predominantly for indexing, Logstash [4] addresses the parsing and storage aspect, Kibana [5] serving the purpose of interface.

All the logs by services require services to be designed to be consistent which relates to the CAP theorem which states that we can either have partition tolerance or high availability [6]. So this requires the data consistency to be managed.

Another issue is when we are trying to address the predictive ability or if we want to calculate the mean time to failure, we don't have a generalized model of the data so we can end up aggregating in temporary tables to reach the final goal.

The challenge is greater when we try to address different environments of products which requires data to be viewed differently. Currently with all the machine learning and the knowledge base we will be able to address the goal of finding MTTF but to view the data is a challenging concept. This paper tries to come up with a data model concept address this and how we can relate hierarchies of levels in log using a structure model.

2 Concept

Here we try to address first the issue of data model where come up with an algorithm to address the case: The data can be from multiple sources and the common challenges involve the scalability of data model and the algorithms that provides the score of elements. To address the data model issue we also designed an architecture to utilize in memory computing power for real time processing of aggregated data [7] (Fig. 1).

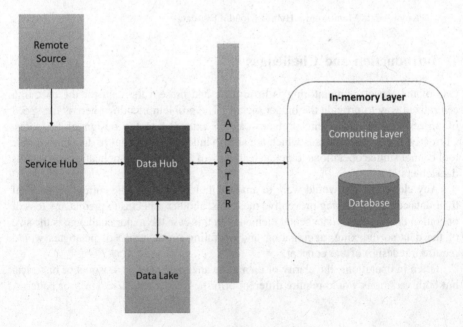

Fig. 1. Architecture

The algorithm proposed is split into two parts where one deals with the depth of the data and the other one deals with the tables/fields count and then we have the mapping between the two sets which helps us in formulating a value table for the equation and this we feed into the central engine which then produces the schema and the data related to the schema tables.

Part 'a' of the algorithm:

Define Parameters = p
Define Level = l
Define Depth = d
Define Sub-Parameters = s
Define entry = e

The restrictions can be defined as:

$p \rightarrow l \rightarrow d \rightarrow s = e$
$p \rightarrow l = e$
$p \rightarrow l \rightarrow l2 \rightarrow d \rightarrow s = e$

Part 'b' of the algorithm:

Define Tables = T
Define Fields = F
Define DataTypes = Y

$T \rightarrow T$ = Relationship
$T \rightarrow F$ = Data type
$F \rightarrow Y$ = Data

The possible relationships can be:

a. $T \rightarrow F \rightarrow Y$
b. $T \rightarrow Y$
c. $T \rightarrow F \rightarrow T \rightarrow F \rightarrow Y$
d. $T \rightarrow T1 \rightarrow T2 \rightarrow F2 \rightarrow Y2$

Overall the complete relationship between the part 'a' and part 'b' of the algorithm:

a. $p = T$
b. $p != Y$
c. $s = F|Y$
d. $e = Y$

Let us say we have the following example:

$p = 5$
$l = 4$
$d0 = 1, d1 = 2, d2 = 1, d3 = 1$
$s0 = 6, s1 = 10, s2 = 20, s3 = 12, s4 = 10$
$s = e$ so, $e0 = 6, e1 = 10, e2 = 12, e3 = 10, e4 = 10$

Now every table in each level can be extended for millions of records.

Here if we visualize it through the example in Fig. 2, we have the fact table at level 1 and all other levels represent the dimension table. The data de duplication in form of hierarchy will help us in sql mutation so we need to generate data in a manner where we also model NULLs for text attributes using enumerate a few more values in the enumerated type with designating them.

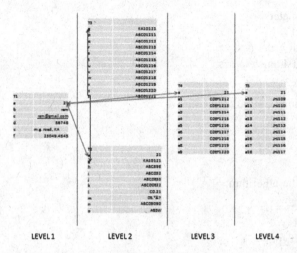

Fig. 2. Example

Now if we now try to query on top of the data then the complex sql queries that will be used will require formal verification and for that we need to base it on comparison with an implementation of a specification. We try to implement the problem of formal verification in the sql domain so as to verify query correctness based on query mutation technique which will also take care of the join mutations, comparison operator mutations and aggregation mutations. This will address the data modeling issue for the log data for disparate sources [8, 9].

3 Conclusion

The Data model can facilitate to understand the infrastructure better and it is also critical to view the data according to certain parameters:

a. Usage evolution for each product per environment per landscape
b. Outage Information trails
c. Point of interest for predicting failure paths

The important aspect of this research is to find out timeline based events and draw out a visual story board for the same. The story board would present layout based on visual variables for spaces of interest in the User Interface for more usability [10, 11].

This will help deduce the characteristics for abnormality help in creating certain maintenance windows and improvements both for infrastructure and products. Currently we are working on realizing the visual techniques to address the parameters so as to get the complete outlook of the overall health of the infrastructure as well as the product.

References

1. Page, A., et al.: Cloud-based secure health monitoring: optimizing fully-homomorphic encryption for streaming algorithms. In: 2014 IEEE Globecom Workshops (GC Wkshps). IEEE (2014)
2. Jia, Z., et al.: Characterizing data analysis workloads in data centers. In: 2013 IEEE International Symposium on Workload Characterization (IISWC). IEEE (2013)
3. Kononenko, O., et al.: Mining modern repositories with Elasticsearch. In: Proceedings of 11th Working Conference on Mining Software Repositories. ACM (2014)
4. Turnbull, J.: The Logstash Book. James Turnbull (2013)
5. Gupta, Y.: Kibana Essentials. Packt Publishing Ltd, Birmingham (2015)
6. Casalicchio, E., Colajanni, M.: A client-aware dispatching algorithm for web clusters providing multiple services. In: Proceedings of 10th International Conference on World Wide Web. ACM (2001)
7. Reelsen, A.: Using Elasticsearch, Logstash and Kibana to create realtime dashboards (2014). Dostupné z: https://secure.trifork.com/dl/goto-berlin-2014/GOTO_Night/logstash-kibana-intro.pdf
8. Dasgupta, S.S., Mahanta, P., Pradeep, S., Subramanian, G.: Reporting optimizations with bill of materials hierarchy traversal in in-memory database domain using set oriented technique. In: Meersman, R., et al. (eds.) OTM 2014. LNCS, vol. 8842, pp. 91–95. Springer, Heidelberg (2014). doi:10.1007/978-3-662-45550-0_13
9. Mahanta, P., Jain, S.: Determination of manufacturing unit root-cause analysis based on conditional monitoring parameters using in-memory paradigm and data-hub rule based optimization platform. In: Ciuciu, I., et al. (eds.) OTM 2015. LNCS, vol. 9416, pp. 41–48. Springer, Heidelberg (2015). doi:10.1007/978-3-319-26138-6_6
10. Burzacca, P., Paternò, F.: Analysis and visualization of interactions with mobile web applications. In: Kotzé, P., Marsden, G., Lindgaard, G., Wesson, J., Winckler, M. (eds.) INTERACT 2013. LNCS, vol. 8120, pp. 515–522. Springer, Heidelberg (2013). doi:10.1007/978-3-642-40498-6_40
11. Tang, D., Stolte, C., Bosch, R.: Design choices when architecting visualizations. Inf. Vis. **3** (2), 65–79 (2004)

Enterprise Interoperability as Framework for Project Knowledge Management

Georg Weichhart[1,2]([✉]), Biljana Roljic[3], Andreas Beham[5,6],
Matthias Frühwirth[4], Robert Steringer[1], Ulrich Neissl[1], Vincent Grote[4],
Johannes Karder[5], and Helmut Zörrer[1]

[1] Profactor GmbH, Steyr, Austria
{georg.weichhart,robert.steringer,ulrich.neissl,
helmut.zoerrer}@profactor.at
[2] Department of Business Informatics/Communications Engineering,
Johannes Kepler University, Linz, Austria
[3] Faculty of Business, Economics and Statistics,
Department of Production and Operations Management with International Focus,
University of Vienna, Vienna, Austria
biljana.roljic@univie.ac.at
[4] Human Research Institut, Weiz, Austria
{matthias.fruehwirth,vincent.grote}@humanresearch.at
[5] Heuristic and Evolutionary Algorithms Laboratory,
University of Applied Sciences Upper Austria, Hagenberg, Austria
{andreas.beham,johannes.karder}@fh-hagenberg.at
[6] Institute for Formal Models and Verification,
Johannes Kepler University, Linz, Austria

Abstract. In this paper we are identifying enterprise interoperability as a possible framework for knowledge management in projects. In particular we are reflecting on research projects, involving small groups of companies and research institutions with heterogeneous backgrounds. The nature of research raises several issues due to the heterogeneous expertise of the project teams. This is in particular true when multiple (semi-formal) models are developed in parallel. In addition to the work evolving over time at the partner's locations, the organisational contexts moved over time, often invisible to the rest of the teams. Interoperability barriers emerge between organisations and models. Enterprise Interoperability can be used to prepare the project teams, supporting the required work on interfaces between models.

Keywords: Enterprise interoperability · Project management · Knowledge management

1 Introduction

The projects NPS2 (Methods and approaches for sustainable decision support in operative production planning) and HOPL (K-project for Heuristic Optimization in Production and Logistics) have been funded to research approaches for

I. Ciuciu et al. (Eds.): OTM 2016 Workshops, LNCS 10034, pp. 190–199, 2017.
DOI: 10.1007/978-3-319-55961-2_19

optimisation of production and logistics schedules following not only straight forward economic performance criteria. In NPS2 also social and human related performance criteria are taken into account in HOPL multiple production and logistics aspects are connected to form an optimisation network. Within the frames of these projects, multiple models stemming from different domains have been developed.

Generally, in projects, domain knowledge of project partners is heterogeneous due to interdisciplinary tasks, efficiency requirements and resource constraints. In research projects, in addition to this, novelty requirements imply that there are no past projects with similar content of work. Project managers face particularly unique situations. Some additional layer of complexity is added by the fact that attainment of the research goals in the required quality is often uncertain.

Despite several tools and knowledge management instruments in place, interoperability on technical/implementation and conceptual/domain level cannot always be reached in the desired quality. The project and the involved agents form an adaptive system, where interoperability is lost over time, and constant effort is needed to re-gain and maintain interoperability [2].

On the overall project level and on the interfaces between participants of different domains abstraction is needed. Despite communication taking place on this abstract layer, interoperability between the theories and models of the different domains needs to be maintained. We analyse model-driven projects from an interoperability point of view and identify aspects where recent developments from enterprise interoperability may support future projects in overcoming problems.

This is an early research, where focus is on identifying potential areas where interoperability frameworks and tools support projects.

The paper is organized as follows. First, we provide our view on the research domain of enterprise interoperability. Second, we provide an overview of the projects in general. The individual, developed models, their interfaces and the issues during integration are analysed using enterprise interoperability as an analysis framework. Finally, we draw the conclusions of using enterprise interoperability as a tool for supporting knowledge management in model driven projects.

2   Enterprise Interoperability for Evolutionary Systems

The nature of research projects implicitly incorporates learning. We focus in the discussion below on approaches and methods that take the evolution of systems into account.

The research domain of Enterprise interoperability is a young discipline with its science base being currently established [8,17]. Interoperability is seen as a systemic approach, which discusses two or more distinct systems that exchange flows and aim at forming a larger system [10,13]. Interoperability is less an overall state, but more a continuous effort requiring adaptation [8]. Enterprise Interoperability understands the overall system not only as a technical system but as a socio-technical system. Organisational interoperability issues are as relevant as issues stemming from information and communication technologies (ICT) [12]. Enterprise interoperability is interested in the information system (IS) which is considered to be a networked system of systems, where humans, software and hardware sensors are connected and consume, generate, and transfer information [15]. Recently more emphasis is placed on the dynamic perspective with complex adaptive systems (CAS) as an underlying theory and the overall goal of sustainable interoperability [2,11].

The complex adaptive system (CAS) theory builds on the notion of autonomous agents, capable of decentralized decision making and collaboration. The Liquid Sensing Enterprise (LSE) [3] and the S^3 Enterprise: Sensing, Smart and Sustainable [15] are examples that build on this theory. The autonomous agents are conceptualised on the technical as well as on the organisational level. Both approaches assume networks of sensors as a basis for smart decision making supported by intelligent agents and informed humans.

The MISE 2 method [4,5] supports any emerging collaborative situation with methods and tools by providing a Mediation Information System (MIS). It supports the evolution of the overall collaboration, the collaborative network and the disruption of the execution of services. It supports the agile adaptation to changes. Its overall design approach uses abstraction layers based on model-driven engineering. The business level consists of a collaborative situation model and a collaborative behaviour model. The technical layer consists of a collaborative workflow model and the deployment and orchestration of these models. At run-time the feedback from the agility layer triggers adaptation in other models and layers.

Existing interoperability measurement methods allow the analysis and assessment of interoperability in projects and at different stages. For example, the Maturity Model for Enterprise Interoperability (MMEI) makes use of the Ontology of Enterprise Interoperability ($OoEI$) and supports modelling situations from an enterprise interoperability point of view [7]. $OoEI$ support to articulate systemic relationships and allows participants to communicate interoperability issues [6,9,10]. MMEI is an a-priori, white-box approach that uses qualitative measurements for EI issues. Experts assess the level of interoperability having insight in the situation (white-box). These assessments are of qualitative nature, where the experts assign a fuzzy level of interoperability (Not Achieved, Partially Achieved, Largely Achieved, Fully Achieved) to a list of interoperability criteria. MMEI is designed to address all organisational, semantic and technical barriers. Maturity levels are identified after expert interviews have been conducted using MMEI [7].

The systemic core of the OoEI has been extended with concepts from complex adaptive systems theory ($OoEI^{CAS}$) [14,16]. This allows to model systems using agents, agent interactions, emergent behaviour, which puts particular emphasis on the dynamics of the described systems. The dynamics may be in the system's behaviour as well as in its structure [16]. The $OoEI^{CAS}$ approach builds on the metamodel, but expresses and formalises the $OoEI$ concepts using a

Domain Specific Language (DSL). The DSL of $OoEI^{CAS}$ allows to model not only structures but also dynamic behaviour of a system and its components [14]. By enabling the dynamic perspective, the $OoEI^{CAS}$ facilitates the integration of interoperability with knowledge management methods and approaches [14,16]. The knowledge management perspective assumes that the system, its components (in particular its agents) and the system's environment is evolving over time.

From a project point of view it is the loose coupling of sub-systems that makes the domain of interoperability an interesting point of view for knowledge management. However, giving the current state of enterprise integration and enterprise interoperability research, in particular in connection with knowledge management, no immediate solution or tool exists that supports projects. We start from the conceptualisation provided by enterprise interoperability and use these for discussion of issues and requirements of possible future solutions of interoperability in projects. Experiences gained in two projects (NPS2, HOPL) provide use cases, based on which requirements for such a support is derived.

3   Project Experiences

The two projects used to gather initial requirements for EI as a tool supporting knowledge management since several teams have been involved in both projects. This implies that the research domains are similar. However, the approach taken on integration and interoperability, the results and processes are quite different. Hence, by comparing these projects, effects of using an enterprise interoperability like point of view can be identified.

3.1   NPS2

In the NPS2 (Methods and approaches for sustainable decision support in operative production planning) project new methods for priority-rule-based guidance and control of flexible, volatile production processes have been researched. To do so, complex priority rules have been automatically synthesised and iteratively optimised using meta-heuristic approaches and simulation models. To specifically define the desired production strategies, several economic, environmental and work psychological indicators have been combined to form a holistic rating model. For the work discussed here, only one use-case of NPS2 on optimisation of production schedules from a holistic perspective taking economic and human resource related performance indicators into account, is considered.

In the considered use-case, a shop floor was investigated, where the percentage of manual operations is very high. These include in particular plastics moulding processes. The global and overall goal was to improve not only the economic performance with respect to scheduling of these production processes, but also to improve the satisfaction of workers. This satisfaction contributes to stress reduction and in return improves productivity of individual workers. However, instruments (tools and methods) that intend to simulate and optimise such production systems have not been available and several research questions remain open with respect to integrating the different models and available approaches from heterogeneous domains.

3.2 HOPL

The HOPL Project was a large project where for the discussion within this paper, we focused on the work in Area 1 where multiple logistics optimisations models have been developed. In this area the overall goal was to integrate isolated problem models, simulation, and mathematical models into a new flexible system for real-world problem modelling and optimisation. Through combining different models, an overarching optimisation methodology has been researched and developed to enable an optimisation of the overall system. That required algorithmic concepts to make multiple sub-problems of complex real-world systems interoperable as an optimisation network. The real-world use-case focused on transport batches for steel slabs after these have been casted. The optimisation depended on the quality level of the slabs, which was hard to predict and required machining. Another model was used to minimise transport to bring slabs to their storage places. Another model simulated the storage, transports and predicted the effect of the optimisation.

4 Interoperability Issues

The (non-linear) research process towards goals are sketched in this section. In both projects some of the teams (organisations) already worked together in a former research project, so they had some basic knowledge on the industrial application domain. However, the involved personnel changed during runtime of both projects.

In the first subsection we sketch project phases which where the same for both projects, in order to give an overview of the abstract process followed. These phases provide only a rough time-line, neglecting permanent changes in all models and of many technical systems. Corrective measures to adapt models to changed situations needed to be taken in both projects.

4.1 Project Interaction Activities

In the first phase of the projects, a lot of industrial production process knowledge had to be transferred to the researchers. In a second Phase conceptual models where developed and introduced to the industrial partner. These conceptual models and the used modelling languages were quite different. One partner developed a discrete event simulation model of the two production sites. Another partner developed for both projects concepts for mathematical rating and optimisation models, taking static and dynamic costs and penalties into account. In NPS2 additionally a qualitative model for determining workers' workplace related health resources was developed based on a questionnaire of workplace related psychological stress and measurements of heart rate variability and sleep quality. All of these developments have been done in parallel, with little interaction between researchers, as each team focused on the conceptual model of its own domain.

In phase three the researchers received feedback from the end-users' point of view. In phase four all developed models have been combined in an integrated or interoperable information system. Here, despite the similarities from the individual modelling phases and project interaction point of view, some major differences between the level of integration is visible among the two considered projects.

4.2   Integrated Approach: NPS2

In NPS2 for the mathematical models and the simulation models, almost all of the required industry data, except for human health resources was already captured in existing ERP (Enterprise Resource Planning) systems.

For research purposes, regular snapshots of the industrial database have been taken and where used for developing the formal Mathematical Economic Performance Measurement Model (MEPMM). This model had a static part capturing traditional cost models and a dynamic part related to alternative scheduling of tasks.

In contrast to this, despite the importance of psychological factors not only for mental but also for physical health, no qualitative or quantitative data about human strain and stress was available. For quantification of effects on human stress a "tank model" was designed. Working tasks that cause strain on human resources deplete the tank, whereas periods of recovery refill it. For reasons of privacy protection, no individual results could enter the final modelling stage.

The heuristic optimisation model taking both the economic and the human stress model into account had been developed by a different partner. The model approach chosen to represent the priority rule was Symbolic Expression Tree [1]. The heuristic method chosen for optimisation was Offspring Genetic Algorithm [1]. From an optimisation model point of view, the specifics of the actual models to be optimised are unknown to the optimisation engine. It provides a decision rule as a parameter to a simulation model which is evaluated by a simulation engine that calculates different performance values. The performance values are combined in a rating model to determine the fitness of a decision rule and are again used by the optimisation engine.

The simulation engine integrated all above heterogeneous models and the industrial database for instantiation of the model. The simulation partner was responsible integrating everything in a single information system, using simulation and optimisation for forecasting future production set-ups. Due to the models being from different domains, the description was quite different. Also the readiness of the different models to be implemented in a concrete platform was very different. That resulted in unexpected high effort and some features not being implemented due to resource constraints.

4.3   Interoperable Approach: HOPL

For the HOPL project, a different approach towards more interoperability was taken. The simulation engine was connected to the mathematical and meta-heuristics optimisation engine and the industrial database through a wrapper-broker system.

Every software component was wrapped and interface specific code was implemented in that wrapper. Each wrapper did run in its own process. Additionally a broker was started. The wrapper "subscribed" to topics and the software packages wrapped received information which was sent to the broker tagged with the topic. A simple interaction protocol was also developed. For this protocol, every data type ("**Transporters**" in the example below) was part of the topic. For very data type CRUD sub-topic existed (**Create Retrieve Update Delete**). A client may now subscribe to the **Transporters** topic or more specifically to **/Transporters/Create**. For every CRUD method a done method existed. For **Transporters** as data type the following topics exist:

- /Transporters/Create
- /Transporters/Retrieve
- /Transporters/Update
- /Transporters/Delete

- /Transporters/Created
- /Transporters/Retrieved
- /Transporters/Updated
- /Transporters/Deleted

Every call to the broker was asynchronous, this includes the acknowledgement messages. For example, after firing "create" one has to listen to the "created" topic (if a particular sequence between "create" and subsequent messages needs to be taken into account). In addition to these topics, data objects (as serialised google protobuf objects have been transferred between applications.

The data level therefore provided a clear, simple and easy to understand interaction protocol. Through the wrappers it was possible to map the interchange format to the needed format. However, on conceptual level, the data still was integrated. The interchange format also carried an agreed upon meaning. The drivers for the development of the exchange data format has been the optimisation model and the industrial database.

5   Towards Systems Interoperability as a Knowledge Management Tool

In this section we discuss initial observations at interfaces between groups and models, as well as knowledge management issues from an enterprise interoperability point of view.

In the NPS2 project, interoperability has not been used as a conceptual tool for analysing and designing interfaces and interactions between models. While it was clear that different (semi-formal) models did exist, no resources have been devoted upfront to clarify interfaces and interactions in detail. Interoperability barriers were discovered late in the project (in particular contrasting NPS2 with HOPL) which lead to an increased and unexpected effort. The economic model had been implemented in the information system. Some data was not available because the existing database tables where empty. This caused several parts of the model to be not integrated in the simulation and optimisation model. There were also some minimal conceptual interoperability issues between the economic model, the simulation model and the optimisation model. It was possible to resolve these issues in the last few months of the project, however, with increased effort. For example the simulation model had no concepts that allowed to capture production orders consisting of multiple parts.

For a few important issues it was not possible to resolve the interoperability problems due to missing resources. One particular issue for example was that the way the simulation engine had been implemented did not meet requirements by the economic rating model. That was discovered late as it involved detail knowledge on the mathematical model.

Several interoperability issues had been observed on conceptual level with the initial model of human health factors. That posed some challenges, when integrating it in the simulation model, for the overall project team and in particular the group working on the human factors related rating model. The initial conceptual model required 24-h information about workers. That type of information was not available in the database, and due to legal incompatibilities (obvious reason not to track the personnel for 24 h), it won't be available in the future. However, it was possible to determine stress levels offsets for different activities on the shop floor. Different activities cause more or less amount of stress, where these levels are the same for all workers. It was possible to assign these indices to machines in the data base model and make use of these for rating of past data and simulating future schedules. That resulted in a conceptually different, but interoperable model which in turn has been integrated in the information system.

For the interoperable project approach, the big picture looked quite different. Due to the early use of the broker infrastructure, it was possible to connect models and discover interoperability issues quite early. The asynchronous interface, and the data transfer objects did influence the design and implementation of the models early on. However, the broker infrastructure with the wrapper needed additional effort. Due to the individual models being modified concurrently and permanently the wrappers needed to be regularly adapted.

6   Conclusions

We have analysed and discussed two quite similar research projects from a systems interoperability point of view. For these projects we where able to identify some positive effects which may be triggered when making use of approaches from enterprise or systems interoperability. Based on observations made through the interoperability lens, we provide some guidelines. In conformity with Vernadat [12], but focusing on model driven research projects, we conclude that when aiming at interoperable models, the following guideline should be taken into account:

- Place application domain model fully at the centre of the architecture to have conceptual interoperability – The application domain is the most stable as it is linked to reality.
- Introduce an abstract level in projects as a common frame of reference for interoperability.
- Keep in mind, that interoperability is not only an issue on technical level, but also on conceptual (semantic) level. These levels need to be taken into account during project runtime.
- Systems architectures should be open with simple interfaces. Best would be to make use of open and agreed upon de facto standards.
- Clear conceptual and technical interfaces of services/application-modules which support flexible operations, respecting model diversity are needed.
- Give priority to continuous improvements and change management policy for models and their interfaces.

An analysis of the project from an interoperability point of view already during the model design phase of the project helps to avoid several of these interoperability issues. From an knowledge management point of view, missing are enterprise interoperability support tools that facilitate better and earlier flows of information between the different teams working in a research project.

Acknowledgements. The work presented here is funded by the Austrian Research Promotion Agency (FFG) through the projects NPS2 "Methods and approaches for sustainable decision support in operative production planning" (Project Number 843638) and HOPL: "K-project for Heuristic Optimisation in Production and Logistics" (Project Number 843532). The authors also wish to thank our colleagues who contributed to the projects, in particular Gerhard Prossliner, Bernhard Puswald, Roland Braune, and all employees at ASMA (NPS2) as well as voestalpine stahl and logserv users (in HOPL).

References

1. Affenzeller, M.: Genetic Algorithms and Genetic Programming: Modern Concepts and Practical Applications. CRC Press, Boca Raton (2009)
2. Agostinho, C., Ducq, Y., Zacharewicz, G., Sarraipa, J., Lampathaki, F., Poler, R., Jardim-Goncalves, R.: Towards a sustainable interoperability in networked enterprise information systems: trends of knowledge and model-driven technology. Comput. Ind. (2015). http://www.sciencedirect.com/science/article/pii/S0166361515300191
3. Agostinho, C., Jardim-Goncalves, R.: Sustaining interoperability of networked liquid-sensing enterprises: a complex systems perspective. Annu. Rev. Control **39**, 128–143 (2015)
4. Bénaben, F., Mu, W., Boissel-Dallier, N., Barthe-Delanoe, A.M., Zribi, S., Pingaud, H.: Supporting interoperability of collaborative networks through engineering of a service-based mediation information system (mise 2.0). Enterp. Inf. Syst. **9**(5–6), 1–27 (2014). doi:10.1080/17517575.2014.928949

5. Bénaben, F., Mu, W., Truptil, S., Pingaud, H., Lorré, J.P.: Information systems design for emerging ecosystems. In: 2010 4th IEEE International Conference on Digital Ecosystems and Technologies (DEST), pp. 310–315, April 2010
6. Guédria, W.: A contribution to enterprise interoperability maturity assessment, Ph.D. thesis, Université Bordeaux 1, L'UNIVERSITE BORDEAUX 1 (2012)
7. Guédria, W.: A Contribution to Enterprise Interoperability Maturity Assessment: Towards an Automatic Approach. LAP LAMBERT Academic Publishing, Saarbrücken (2012)
8. Jardim-Goncalves, R., Grilo, A., Agostinho, C., Lampathaki, F., Charalabidis, Y.: Systematisation of interoperability body of knowledge: the foundation for enterprise interoperability as a science. Enterp. Inf. Syst. **7**(1), 7–32 (2013). http://www.tandfonline.com/doi/full/10.1080/17517575.2012.684401
9. Naudet, Y., Guédria, W., Chen, D.: Systems science for enterprise interoperability. In: International Conference on Interoperability for Enterprise Software and Applications, China, 2009, IESA 2009, pp. 107–113 (2009)
10. Naudet, Y., Latour, T., Guédria, W., Chen, D.: Towards a systemic formalisation of interoperability. Comput. Ind. **61**, 176–185 (2010)
11. Tu, Z., Zacharewicz, G., Chen, D.: A federated approach to develop enterprise interoperability. J. Intell. Manuf. **27**(1), 11–31 (2014). http://dx.doi.org/10.1007/s10845-013-0868-1
12. Vernadat, F.: Interoperable enterprise systems: principles, concepts, and methods. Annu. Rev. Control **31**(1), 137–145 (2007). http://www.sciencedirect.com/science/article/pii/S1367578807000132
13. Vernadat, F.B.: Technical, semantic and organizational issues of enterprise interoperability and networking. Annu. Rev. Control **34**(1), 139–144 (2010)
14. Weichhart, G., Guédria, W., Naudet, Y.: Supporting interoperability in complex adaptive enterprise systems: a domain specific language approach. Data Knowl. Eng. (2016, accepted for publication)
15. Weichhart, G., Molina, A., Chen, D., Whitman, L., Vernadat, F.: Challenges and current developments for sensing, smart and sustainable enterprise systems. Comput. Ind. (2015, inprint). http://www.sciencedirect.com/science/article/pii/S0166361515300208
16. Weichhart, G., Stary, C.: A domain specific language for organisational interoperability. In: Ciuciu, I., Panetto, H., Debruyne, C., Aubry, A., Bollen, P., Valencia-García, R., Mishra, A., Fensel, A., Ferri, F. (eds.) OTM 2015. LNCS, vol. 9416, pp. 117–126. Springer, Heidelberg (2015). doi:10.1007/978-3-319-26138-6_15
17. Zacharewicz, G., Diallo, S.Y., Ducq, Y., Agostinho, C., Jardim-Goncalves, R., Bazoun, H., zhongjie Wang, Doumeingts, G.: Model-based approaches for interoperability of next generation enterprise information systems: state of the art and future challenges. Inf. Syst. E-Bus. Manag. 1–28 (2016). doi:10.1007/s10257-016-0317-8

Environment Aware Resource Allocation with Intelligent Provisioning Workflow Framework Concept

Prabal Mahanta[✉], Sandeep Manjunath, and Akhilesh Kumar

SAP Labs India Pvt Ltd, Bangalore 560076, Karnataka, India
{p.mahanta, sandeep.manjunath,
akhilesh.kumar02}@sap.com

Abstract. With the introduction of Dev-ops, there has been lot of research on how to stabilize the cloud for better support and define the characteristics of the environments surrounding them. The hybrid cloud presents the challenge of creating a framework which can formalize build deployment activities with minimal errors. This paper will focus on delivering the concepts of a stable framework with ability to handle product landscapes for variable environments. We will also present the approach to realize the concept of standardization by defining rules for automated healing. Lifecycle of any deployment relies heavily on support and virtual environment performance along with developmental improvements. The framework would define the life cycle of the jobs and the parameters that affect the hardware level performance and intelligently provision resources for optimal usage.

Keywords: DevOps · Hybrid-cloud · Framework

1 Introduction

DevOps culture has contributed to an influx of automation tooling and presented us with the paradigm where application is brought closer to datacenter environment. The primary goal of any kind of automation is to enable lesser human errors and cyclic feedback to bridge both the development and operations [1].

Tooling comes with several aspects so like any new technology at the beginning there would be several entrants and the numbers rise to attain a peak period and then eventually couple of major competitors remain. In context of the current scenario of the Dev-ops tooling, there are certain standardization topics that are still to be realized. Automation carries the critical dimension of providing the solution for continuous delivery [2].

With automation, we can have precise application resource management with required rules and stabilize migration costs which can be quantifiable like hardware and software or non-quantifiable parameters. To auto-scale we need to measure or monitor the performance of cloud and its related services which can be on a base requirement which can be daily to yearly. This information is very critical in determining resource requirements and over analysis we can optimize the utilization but achieve this in a

© Springer International Publishing AG 2017
I. Ciuciu et al. (Eds.): OTM 2016 Workshops, LNCS 10034, pp. 200–205, 2017.
DOI: 10.1007/978-3-319-55961-2_20

monolithic landscape is a distant dream as there is a need to standardize modules like virtual machine management, provisioning requirement. Applications are often not mapped to the infrastructure so dynamically configure resources as per the load of a virtualized environment is one of the challenges [3].

The idea here is to present a concept framework which can be implemented independent of the infrastructure to ensure secure and reliable services with ability to fault tolerance and self-healing as per product environments.

2 Designing Automated Framework for Provisioning

There are various research done on enabling deployment and making a strong operational unit based out of automated techniques. There are several factors out of which we would concentrate on:

- Scalability
- Availability
- QoS

The main issue that currently resides in all the framework is the ability to stitch the steps together with the causal feedback loop for environment awareness. Apart from the environment awareness, managing all the nodes is also one aspect that orchestration engine has to address [4, 5].

There are many ways to approach this problem, one of the ways can be:

a. Manage node information in orchestrator and automation framework without any disparity or duplication.
b. Create a centralized rule repository for storing resource calculations for all products and environments
c. Resource analysis with in depth log analysis for hierarchical analysis from hardware and software levels
d. Automated verification of build deployment based on pre-defined deployment scheduled
e. Workflow management for automation artifacts and monitoring modules.

The proposed framework is presented as started with Fig. 1 where product resource analysis module which starts with product resource analysis. Here the product logs from earlier deployments and infrastructure monitoring.

Resource analysis is based on analyzing all the logs from various sources using aggregation to a generalized model via data services and then running the rules on top of the data for creating threshold groups for different products based on engine.

The flow of analysis of logs would be to create a cluster based on product/environment and create rules accordingly for monitoring modules to cause alerts when the threshold percentages are about to reach (Fig. 2).

The next step is to have an automated application level where monitoring and automation framework artifacts are synchronized as follows as shown in Fig. 3:

Now after this steps the concept of auto healing should be realized. In this case, we know that compute resources for any infrastructure is restricted to hardware and

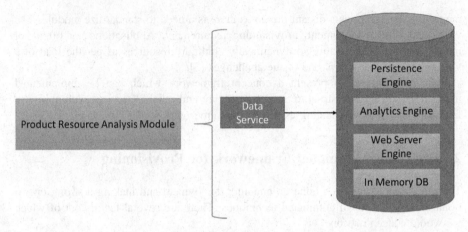

Fig. 1. Resource analysis

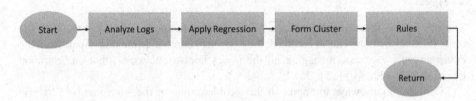

Fig. 2. Steps for analysis and rule generation

software limitations so this step cannot be completely automated but this can be made customized to alerts. The framework tackles this issue with the concept of flow described in the Fig. 4.

The customized workflow which can be made environment aware and automation framework independent where we can make chef [6] or puppet [7], rundeck [8] based artifacts work independently as per the environment requirements. These artifacts are realized using concept of idempotence of the delivery modules.

One of the biggest challenges for any organization is to have an updated database of inventory provisioned virtual machines so this framework forces the deployments to add the inventory details or update the inventory details from IPAM database [9] as per provisioning or decommissioning requirements. The flow is depicted in Fig. 5.

The overall steps would take care of availability and automated deployments as there are instances where we need to manage our monitoring alerts.

3 Looking Ahead

The concept of frameworks applies to distributed compute resources including parameters for self-healing and fault tolerance using recoverable step based feedback loops in delivery artifacts.

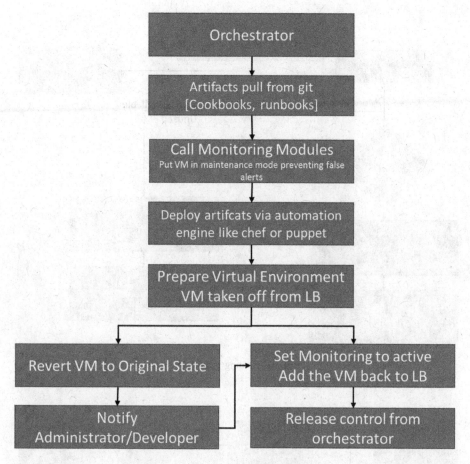

Fig. 3. Workflow for preparing a new server for deploying new build (*LB = Load Balancer)

For dynamic changes or new feature the framework will provision for pluggable or substitute modules. This will also help to understand as per the organization cloud strategy which are the modules or tool sets will optimize their overall delivery experience.

Our approach is to adopt this framework to various landscapes and currently we were successful in a simulated arena. To realize it in a productive environment we need to map artifact dependency on environment and scheduling tasks. This would also be required to map cluster based resources to accommodate both computing paradigm where once can manage a homogenous and heterogeneous cloud [10].

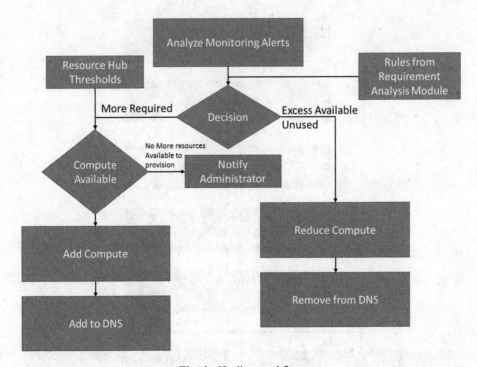

Fig. 4. Healing workflow

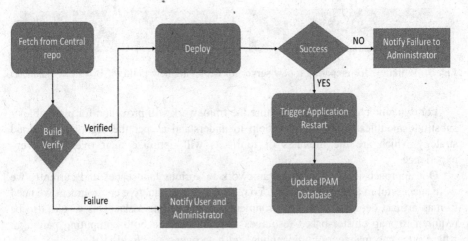

Fig. 5. Flow for build deployment

References

1. Wettinger, J., Andrikopoulos, V., Leymann, F.: Automated capturing and systematic usage of devops knowledge for cloud applications. In: 2015 IEEE International Conference on Cloud Engineering (IC2E). IEEE (2015)
2. Wettinger, J., Breitenbücher, U., Leymann, F.: Standards-based devops automation and integration using TOSCA. In: Proceedings of the 2014 IEEE/ACM 7th International Conference on Utility and Cloud Computing. IEEE Computer Society (2014)
3. Andrikopoulos, V., et al.: How to adapt applications for the Cloud environment. Computing 95(6), 493–535 (2013)
4. Garg, S.K., et al.: Environment-conscious scheduling of HPC applications on distributed cloud-oriented data centers. J. Parallel Distrib. Comput. 71(6), 732–749 (2011)
5. Buyya, R., Ranjan, R., Calheiros, Rodrigo, N.: InterCloud: utility-oriented federation of cloud computing environments for scaling of application services. In: Hsu, C.-H., Yang, Laurence, T., Park, J.H., Yeo, S.-S. (eds.) ICA3PP 2010. LNCS, vol. 6081, pp. 13–31. Springer, Heidelberg (2010). doi:10.1007/978-3-642-13119-6_2
6. Marschall, M.: Chef Infrastructure Automation Cookbook. Packt Publishing Ltd, Birmingham (2013)
7. Loope, J.: Managing Infrastructure with Puppet. O'Reilly Media, Inc, Sebastopol (2011)
8. Spinellis, D.: Service orchestration with rundeck. IEEE Softw. 31(4), 16–18 (2014)
9. Brenner, M., et al.: Replace or integrate?-Decision support for building a federated configuration management database. In: 16th International Conference of European University Information Systems (EUNIS) (2010)
10. Sanaei, Z., et al.: Heterogeneity in mobile cloud computing: taxonomy and open challenges. IEEE Commun. Surv. Tutorials 16(1), 369–392 (2014)

Development of a Virtual Reality Based Simulation Environment for Orthopedic Surgical Training

J. Cecil[1(✉)], M.B. Bharathi Raj Kumar[1], Avinash Gupta[1], M. Pirela-Cruz[2], E. Chan-Tin[1], and J. Yu[1]

[1] Center for Cyber Physical Systems, Oklahoma State University, Stillwater, USA
j.cecil@okstate.edu
[2] Texas Tech University Health Sciences Center, El Paso, Texas, USA

Abstract. Virtual Reality (VR) based simulation environments are becoming more widely used in the field of medical surgery. Typically, medical residents practice on cadavers or animals or observing a master surgeon perform surgery. The creation of VR based simulation environments holds the potential in improving the quality of training while decreasing the time needed for training. In this paper, the design and development of a Virtual Surgical Environment (VSE) is described which is used to train medical residents in an orthopedic surgery process known as LISS plating. A discussion of the overall system architecture along with an overview on the adoption of Next Generation Internet frameworks is provided. The results of the initial validation activities is discussed along with a brief outline of the process of designing and building the VSE.

Keywords: Virtual reality · Surgical simulator · Orthopedic surgery

1 Introduction

One of the recent trends in the field of medicine involves the use of VR based simulators for various surgical applications. Typically, medical surgery training involves practicing on cadavers or small animals. Other training activities involve the residents observing a surgery carried out by a master surgeon and then performing the same procedures. These approaches have several drawbacks; for example, cadavers can be the cause of various infections. Practicing on animals is not very effective due to the difference in anatomy of animals and humans. Further, the field of orthopedic surgery lags behind other fields in adopting the use of virtual training environments [1]. This paper discusses the design and development of a simulation environment called the Virtual Surgical Environment (VSE) for the Less Invasive Stabilization System (LISS) plating orthopedic surgical process.

2 Literature Review

A brief review of literature related to VR in orthopedic surgery is presented in this section. An overview of the recent trends in the field of orthopedic surgery simulation

I. Ciuciu et al. (Eds.): OTM 2016 Workshops, LNCS 10034, pp. 206–214, 2017.
DOI: 10.1007/978-3-319-55961-2_21

and the challenges associated with it is presented in [2]. Other research efforts have developed VR based simulators to support orthopedic surgical processes [3–9, 21–26, 28]. Cecil and Pirela-Cruz [10] developed an information model for virtual micro surgery which could play vital role in planning and executing the development process in an effortless manner. Other researchers have explored surgical planning approaches for treating fractures and other conditions [11–17]. Ruthenbeck and Reynolds [18] briefly described about various software tools required for the design and development of a virtual surgical simulator. Wolfson et al. [19] provided an overview of the conventional surgical training systems and the role and impact of VR surgical simulations in advancing surgical education. Haptic technologies have been explored by researchers as part of surgical simulation systems [20, 27].

Several voids were identified based on our literature survey. In general, the field of orthopedic surgery lags behind other surgical domains when it comes to utilization of VR based simulators. Most of the VR simulators for orthopedic surgery have focused on arthroscopy procedures; there is a need to develop simulators for training residents in treating fracture related surgical processes. This research approach discussed in this paper deals with LISS plating surgery which has not been addressed by any prior research. Past research has not focused on developing an information centric basis which is critically needed prior to designing and building such VR based simulators. In our research approach, we propose the use of information modeling techniques which has the potential to provide a structured basis to design and build such VSEs.

3 Surgery Background

The focus of the scope of the Virtual Surgical Environment (VSE) is limited to a process called Less Invasive Stabilization System (LISS) surgery; this orthopedic surgical process is performed to treat fractures of a femur bone.

The LISS plating based surgery has several steps (Fig. 1). Initially, the preoperative steps are performed and proper implants are chosen for the observed fracture. Subsequently, the surgeon attempts to reduce the fracture [29]. After the fracture has been reduced, the LISS plate is inserted into its proper position using an insertion guide. The attachment of the LISS plate to the bone using different types of surgical screws is the next step and considered the most important step of the surgery. The insertion guide is

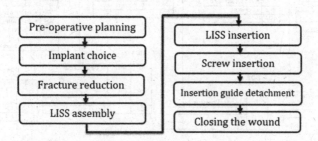

Fig. 1. LISS plating surgery step

Fig. 2. LISS components (from synthes manual [29])

detached from the LISS plate when the LISS plate is placed properly over the femur. Subsequently, the surgical incisions are closed (Fig. 2).

4 Designing and Building the VSE

The use of information modeling approaches to design and build complex simulation environments is relatively new for various engineering applications [30, 31]. To design the VSE outlined in this paper, the engineering Enterprise Modeling Language (eEML) has been used. For information modeling activities, there are a variety of modeling languages and methodologies including the IDEF suite of methods, the Unified Modeling Language, Business Process Modeling Language (BPML), among others.

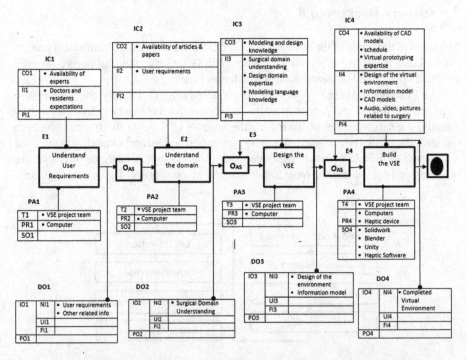

Fig. 3. eEML model showing the overall VSE development process (except validation)

Any modeling language can be used as part of our proposed approach. We are using eEML to design VSE as we have used it in prior simulation based projects to analyze data exchange tasks and design VR based software systems for different domains [32]. Figure 3 shows the top level view of the eEML model used to plan the process of designing, building and validating the VSE. The team involved in the development of the VSE is multi-disciplinary comprising of engineers, IT experts and surgeons working collaboratively. The eEML model provides a structured foundation to design and build the VSE.

The eEML model consists of functional entities and associated attributes essential to identified tasks. Each entity corresponds to a functional task; e.g. E1 corresponds to "understand user requirements". For each task, a set of associated information attributes are identified which include influencing criteria (IC), performing agents (PA) and decision objects (DO). The IC can be sub-grouped into constraints (CO), information inputs (II) and physical inputs (PI). The sub-categories of PA are teams (T), physical resources (PR) and software resources (SO). The decision objects consist of information outputs (IO) and physical outputs (PO) [31]. A description of the five phases involved in building the VSE follows.

In task E1, the focus is to understand users' preferences and requirements. In E2, the focus is on understanding the surgical domain by reading books, articles, watching videos, etc. The E3 task involves the designing of the VSE's architecture, identifying and designing of the various modules and their capabilities. In E4, the emphasis is on building the VSE using various software tools and VR hardware. The last task involved validating the built VSE by interacting with expert surgeons and residents (this task has been modeled but has not been included in Fig. 3).

Both the haptic and non-haptic environment have been built using the Unity 3D™ game engine. The simulation environment was created with application related programs written in C# and Javascript.

5   System Architecture

The overall architecture of the VSE is shown in the Fig. 4 and a discussion of the key modules follows.

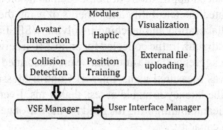

Fig. 4. VSE system architecture

5.1 System Architecture

The training modules enable residents to become skilled in these surgical tasks: Assembly of LISS plate, Fracture reduction, Insertion of LISS plate, positioning and fixing of the LISS plate to the broken bone with screws and removal of the insertion guide. A view of the VSE (which also uses avatars to help interactions) is shown in Fig. 5. For purposes of brevity, a description of only one training module (the position training module) is provided.

Fig. 5. A view of the VSE

The position training module (Fig. 6) focuses on enabling residents to become skilled at positioning the LISS plate with respect to the bone (femur) and surgical implants. This helps residents become familiar with positioning of the LISS plate with respect to the bone and surgical implants. As shown in Fig. 6, an indicator turns green when the implant is in the correct position. When the resident exceeds the accepted boundary and places the plate in an incorrect position and orientation, the color of the indicator turns red; residents can practice this important task interactively. A haptic interface (using the Geomagic Touch™) can be used (Fig. 7) to practice assembling the LISS plate and other steps. The VSE can also be accessed from different locations; a master surgeon can interact with medical residents in other locations and train them interactively. As part of US Ignite (usignite.org) and GENI (geni.net) projects, we are studying the feasibility of Next Generation Internet frameworks which can support low latency high gigabit data exchange for advanced applications in fields such as medicine [33, 34]. We have successfully demonstrated the feasibility and benefits of using the GENI framework to support distributed collaboration and teaching involving VSE. Figure 8a and b shows the data latency and bandwidth traffic collected for almost 10 h between two GENI nodes located at the same site aggregate. Measurements were performed using GENI Desktop and network latency was measured using Internet Control Message Protocol (ICMP) ping. As can be seen, the latency is stable at less than 1 ms. Even with two nodes, the network traffic is significant, highlighting the need for the use of next generation Internet with higher bandwidth capacity.

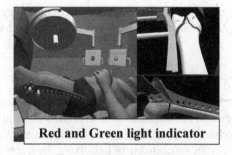

Red and Green light indicator

Fig. 6. Position control module (Color figure online)

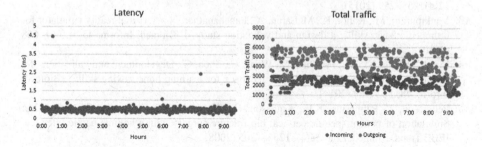

Fig. 7. A resident using haptic device

Latency | Total Traffic

Fig. 8. (a) Latency (milliseconds) and (b) traffic (in Kilobytes)

6   Validation and Discussion

The usefulness of the VSE was validated through a set of activities involving eleven orthopedic residents (coordinated by Dr. M. Cruz) at the Texas Tech University Health Sciences Center in El Paso, Texas. The participants were first pre-tested on their knowledge/skills of the LISS plating process. Subsequently, they interacted and used the VSE to become familiar and knowledgeable about the LISS surgery. Then, the participants were evaluated through post-tests based on the understanding acquired through using the VSE. Post-test evaluations indicated that eight of eleven residents showed significant improvements in their understanding of the LISS surgical process. The results demonstrated that the VSE training improved the skills compared with normal learning methodologies. However, additional validation tests are continuing which will compare the impact of using haptic based environments versus non haptic based simulation environments.

7 Validation and Discussion

In this paper, the design and development of a VR based surgical environment (VSE) was discussed. The architecture was discussed along outcomes of a validation study which indicated that the VSE was capable of improving the learning skills of residents. As part of US Ignite and GENI projects, we demonstrated the use of Next Generation Internet technologies which supported feasibility of surgeons and residents interacting with VSE from different locations.

Acknowledgments. Funding was received from the National Science Foundation through grant numbers 1257803, 1447237 and 1547156.

References

1. Vaughan, N., Dubey, V.N., Wainwright, T.W., Middleton, R.G.: A review of virtual reality based training simulators for orthopedic surgery. Med. Eng. Phys. **38**(2), 59–71 (2016)
2. Mediouni, M., Volosnikov, A.: The trends and challenges in orthopedic simulation. J. Orthop. **12**(4), 253–259 (2015)
3. Vankipuram, M., Kahol, K., McLaren, A., Panchanathan, S.: A virtual reality simulator for orthopedic basic skills: a design and validation study. J. Biomed. Inform. **43**(5), 661–668 (2010)
4. Lin, Y., Wang, X., Wu, F., Chen, X., Wang, C., Shen, G.: Development and validation of a surgical training simulator with haptic feedback for learning bone-sawing skill. J. Biomed. Inform. **48**, 122–129 (2014)
5. Pettersson, J., Palmerius, K.L., Knutsson, H., Wahlstrom, O., Tillander, B., Borga, M.: Simulation of patient specific cervical hip fracture surgery with a volume haptic interface. IEEE Trans. Biomed. Eng. **55**(4), 1255–1265 (2008)
6. Sabri, H., Cowan, B., Kapralos, B., Porte, M., Backstein, D., Dubrowskie, A.: Serious games for knee replacement surgery procedure education and training. Procedia-Soc. Behav. Sci. **2**(2), 3483–3488 (2010)
7. Zhu, B., Gu, L., Peng, X., Zhou, Z.: A point-based simulation framework for minimally invasive surgery. In: Bello, F., Cotin, S. (eds.) ISBMS 2010. LNCS, vol. 5958, pp. 130–138. Springer, Heidelberg (2010). doi:10.1007/978-3-642-11615-5_14
8. Citak, M., Gardner, M.J., Kendoff, D., Tarte, S., Krettek, C., Nolte, L.P., Hüfner, T.: Virtual 3D planning of acetabular fracture reduction. J. Orthop. Res. **26**(4), 547–552 (2008)
9. Qin, J., Pang, W.M., Chui, Y.P., Wong, T.T., Heng, P.A.: A novel modeling framework for multilayered soft tissue deformation in virtual orthopedic surgery. J. Med. Syst. **34**(3), 261–271 (2010)
10. Cecil, J., Pirela-Cruz, M.: An information model based framework for virtual micro surgery. Int. J. Virtual Reality **10**(2), 17–31 (2011)
11. Jun, Y., Park, S.: Polygon-based 3D surgical planning system for hip operation. Int. J. Precis. Eng. Manuf. **12**(1), 157–160 (2011)

12. Kovler, I., Joskowicz, L., Weil, Y.A., Khoury, A., Kronman, A., Mosheiff, R., Liebergall, M., Salavarrieta, J.: Haptic computer-assisted patient-specific preoperative planning for orthopedic fractures surgery. Int. J. Comput. Assist. Radiol. Surg. **10**(10), 1535–1546 (2015)

13. Nahvi, A., Moghaddam, M., Arbabtafti, M., Mahvash, M., Richardson, B.: Virtual bone surgery using a haptic robot. Int. J. Rob. Theory Appl. **1**(1), 1–12 (2016)

14. Seah, T.E.T., Barrow, A., Baskaradas, A., Gupte, C., Bello, F.: A virtual reality system to train image guided placement of kirschner-wires for distal radius fractures. In: Bello, F., Cotin, S. (eds.) ISBMS 2014. LNCS, vol. 8789, pp. 20–29. Springer, Heidelberg (2014). doi: 10.1007/978-3-319-12057-7_3

15. Park, S.H., Yoon, Y.S., Kim, L.H., Lee, S.H. and Han, M.: Virtual knee joint replacement surgery system. In: 2007 Geometric Modeling and Imaging, GMAI 2007, pp. 79–84. IEEE, July 2007

16. Rasool, S., Sourin, A.: Image-driven virtual simulation of arthroscopy. Vis. Comput. **29**(5), 333–344 (2013)

17. Cimerman, M., Kristan, A.: Preoperative planning in pelvic and acetabular surgery: the value of advanced computerised planning modules. Injury **38**(4), 442–449 (2007)

18. Ruthenbeck, G.S., Reynolds, K.J.: Virtual reality surgical simulator software development tools. J. Simul. **7**(2), 101–108 (2013)

19. Wolfson, T.S., Atesok, K.I., Turhan, C., Mabrey, J.D., Egol, K.A., Jazrawi, L.M.: Animation and surgical simulation in orthopedic education. In: Doral, M.N., Karlsson, J. (eds.) Sports Injuries: Prevention Treatment and Rehabilitation Diagnosis, pp. 3047–3063. (2015)

20. Shi, Y., Xiong, Y., Hua, X., Tan, K., Pan, X.: Key techniques of haptic related computation in virtual liver surgery. In: 2015 8th International Conference on Biomedical Engineering and Informatics (BMEI), pp. 355–359. IEEE, October 2015

21. Maciel, A., Halic, T., Lu, Z., Nedel, L.P., De, S.: Using the PhysX engine for physics-based virtual surgery with force feedback. Int. J. Med. Robot. Comput. Assist. Surg. **5**(3), 341–353 (2009)

22. Gomoll, A.H., O'Toole, R.V., Czarnecki, J., Warner, J.J.: Surgical experience correlates with performance on a virtual reality simulator for shoulder arthroscopy. Am. J. Sports Med. **35**(6), 883–888 (2007)

23. Braman, J.P., Sweet, R.M., Hananel, D.M., Ludewig, P.M., Van Heest, A.E.: Development and validation of a basic arthroscopy skills simulator. Arthrosc.: J. Arthrosc. Relat. Surg. **31**(1), 104–112 (2015)

24. Andersen, C., Winding, T.N., Vesterby, M.S.: Development of simulated arthroscopic skills: a randomized trial of virtual-reality training of 21 orthopedic surgeons. Acta Orthop. **82**(1), 90–95 (2011)

25. Rose, K., Pedowitz, R.: Fundamental arthroscopic skill differentiation with virtual reality simulation. Arthrosc.: J. Arthrosc. Relat. Surg. **31**(2), 299–305 (2015)

26. Stunt, J.J., Kerkhoffs, G.M.M.J., van Dijk, C.N., Tuijthof, G.J.M.: Validation of the ArthroS virtual reality simulator for arthroscopic skills. Knee Surg. Sports Traumatol. Arthrosc. **23**(11), 3436–3442 (2015)

27. Akhtar, K., Sugand, K., Sperrin, M., Cobb, J., Standfield, N., Gupte, C.: Training safer orthopedic surgeons: construct validation of a virtual-reality simulator for hip fracture surgery. Acta Orthop. **86**(5), 616–621 (2015)

28. Willaert, W.I., Aggarwal, R., Van Herzeele, I., Cheshire, N.J., Vermassen, F.E.: Recent advancements in medical simulation: patient-specific virtual reality simulation. World J. Surg. **36**(7), 1703–1712 (2012)

29. SYNTHES, Less Invasive Stabilization System (LISS) (2000). http://www.synthes.com

30. Muthaiyan, A., Cecil, J.: A virtual environment for satellite assembly. Comput.-Aided Des. Appl. **5**(1–4), 526–538 (2008)
31. Cecil, J.: Modeling the process of creating virtual prototypes. Comput.-Aided Des. Appl. **6**(1–4), 1–4 (2015)
32. Cecil, J., Pirela-Cruz, M.: Development of an information model for a virtual surgical environment. In: Proceedings of the TMCE 2010, 12–16 April. Ancona, Italy (2010)
33. Cecil, J., Ramanathan, P., Rahneshin, V., Prakash, A., Pirela-Cruz, M.: Collaborative virtual environments for orthopedic surgery. In: 2013 IEEE International Conference on Automation Science and Engineering (CASE), pp. 133–137. IEEE, August 2013
34. Cecil, J., Gupta, A., Pirela-Cruz, M., Rajkumar, M., Ramanathan, P.: Presentation at 2016 IEEE International Conference on Automation Science and Engineering (CASE). IEEE (2016)

International Workshop on Methods, Evaluation, Tools and Applications for the Creation and Consumption of Structured Data for the e-Society (Meta4eS) 2016

Meta4eS 2016 PC Co-chairs' Message

The future eSociety, addressed with our workshop, is an e-inclusive society based on the extensive use of digital technologies at all levels of interaction between its members. It is a society that evolves based on knowledge and that empowers individuals by creating virtual communities that benefit from social inclusion, access to information, enhanced interaction, participation and freedom of expression, among other.

In this context, the role of the ICT in the way people and organizations exchange information and interact in the social cyberspace is crucial. Large amounts of structured data – Big Data and Linked (Open) Data – are being generated, published and shared on the Web and a growing number of services and applications emerge from it. These initiatives take into account methods for the creation, storage and consumption of increasing amounts of structured data and tools that make possible their application by end-users to real-life situations, as well as their evaluation. The final aim is to lower the barrier between end-users and information and communication technologies via a number of techniques stemming from the fields of semantic knowledge processing, multilingual information, information visualization, privacy and trust, etc.

To discuss, demonstrate and share best practices, ideas and results, the 5th International IFIP Workshop on Methods, Evaluation, Tools and Applications for the Creation and Consumption of Structured Data for the eSociety (Meta4eS 2016), an event supported by IFIP TC 12 WG 12.7 and The Big data roadmap and cross-disciplinarY community for addressing socieTal Externalities (BYTE) project, with a special focus on cross-disciplinary communities and applications associated with Big Data and their impact on the eSociety, brings together researchers, professionals and experts interested to present original research results in this area.

We are happy to announce that, for its fifth edition, the workshop raised interest and good participation in the research community. After a thorough review process, with each submission refereed by at least three members of the workshop Program Committee, we accepted 6 full papers and 3 short papers covering topics such as ontology engineering, Big Data, smart knowledge processing and extraction, social semantics, decision making, service discovery, user interfaces, and applied to the fields of education, safety information management, e-Health and ambient assisted living.

We thank the Program Committee members for their time and effort in ensuring the quality during the review process, as well as all the authors and the workshop attendees for the original ideas and the inspiring discussions. We also thank the OTM 2016 Organizing Committee members for their continuous support. We are confident that Meta4eS will bring an important contribution towards the future eSociety.

September 2016

Ioana Ciuciu
Anna Fensel

Artificial Neural Network for Supporting Medical Decision Making: A Decision Model and Notation Approach to Spondylolisthesis and Disk Hernia

Lorenzo Servadei[✉], Rainer Schmidt, and Florian Bär

Department of Computer Sciences and Informatics, Munich University of Applied Sciences,
Lothstraße 64, 80335 Munich, Germany
lorenzo.servadei@hm.edu

Abstract. E-health is a key factor in the E-society. E-health, in fact, enhances the efficiency and reduces the costs of the health services. In the diagnostic field, E-health can avail of several Machine Learning (ML) algorithms, as Artificial Neural Networks (ANNs) for instance, which often demonstrated a high classification accuracy. Although ANNs have already been applied for medical diagnosis, their influence on the Decision Making Process (DMP) has not been investigated in detail. Therefore, this paper focuses on the impact of ANNs on the DMP for a special kind of medical diagnosis called Spondylolisthesis and Disk Hernia. Through the Decision Model and Notation standard (DMN), the DMP is described, offering a model for possible health policies. In this way ANNs supported decision making for Spondylolisthesis and Disk Hernia diagnosis improve efficiency and quality of health service, especially in developing countries.

1 Introduction

A society which uses digitalization in most of the relationships (among peers, customers to business, business to business) takes the name of E-society [1] In the context of the E-society, the healthcare system provides transferring of resources and information by electronic mean and defines this process as E-health [2]. It has been pointed out in scientific papers how an E-health based healthcare system improve health services [3]: this potentiality seems to be more successfully profited by developed countries than by developing ones [2]. Among the causes of this disparity, there have been identified economic resources, high usage prices, but also lack of governmental policies for E-health [2]. Machine Learning (ML) has often been used as an approach to e-Health issues and automatic diagnostic problems in medicine. One example of this is the application of ML in the sagittal panoramic radiography[1] (SPR) to detect anomalies on the vertebral column [4]. As a result, recent papers show an accuracy of ≈93% on public available dataset for ternary classification (normal, spondylolisthesis, disk hernia) through ANNs [5] and an even higher accuracy of ≈96.55% by binary classification (normal, abnormal) with AdaBoost and improved RIPPER algorithms [6]. These

---

[1] Wide angle X-ray imaging of the sagittal plane, which divides the body in left and right halves.

© Springer International Publishing AG 2017
I. Ciuciu et al. (Eds.): OTM 2016 Workshops, LNCS 10034, pp. 217–227, 2017.
DOI: 10.1007/978-3-319-55961-2_22

outcomes can be very useful in the praxis, because sagittal radiographs are 2D imaging instruments which are available worldwide and allow a less expensive imaging [7] if compared to more advanced systems such as CT or MRI [8, 9]. This means that the cost of a SPR is more sustainable for the patient and for the healthcare system, especially in countries with lower expenditure (globally and per capita) on healthcare [10, 11]. With the result of the SPR and the ternary classification through ANNs [5], the doctor is aided in detecting a disk hernia through six biomechanical features obtained. This optimizes the decision process despite of a conservative access to the MRI or CT and leads to an effective and prompt therapy decision [12].

The proposition of this paper is to integrate a ML based E-health system into a DMP, which contributes to design a specific health policy for vertebral column disorders in low budget healthcare systems. In order to represent the DMP in a repeatable method, the standard DMN from the OMG has been used [13]. The DMN integrates BPMN services fully, giving thus a framework for multiple use cases [13]. A description of a DMP through the DMN is a solid basis for the realization of a health policy: by definition of the World Health Organization (WHO) in fact, the DMP is an essential part of a health policy, and constitutes, together with plans and actions for an health goal, the very core of it [14].

2   Related Works

The ML supported DMP in the medical field is an interdisciplinary area of research. For this reason, the paper is based on the following key areas of research: ML applied to vertical column pathologies, vertical column diagnostic, healthcare systems and policies, decision processes descriptions (Table 1).

Table 1. Selection of literature, categorized by the main topic of interest.

ML applied to vertebral column pathologies	Vertebral column diagnostic	Healthcare systems and policies	Decision making
[4]–[6], [15]–[17]	[18]–[24]	[7]–[12]	[13], [25]–[27]

Regarding the ML algorithms applied to vertebral column pathologies, the fundament of this paper lays on the UCI ML dataset [16] for vertebral column, the first paper published on the classification of these data [4] and on a ML approach on the detection issue [17]. Furthermore, an article about a comparative ML approach on Feed Forward Neural Networks (FFNNs), Generalized Regression Neural Networks (GRNNs) and Support Vector Machines (SVM) has been critical for identifying the main role of ANNs in a ternary classification based on their compared accuracy [5]. Other approaches to binary classification (sorting normal and abnormal patients) have shown a superior accuracy, 96.55%, higher sensitivity and specificity (respectively 0.966 and 0.987) on the same dataset with the AdaBoost and improved RIPPER ML algorithms [6]. On the field of vertebral column diagnostic, the paper bases on the correlation among pelvic and lumbar adjacent orientation and shape parameters in detecting pathologic conditions of the spine and pelvis [18]. Regarding spondylolisthesis, as a deepening on clinical evaluation and imaging, a medical paper on determination by clinical evaluation [19] and one on the imaging of lumbar spondylolisthesis [20] have been consulted. Concerning the treatment of the spondylolisthesis, a source to compare surgical and non-surgical treatment of it [20] has been used. Over disk hernia, it has been adopted the same sources retrieval design as for spondylolisthesis, first focusing on diagnosis and imaging of disk hernia [21–23] and then on the surgical or non-operational treatment [24]. Directly related to the surgical and non-surgical treatment of the disk herniation, papers related to the cost-effectiveness and cost-utility of the disk hernia treatment have been retrieved [7, 12]. These sources, together with papers and statistics about pro-capita healthcare expenditure in each country [10] and health expenditure per country [11], allowed me an overview on general healthcare policies and a specific insight on the field of the disk hernia. To complete this framework, the distribution over countries of medical imaging machines for MRI [8] and CT [9] have been gathered. The last area of my sources retrieval it is focused on the DMP. Decision making has been a widely treated topic in healthcare [25, 26] and in the last years, the decision making in clinical fields has been taking into account fewer parameters to reach higher success expectation [27]. This helped me to describe through the DMN, a recent standard proposed by the Object Management Group, a DMP based on ML support for the detection of spondylolisthesis and disk hernia.

2.1 Importance of the Research and Research Questions

As pointed out in the previous section, the paper bases on the correlation between shapes and orientation of lumbar and pelvic segments and state of spinal anomalies [18]. This paper aims to integrate the geometric features of the body into an ANNs driven diagnosis [5] for an E-health DMP. How and in which case can the ANNs driven diagnosis be implemented in a DMP? In which way would it support the therapy and enhance the expectations of a successful treatment?

3 Research and Methodologies

3.1 Biomechanical Features and the Dataset

The human vertebral column is composed of irregularly shaped units of bones and hyaline cartilage, called vertebrae, separated by intervertebral fibrocartilage (intervertebral disks) [28]. Facet joints, muscles, medulla and nerves are completing the composition of the vertebral column [17], which counts in humans usually 33 vertebrae in total [28]. The vertebrae are divided in 7 cervical, 12 thoracic, 5–6 lumbar, 5 fused called sacrum, and 3 named coccyx. The main function of the vertebral column is to protect the spinal cord, nerves and internal organs, provide support and balance to the muscles and enable flexibility in motion and posture in standing [17]. As each one of these functions could be endangered, the diagnostic of vertebral column pathologies has been researched, and results of scientific papers have shown how the pelvic-spine system and its morphological anomalies influence vertebral column disorders [18]. The selection of relevant parameters for the correlation of pelvic-spine system has been chosen by the

Pearson coefficient P and r at the level of significance for P < 0.01. The correlation values point the correlation of three pelvic parameters to the spinal ones (in particular, on the lumbar spine section) [4, 17]. The first three biomechanical attributes chosen, Pelvic Incidence (PI), Sacral Slope (SS) and Pelvic Tilt (PT), are the one named in the literature as the Duval-Beaupère's pelvic parameters [29]. The PI has a main role for sagittal spinal balance and corresponds to the angle between the line perpendicular to the sacral plate at its midpoint, and the line connecting this point to the axis of the femoral heads [29]. The PI stays constant in grown up humans and decides the parameters of sacral slope (SS) and pelvic tilt (PT). PT is defined by the angle between the line connecting the midpoint of the sacral plate to the bi-coxo-femoral axis and the vertical line. The sacral slope is the angle between the sacral plate and the horizontal line [29]. The last three parameters are the lordosis angle, calculated through the Cobb's angle and representing the Sagittal Angle in Lumbar Lordosis (SALL), the Pelvic Radius (RP). Last, the Grade of Slipping (GS) is defined as the percentage of slipping of the vertebra L5 and the sacrum [17]. The dataset has been supplied by the Centre Médico-Chirurgical de Readaptation des Massues, by Dr. Henrique da Mota [16]. The data were collected by measuring six parameters in a SPR (PI, SS, PT, RP, SALL, RP, GS) on a total of 310 patients. Patients were previously divided in 100 without any spine pathology (normal), 150 with spondylolisthesis (abnormal), and 60 with disk hernia (abnormal). Even if reduced, a dataset of 310 patients, given only six features and three possible outcomes, has been considered sufficient [4, 17].

3.2 Classification Through Artificial Neural Networks

In the paper it has been treated the case of ternary classification (as it is believed to have further relevance for a DMP). ANNs have shown in the literature over this dataset major accuracy and generally better multi-classification performances [5, 15]. ANNs consist of biologically inspired computational networks, which avails of an amount of units, also called artificial neurons, able interact with each other and generate a number of outputs for the given inputs. The architecture consists of an input layer, for complex tasks, one or more hidden layer (none in case of single-layer perceptron) and an output layer [30]. The Multi-Layer Perceptron (MLP) Feed Forward Neural Network (FFNN) is an often used architecture for neural networks. In the FFNN, neurons of one layer are connected with neurons of the subsequent layer, each neuron having an activation function and multiplying in the given synapsis for a specific parameter, also called weight (and generating thus the activity of the network) [30].

$$a_k = g_k(b_k + \sum_j g_j\left(b_j + \sum_i a_i w_{ij}\right)w_{jk}) \tag{1}$$

The formula (1) provides an example of computation for a neural network with one hidden layer. The feed-forward computations entail the multiplication of the inputs from the input layer a_i for the fully connected weights w_{ij} to each neuron of the hidden layer. Each neuron of the hidden layer received contribute by each weight and, together with the other neuron in the hidden layer and added to a bias unit (specific for the layer), will be equal to the activity $z_j = b_j + \sum_i a_i w_{ij}$ of the hidden layer. Successively, the activation function g_j will be applied to the activity. The same procedure will be repeated a second time, but instead of the inputs a_i, the activation of the layer a_j will be multiplied by the weights. As a result of the last activation function g_k, one or more outputs will be computed [30]. As a MLP ANN is used to compute outputs, what is mainly important in order to have good predictions is to choose proper parameters (or weights) and proper hyper parameters (architecture of network, learning rate, batch-size, etc.). For accomplishing the first task, which is related to the problem of the least squared error, in MLP is often used the matrix of weights which produce the littler error and minimize the cost function given by the mean squared error (MSE) [30]. In the formula (2), the $\hat{Y}_i$ indicates the output prediction given the hypothesis function, whereas Y_i points out the actual output from the inputs given. In order to do that, is often used the backpropagation algorithm, which is called gradient descent. It back propagates the error to the whole parameters of the neural networks, trying to find which parameter has to be changed and how, in order to converge, through the first order derivative direction of the parameters, to the global minimum. In order to avoid little steps by bigger steeps, it has been introduced the concept of momentum, which rules the variation of the weight update for each step. In the formula (3), Δw_i corresponds to the variation of the weight. The constant γ is the momentum, whereas α is the learning rate and gW the gradient for the weight [31].

$$MSE = \frac{1}{n} \sum_{i=1}^{n} (\hat{Y}_i - Y_i)^2 \tag{2}$$

$$\Delta w_i = \gamma \Delta w_{i-1} + (1 - \gamma)\alpha gW \tag{3}$$

For each neural networks will be provided the overall accuracy of the model, which focuses on the fitting of the model for the given classification, computing the addition of true positives and true negatives, and dividing for the amount of the classifications. Other two values we will avail are the sensitivity and the specificity, described as follow. The values proposed have been pointed out to measure the performance of medical classification tests [32].

$$Specificity = \frac{TN}{TN + FN} \tag{4}$$

$$Sensitivity = \frac{TP}{TP + FP} \tag{5}$$

$$Accuracy = \frac{TP + TN}{TP + TN + FP + FN} \tag{6}$$

The measurement will be computed through the confusion matrix which, in each classification, outline how many true positives (correctly positively classified), true negatives (correctly negatively classified), false negatives (erroneously classified negative) and false positives (erroneously classified positive) are present.

3.3   ANNs Classification Compared

In order to provide a good performance for classification for the ANNs, different cost functions and optimization methods have been tested. In the first trial, a FFNN with one hidden layer of ten neurons has been designed [33]. The data, already cleaned as part of a well-known public ML dataset [16], have been divided in 50% ratio for training, 15% for cross-validation scope and 35% for the test. The training, per default, stops after reaching 1000 epochs. The cross validation set takes the main function of avoiding overfitting and have the role to test the hypothesis, so that is not excessively modeled by the training set. The final performance measurement has been computed on an average of one hundred training so that the performance results have been stabilized. The first optimization function used has been the gradient descent, which updates the function in the direction of the steepest way into a minimum (taking thus the negative of the gradient). This algorithm tries to take to 0 each derivative of the cost function with respect to each parameter, as we are heading to a (global) minimum of the cost function. Through gradient descent and mean squared error cost function (MSE), using as activation function for the neurons the tan-sigmoid functions (7), the accuracy reached has been 78,4%. This result could be better if some hyper parameter changes to adapt better to our multi-classification case. The possibility to reach faster the global minimum has been guaranteed by the search for conjugate directions, which enable a faster convergence than the steepest direction of the gradient descent [39]. Performance result obtained are better: with a conjugate gradient descent training, results for accuracy have been 87,4% while for the sensitivity, first class 81,82%, second class 73,68% and third class 86,10%, while specificity for the first class is 91,00%, 92,89% for the second one and 98,72% for the last one. This value is very important for two last classes in this medical test, because it specifies how many people had actually this pathology, but they were not properly classified, with higher risk for the patient. The conjugate gradient descent converges fast but, could be, in some case, not the best optimization solution. In some loss functions it is important in fact to take into account the second derivative with respect to the parameters, which means the curvature of the function, thus avoiding different steps for different parameters and ending up to bowl like areas of the function curve [34]. To overcome this problem, it has been used the Levenberg–Marquardt optimization algorithm, which combines the gradient descent to the Gauss-Newton Algorithm [35]. In doing this, we reached the following results: overall accuracy 88,7%, with first class sensitivity of 82,18%, second class of 75,44% and third class of 96,71%; specificity has been of 91,87% for the first class, 93,28% for the second and 98,10% for the third one. In the formula (8), it is seen that the update of the weight follows the following pattern: under the assumption that the loss function is a mean or sum of squared errors, to the former weight w_k is going to be subtracted to the inverse of the approximation of the Hessian matrix $J^T J$ added to the I identity matrix, multiplied for the transpose of the Jakobian Matrix J^T multiplied for the error e.

$$\text{tansig}(n) = \frac{2}{1 + e^{-2n}} - 1 \tag{7}$$

$$w_{k+1} = w_k - [J^T J + \mu I]^{-1} J^T e \tag{8}$$

$$C(k) = \beta Ed + \alpha Ew \qquad (9)$$

As taken from literature, the Bayes regularization is using the Levenberg–Marquardt algorithm but has a different way to calculate the combination of errors and weights. In fact, it tries not only to minimize the error in the cost (or loss) function but also to minimize the weights used [36]. In the formula (9), the cost function $C(k)$ depends on the sum of the squared errors E_d and on the sum of the squared weights E_w. The ensemble the advantages of Levenberg–Marquardt to a different approach of optimization, which is slower as algorithm but with great accuracy. In fact, the result obtained show this: 96,1% accuracy, which is believed to be, on the knowledge of the author, a better ternary classification accuracy for this dataset through ANNs than in the literature known. First class sensitivity is 94,95%, second class of 93,44% and third class of 98,00%; the specificity has been of 97,16% for the first class, 98,80% for the second and 98,12% for the third one.

3.4   Artificial Neural Networks Supported DMP

Using the DMN standard [13], the DMP is modeled and formalized. The DMN standard is flexible, and can be integrated, for describing the decision making inside a broader process, into the Business Process Model and Notation (BPMN) framework [37]. BPMN is, exactly as the DMN, an OMG standard [37]. Through a BPMN 2.0 diagram, it has been pointed out the context of the distinct decision-making processes and the single steps which compose a physician medical examination, where there is a suspect of Hernia or Spondylolisthesis (symptoms of the two pathologies are often confused [15]). In the graphically represented flow objects (see Fig. 1), two exclusive gateways rule the Diagnostic Imaging Method (DIM) and the ANNs suggested diagnosis.

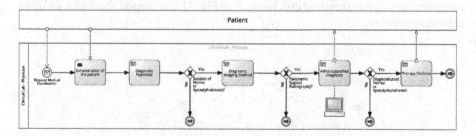

Fig. 1. BPMN overall medical examination process.

Of the four different DMPs pointed out in the BPMN diagram, namely "Diagnostic Hypothesis", "Therapy Decision", "Diagnostic Imaging Method" and "ANNs supported diagnosis", it is important to focus in this paper on the last two, which are the necessary condition and the actuation of our ANNs approach. Regarding the first decision process, the decision of an optimal DIM, it is based on five inputs, namely the symptoms, the budget, the patient condition, the Availability of the Imaging Method. The only output, in this decision logic, is the imaging method. The input parameters are the *Symptoms*, taken as a constant (back pain), the *Budget* (budget available for the imaging test, increasingly for SPR, CT and MRI) and *Patient Conditions* ("at Radiation Risk", or "good"). The last one is *Availability Imaging*: taken as a constant, as it is supposed that CT, MRI or SPR are available imaging methods. The output of the DMP is the appropriate imaging method (*Imaging*). The resulting decision-making diagram has been presented in Fig. 2.

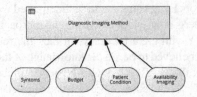

Fig. 2. Diagnostic imaging method – decision model diagram.

The decision logic table, containing the rules for a DMI output, shows that the SPR corresponds to the output case, where the budget at disposal is low and the patient condition is not at radiation risk. In fact, by high budget, the MRI is preferred because of low radiations emitted and precision in detecting pathologies on muscles and tissue [38, 39]. At the same time, when the budget is on medium level but there is no risk for radiations, the CT is the preferred method, being, in fact, superior to traditional medical X-ray machines [22]. Unfortunately concerning imaging for patients with risk for absorbing X-rays and a medium or low budget, none of MRI, CT or traditional X-ray equipment seems to be proper. In further considerations of the BPMN diagram, it has been treated the choice of SPR, where the budget available is low but there is no contra-indication to the use of X-ray. The possibility, through a radiography, to measure six features which let the ANNs to classify, with an accuracy of 96,1%, the status of normality, spondylolisthesis, or disk hernia (see Fig. 3), can support the doctor on more accurate diagnosis.

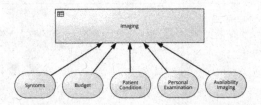

Fig. 3. Knowledge base for diagnostic classification support.

In our DMP the final diagnosis is determined by the contribution of the personal examination to the knowledge base given by the ANNs classification of the six parameters from the SPR, as shown in Fig. 4.

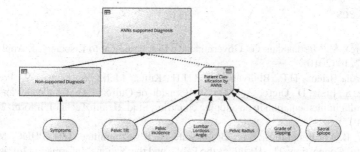

Fig. 4. ANNs supported diagnosis.

The ANNs supported diagnosis output will become, in the next DMP for a therapy decision, the input on which the doctor avails on. The diagnostic output will be determined by ANNs diagnosis and by the non-supported one.

4   Conclusions and Further Work

Improving quality and efficiency of decision-making is an important pillar of E-health and an important contribution to the development of an E-society. Providing models for IT supported medical decision processes and defining a context for the application of E-health related policies is a condition for the development of the E-society. The difficulty for E-health systems to spread in developing countries is shown to be due to a lack of proper health policies as well as economical resources [2]. As E-health is improving significantly healthcare systems performances and diminishing costs [3], the implementation of E-health affine DMP can contribute to increase health standards in developing countries [3]. Through the DMPs presented in the BPMN diagram in Fig. 3, we have shown the direct contribution of the ANNs supported diagnosis to a decision for a proper therapy. As possible hypothesis in a low budget healthcare model, the doctor could prescribe an MRI only in cases of a disk hernia diagnosis. Or he could directly opt for further exam for a surgical therapy, as shown to be less expensive for the healthcare system [12]. At the same time, in case of difficulty on availing on a surgical treatment, the doctor could attempt a prompt non-surgical therapy. Different treatments could be opined in case of a spondylolisthesis detection. The case of ML detection of spinal normality instead can aid the doctor in the decision of a new physical examination or the use of other diagnostic systems. As we have pointed out, a very high ternary classification accuracy can be reached (96,1%) through FFNNs on the dataset, overcoming previous results.

In further works, it would be interesting to evaluate the impact of DMPs in e-Health systems and the benefit on accuracy of diagnosis, treatment timing, therapy response and success. A review of e-Health based DMP and available use cases could better quantify their relevance in e-Health implementations. A particularly interesting topic for research is the implementation of other ML algorithms on diagnostic systems to overcome through Soft Computing predictions common difficulties in availing of expensive medical equipment for low budget healthcare systems.

References

1. Jayashree, S., Marthandan, G.: Government to E-government to E-society. J. Appl. Sci. **10**, 2205–2210 (2010)
2. Mandirola Brieux, H.F., Bhuiyan Masud, J.H., Kumar Meher, S., Kumar, V., Portilla, F., Indarte, S., Luna, D., Otero, C., Otero, P., Bernaldo de Quirós, F.G.: Challenges and hurdles of eHealth implementation in developing countries. Stud. Health Technol. Inform. **216**, 434–437 (2015)
3. Lasker, R.D., Humphreys, B.L., Braithwaite, W.R.: Committee, U.S.–PHDC. Making a Powerful Connection: The Health of the Public and the National Information Infrastructure. https://www.nlm.nih.gov/pubs/staffpubs/lo/makingpd.html
4. Neto, A.R.R., Barreto, G.A.: On the application of ensembles of classifiers to the diagnosis of pathologies of the vertebral column: a comparative analysis. IEEE Lat. Am. Trans. **7**, 487–496 (2009)
5. Ansari, S., Sajjad, F., ul-Qayyum, Z., Naveed, N., Shafi, I.: Diagnosis of vertebral column disorders using machine learning classifiers, June 2013
6. Mandal, I.: Developing new machine learning ensembles for quality spine diagnosis. Knowl.-Based Syst. **73**, 298–310 (2015)
7. Tosteson, A.N.A., Skinner, J.S., Tosteson, T.D., Lurie, J.D., Andersson, G.B., Berven, S., Grove, M.R., Hanscom, B., Blood, E.A., Weinstein, J.N.: The cost effectiveness of surgical versus nonoperative treatment for lumbar disc herniation over two years: evidence from the spine patient outcomes research trial (SPORT). Spine **33**, 2108–2115 (2008)
8. OECD: Magnetic resonance imaging (MRI) units. OECD Publishing (2015)
9. OECD: Computed tomography (CT) scanners. OECD Publishing (2015)
10. OECD: Health expenditure per capita. In: Health at a Glance 2013, pp. 154–155. OECD Publishing (2013)
11. OECD: Health spending. OECD Publishing (2014)
12. Hansson, E., Hansson, T.: The cost–utility of lumbar disc herniation surgery. Eur. Spine J. **16**, 329–337 (2007)
13. DMN 1.1. http://www.omg.org/spec/DMN/1.1/
14. WHO | Health policy. http://www.who.int/topics/health_policy/en/
15. Oyedotun, O.K., Olaniyi, E.O., Khashman, A.: Disk hernia and spondylolisthesis diagnosis using biomechanical features and neural network. Technol. Health Care **24**, 267–279 (2016)
16. Bache, K., Lichman, M.: UCI machine learning repository, p. 901 (2013). http://archive.ics.uci.edu/ml/
17. Rocha Neto, Ajalmar, R., Sousa, R., A. Barreto, G., Cardoso, Jaime, S.: Diagnostic of pathology on the vertebral column with embedded reject option. In: Vitrià, J., Sanches, J.M., Hernández, M. (eds.) IbPRIA 2011. LNCS, vol. 6669, pp. 588–595. Springer, Heidelberg (2011). doi:10.1007/978-3-642-21257-4_73
18. Berthonnaud, E., Dimnet, J., Roussouly, P., Labelle, H.: Analysis of the sagittal balance of the spine and pelvis using shape and orientation parameters. J. Spinal Disord. Tech. **18**, 40–47 (2005)
19. Kalpakcioglu, B., Altinbilek, T., Senel, K.: Determination of spondylolisthesis in low back pain by clinical evaluation. J. Back Musculoskelet. Rehabil. **22**, 27–32 (2009)
20. Vibert, B.T., Sliva, C.D., Herkowitz, H.N.: Treatment of instability and spondylolisthesis: surgical versus nonsurgical treatment. Clin. Orthop. **443**, 222–227 (2006)
21. Humphreys, S.C., Eck, J.C.: Clinical evaluation and treatment options for herniated lumbar disc. Am. Fam. Physician **59**, 575–582 (1999). 587–588

22. Killeen, K.L., Girard, S., DeMeo, J.H., Shanmuganathan, K., Mirvis, S.E.: Using CT to diagnose traumatic lumbar hernia. Am. J. Roentgenol. **174,** 1413–1415 (2000)
23. D'Andrea, G., Trillò, G., Roperto, R., Celli, P., Orlando, E.R., Ferrante, L.: Intradural lumbar disc herniations: the role of MRI in preoperative diagnosis and review of the literature. Neurosurg. Rev. **27**, 75–80 (2003)
24. Daffner, S.D., Hymanson, H.J., Wang, J.C.: Cost and use of conservative management of lumbar disc herniation before surgical discectomy. Spine J. **10**, 463–468 (2010)
25. Kaplan, R.M., Frosch, D.L.: Decision making in medicine and health care. Ann. Rev. Clin. Psychol. **1**, 525–556 (2005)
26. Bates, D.W., Kuperman, G.J., Wang, S., Gandhi, T., Kittler, A., Volk, L., Spurr, C., Khorasani, R., Tanasijevic, M., Middleton, B.: Ten commandments for effective clinical decision support: making the practice of evidence-based medicine a reality. J. Am. Med. Inf. Assoc. **10**, 523–530 (2003)
27. Marewski, J.N., Gigerenzer, G.: Heuristic decision making in medicine. Dialogues Clin. Neurosci. **14**, 77–89 (2012)
28. Clemente, C.: Gray's Anatomy of the Human Body. Lea & Febiger, Philadelphia (1985)
29. Barrey, C.: Current strategies for the restoration of adequate lordosis during lumbar fusion. World J. Orthop. **6**, 117 (2015)
30. MacKay, D.J.C.: Information Theory, Inference and Learning Algorithms. Cambridge University Press, Cambridge (2003)
31. Qian, N.: On the momentum term in gradient descent learning algorithms. Neural Netw. **12**, 145–151 (1999)
32. Pewsner, D.: Ruling a diagnosis in or out with SpPIn and SnNOut: a note of caution. BMJ **329**, 209–213 (2004)
33. lm.dvi - lm.pdf. https://www.cs.nyu.edu/~roweis/notes/lm.pdf
34. Shirangi, M.G., Emerick, A.A.: An improved TSVD-based Levenberg–Marquardt algorithm for history matching and comparison with Gauss-Newton. J. Pet. Sci. Eng. **143**, 258–271 (2016)
35. Burden, F., Winkler, D.: Bayesian regularization of neural networks. Methods Mol. Biol. **458**, 25–44 (2008). Clifton
36. BPMN 2.0. http://www.omg.org/spec/BPMN/2.0/
37. Butt, S., Saifuddin, A.: The imaging of lumbar spondylolisthesis. Clin. Radiol. **60**, 533–546 (2005)
38. Forristall, R.M., Marsh, H.O., Pay, N.T.: Magnetic resonance imaging and contrast CT of the lumbar spine: comparison of diagnostic methods and correlation with surgical findings. Spine. **13**, 1049–1054 (1988)
39. MathWorks – Makers of MATLAB and Simulink - MathWorks Deutschland. http://de.mathworks.com/

KSD: An Ontology-Driven Yet Semantically Transparent Application Development Tool

Dibyanshu Jaiswal[✉] and Sounak Dey

TCS Research and Innovation Labs, Kolkata, India
{dibyanshu.jaiswal,sounak.d}@tcs.com

Abstract. To come up with a semantic web application, it requires skills from two major backgrounds: (*a*) domain experts to model and populate a semantic knowledge base; and (*b*) application developers to understand the domain ontology and then build an interface for end users. Learning and using such tools is an overhead and slows down the development process. To address these problems, our paper proposes KSD - Knowledge Serializer and De-serializer tool, that takes an ontology as an input and represents it in a structured form (like JSON, XML) while preserving the underlying semantic information. This format is adaptable to the changes in the underlying ontology and can be used to create user interface, web services and other application modules.

Keywords: Serialization · Semantic user interface · Ontology-driven user interface · Semantic data processing

1 Introduction

Application development in the age of Internet of Things (IoT) requires knowledge and data exchange within and across multiple domains like healthcare, transportation etc. A common data representation format (like RDF) combined with a knowledge schema (like an ontology) is a popular way to handle this issue, which helps to understand the underlying semantics of the data. Though many ontologies are available from various sources in multiple domains, selecting proper ontology to address application requirements is the first hurdle for an application developer.

Once the ontologies are selected, next challenge is populating it with relevant data, which require domain experts to be well versed with (i) semantic data representation techniques like OWL, Turtle, N3 etc.; and (ii) understand how tools like Protégé[1], TopBraid Composer[2] etc. work. This initial learning barrier, slows down the application development process. Not only this, insufficient knowledge of such tools may lead to asserting wrong entailments, causing inconsistencies and effect reliability of the end application.

---

[1] http://protege.stanford.edu/.

[2] http://www.topquadrant.com/tools/modeling-topbraid-composer-standard-edition/.

© Springer International Publishing AG 2017
I. Ciuciu et al. (Eds.): OTM 2016 Workshops, LNCS 10034, pp. 228–235, 2017.
DOI: 10.1007/978-3-319-55961-2_23

On the other hand, similar depth of knowledge is also required by the application developers for (a) using the ontology to implement different business logic and rules and (b) for coming up with an user friendly interface for the underlying ontology. In most of the cases, an application concentrates on few particular concepts and relations from an ontology. Furthermore, any change in ontology (say addition, deletion of a concept or property) becomes an overhead for the application/interface to adapt with. The authors of this paper strongly feel that the development of a semantic web application can be automated to a certain extent, independent to changes in the underlying concept and relations.

This paper proposes **KSD - Knowledge Serializer and De-serializer** tool - an ontology broker capable of representing ontological entities in an easily interpretable way for the application developers. KSD utilizes the inherent structure of the ontology. i.e. (a) taxonomical relationships; (b) properties; (c) restrictions; and (d) property characteristics for this purpose. The paper is organized as follows: Sect. 2 addresses the state of the art for creating such dynamic tools. Section 3 describes the architecture, inherent processes and implementation of the KSD tool. Finally, Sect. 4 concludes the paper.

2 Related Work

To create and interact with ontologies there are some useful tools like Protégé, TopBraid Composer etc. Though they are rich in feature, but for a layman it is hard to understand and use these tools effectively to populate or modify the ontology. Another set of tools such as Jena Fuseki server[3], OpenLink Virtuoso [6] server enable query endpoints for knowledge bases but that requires expert knowledge of SPARQL and the ontology structure. Various efforts as discussed below, have been made to ease up aforesaid overheads.

OntoPlay [5], is a framework that allows dynamic creation of user interfaces that guide naïve users to define new class restrictions and individuals. It uses a *Condition Builder* to define conditions on given root class w.r.t different properties and its corresponding range values, listed as nested drop down menus. The major limitation of the framework is the condition builder being tightly coupled with a specified root class. Though the framework can adapt to the changes in the ontology, but that requires restarting the application to see the changes.

The Event Dashboard [8] is another example of an ontology driven user interface. It uses SSN ontology and event constraints of sensor observations. It only allows creation of observation constraints (no individuals). Furthermore, the user interface provided with this is tightly coupled with the specific classes of SSN ontology and hence cannot be used as a generic tool.

Authors in the paper [1] uses the concept of model driven engineering to derive user interface from a domain ontology. It uses a presentation model, tightly coupled with the domain ontology, to highlight different aspects of that ontology. But it requires the domain ontology to be extensively annotated w.r.t. user interface components.

---

[3] http://jena.sourceforge.net/.

3   Knowledge Serializer and De-serializer (KSD)

KSD is a tool aimed to ease the semantic application development process. It takes an annotated ontology as an input and provides APIs (both Java and RESTful web services), to represent the semantics asserted in the ontology in a serialized representation (such as JSON, XML etc.), which is semantically transparent, easy to use and better understood by the application developers. The reverse protocol may be used to modify content of ontology via this representation. Since the developers interact with the serialized representations only, it saves the initial overhead of learning semantic technologies.

In next few sub sections, we discuss the architecture, working and implementation of the KSD tool, with JSON as an example serialization format and Algopedia ontology [4, 7].

3.1   Architecture of KSD

Figure 1 shows an architecture block diagram of KSD tool. It consists of three major blocks interacting with each other.

Knowledge Base: is the physical knowledge repository created from the input ontology.

Serializer: responsible to produce a serialized representation (like JSON) of a specified entity in the knowledge base. This representation consists of the properties of a given entity, along with its corresponding type and values the property may take.

De-serializer: is the block responsible to parse the incoming serialized representation back to the semantic representation of knowledge base.

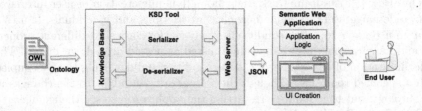

Fig. 1. KSD architecture

The tool as a whole communicates via either Java APIs or RESTful Web Services with an application. In broad sense, KSD tool can be treated as a broker which leverage the advantages of semantic technologies, in a transparent manner without the need to indulge in details of semantic technologies. The serialized representation can then be used by application developers to make user interfaces and write application logic to create, modify, query application entities.

3.2   Working of KSD Tool

KSD uses the inherent semantic structure of the ontology i.e. its taxonomical relationships, properties, restriction and annotations. Based on application requirement, Serializer transforms the inherent semantic structure to a JSON representation. Each such a serialized representation is a semantic independent representation of a given entity in the ontology, obtained from ontological entailments. In case of JSON, one can add/modify the <key,value> pairs and revert back to the De-serializer that transforms the serialized representation back to the semantic representation. Thus, serialized representation structure is used as a protocol to send and receive information between developers and KSD tool.

Not only this, the protocol is dynamic in nature, independent of any given class and is adaptable to the changes in the ontology. Any addition or deletion of concepts and properties made to the knowledge base, automatically reflects back in the serialization reproduced hence forth, without any further coding effort made. For every invocation, with a class as an input, the system iterates over each of the properties asserted for the given class and adds a <key,value> pair to construct its corresponding JSON representation, as discussed in detail below.

Serializer: Knowledge Base to JSON - The job of the Serializer is to take a class or an individual as an input *object*, parse the ontology for the assertions made against it and hence represent them in terms of <key,value> pairs to return a JSON representation of the input *object*, based on different ontology structures.

Taxonomical structure of a given class, is represented as a JSON object, with the class name as *key* and its *value* being an array of JSON objects representing its subclasses. Given an input class, Serializer iterates over its subclasses (recursively), to create an array of JSON objects representing the sub classes. If there is no subclass, then *value* is set to *Leaf*. Figure 2, shows the snapshot of Protégé class hierarchy of a class say, Algorithms, and its corresponding JSON representation.

Object and *datatype* **properties** of a given class are also represented as a JSON object by Serializer. Each such property is represented via a <key,value>

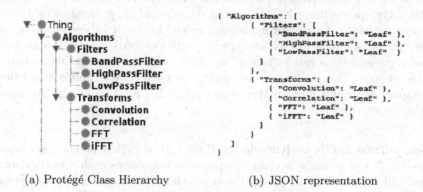

(a) Protégé Class Hierarchy   (b) JSON representation

Fig. 2. Class hierarchy serialization

Table 1. Properties to JSON representation

Case	Property type	Is functional	Range type	JSON representation of range as *value*
1	Object	Yes	Class	JSON object property representation of the range class
2	Object	No	Class	Array of JSON object property representation when the property is functional
3	Object	Yes	Enumerated class	Array of URI's/names of the individuals of the enumerated class
4	Object	No	Enumerated class	Array of JSON object property representation when the property is functional
5	Datatype	Yes	Built in dataype	String asserting the range
6	Datatype	No	Built in dataype	Array of JSON representation when the property is functional

pair, with *key* denoting property name or property URI and the *value* being a JSON representation of the corresponding range of the property. For a given class as an input, the Serializer iterates over each asserted properties. If the range of the property is an object, Serializer recursively obtains the JSON representation of the range class. The JSON representation of the range depends on certain factors such as (*a*) the type of the property (i.e. whether it is a object or datatype property), (*b*) whether the property is functional or not, and (*c*) if the range of property is an enumerated class or not. Table 1 lists the different combinations of the above factors and their corresponding *value* representation in JSON.

Figure 3a shows the graph view of the property *has ConfigurationParameter* for *Algorithms* class. The corresponding JSON representation as shown in Fig. 3b is obtained by following the rules stated in Table 1 above. In case of **individuals**, Serializer has a similar output (Fig. 3c) showing instance values for *ConfigurationParameters*. **Restriction** are represented in a similar fashion as for object and datatype properties, with appropriate domain and range of values as defined by the constraints. **Annotations**, being a special kind of datatype property, are represented in a similar way as datatype properties as listed in Table 1. Such Serialized representations can be treated as blank template representing an entity in the ontology. This can be used in creating user interface for different entities. A template with user input is then sent back to the KSD tool to be processed by the De-serializer.

De-serializer: JSON to Knowledge Base - De-serializer accepts user input data (Fig. 3c) in a similar serialized representation, parses each <key,value> pairs, and creates new instances based on the attributes like type of property (*key*) and JSON element in the *value*. Table 2, lists different cases of

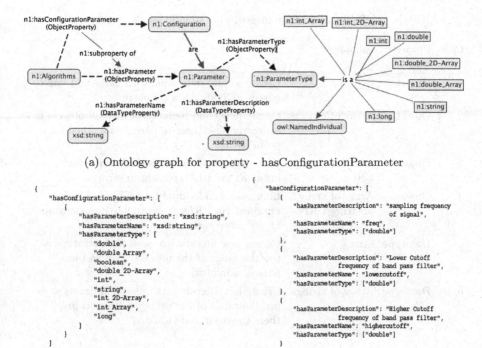

(a) Ontology graph for property - hasConfigurationParameter

```
{
    "hasConfigurationParameter": [
        {
            "hasParameterDescription": "xsd:string",
            "hasParameterName": "xsd:string",
            "hasParameterType": [
                "double",
                "double_Array",
                "boolean",
                "double_2D-Array",
                "int",
                "string",
                "int_2D-Array",
                "int_Array",
                "long"
            ]
        }
    ]
}
```

```
{
    "hasConfigurationParameter": [
        {
            "hasParameterDescription": "sampling frequency
                                        of signal",
            "hasParameterName": "freq",
            "hasParameterType": ["double"]
        },
        {
            "hasParameterDescription": "Lower Cutoff
                            frequency of band pass filter",
            "hasParameterName": "lowercutoff",
            "hasParameterType": ["double"]
        },
        {
            "hasParameterDescription": "Higher Cutoff
                            frequency of band pass filter",
            "hasParameterName": "highercutoff",
            "hasParameterType": ["double"]
        }
    ]
}
```

(b) Serialized representation of concept   (c) Serialized representation of instance

Fig. 3. Serialization example

<key,value> pairs and their corresponding interpretation. Each of the cases (as in Table 2) can be mapped to the corresponding cases in Table 1, hence preserving the semantics of the information being gathered from the user.

3.3   Implementation of KSD

KSD tool is a Java based RESTful web service application that takes ontology as an input and exposes REST APIs corresponding to the ontology. It uses Apache Jena[4] framework to connect and interface with the ontology and GSON[5] library for JSON representation. To expose the functionalities as REST APIs it makes uses of Java API for RESTful Web Services (JAX-RS)[6].

APIs such as *classHierarchy* - to get class hierarchy of concepts (Fig. 2b), *prototypeInstance* - to get a template of a concept for an instance (Fig. 3b), *instances* - to add, browse, delete an instance (Fig. 3c), *editInstance* - modify an instance, *query* - to query the database (in SPARQL) are made available. Using the above APIs, one can develop a complete web application to browse,

---

[4] Apache Jena - https://jena.apache.org/.
[5] Google GSON - https://github.com/google/gson.
[6] JAX-RS - https://jax-rs-spec.java.net/.

Table 2. JSON representation to individuals

Case	Property type	*value* type	Task
1	Object	Object	Create a child individual with *value* and link to parent individual via property *key*
2	Object	Array of objects	Create new child individuals with all objects in array and link them to parent individual via property *key*
3	Object	Array of string URI's	Link parent individual to child individuals obtained via URI's present in strings
4	Object	Array of array of string URI's	Link parent individual to child individuals obtained via URI's present in strings elements of the subsequent arrays
5	Datatype	String	Create new literal with *value* and datatype as per the range of the property *key* and link to parent individual
6	Datatype	Array of strings	Create new literals with *value* and datatype as per the range of the property *key* and link them to parent individual

populate and query entities of a semantic web application, without the need of indulging into semantic technologies. Currently deployed instance of KSD tool can be found in [2, 3, 7].

4   Conclusion

In this paper, we described a serialization-deserialization based generic tool, named KSD, to represent and modify semantic information in easy-to-understand manner for any given ontology. This tool enables naïve application developers to exploit the advantages of semantic technologies without having any prior knowledge of related tools and technologies. At present, we are trying to implement an ontology marketplace as a crowd-sourced collection of different ontologies. For any given ontology, same set of APIs, will be made available. This will be leveraged by the KSD tool. Naïve developers can use these APIs from the marketplace to use in their own application.

References

1. Caadas, J., Palma, J., Tnez, S.: Model-driven rich user interface generation from ontologies for data-intensive web applications (2011)
2. Dey, S., Jaiswal, D., Dasgupta, R., Misra, A.: A semantic sensor network (SSN) ontology based tool for semantic exploration of sensor. In: Semantic Web Challenge Competition ISWC (2014)

3. Dey, S., Jaiswal, D., Dasgupta, R., Mukherjee, A.: Organization and management of semantic sensor information using SSN ontology: an energy meter use case. In: 2015 9th International Conference on Sensing Technology (ICST). IEEE (2015)
4. Dey, S., Jaiswal, D., Paul, H.S., Mukherjee, A.: A semantic algorithm repository and workflow designer tool: signal processing use case. In: Mandler, B., et al. (eds.) IoT360 2015. LNICSSITE, vol. 170, pp. 53–61. Springer, Heidelberg (2016). doi:10. 1007/978-3-319-47075-7_7
5. Drozdowicz, M., Ganzha, M., Paprzycki, M., Szmeja, P., Wasielewska, K.: Onto-Play - a flexible user-interface for ontology-based systems. In: AT (2012)
6. Erling, O., Mikhailov, I.: OpenLink Virtuoso: Open-Source Edition: RDF Support in the Virtuoso DBMS. http://virtuoso.openlinksw.com
7. Jaiswal, D., et al.: Demo: a smart framework for IoT analytic workflow development. In: Proceedings of the 13th ACM Conference on Embedded Networked Sensor Systems. ACM (2015)
8. Yu, J., Taylor, K.: Event dashboard: capturing user-defined semantics events for event detection over real-time sensor data (2013)

Using Extended Stopwords Lists to Improve the Quality of Academic Abstracts Clustering

Svetlana Popova[1,2(✉)] and Vera Danilova[3]

[1] ITMO University, Saint-petersburg, Russia
svp@list.ru
[2] St. Petersburg State University, St. Petersburg, Russia
[3] Russian Presidential Academy of National Economy and Public Administration,
Moscow, Russia
vera.danilova@e-campus.uab.cat

Abstract. Knowledge extraction from scientific documents plays an important role in the development of academic databases and services. We focus on the processing of abstracts to academic papers for the purposes of research data structuring that includes various subtasks, such as key phrase extraction and clustering. The use of abstracts is beneficial, because authors keep up with formal and stylistic requirements imposed by the publishers, and, therefore, informational and language patterns can be revealed. From our viewpoint, the existence of these patterns makes it possible to perform the cross-task application of techniques used for abstracts processing. The aim of the paper is to show it.

Keywords: Clustering · Stopwords · Document representation · Extended stopwords list construction · Natural Language Processing

1 Introduction and Experiment Description

These experiments aim at studying whether it is possible to enhance the academic abstracts clustering performance by applying extended stopwords lists obtained during key phrase extraction optimization on another collection. The hypothesis is that in both cases (clustering and key phrase extraction) the elimination of common lexicon in abstracts leads to the performance quality improvement. We have assumed that similar approaches and tools can be used for both key phrase extraction and clustering, which allows us to conclude that the cross-task application of results is possible.

Our previous study shows that key phrase extraction performance can be enhanced by using an extended stopwords list [5]. Additional a number of studies have shown that in the field of document annotation with key words/phrases nouns and adjectives are the parts of speech that should form the document

The reported study was funded by RFBR according to the research project No. 16-37-00430 mol_a and partially supported by the Government of Russian Federation, Grant 074-U01.

I. Ciuciu et al. (Eds.): OTM 2016 Workshops, LNCS 10034, pp. 236–241, 2017.
DOI: 10.1007/978-3-319-55961-2_24

representation for the effective key phrase extraction [6–10]. This observation has allowed for a hypothesis on the improvement of clustering quality by using only nouns and adjectives for document representation and extended stopwords list. A hierarchical agglomerative clustering method (average-link algorithm) from the Weka package[1] has been chosen, because it is known to achieve good results in short-text clustering. The experiment has the following structure:

1. clustering of academic abstracts collections using a standard stopwords list (baseline);
2. clustering of academic abstracts collections using an extended stopwords list;
3. clustering of academic abstracts collections using a standard stopwords list when the documents are represented by nouns and adjectives;
4. clustering of academic abstracts collections using an extended stopwords list when the documents are represented by nouns and adjectives.

2   Description of the Datasets

Testing and quality evaluation of the approach have been performed on the CICling, EasyAbstracts and SEPLN-CICling collections, which are frequently used by the research community for testing (narrow-domain) short-text clustering algorithms [1–4][2]. All of the collections contain academic abstracts that have been manually divided by the experts into 4 classes. Gold standards are known for each of the collections. The size of each collection is of 48 documents. The link to the collections that we have given before refers to the pre-processed collections, where punctuation and stopwords are removed and partial stemming is performed. We have formed the same collections, however, containing original abstracts without any pre-processing. In the next step, part-of-speech tagging has been done using the Stanford PoS tagging tool[3].

The extended stopwords list has been constructed on the basis of INSPEC [5–7,9,10], one of the main collections for key phrase extraction from abstracts. A detailed description of INSPEC is given in [6]. It contains subcollections: "trial" (1000 documents) "test" (500 documents). Each of the collections has a gold standard - the result of the document annotation with key phrases.

3   Construction of the Extended Stopwords List

We first define the algorithm of key phrase extraction similar to the one used in [5]. Key phrases are extracted from text as maximum-length continuous sequences of nouns and adjectives. Punctuation marks, stopwords and words that belong to a part of speech other than noun or adjective are considered delimiters between key phrases. The sequences containing less than two words are ignored.

---

[1] Weka package: http://www.cs.waikato.ac.nz/ml/weka/.

[2] Pre-processed collections: http://sites.google.com/site/merrecalde/resources.

[3] Stanford PoS tagging tool: http://nlp.stanford.edu/software/tagger.html.

Secondly, the method of key phrase extraction evaluation should be defined. Each INSPEC text is represented by a list of key phrases, annotated by the experts. The results of the automatic key phrase extraction are compared to this expert annotation by using F_{score} (full description [5]).

INSPEC "trial" has been used for the construction of the extended stopwords list as follows. Nouns and adjectives from the collection dictionary are added to the standard stopwords list sequentially, one at a time. Next, the above described key phrase extraction algorithm (detailed description [5]) is run on the "trial" and in case the addition of a specific word to the stopwords list leads to an improvement of key phrase extraction quality of more than a threshold n, the added word is marked as "bad". Sample "bad" words are: *results, such, novel, other, new, several, study, various, previous, main, many, different* and others. This procedure is applied to all nouns and adjectives from the "trial" dictionary, and the resulting "bad" words get added to the standard stopwords list. The extended stopwords list obtained in this way has been used in [5] for key phrase extraction from the "test" subcollection and allowed to significantly improve the performance as compared to the case of the standard stopwords list use. In this study we apply the extended stopwords list for clustering purposes.

4   Clustering Quality Evaluation

To evaluate the clustering quality a standard metrics based on F_{score} was used

$$F = \sum_i \frac{|G_i|}{|D|} \max_j F_{ij}, \tag{1}$$

where: $F_{ij} = \frac{2 \cdot P_{ij} \cdot R_{ij}}{P_{ij} + R_{ij}}$, $P_{ij} = \frac{|G_i \cap C_j|}{|G_i|}$, $R_{ij} = \frac{|G_i \cap C_j|}{|C_j|}$, $G = \{G_i\}_{i=1,...,n}$ - automatically obtained clusters, $|D|$ - the amount of documents in the collection, $C = \{C_j\}_{j=1,...,n}$ - classes, created manually by an expert.

Document representation for clustering. The original texts of academic abstracts are tagged with part-of-speech information and lower-cased, punctuation, stopwords are removed and documents are stemmed with the Porter Stemmer[4]. Each document is represented by a feature vector (the feature space is formed on the basis of the collection dictionary). TF-IDF is used to evaluate the weight of each feature in each of the documents. The similarity between feature vectors is measured using the cosine similarity. The number of clusters is the same as in the gold standard.

Results. The results of the experiments are shown in the Tables below and are related to two stages: (1) stopwords extraction on the basis of the corpus

---

[4] Porter Stemmer: http://tartarus.org/martin/PorterStemmer.

annotated with key phrases; (2) clustering of text collections using the obtained stopwords lists. The following notation is used: n corresponds to the value of the key phrase extraction quality improvement in case of the addition of a word to the standard stopwords list (see Sect. 4). *Baseline* is the result of clustering in case the standard stopwords list is used. *PoS text* denotes the case, where the texts are represented only by nouns and adjectives. *Original text* is the option, where the other parts of speech are not excluded. In Table 1 the results of clustering with the extended stopwords list are shown.

Table 1. Clustering performance with the extended list of stopwords

$n\rightarrow$	Baseline	0005	0002	0001	00007	00005	00001	000007	000001
CICling 2002									
Original text	0.56	0.55	0.55	**0.57**	0.56	0.54	0.56	0.56	0.56
POS text	0.50	0.68	**0.70**	**0.70**	0.55	0.55	0.53	0.53	0.53
SEPLN-CICling 2002									
Original text	0.86	0.86	0.87	0.86	**0.88**	**0.88**	0.86	0.86	0.86
POS text	0.76	0.77	0.77	0.77	0.77	0.77	**0.79**	**0.79**	**0.79**
EasyAbstracts									
Original text	0.76	**0.92**	0.90	0.76	0.71	0.76	0.76	0.76	0.76
POS text	**0.96**	**0.96**	**0.96**	0.94	0.94	0.94	**0.96**	0.94	0.94

These results show that in most cases the extended stopwords list either positively influences the results or makes no effect. In some cases a considerable improvement can be seen. However, for certain values of n the performance drops. In attempt to understand the cause, we have considered the influence of n on the obtained list. Indeed, for large values of n (e.g., $n = 0.005$) the standard stopwords list gets populated with the words that ensure the maximum improvement of the key phrase extraction quality (general lexicon in the first place), while the smaller the values of n - the more domain-specific words end up into the list. Therefore, the use of very small values ($n < 0.0001$) does not make sense. It is also of importance that the stopwords source collection should not be topically close to one or several clusters of the clustered collection, because the words that are specific to one of the clusters may fall into the stopwords list and cause a performance drop. As a solution, we have taken the maximum-length stopwords list (for $n = 0.000001$) and left only those words that are present in the dictionaries of all three test clustering collections. For the obtained short list of additional stopwords, the evaluation of clustering quality has been performed. The results are in Table 2 in the row "Short list". The manual checking of the short list has shown that almost all of the domain-specific words have been removed, except *sense, entropy, formalism, formalization, target, extension, form, features*. We have excluded them and run the clustering algorithm once again. The results are in the row "Short list cleaned".

Table 2. Clustering performance with the short list of additional stopwords

	CICling 2002		SEPLN-CICling		EasyAbstracts	
	Original text	POS text	Original text	POS text	Original text	POS text
Shot stop list	0.54	0.70	0.81	0.79	0.90	0.96
Shot stop list cleaned	0.56	**0.70**	**0.86**	0.79	0.90	**0.98**

5   Discussion of Results and Conclusions

The results of academic abstracts clustering achieved using the average-link algorithm, an extended stopwords list and document representation by nouns and adjectives allowed to get very good results in compare with the state of the art. The study has shown that the set of general-purpose terms is more or less the same for different collections, which allows for the cross-task application. Stopwords have been extracted on the basis of the INSPEC. On the one hand, the lower the values of n, the more general-purpose words get into the stopwords lists. On the other hand, the lower the values of n, the more domain-specific terms fall into the lists. In case the obtained lists are used to process a topically unrelated collection, the presence of these domain-specific terms will have no influence on the results, because they will not form part of the collection dictionary. However, if they are in the dictionary, the results will be distorted. Our solution is to remove these words from the list and leave only those that are domain- and study-independent. The final version of the stopwords list includes 386 terms (inluding the standard list).

References

1. Cagnina, L., Errecalde, M., Ingaramo, D., Rosso, P.: A discrete particle swarm optimizer for clustering short text corpora. In: BIOMA 2008, pp. 93–103 (2008)
2. Errecalde, M., Ingaramo, D., Rosso, P.: ITSA[*]: an effective iterative method for short-text clustering tasks. In: García-Pedrajas, N., Herrera, F., Fyfe, C., Benítez, J.M., Ali, M. (eds.) IEA/AIE 2010. LNCS (LNAI), vol. 6096, pp. 550–559. Springer, Heidelberg (2010). doi:10.1007/978-3-642-13022-9_55
3. Pinto, D.: Analysis of narrow-domain short texts clustering. In: Research report for Diploma de Estudios Avanzados (DEA), Department of Information Systems and Computation, UPV (2007). http://users.dsic.upv.es/~prosso/resources/PintoDEA.pdf. Accessed 31 Mar 2016
4. Pinto, D., Rosso, P., Jimnez, H.: A self-enriching methodology for clustering narrow domain short texts. Comput. J. **54**(7), 1148–1165 (2011)
5. Popova, S., Kovriguina, L., Muromtsev, D., Khodyrev, I.: Stop-words in keyphrase extraction problem. In: Proceedings of 14th Conference of Open Innovations Association FRUCT Helsinki, Finland (2013)

6. Hulth, A.: Improved automatic keyword extraction given more linguistic knowledge. In: 2003 Conference on Empirical Methods in Natural Language Processing, pp. 216–223 (2003)
7. Mihalcea, R., Tarau, P.: TextRank: bringing order into texts. In: 2004 Conference on Empirical Methods in Natural Language Processing, pp. 404–411 (2004)
8. Xiaojun, W., Xiao, J.: Exploiting neighborhood knowledge for single document summarization and keyphrase extraction. ACM Trans. Inf. Syst. **28**(2), Artical ID 8 (2010)
9. Zesch, T., Gurevych, I.: Approximate Matching for Evaluating Keyphrase Extraction. In: 2009 International Conference RANLP, pp. 484–489 (2009)
10. Popova, S., Khodyrev, I.: Ranking in keyphrase extraction problem: is it useful to use statistics of words occurrences? In.: proceedings of the Institute for System Programming of the RAS, book 26, 2014, 4 (2014)

Towards Ontology-Based Safety Information Management in the Aviation Industry

Bogdan Kostov[✉], Jana Ahmad, and Petr Křemen

Faculty of Electrical Engineering,
Czech Technical University in Prague, Praha, Czech Republic
{bogdan.kostov,jana.ahmad,petr.kremen}@fel.cvut.cz

Abstract. Aviation is a high risk industry where safety management is mandatory for organizations. On a global scale, safety management is hierarchical, i.e. national authorities manage safety of the sector, controlling organizations which in turn manage safety of their operations, as well as the safety of their organizational units. It is apparent that safety information management is a key factor to the success of safety management. Improving safety information management in aviation can be achieved by the systematic documentation of safety information and its seamless sharing vertically as well as horizontally through the management hierarchy. Despite attempts to tackle this problem, the industry still suffers from information management issues, e.g. usage of terminologically incompatible safety management frameworks. As a result diverse information repositories, e.g. investigation reports, safety recommendations, or audit reports managed by these frameworks, cannot be efficiently explored and compared. We apply Linked Data principles, e.g. searchability and explorability based on dataset descriptors, to help solving the problem. In this work we propose an ontology-based safety information management for the aviation industry. To achieve this we develop the Aviation Safety Ontology that is modular and covers the contexts of the organization types aerodrome, airline, air traffic management, maintenance and the state civil aviation authority. We test the appropriateness of the proposed ontology by representing safety data in terms of the ontology.

1 Introduction

Aviation is a high risk industry where safety management is mandatory for organizations. Since the first steps towards aviation safety starting with regulations published in the 1920s in the USA, the industry observes reduction of the incident/accident rates [2]. Lower incident rates and the effort to further improve the quality of safety took the industry on a road towards adopting the proactive rather than the reactive safety approach. The reactive approach is based on dealing with incidents after they happen. Proactive safety tries to predict and prevent incidents before they happen. In his work [22], Reason argues that proactive safety can be achieved trough tackling safety breaches using the system approach. Safety management in the aviation industry, on a global scale, is

© Springer International Publishing AG 2017
I. Ciuciu et al. (Eds.): OTM 2016 Workshops, LNCS 10034, pp. 242–251, 2017.
DOI: 10.1007/978-3-319-55961-2_25

hierarchical and highly distributed, e.g. national authorities manage safety of the sector, controlling organizations which in turn manage safety of their operations, as well as the safety of their organizational units. Implementing Reason's ideas on a global scale in practice requires seamless Safety Information Management and Sharing (SIMS) [23]. Despite efforts towards improvement, the problem of global and seamless SIMS remains. A key factor of the quality of SIMS is that the design and implementation of safety data management systems is based on safety standards, manuals and legislation which use incompatible terminologies, hence inducing the information silos problem [13].

Linked Data principles address the information silos problem found in SIMS. In this work we present the Aviation Safety Ontology (ASO), a candidate shared ontology. We present an evaluation of ASO by integration of incident and audit reports. Furthermore, the resulting datasets are used to design content based dataset descriptors, such as summary descriptors [9], which will improve searchability and explorability of safety data.

The rest of the paper is structured as follows. In Sect. 2 we discuss the state of art and point out our contributions. In Sect. 3 we briefly describe our ontology engineering methodology. Section 4 presents the modules of ASO. Section 5 presents core modules of ASO. Subsect. 5.1 describes the aviation domain ontology. Subsect. 5.2 describes the Safety task ontology. In Sect. 6 presents the evaluation methodology of ASO. In Sect. 7, we conclude and discuss future work.

2   Related Work

In practice, there are many safety standards and manuals, [4,5,21] to name a few. Other initiatives try to define vocabularies where common aviation safety terms are defined, e.g. [1,3,11]. The ECCAIRS system [11] stands out because it defines an XML based machine communication interface [12]. The main problem is however that they target specific use-cases and use incompatible terminologies. Although these documents and tools are based on a common conceptualization and help unify and improve the safety management process, they use incompatible terminologies.

In the paper [6] the authors describe the development of an aircraft design ontology designed to facilitate the collaboration among experts. This work is relevant in the domain of aviation and it covers some common concepts like the Aircraft and its sub-components.

In the paper [19] the authors propose an ontology for Operational Risk Management (ORM) to facilitate the ORM related information sharing across organizational unit boundaries. The proposed ontology is domain independent and it defines the relevant generic concepts used on ORM. An essential part of ORM is the documentation of events. The work found in [16,17] lays the ontological foundations for the representation events and it allows for the representation of event instances (such as incidents and audit findings) as well as event types (such as risk and hazards).

In our work we contribute by designing an Aviation Safety Ontology. We design the ontology based on domain terminology found in aviation safety standards and manuals (e.g. [1,3,5,11]) as well as safety data found in incident and audit reports. We combine the domain terminology with relevant and well defined state of art conceptualizations.

3   Ontology and Ontology Engineering Methodology

The term ontology (in other words the study of existence) originates in philosophy. In computer science, there are several definitions of what is an ontology. We adopt the definition found in [24] – "*An ontology is a formal, explicit specification of a shared conceptualisation*".

There are four different types of ontologies, i.e. foundational ontologies, domain ontologies, task ontologies and application ontologies. Foundational ontologies provide definitions of fundamental concepts and relations used to describe reality, e.g. Endurant, Perdurant or Universal, see Sect. 3.1. Domain ontologies focus on a specific domain of discourse and should use a foundational ontology to describe the terminology of the domain. Task ontologies focus on a specific task which might be shared across multiple domains. And finally, an application ontology is one that specifies the application of a given task in a given domain.

We can divide the development of ASC in two main activities. The first is identifying and developing domain and task ontologies, further referred to as *core ontologies*, that cover well defined conceptualizations of the studied problem aligned with the foundational ontology. The second activity is developing application ontologies based on different use-cases. In this work we consider application ontologies which are found in five different contexts, i.e. aerodrome, airline, air traffic management, maintenance and the state civil aviation authority contexts. We employ an agile methodology based on RapidOWL [7] and Methontology [14].

3.1   Unified Foundational Ontology (UFO)

We build our ontology on top of the Unified Foundational Ontology (UFO) [15]. We choose to use UFO because it is grounded in literature from the fields of Formal Ontology, Cognitive Psychology, Linguistics, Philosophy of Language and Philosophical Logics. To the best of our knowledge UFO modules are not distributed as OWL 2 ontologies, the implementation language of our choice. Although there are transformations between from UFO to OWL [8] they are consider only on the UFO-A module. Our implementation of UFO modules, including UFO-B and UFO-C, in OWL 2 is based on the OLED's simple transformation [8].

UFO consists of a static object model part (UFO-A) [15], an event model part (UFO-B) [17] and a social and agent model part (UFO-C) [20]. The ontology particulars are split into endurants and perdurants, where endurants are:

- Agent: is a proactive object, it has its own beliefs, intentions, and goals.
- Physical object: which is a complex of:
  - Spatial Object: An object with spatial extent. It can provide reference for locating other objects.
  - Technical System: (such as Equipment, Power System, Vehicles)
- Service: service which is provided by some agent to another agent.
- Data, Weather

and perdurants are:

- Event: temporal entity, e.g. a runway incursion is an event that describes incorrect entrance of an object on the runway
- Object Snapshot: is an immutable state description of an object within a situation.
- Situation: is a snapshot of object states valid in the given temporal range.

The overall structure of the UFO ontology is shown in the Fig. 1.

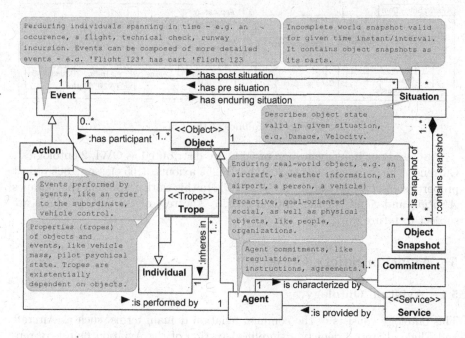

Fig. 1. Main concepts of the UFO ontology

4   Aviation Safety Ontology

The ASO ontology we present emerges from the requirements we designed in the Aviation Domain analysis phase. Our observation is that most safety related data and information deals with the description perdurant types (e.g. factor types, risks, barriers) and of their instances (e.g. incident, audit finding). Obviously perdurant descriptions are based on endurants, e.g. persons pilot role in an flight event or the the level traffic flow in a situation. Upon review of safety manuals and standards we reveal that there are many vocabularies and taxonomies. Alignment of terminology found in these documents is done with the help of experts.

During the analysis of the aviation safety domain we identify several modules and relationships among them, see Fig. 2. The modules in the figure are divided in two, the Safety Aviation Core (ASC) ontology (on the left) and Application Onotologies (on the right). The ASC ontology contains concepts and relations common in the domain. ASC is composed of the modules containing Aviation, Safety, Documentation, Communication and Organizational Process.

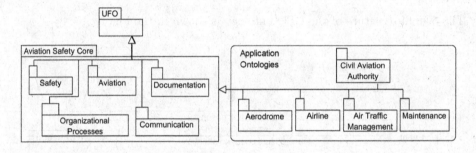

Fig. 2. Modules of the ASC

ASO and our implementation of UFO are distributed as OWL 2 ontologies[1]. Currently the ontology has ontology has 11255 axioms, 3165 classes, 1865 object properties and its expressivity is $\mathcal{SHIQ}(\mathcal{D})$. In this work we present the modules *Aviation* and *Safety* of the ASC in Sect. 5. The rest of the ASC modules are subject to future work.

5   Aviation Safety Core

5.1   Aviation Ontology

This ontology consists of the common aviation domain terms, such as Aircraft and Flight. Figure 3 depicts a simplified version of the Aviation Ontology represented in UFO. The *Object* classes (those that belong to the class hierarchy with root class *Object* or their parts) are aircraft, vehicle, agent, aerodrome part, equipment, etc. Agent actions are on the left side. On the right, we have a categorization of safety events and also other operational events such as *Flight Stage*.

---

[1] http://www.inbas.cz/aviation-safety-ontology.

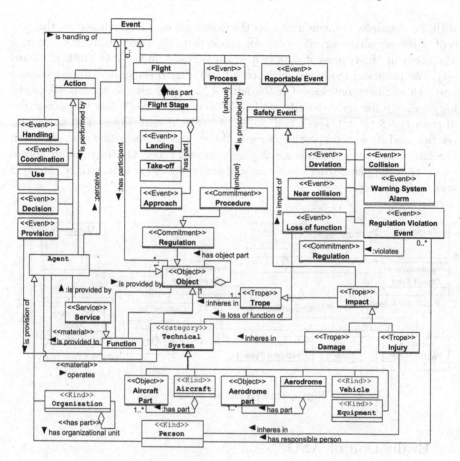

Fig. 3. Aviation domain ontology

The purpose of this conceptualization is to serve as a definition language for safety aviation application ontologies. This can help define specific application classes in a more compatible fashion across different applications. For example terms for aircraft parts such as *engine* or *fuel system* refer to the same meaning regardless of the context, e.g. maintenance or flight operator context.

5.2 Safety Ontology

This ontology consists of the fundamental conceptualizations necessary for the management of safety information. Generally the concept of safety can be defined as *the state of acceptable level of risk*. Safety management can be defined as a *process which improves the level of safety*. In the aviation industry, safety is concerned only with flight risks. Such risks are for example considers risk of aircraft damage, property damage and loss of life during the servicing of regular commercial flight operation. On the other hand aviation safety does not count with, for example, financial risks. As the definition of safety is based on the concept of risk we align our safety ontology module to the conceptualization of Risk Management (RM) presented in [19] which is based on the ISO 31000 standard [18]. The proposed module is enriched by UFO based semantics. Figure 4 shows part of the Safety ontology. On the left we have present the conceptual model for necessary for term definitions, i.e. *Term Type* [2]. We define two categories of term types *Object Types* and *Safety Aviation Event Types*. The *has factor* relation and its sub properties *is contribution* and *is mitigation* (not shown in the figure), are used to define a *risk graph* of event types. On the right are shown events that happen during *Operation* and are typically documented, i.e. *Incident* and *Audit finding*.

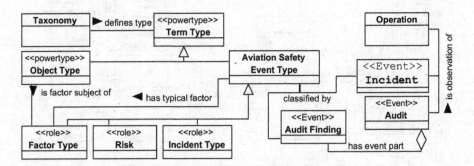

Fig. 4. Conceptual model of factors

6   Evaluation of ASO

The evaluation of ASO is twofold, first by building application ontologies we evaluate the ASC modules and second we conduct an application based evaluation. The application ontologies created for each organization type should represent the organizational structure, its documentation, operational processes and their risk management strategies. Our goal is to be able to represent *incident/risk graphs*, i.e. event/event-types which are factors of incidents/risks. The relevant contents of the application ontologies in this context is taxonomies of relevant entity types, e.g. taxonomy of factors and incidents, type of operations, types of equipment. We look for such taxonomies in the following sources: data schema and taxonomies used in the European Coordination Center for Accident and Incident Reporting System (ECCAIRS) [11]; The Ramp Error Decision Aid (REDA) [5].

For the sake of brevity we will discuss the task ontology only for the Aerodrome organization type and REDA safety manual. The evaluation in the other organization types is similar. REDA describes the investigation of incidents caused by worker performance that occurred during the receiving, unloading,

---

[2] *Powertypes* are classes whose instances of are also classes.

servicing, maintaining, uploading, and dispatching of commercial aircraft at an airport. The manual systematically decomposes the ramp operational process and its environment into components such as involved agents, agent operations and systems. Based on this description the manual further defines safety event categories, i.e. taxonomy of human factors, system failures and incidents. Listing 1 shows an example of the knowledge found in REDA.

Listing 1. Representation of Knowledge found in REDA shown in Turtle [10] (RDF serialization format)

```
1  Incident  asc:hasTypicalContributingFactor  SystemFailure ,
        ContributingFactor .
2  ContributingFactor  asc:hasTypicalContributingFactor  InformationNotUsed ,
3     InformationNotUnderstood , InformationUnderstood .
4  Incident  asc:hasTypicalMitigatingFactor  InformationUnderstood .
5  Information  aso:isFactorSubjectOf  InformationNotUsed ,
6     InformationNotUnderstood .
```

Line one in Listing one to four 1 shows the usage of the properties *asc:hasTypi-calContributingFactor* and *asc:hasTypicalMitigatingFactor* (sub properties of *asc: hasTypicalFactor*) to represent the typical factor graph found in REDA. Lines five to six show how to associate factors with their subject subject.

Furthermore, we conduct an application based evaluation of ASO. Experts evaluate ontology data using a web based application developed for the purpose of viewing and editing reports. We import heterogeneous structured data into the ontology using a schema to ontology mapping. The resulting data is then revised by domain experts through the application. ASO's coverage of the domain is evaluated by enriching imported structured data with additional information about factors, events, participants and their tropes found in full-text descriptions. This way experts discover limitations which are taken as requirements for the next update of ASO. Currently the dataset contains over 250 K triples. Table 1 shows instance count per individual ASO classes.

Table 1. Dataset statistics

Type	Count
Aerodrome	555
Air traffic service	555
Loss of separation	374
Occurrence	587
Runway	187
License	187
Factor	67

7 Conclusion

In this work we analyze the domain of Aviation for the purpose of SIMS. We confirm that the information silos problem is a key factor of the quality of SIMS. We address this factor using Linked Data principles. Specifically we design and develop the Aviation Safety Ontology (ASO) to be used to align diverse aviation safety information. The designed ontology is modular. The part of ASO presented in this paper targets the description of events and event types which is the most common type of information found in aviation safety.

In future work we will target the rest of the modules of ASC. Furthermore, usage of ASO for representing safety data set descriptors will be elaborated. For example, the Air Accidents Investigation Institutes of the Czech Republic maintains a set of aviation investigation reports that might be formally described by an index of *Reports* describing *Safety Events* having *Aircrafts* present in the *Czech Republic* or registered in the *Czech Republic* as participants. Such descriptors might be used to efficiently retrieve relevant aviation safety data sets.

Acknowledgment. This work was supported jointly by grants No. GA 16-09713S Efficient Exploration of Linked Data Cloud of the Grant Agency of the Czech Republic and No. TA04030465 Research and development of progressive methods for measuring aviation organizations safety performance of the Technology Agency of the Czech Republic.

References

1. Lexicon, A.T.M.: www.eurocontrol.int/lexicon/lexicon/en/index.php/Main_Page. Accessed 1 Aug 2016
2. Causes of Fatal Accidents by Decade. http://www.planecrashinfo.com/cause.htm. Accessed 1 Aug 2016
3. Glossary, I.: www.intlaviationstandards.org/apex/f?p=240:1:15338757287208:: NO::P1_X:Glossary. Accessed 1 Aug 2016
4. International Air Transportation Association (IATA) Standards, Manuals and Guidelines. http://www.iata.org/publications/Pages/standards-manuals. aspx. Accessed 1 Aug 2016
5. Ramp Error Decision Aid (REDA) User's Guide, 2013. http://www.faa.gov/ about/initiatives/maintenance_hf/library/documents/media/media/reda_users_ guide_v-8_september2013.pdf. Accessed 1 Aug 2016
6. Ast, M., Glas, M., Roehm, T., Luftfahrt, B.: Creating an ontology for aircraft design. Deutscher Luft- und Raumfahrtkongress 2013 (2013)
7. Auer, S., Herre, H.: RapidOWL — an agile knowledge engineering methodology. In: Virbitskaite, I., Voronkov, A. (eds.) PSI 2006. LNCS, vol. 4378, pp. 424–430. Springer, Heidelberg (2007). doi:10.1007/978-3-540-70881-0_36
8. Barcelos, P.P.F., Dos Santos, V.A., Silva, F.B., Monteiro, M.E., Garcia, A.S.: An automated transformation from OntoUML to OWL and SWRL. CEUR Workshop Proc. **1041**, 130–141 (2013)

9. Blaško, M., Kostov, B., Køemen, P.: Ontology-based dataset exploration - a temporal ontology use-case. In: Intelligent Exploration of Semantic Data (IESD 2016), Kode (2016)
10. Carothers, G., Prud'hommeaux, E.: RDF 1.1 Turtle. W3C Recommendation, W3C, February 2014
11. J.R. Center. European Coordination Center for Accident and Incident Reporting (ECCAIRS)
12. ECCAIRS: ECCAIRS data bridge. Technical report, Joint Research Centre of the European Commission (2015)
13. Ensor, P.S.: The functional silo syndrome. AME Target **16**((Spring Issue)), 16 (1988)
14. Fernández-López, M., Gómez-Pérez, A., Juristo, N.: Methontology: from ontological art towards ontological engineering, March 1997
15. Guizzardi, G.: Ontological foundations for structural conceptual models. Ph.D. thesis, University of Twente, The Netherlands, March 2005
16. Guizzardi, G., Wagner, G.: Towards an ontological foundation of agent-based simulation. In: Proceedings of the Winter Simulation Conference, Phoenix, Dec. Winter Simulation Conference, pp. 284-295 (2011). http://dl.acm.org/citation.cfm?id=2431518.2431549
17. Guizzardi, G., Wagner, G., Almeida Falbo, R., Guizzardi, R.S.S., Almeida, J.P.A.: Towards ontological foundations for the conceptual modeling of events. In: Ng, W., Storey, V.C., Trujillo, J.C. (eds.) ER 2013. LNCS, vol. 8217, pp. 327–341. Springer, Heidelberg (2013). doi:10.1007/978-3-642-41924-9_27
18. ISO: ISO/FDIS 31000 risk management-principles and guidelines. Technical report, International Organization for Standardization, Geneva, Switzerland (2009)
19. Lykourentzou, I., Papadaki, K., Kalliakmanis, A., Djaghloul, Y., Latour, T., Charalabis, I., Kapetanios, E.: Ontology-based operational risk management. In: 13th IEEE Conference on Commerce and Enterprise Computing, CEC 2011, Luxembourg-Kirchberg, Luxembourg, 5–7 September 2011, pp. 153–160 (2011)
20. Nardi, J.C., Falbo, R.d.A., Almeida, J.P.A., Guizzardi, G., Pires, L.F., van Sinderen, M.J., Guarino, N.: Towards a commitment-based reference ontology for services. In: 2013 17th IEEE International Enterprise Distributed Object Computing Conference, pp. 175–184. IEEE, September 2013
21. International Civil Aviation Organization: Safety Management Manual (SMM) (2013)
22. Reason, J.: Human error: models and management. BMJ (Clin. Res. ed.) **320**(7237), 768–770 (2000)
23. Rodriguez, E., Edwards, J.: People, technology, processes and risk knowledge sharing. Electron. J. Knowl. Manag. **8**(1), 139–150 (2010)
24. Studer, R., Benjamins, V., Fensel, D.: Knowledge engineering: principles and methods. Data Knowl. Eng. **25**(1–2), 161–197 (1998)

CASD: A Framework for Context Aware Service Discovery and Selection

Altaf Hussain[1]($\boxtimes$), Wendy MacCaull[1], and Yngve Lamo[2]

[1] St. Francis Xavier University, Antigonish, Nova Scotia, Canada
altaf_sust_82@yahoo.com, wmaccaul@stfx.ca
[2] Bergen University College, Bergen, Norway
yngve.lamo@hib.no

Abstract. We present the architecture for a framework for semantic web-based service discovery, suitable for integration with relational database systems. Existing discovery algorithms often lead to poor results due to limitations of the service description used and lack of domain data. Our framework incorporates context aware service discovery vis a vis dynamic (run-time) update using relational (domain) data from a legacy system. A template for service ontologies is provided, so the user may represent their services and the interrelationships between them. The domain data is represented as an OWL-ontology. The systems takes information in the service and domain ontologies and performs rule based reasoning using rules articulating inter-service dependencies as well as dependencies between services and domain data. An aggregation over service quality properties allows the aggregated selection of the best-suited services. The framework is implemented as a web application following the Service Oriented Architecture; extensive testing shows that the system is robust. Features of the framework are illustrated using a detailed case study for the health-care domain.

Keywords: Ontology · Data integration · Dynamic context representation · Context aware service discovery · Domain and Service Integration

1 Introduction

Nowadays, people are dependent on services which are entities that offer value to consumers. Web Service (WS) [10] is the technology that makes various services available as consumable entities, accessed and consumed through computers, such as the Email Service. WS technology, backed by Service Oriented Architecture (SOA) [16] has gained a lot of focus and popularity in the commercial computing sector as an enabling technology for service planning, development, delivery and management methodology. In addition, with the advancement of Relational Database technology, businesses have invested in and developed data

Acknowledgment: The second author was supported by grant by the Natural Sciences and Engineering Research Council of Canada.

© Springer International Publishing AG 2017
I. Ciuciu et al. (Eds.): OTM 2016 Workshops, LNCS 10034, pp. 252–264, 2017.
DOI: 10.1007/978-3-319-55961-2_26

driven dynamic applications resulting in a new spectrum of web applications supporting business-to-business integration, e-commerce, and industry wide collaboration. These applications are empowered by the WS technology, which provides a platform of independent communication and machine-to-machine interaction. However, WS technologies need extensive human involvement for optimizing service discovery, selection and composition [16].

In recent years, a new paradigm has evolved, called the Semantic Web (SW) [18], which supports machine-readability through an Artificial Intelligence inspired content markup language based on the Web Ontology Language (OWL) [17]. Its ability to express logical relations among entities on the web has led to a new kind of WS technology called the Semantic Web Service (SWS) [18]. Due to the lack of adequate service description, many discovery approaches often lead to poor discovery results. Most current approaches for service discovery perform syntactic matching and semantic Input/Output matching which retrieve services using a description that contains particular keywords from the user's service query. Context aware service discovery approaches provide a promising way to more accurately discover services based on the domain or user's context. Contextual information, by nature, is dynamic and can reflect the current state and condition of the domain. However, existing context aware service discovery approaches provide limited support for the mechanisms required to dynamically represent and update the context.

Here, we present a framework called CASD for context aware, domain data dependent and inter-service relationship based service discovery, which automatically selects the best suited services via aggregation over service quality properties. This paper is organized as follows: first we provide a motivating example. Section 2 provides an overview of the CASD framework. Section 3 provides a brief description of the knowledge base of the framework. Sections 4 and 5 provide the system architecture and performance analysis of the framework, respectively. Related and future work are provided in Sect. 6.

1.1 Motivating Example

Suppose a person gets injured in an accident. Depending on the status of the patient (i.e., context), paramedics need to decide how to relocate the patient to a medical facility. For example, if the patient's condition is critical, the fastest mode of relocation should be used, otherwise the cheapest relocation service may be used. However if the patient has respiratory problems, oxygen supply should be ensured. Suppose the paramedics have the option to select from an *Ambulance-Service*, a *HelicopterService*, and a *BusService*. Among these services suppose the *HelicopterService* is the fastest service, the *BusService* is the cheapest, but only the *Ambulance Service* has oxygen supply. Now, if the paramedics decide that the patient's condition is normal and does not require oxygen, the *BusService*, i.e., the cheapest service is the best option for the context. On the other hand, if patient's condition is critical and he is not suffering from respiratory problems, paramedics can select the fastest service for relocation, that is, the *HelicopterService* service.

However, if the patient's condition is critical and he is also suffering from respiratory problems the *Ambulance Service* should be selected as that is the only service that provides oxygen. Here we have provided a simplified imaginary emergency care guideline. Real-world guidelines for emergency care, response and life support are obviously much more complex [7,8].

In the above example, the patient status after the accident such as: *Patient Condition is critical, Patient shows Respiratory Problems* is referred as the *Context*. The 'if-else' rules on which the paramedics decide what to do are called *Context Based Rules*. The quality the paramedics seek in a specific service such as the fastest service, or the cheapest service, is found by performing quantitative reasoning over some of the service properties say: the cost or speed of the relocation. We refer to *Cost and Speed* as Quality of Service (QoS) properties. This type of discovery and selection of services is referred to as *Context Aware Service Discovery*. The selection of *Ambulance Service* which enables *Oxygen Supply Service* is based on the relationships between these two services which we refer as an *Inter-Service relationship*. In addition, selection of a service may differ based on patient clinical history or age, which may restrict consumption of a service. Eg., humidified oxygen supply may be required if the patient is a child. Hence, the service discovery process should also take the domain data (in this case, patient data) into consideration. We refer to this type of service discovery as *Domain Data Dependency based Discovery*.

2   CASD Framework: Features and Approach Overview

In this section we briefly discuss the features and provide an overview of the service discovery approach of our framework. The features include:

1. Interoperability Between Legacy Systems and SW Systems: The CASD framework provides automatic integration with a legacy system's relational database (RDB) or domain database and SW system. The CASD framework provides and uses a tool called "RDB2O" to convert a domain database to semantic web accessible data or ontology (called Domain ontology).
2. Dynamic Context Representation and Update: Domain database schema can be used as a source of vocabulary for concept and relationships to create the Domain ontology, which eventually represents the context. As we create a Domain ontology from a domain database automatically, the CASD framework can represent the context dynamically for a domain.
3. Service Ontology Template: In the CASD framework, we provide a Service ontology template, which provides the concepts and relationships necessary to include services that can be accessible in a domain, the service quality properties (QoS) and the inter-service dependency properties. The inter-service relationships express whether a consumer can consume a service depending on the consumption history of another service by the consumer.
4. Context Aware Service Discovery and Aggregated Selection: By combining the domain and the service ontologies we can define service discovery and selection rules using relations and concepts from both ontologies. The CASD

framework utilizes the context present at runtime in the domain ontology to discover and automatically select the best-suited services. The context aware discovery process uses rule based reasoning through the Pellet reasoner [19] for discovery of services.

(a) Domain Data Dependent Discovery and Selection: The CASD framework can discover and select services not only based on the QoS properties, but also on the domain data. For example, in the health-care domain, depending on whether a patient's condition is *critical* or not, the CASD framework can select the *fastest* or the *cheapest* service.

(b) Inter-service Relationship based Service Discovery: Based on service relationships, there might be services which may not allow consumption of other services or there might be services that have to be consumed with another service. In the motivating example, we have to select the second fastest service, the *Ambulance Servie*, which is the only service that allows the consumption of the required *OxygenSupplyService*.

5. Accessibility and Extendability of the CASD framework: The CASD framework is designed and developed as a web application, which is easily accessible through browsers.

3   Knowledge Base and Context Aware Service Discovery

The KB used in the CASD framework consists of the following:

1. Domain Ontology: We create the Domain ontology from a domain database automatically using our tool, RDB2O. RDB2O creates the ontology T_{Box} by converting the domain database schema. The T_{Box} contains the concepts and relationships which are created based on a database-ontology conversion mapping algorithm in RDB2O. The Domain ontology A_{Box} consisting of facts, is populated with domain data at the runtime.

2. Service Ontology: The Service Ontology T_{Box} provides concepts and properties for domain services. The user can instantiate related A_{Box} or instances of services and their relationships based on the services offered by the domain. The Service ontology also contains another type of service called the RuntimeQoSFlagService, which is not consumable and is created at runtime by CASD framework based on QoS properties of individual domain services.

3. Context Based Rules: We express context based rules using the Semantic Web Rule Language (SWRL) [12], which is an expressive OWL-based rule language. SWRL includes a high-level abstract syntax for Horn-like rules. We can write context based rules using concepts and properties from both the Domain and Service ontologies. The following is a rule expressed in SWRL:
If the the patient's condition is critical, select the fastest relocation service:
Patient(?p) ∧ hasCondition(?p,"Critical") ∧ MaxSpeedQoSFlagService (?maxSpeedServ) → SelectedService(?maxSpeedServ).

Figure 1 shows the items in the CASD process for discovery and selection of services, which are briefly described below:

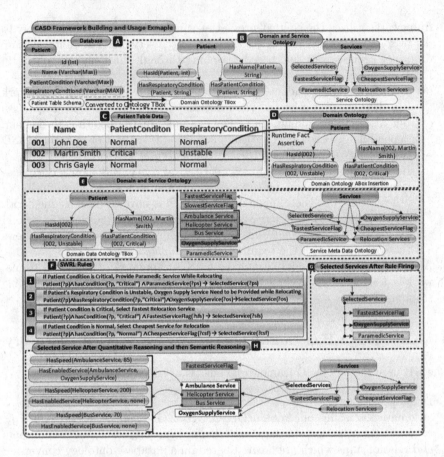

Fig. 1. Example of setup steps and usage of the CASD framework

A. Here we see an example legacy system relational database schema that is to be used as domain data provider. In the figure, the schema of a *Patient* table is shown, which is part of a *health-care* application, eg., the *EHR* [2]. We convert the schema of the database into an ontology to get the Domain ontology.

B. In this item, we combine the Domain ontology, the Service ontology and the Context Based Rules to create the KB.

C. Shows example data in the *Patient* table.

D. Based on the user query and rules in the domain, we gather data from the legacy system database and assert them into the Domain ontology i.e., into the KB. Item D shows how the data for the requested patient, whose id is 002, is collected from the domain database and asserted in the Domain ontology.

E. Shows examples of populated Domain and Service ontologies with required patient data and service instances, respectively.

F. Shows rules the reasoner applies to discover services for the current context.

G. In this item, the services that are required to be selected are shown which resulted from executing the rules in the reasoner. From rule 1, the reasoner concluded that the patient needs OxygenSupplyService. From rule 2, it is reasoned that the patient requires the fastest service for relocation. Combining these results we can conclude that the user needed to be relocated using the fastest service that enables OxygenSupplyService.

H. In item H, the CASD applies aggregation over the QoS property *Speed*, to find the fastest service that enables OxygenSupplyService. Here the AmbulanceService is the fastest service that supports, i.e., enables the OxygenSupplyService.

4 Architecture

We design the CASD framework following the SOA and N-tier architecture which makes integration of different components easier while providing better separation among user interface, logic layers and data layers. We have developed the framework using *C#.NET, ASP.NET* and *Java*. For ontology and rule processing we use DotNetRDF API [20], OWLAPI and Jena API [4]. The CASD frame-

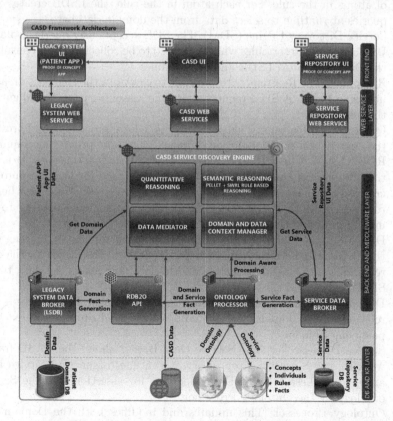

Fig. 2. Full architecture of the CASD framework

work provides the RDB2O tool [13] and uses it as an API to easily convert and integrate legacy system data and can leverage real-time data to generate ontology facts and represent context using an ontology. The architecture of the CASD framework is given in Fig. 2 and has the following tiers:

1. CASD Front End: The CASD front end is developed as a web application which can be accessed from browsers. We have also provided integration of the CASD framework with two other applications, namely, a simple healthcare system and a service repository.
2. Web Service Layer: We provide service discovery functionalities of the CASD framework as web services. This layer also provides web services for a healthcare system and service repository, which are used for integration with the CASD framework.
3. The Back End and Middle-ware Layer: The back end tier and the middle-ware layer components of the CASD framework are responsible for service discovery and selection, data conversion, accessing data and updating ontologies at runtime.
   (a) Legacy System Data Broker (LSDB): This collects data from a domain database depending on the rules using algorithms specified based on types of atoms in the rule. For each atom in the rule, the LSDB creates SQL queries at runtime to select data from the domain database.
   (b) Service Discovery Engine (SDM): The SDE accepts user queries from the UI module and determines what data need to be collected, after consulting the Data Mediator, LSDB and KB modules.
   (c) Reasoning: The Reasoner is responsible to carry out the rule based reasoning using Pellet. A SDM request starts the reasoning process and gathers the result.
   (d) Quantitative Reasoner: This performs procedural processing and provides the aggregation functionality and, indeed, any post processing required.
   (e) RDB2O API: The RDB2O API allows the CASD framework to access the database to ontology conversion mapping used for Domain ontology creation at runtime and thus allows the Ontology Processor (see below) to assert facts in the Service and Domain ontologies according to the mapping used in conversion.
   (f) Data Mediator: The Data Mediator is responsible for communicating with the LSDB. It passes the request from the SDM to the LSDB for the data required for the SDM and also collects data and relays the data to the SDM.
   (g) Domain Data and Context Manager: The Manager keeps records and relationships of domains, associated ontologies and runtime context for a particular domain.
   (h) Service Data Broker: The Service Data Broker allows the CASD framework to access a service repository at runtime to generate service facts and passes these facts to Data Mediator for assertion into the Service ontology by the Ontology Processor.
   (i) Ontology Processor: This updates and modifies both the Domain and Service ontologies as facts become available at runtime.

4. Data and Knowledge Representation (KR) Layer: The Data and KR layer contains the domain database (patient database), the service repository, the database for the CASD application and the Domain and Service ontologies.

5 Robustness and Performance of the CASD Framework

In this section we provide a performance analysis of the framework with basic functional testing and load based testing. The CASD framework is deployed as a web application on IIS 7.0 on a Lenovo ThinkPad running on Windows 7 64 bit. The computer has 12 GB ram, Intel(R) Core (TM) i5 @ 2.50 GHz.

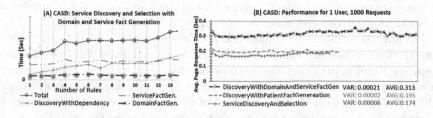

Fig. 3. Testing and performance analysis of the CASD framework

There are settings in the CASD framework called "GenerateServiceFacts" and "GenerateDomainFacts", which, respectively, determine whether to generate service facts to insert into the Service ontology with updated QoS properties from the service repository and domain facts to update the domain ontology or context with up-to-date domain data at runtime. Otherwise, it reuses the facts from the previous run and can save time for service and/or domain facts generation.

Figure 3(A), shows the time required for service discovery and selection (line: ..+..), for domain fact generation (line:–X–X–), for service fact generation (line: –..–..) and total time for discovery and selection when both domain facts and service facts generation are enabled (line:- -o- -o- -), as we gradually increase the number of rules from 1 to 15. Effectively, the total time for discovery is the sum of time required for service discovery and selection, domain fact generation, and service fact generation. As we can see from the graph, the time for domain fact generation (line:–X–X–) remains flat as we apply services for only one patient and for each request, the CASD framework generates the domain ontology for the same patient (or domain object) regardless the number of services to discover or number of patients in the database. The time required for discovery and services (line:..+..+..) increases as the number of rules (for this domain, executing 15 rules, discover 13 services) increases, as more QoS properties and more inter-service dependencies by quantitative reasoning have to be satisfied. The time required for runtime service facts generation (line: –..–..) increases in a linear fashion as the number of services in the repository increases.

We measured the performance of the CASD framework for 1000 requests to execute 10 rules by a single simulated user using the Visual Studio 2013 load test tool. The graph in Fig. 3(B) shows the average page response time for the different settings discussed above. The page response time constitutes the time required for posting the request to the server for a particular patient, receiving response or rules execution result, rendering discovery and selection of services. The time required for service discovery and selection without service and patient facts generation (line: .+.+.+.) remains flat over the time of tests resulting in a fixed page response time. The time for required for discovery and selection of services with only domain (patient) facts generation (line:......) is somewhat higher, than the time required with no facts generation (line .+...+..+.). The time required for service discovery and selection with both service facts and patient facts generation enabled is shown using line:-o-o-o-o-, which is somewhat higher than other two test criteria.

We have also tested the framework with more scenarios (due to space limitations these results are not included) such as: (i) Load test for 10 vs 15 user executing 10 rules, (ii) Executing 10 rules for a fixed patient vs a different patient for each run, and (iii) Load test for 1 vs 10 vs 15 users using the system to execute 1000 requests with 15 rules. For each of these test cases, we found the result is satisfactory and consistent (see the first author's Masters thesis, [13]).

6 Related and Future Work

The desirability for automation in service discovery and collaboration backed the escalation of the SWS with the maturity of the SW. The most widely used conceptualizations of the SWS are the OWL-S [18], the WSMO [11] and the SADI framework [21]. OWL-S helps software agents discover web services that satisfy some specified quality constraints (QoS) in terms of Input, Output, Pre-conditions, Post-condition and Effects (IOPEs). OWL-S also helps the service composition and service interaction by providing a minimal set of composition templates including: Sequence, Split, Unordered, Split+Join, etc. OWL-S does not provide any methodology for domain data integration with service model, thus does not support service discovery based on domain data, which is supported by the CASD framework. On the other hand, WSMO provides a concept vocabulary to express service description in terms of IOPEs and currently only supports syntactical matching of a user's goal against service descriptions. The WSMO supports selecting a service based on one or the other of two criteria, namely, "always the first" or multi-criteria selections, which depends on nonfunctional properties like reliability, and security. The SADI [21] framework discovers services based on IO matching and can make dynamic composition of services to match service IO requirements. The CASD framework discovers services based on dynamic QoS properties, inter-service dependency relationships, and domain context and automatically selects best-suited services.

OWLS-MX [15] and WSMX [11] are the SWS execution and testing environments for the OWL-S and WSMO approaches, respectively. OWLS-MX implemented the hybrid service discovery matchmaking (semantic matching of service description and user query provided) using the OWL-2 reasoner, Pellet. The OWL-S API uses the Jena Semantic Web Framework under the hood to modify the OWLS-MX matchmaker ontology. WSMX can work with Pellet. We are using Pellet and Jena and the OWL-API for reasoning, ontology manipulation, fact writing, and running SWRL rules.

In [9], several types of inter-process dependencies are modeled using UML including Enabling, Canceling, Triggering, and Disabling dependencies. However, no implementation was provided. We have integrated two of these service dependencies in the CASD framework by implementing the Enabling and Disabling dependencies.

In Table 1 we summarize features of the different frameworks for service discovery and selection (Based on literature provided). Due to space limitations we are not providing comparison with OWLS-MX.

Table 1. Comparisons among different frameworks for service discovery and selection

Features	CASD	WSMX	SADI
Service ontology	Service QoS and Inter-service rel	WSMO ontology	Service IO
Domain data integration	Domain ont. (run-time) d	Not supported	Not supported
Context rep	Service and domain ont.(dynamic)	Not supported	Not supported
Context data source	RDB (run-time data)	Not supported	Not supported
Reasoning support	Yes (rule based)	Semantic IO matching	Yes (SPARQL Query)
Domain setup by user	Yes	No	Limited
User SW knowledge req	Not needed for basic user	Required	Required
Context aware discovery	Yes	No	No
Aggregated selection	Yes	No	No
Inter-service rel. discovery	Yes	No	No
Discovery focus	Which service, when to use	Which service	Which service
Legacy system integration	Yes	Not supported	Not supported
Security support	Implemented	No	Implemented
Accessibility and extendibility	Web based, Web APIs, SOA	Desktop application	Web based, Web APIs

S. Cuddy et al. proposed a context aware service discovery technique base on static and dynamic service properties in [5]. This approach provides dynamic context representation with XML, using weighted service properties based on the user preferences, which must be provided for each discovery request. Also, if multiple services are discovered from a request, the approach randomly selects a service without taking the most suitable service into account. The CASD framework discovers services based on context represented from real-time domain data as well as dynamic service properties and inter-service dependencies. The CASD framework also features automatic service selection using aggregation over service properties. T. Broens et al. proposed another context aware service discovery approach which represents the context using an ontology [1]. This approach proposed using a pre-defined vocabulary for a domain built by consensus from a related community. The approach proposed by Xiao et al. [22] also represents context using an ontology, but uses some static features of the services such as location, keywords, etc. In our framework, we use a dynamic context representation using an ontology, that uses vocabulary directly from the Domain ontology which we gather by converting the domain database. Moreover, our framework supports most up-to-date context values as the framework can access the domain data and update the Domain ontology to reflect the changes in the context. Table 2 provides comparisons among different context aware service discovery and selection approaches with the CASD framework (comparisons are provided based on the literature provided). A more comprehensive analysis of related work can be found in [13].

Table 2. Comparisons among different approaches for context aware service discovery and selection

Features	CASD framework	S. Cuddy et al.	Xiao et al.
Context representation	Service and domain ontologies	XML	Ontology
Dynamic context vocabulary	Yes (service and domain onto.)	Partially dynamic (QoS)	Pre-defined
Runtime context update	Converted from RDB (at run-time)	User defined	User defined
Discovery criteria	QoS and domain context	QoS (IO matching)	QoS
Domain data integration	Yes	No	No
Data dependent discovery	Yes	No	No
Inter-service rel. discovery	Yes	No	No
QoS based discovery	Yes (dynamic QoS, aggregation)	Yes (partially dynamic)	Yes (static QoS)
Automatic service selection	Yes (fully automatic)	Random	Yes (static QoS)

To provide integration of legacy systems with SW systems, we need a tool that can convert a database to an ontology and can be used as an API for runtime data conversion. There are tools like [3,6] that can provide mappings of domain databases to ontologies. However, there are not many implemented tools available but some require intermediate manual mapping via bridge programming and do not provide run-time data conversion as an API. DB2OWL [6] and RDB2OWL [3] each provides an easy mapping process but the first can not handle self-reference of Tables and the second requires a manual mapping process. In our RDB2O tool, the mapping is based on the relationships and constraints specification among tables which can provide a database to ontology conversion automatically (without any manual mapping) and can be used as an API for run-time data mapping. We implement RDB2O using *C#.NET* and it can convert MS-SQL Server databases.

Our approach is still preliminary and some improvements can be made. The generation of ontological facts at runtime from a domain database is based on a serial algorithm. For larger domain databases, we may gain significant performance benefits if the fact generation process can be parallelized. Also when running multiple rules, which results in the discovery and selection of multiple secondary services, the discovery process is dependent on the sequence of the specific rule execution. This situation arises when we try to satisfy inter-service dependencies. A promising way go to froward is by defining discovery priorities based on service types for secondary services based on domain data.

Earlier [14] we discussed providing Service Enabled Workflow (SEW) leveraging the CASD framework. SEW imagines workflow as a collection of tasks with control flows where tasks are carried out as services. A workflow task has defined specifications, which can be imagined as a user query for the discovery of services to the CASD framework. The workflow user may select a service to execute from the discovered list of services against a task specification. Continuing in this fashion, we can provide dynamic composition of services: the overall result is SEW. In order to achieve SEW support using the CASD framework, we need to implement a workflow engine to provide control flow and develop an interconnection with the workflow engine and CASD framework for service discovery and selection for discovering services based on workflow task specification.

References

1. Broens, T., Pokraev, S., Sinderen, M., Koolwaaij, J., Dockhorn Costa, P.: Context-aware, ontology-based service discovery. In: Markopoulos, P., Eggen, B., Aarts, E., Crowley, J.L. (eds.) EUSAI 2004. LNCS, vol. 3295, pp. 72–83. Springer, Heidelberg (2004). doi:10.1007/978-3-540-30473-9_7
2. Canada Health Infoway: EHRS Blueprint Version 2. https://www.infoway-inforoute.ca/en/component/edocman/391-ehrs-blueprint-v2-full/view-document. Accessed Mar 2016
3. Čerāns, K., Būmans, G.: RDB2OWL: a language and tool for database to ontology mapping. In: 27th International Conference on Advanced Information Systems Engineering (2015). http://ceur-ws.org/Vol-1367/paper-11.pdf
4. Clark, P.: The OWL API. http://owlapi.sourceforge.net/. Accessed Mar 2016
5. Cuddy, S., et al.: Context-aware service selection based on dynamic and static service attributes. In: Wireless and Mobile Computing, Networking and Communications, vol. 4, pp. 13–20. IEEE (2005)
6. Cullot, N., Ghawi, R., Yétongnon, K.: DB2OWL: a tool for automatic database-to-ontology mapping. In: 15th Italian Symposium on Advanced Database Systems (SEBD 2007), pp. 491–494 (2007)
7. Emergency Health Service Branch, Ministry of Health, Long-Term Care: Basic life support patient care standard. http://www.health.gov.on.ca/. Accessed Mar 2016
8. Emergency Medical Services, Manitoba Health, Province of Manitoba: Emergency treatment guidelines. http://www.gov.mb.ca/health/ems/guidelines/etg.html. Accessed Mar 2016
9. Grossmann, G., et al.: Modeling inter-process dependencies with high-level business process modeling languages. In: Hinze, A., Kirchberg, M. (eds.) 5th Asia-Pacific Conference on Conceptual Modelling, vol. 79, pp. 89–102 (2008)
10. Haas, H., et al.: Web services glossary. W3C Working Group Note (2004)
11. Herold, M.: WSMX documentation. Digital Enterprise Research Institute Galway, Ireland 3 (2008). http://www.wsmx.org:8080/wsmxsite/papers/documentation/WSMXDocumentation.pdf
12. Horrocks, I., Boley, H., et al.: SWRL: a semantic web rule language combining OWL and RuleML. W3C Member Submission 21, 79 (2004)
13. Hussain, A.: A framework for context aware service discovery and selection, MSc. thesis. St. Francis Xavier University (2016)
14. Hussain, A., MacCaull, W.: Context aware service discovery and service enabled workflow. In: 4th Canadian Semantic Web Symposium, CEUR-WS pp. 45–48 (2013). http://ceur-ws.org/Vol-1054/paper-11.pdf

15. Klusch, M., et al.: OWLS-MX: A hybrid semantic web service matchmaker for OWL-S services. Web Semant. Sci. Serv. Agents World Wide Web **7**(2), 121–133 (2009)
16. Krafzig, D., Banke, K., Slama, D.: Enterprise SOA: Service-Oriented Architecture Best Practices. Prentice Hall Professional, Upper Saddle River (2005)
17. McGuinness, D.L., Others: OWL web ontology language overview. http://static.twoday.net/71desa1bif/files/W3C-OWL-Overview.pdf. Accessed Mar 2016
18. McIlraith, S.A., et al.: Semantic web services. Intell. Syst. IEEE **16**(2), 46–53 (2001)
19. Sirin, E., et al.: Pellet: a practical OWL-DL reasoner. Web Semant. Sci. Serv. Agents World Wide Web **5**(2), 51–53 (2007)
20. Vesse, R., Team: dotNetRDF - semantic web, RDF and SPARQL library for C-sharp/.Net, http://www.dotnetrdf.org/. Accessed Mar 2016
21. Wilkinson, M.D., et al.: The semantic automated discovery and integration (SADI) web service design-pattern, API and reference implementation. J. Biomed. Semant. **2**(1), 1–23 (2011)
22. Xiao, H., Zou, Y., et al.: An approach for context-aware service discovery and recommendation. In: 2010 IEEE International Conference on Web Services, pp. 163–170. IEEE (2010)

A Case Study on Linked Data for University Courses

Barnabás Szász[1], Rita Fleiner[2], and András Micsik[3(✉)]

[1] University of Debrecen, Debrecen, Hungary
bszasz@gmail.com
[2] Óbuda University, Budapest, Hungary
fleiner.rita@nik.uni-obuda.hu
[3] Department of Distributed Systems, MTA SZTAKI, Budapest, Hungary
micsik@sztaki.mta.hu

Abstract. Óbuda University wanted to build a linked dataset describing their courses in the semester. The concepts to be covered included curricula, subjects, courses, semesters and educators. A particular use case needed the description of lecture rooms and events as well. Although there are several ontologies for the mentioned domains, selecting a set of ontologies fitting our use case was not an easy task. After realizing the problems, we created the Ontology for Linked Open University Data (OLOUD) to fill in the gaps between re-used ontologies. OLOUD acts as a glue for a selection of existing ontologies, and thus enables us to integrate data from several sources and to provide practical information services for students and lecturers.

Keywords: Ontology · Linked Open Data · Linked Open University Data · SPARQL

1 Introduction

In this paper we focus on a special segment of open data at the university domain: university courses. We aim to facilitate the implementation of Smart Universities [1] by defining a common data model for course information. Ontological representation as the most modern description method for the problem domain was chosen. Originally our objective was to develop a generic data model for university course related data. During our work we noticed that though the Bologna Process ensures a certain level of compatibility for education systems in the EU, this does not reach deeper constructs regarding the educational model. We found that the meaning of the main concepts (like course, subject and study programme) is quite different in currently available educational models in Europe.

Presenting course related information requires a lot of data originating from multiple information systems at a typical university. As these systems are usually not fully integrated and the access to the data is limited, significant effort is necessary to successfully navigate through the potential difficulties. Foreign students, who are not aware of the local specialties can find it even more cumbersome. With our data model

© Springer International Publishing AG 2017
I. Ciuciu et al. (Eds.): OTM 2016 Workshops, LNCS 10034, pp. 265–276, 2017.
DOI: 10.1007/978-3-319-55961-2_27

we would like to support the generation and the management of integrated university data and also the appearance of future mobile and web applications building on the use of this data.

In Sect. 2 use cases are explored for the planned course dataset. Section 3 is about existing work related to our goals. Section 4 clarifies the terminology and describes how our new "glue" ontology was built and how it re-uses other existing ontologies. Finally, we summarize results in Sect. 5.

2 Use Case

In the following we list some of the tasks we aim to support with our Linked Data approach.

Courses. Courses are organized into a series of lectures and lab exercises, either in a weekly or in a custom cadence within a semester. There might be multiple labs advertised for a course, so students can choose the most suitable to their circumstances. This creates the challenge of assembling a personal timetable for students and lecturers avoiding conflicts and considering personal preferences and requirements.

Students could benefit from an integrated view containing course description (title, identifier, abstract, dependencies), course time, location, and learning resources. A personal information service may provide students with on-demand information about their daily schedule, navigation to the next lecture, overlaps of classes, etc. We also consider accessible way-finding to course locations.

Curriculum fulfillment. There is a need for long term planning of studies as well. Quite often there are no predefined course timetables at Hungarian universities, just a list of courses to be completed, and a dependency graph among the courses, which defines the prerequisites for each. Some courses are advertised in every second semester only. Some universities recommend a specific order of courses, but following such an order breaks easily if for example a single course is not completed in the suggested semester. Thus, students face a kind of constraint satisfaction problem to solve at each semester start.

For this purpose, students need a personal advisor recommending the best way for them to fulfill the curriculum requirements. This advisor needs to consider where the student is on his roadmap, what courses they should focus on, what are the personal preferences (e.g. preferred number of courses or credits per semester) and what courses are being advertised.

Resource reservation. University resources (rooms, equipment) are used by multiple faculties. They can be booked for regular courses, exams in the exam period and other events. Different types of events may have separate registries, thus blocking an overall view of anticipated resource usages. One needs an overall list of reservations by reserving person, location and date at least.

3 Related Work

Linked Universities[1] and Linked Education[2] are two European initiatives created to enable education with the power of Linked Data. Linked Universities is an alliance of European universities engaged into exposing their public data as linked data. LinkedEducation.org is an open platform aimed at further promoting the use of Linked Data for educational purposes. However, we did not find any existing solution or vocabulary at these websites fulfilling our needs for the data model.

The Open University in the UK was the first university that created a linked data platform to expose information from its departments [2]. The Open University datasets can be classified in the following six groups: open educational resources, scientific production, social media, organizational data, research project output, publication metadata. The main difference with Óbuda University is the lack of navigation and timetable data at the Open University.

The general process for building linked open university data and a use case at Tsinghua University are described in [3]. Procedures like choosing datasets and vocabularies, collecting and processing data, converting data into RDF and interlinking datasets are studied. The datasets unfortunately are not available through public SPARQL endpoint.

The Lucero project analyzed open educational datasets in 2012 [4]. Linked Open Datasets in four universities and four broader educational projects were studied and the most commonly used vocabularies, classes and properties were described. In this case no representations for course, semester or lecture room concepts were found. The general state of linked data for education is studied in [5] containing statistics on vocabulary re-use. We found another very useful review of ontologies for modelling course information in higher education [6].

AIISO (Academic Institution Internal Structure Ontology) [7] provides classes and properties to describe the structure of an academic institution. It is designed to be used in conjunction with the Participation ontology [8] which stands for describing the roles that people play within groups.

TEACH [9] is a lightweight vocabulary providing detailed properties in order to describe a course, but it doesn't model the provider of the course. The concepts in TEACH lack some important features that are essential for our purposes. For example, in order to describe university courses the concept of Subject is necessary, which doesn't exist in TEACH.

XCRI-CAP [10] is the abbreviation for eXchanging Course Related Information, Course Advertising Profile. It is the UK standard for describing course marketing information. XRI-CAP doesn't make a distinction between a module, a course, a subject or a study program.

The Metadata for Learning Opportunities (MLO) Advertising ontology [11] aims to standardize the specifications for describing and exchanging information about courses and learning opportunities. It can be considered the European equivalent of the British

---

[1] http://linkeduniversities.org.

[2] http://linkededucation.org.

Standard XCRI-CAP for advertising courses. MLO-Adv contains very abstract and general concepts and misses many properties for courses and curricula.

After reviewing the above ontologies, we realized that there are many ontologies defining Course, Subject, Curriculum and Degree, but neither provides a full coverage and there are missing relations between the concepts. We concluded that the AIISO ontology provides the best coverage, and its structure fits our concrete use case, thus it can be reused and extended with the necessary terms.

4 Implementation

The major concepts for university students and teachers in our use case are depicted in Fig. 1.

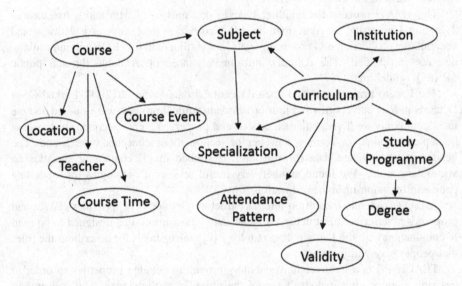

Fig. 1. Main concepts for our use cases

A Curriculum stands in many-to-one relationship with a **Study Programme** (e.g. Applied Mathematician), offered by the university. Each Curriculum has a specific **Attendance Pattern** (full-time, part-time, correspondence, etc.). A Study Programme determines the qualification and a specific **Degree** (BSc, MSc, BA, MA, PhD, etc.) that students will get after the successful completion of their studies. A Study Programme must be accredited by an external body. The curriculum is the specification how the Study Programme can be completed. A Curriculum is valid for a given time interval, meaning that a student can be assigned to it only if his enrollment time falls into this period of time. For each Subject there is an **Organizational Unit** responsible for it. **Courses** are advertised based on a Subject, have temporal (**Course Time**) and spatial (**Location**) attributes and one or more assigned **Teacher**(s). **Course Events** are individual sessions such as lectures or practice held often on a weekly basis, and courses may also have some special, associated events, for example exams. Additionally, learning material (**Learning Resource**) can be assigned to specific courses and subjects.

Course is the elementary unit of the educational process, where students, teachers, location and date are assigned. Subject is a higher level component of the training process, it represents a part of knowledge students need to acquire.

As seen in Sect. 3, we had to extend and connect existing ontologies for our domain model. The result is the Ontology for Linked Open University Data (OLOUD) presented in the rest of the section. Figure 2 depicts the main classes as ovals and the most significant attributes as arrows in OLOUD.

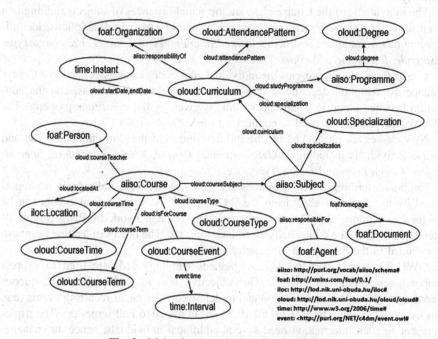

Fig. 2. Main classes and properties in OLOUD

The prefixes for classes and properties clearly show what has been reused and where we had to fill missing links. We selected to reuse the following ontologies: AIISO for the description of university faculties, courses, subjects and roles; FOAF for the description of persons; OWL Time for temporal definitions; Event for describing events and Dublin Core for generic properties such as language.

Curriculum, Subject, Course and *CourseEvent* are the most important classes in OLOUD. In the following the description of the classes are given with their direct connections. Curricula contain the list of subjects with their dependencies, since each subject can have various prerequisite subjects. The faculty of the university responsible for the Curriculum is given by the *aiiso:responsibilityOf* property. S*tartDate* and *endDate* properties determine the period, when a Curriculum is valid. The possible Specializations, the Degree, the Attendance pattern and the Study programme of the study are given by the corresponding *specialization, degree, attendancePattern and studyProgramme* properties. The language of the studies is given with the *dcterms: language* property.

Subjects are described by their name, code, credit number, person and organization responsible for it: *foaf:name, aiiso:code, subjectCredit, aiiso:responsibilityOf.* The connection between a Subject and its Courses is given by the *courseSubject* attribute. The prerequisite conditions between Subject entities are set by the *hasPrerequisite* property.

The individuals of the Course class are the actual instances of subjects running in a given semester (*courseTerm*) having spatial, temporal and type descriptions, identification number, name and instructor: *locatedAt, courseTime, courseTerm, courseType, aiiso:code, foaf:name* and *courseTeacher.*

CourseEvent class represents the individual classes or exams associated to a Course instance. Its temporal description is given by the *event:Interval* class, and the connection between a course event and its time is given by the *event:time* property. The *isForCourse* property is used to connect a *CourseEvent* with a *Course.*

New classes are introduced for the full description of the Curriculum, Subject and Course individuals including *StudyProgramme, Degree, AttendancePattern, Specialization, CourseTerm* and *CourseType.*

Entities describing indoor locations for Course and Event individuals are represented by the *Location* class from the iLOC[3] ontology. Courses and events can be assigned to Rooms, and Rooms are connected via a network of POIs (Points of Interest), which can be doors, hallway connections, etc. The offices of lecturers can also be included in the description of campus buildings.

OWL Time [12] and the TimeAggregates Ontology [13] are used to express temporal descriptions of courses. Our objective was to enable SPARQL queries according to date, time and duration and to define course time as recurring events (e.g. labs on every Tuesday from 9 am till 10.30 am in the 2016 Fall semester). The triples representing such information need several additional individuals, hence the management of such information is time consuming and error prone. The generation of course time data was implemented using an automatized process described in [14] and complete examples can be found on the web[4].

---

[3] http://lod.nik.uni-obuda.hu/iloc/iloc.html.

[4] http://lod.nik.uni-obuda.hu/unfolding/example.html.

The advantage of OLOUD as a common vocabulary is the ability to integrate databases covering only parts of university life. Then, the unified data can be queried using SPARQL to find answers for complex queries relating multiple aspects such as timetable, location, curriculum, etc. simultaneously. The next part of our research is to further investigations on OLOUD as a common model, and to discover constraints and rules for university domain, resulting in a unified knowledge base which can be used for inferencing new facts and for finding inconsistencies, problems in campus data. Reasoners may reveal problems in current data such as course overlaps, missing courses for subjects, or cycles in subject prerequisites (see following example rules).

```
hasPrerequisite(?x, ?y), hasPrerequisite(?y, ?z) -> hasPrerequisite(?x, ?z)
Subject(?x), hasPrerequisite(?x, ?x) -> SelfDependentSubject(?x)
```

Finally, rules run on temporary facts can be used to generate personal short or long-term tuition plans for students.

5 Results

Protégé[5] was used for validation purposes, as it revealed problems in the imported ontologies and in our ontology as well. The OOPS! Ontology Pitfall Scanner was also used to check our OWL [15], and the found small problems were fixed.

Linked data triplets were created based on public data[6] at the Óbuda University. The location data was created manually based on building layout diagrams of the university, while the subject and course data were converted using custom PHP scripts from relational database dumps extracted from the electronic administration system (Neptun) of the Óbuda University. The entities of the Person class and their personal data were scraped from the personal webpages. The university event descriptions were generated with a crawler from the OU webpage. The dataset was also extended with links to the GeoNames geographic dataset. At this moment, the database contains about 1000 entities with more than 6000 triples.

As an example, we provide a sample Course, Subject and Curriculum description:

---

[5] http://protege.stanford.edu/.

[6] http://lod.nik.uni-obuda.hu/marmotta/.

```
:AB0_LA_01_E_2014-15-1 rdf:type aiiso:Course,
aiiso:code "AB0_LA_01_E"@hu ;
foaf:name "Adatbázisok"@hu ;
oloud:courseSubject :NAIAB0SAED ;
oloud:locatedAt :PC_Labor_220 ;
oloud:courseTeacher :Dominika_Fleiner ;
oloud:courseTime
odata:CourseTime;courseTerm=2014Fall;hour=17;minute=55;durationHour=1;duration
Minute=35;dayofweek=1 ;
oloud:courseType :Lab ;
oloud:courseTerm :2014Fall .

:NAIAB0SAND rdf:type aiiso:Subject,
oloud:subjectCredit "4.00"^^xsd:Integer;
foaf:homepage "http://users.nik.uni-obuda.hu/to/tantargy/adatbazisok-0" ;
aiiso:code "NAIAB0SAND" ;
foaf:name "Adatbázisok"@hu ;
aiiso:responsibilityOf :Rita_Fleiner ;
oloud:specialization :ObligatoryPart ;
oloud:subjectCredit "4"^^xsd:int ;
oloud:subjectLabNo "2"^^xsd:int ;
oloud:subjectLectureNo "2"^^xsd:int ;
oloud:subjectSeminarNo    "0"^^xsd:int ;
oloud:subjectWeeklyHours   "4"^^xsd:int ;
oloud:hasPrerequisite       : NAIPR1SAND ;
oloud:recommendedSemester   "3"^^xsd:int ;
dcterms:language "hu" ;
oloud:subjectTerm :2014Fall;
oloud:hasAssessmentMethod oloud:exam;
oloud:curriculum :MérnökInformatikusBSc_2012 .

:MérnökInformatikusBSc_2012 rdf:type oloud:Curriculum ,
foaf:name "Mérnök Informatikus BSc (2012)"@hu ;
aiiso:responsibilityOf :AII ;
oloud:studyProgramme :ComputerEngineer ;
oloud:attendancePattern :FullTime ;
dcterms:language "hu" ;
oloud:degree :bsc ;
oloud:startDate odata:UnitDayInstant;year=2012;month=9;day=1.
```

Figure 3 provides a visualization of a part of the linked data graph. Browsing the dataset with a LOD tool such as LODmilla [16] provides access to useful integrated data for students. Furthermore, an in-door way finding service for students is also available, providing a simple itinerary to the place of the given lecture. It is available as a mobile app, and backed by an open SPARQL endpoint.

We tested the complex use cases with implementing different SPARQL queries answering the questions in Sect. 2. For example, one can ask about the courses for a given subject in a specific semester:

```
PREFIX oloud: <http://lod.nik.uni-obuda.hu/oloud/oloud#>
SELECT DISTINCT ?course WHERE {
    ?course a <http://purl.org/vocab/aiiso/schema#Course>.
    ?course oloud:courseSubject <http://lod.nik.uni-obuda.hu/data/NAIAB0SAND>.
    ?course oloud:courseTerm <http://lod.nik.uni-obuda.hu/data/2014Fall>.
}
```

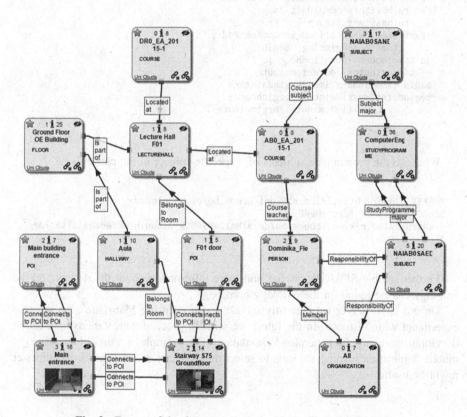

Fig. 3. Extract of the dataset presented with the Lodmilla browser

What is the course schedule (with course identifier, time and lecturer) for a specific lecture hall or lab?

```
PREFIX oloud: <http://lod.nik.uni-obuda.hu/oloud/oloud#>
PREFIX ta: <http://ontology.ihmc.us/temporalAggregates.owl#>
PREFIX time: <http://www.w3.org/2006/time#>
PREFIX iloc: <http://lod.nik.uni-obuda.hu/iloc/iloc#>

SELECT DISTINCT ?course ?room ?day ?beginhour ?beginminute ?teacher WHERE {
    ?room a iloc:Room.
    ?course oloud:locatedAt ?room;
            oloud:courseTeacher ?teacher;
            oloud:courseTime ?ct .
    ?ct ta:hasTemporalAggregateDescription ?tad .
    ?tad ta:hasithTemporalUnit ?day ;
        ta:hasStart ?start .
    ?start time:hasDurationDescription ?dd ;
          time:hasBeginning ?begin .
    ?dd time:hours ?durationhour ;
        time:minutes ?durationminute .
    ?begin time:inDateTime ?begindatetime .
    ?begindatetime time:hour ?beginhour ;
                   time:minute ?beginminute .
}
```

What are the prerequisite subjects of a specific subject in the curriculum?

```
PREFIX oloud: <http://lod.nik.uni-obuda.hu/oloud/oloud#>
SELECT DISTINCT ?dep WHERE {
  <http://lod.nik.uni-obuda.hu/data/NAIDR0SAND> oloud:hasPrerequisite ?dep
}
```

Further sample SPARQL queries and more information about the dataset and the ontology can be found on the ontology homepage[7].

On our LOD server we currently serve the dataset using Marmotta[8], but we also experiment with Virtuoso. In the future we wish to proceed with various application developments using the generated LOD dataset. For example, a 'curriculum assistant' mobile application helping students to select their courses at the start of the semester might be useful.

---

[7] http://lod.nik.uni-obuda.hu/oloud/.

[8] http://marmotta.apache.org/.

6 Conclusions

With an initial goal to implement useful, "smart" services for university students based on linked data, we soon realized that there are many ontologies or vocabularies for the domain, yet none of them is suitable for our purpose. The biggest problems we found were the missing discriminations between subjects and courses and curricula and study programs. We created the OLOUD ontology which amalgamates selected ontologies and facilitates the full description of course-related information. Hence, we think our work helps to better clarify the role of concepts frequently used in this domain.

The OLOUD ontology provides the basis of several ongoing student projects, which either integrate new datasets for the university or implement new services on top of the OLOUD dataset. Furthermore, OLOUD aims to become more than a vocabulary and to exploit the modeling power of description logic by exploring and describing the constraints and details of concepts in this domain.

References

1. Rohs, M., Bohn, J.: Entry points into a smart campus environment-overview of the ETHOC system. In: Proceedings of the 23rd International Conference on Distributed Computing Systems Workshops, pp. 260–266. IEEE (2003)
2. Daga, E., d'Aquin, M., Adamou, A., Brown, S.: The Open University Linked Data - data. open.ac.uk. Semantic Web Journal 7(2), 183–191 (2015)
3. Ma, Y., Xu, B., Bai, Y., Li, Z.: Building linked open university data: Tsinghua University open data as a showcase. In: Pan, J.Z., Chen, H., Kim, H.-G., Li, J., Wu, Z., Horrocks, I., Mizoguchi, R., Wu, Z. (eds.) JIST 2011. LNCS, vol. 7185, pp. 385–393. Springer, Heidelberg (2012). doi:10.1007/978-3-642-29923-0_28
4. The Lucero project: So, what's in linked datasets for education (2012). http://lucero-project. info/lb/2012/04/so-whats-in-linked-datasets-for-education/
5. d'Aquin, M., Adamou, A., Dietze, S.: Assessing the educational linked data landscape. In: Proceedings of the 5th Annual ACM Web Science Conference, pp. 43–46. ACM (2013)
6. Barker, P.: A short project on linking course data (2015). http://blogs.pjjk.net/phil/a-short-project-on-linking-course-data/
7. Styles, R., Shabir, N.: Academic institution internal structure ontology (AIISO) (2008). http://vocab.org/aiiso/schema
8. Styles, R., Wallace, C., Moeller, K.: Participation ontology (2008). http://vocab.org/participation/schema
9. Kauppinen, T., Trame, J., Westermann, A.: Teaching Core Vocabulary Specification (TEACH ontology) (2012). http://linkedscience.org/teach/ns/
10. Stubbs, M., Wilson, S.: eXchanging Course-Related Information: a UK service-oriented approach (2006). http://hdl.handle.net/1820/837
11. EN 15982:2011 Metadata for Learning Opportunities (MLO)-Advertising (2011)
12. OWL Time Ontology (2006). https://www.w3.org/TR/owl-time/
13. Pan, F.: Temporal aggregates for Web services on the semantic Web. IEEE International Conference on Web Services (ICWS 2005), pp. 831–832. IEEE (2005)

14. Szasz, B., Fleiner, R., Micsik, A.: Linked data enrichment with self-unfolding URIs. In: 2016 IEEE 14th International Symposium on Applied Machine Intelligence and Informatics (SAMI), pp. 305–309. IEEE (2016)
15. Poveda-Villalón, M., Suárez-Figueroa, M.C., Gómez-Pérez, A.: Validating ontologies with OOPS!. In: Knowledge Engineering and Knowledge Management, pp. 267–281. Springer, Heidelberg (2012)
16. Micsik, A., Turbucz, S., Györök, A.: LODmilla: a Linked Data Browser for All. In: Proceedings of the Posters and Demos Track of 10th International Conference on Semantic Systems - SEMANTiCS 2014. CEUR Workshop Proceeding, pp. 31–34 (2014)

A Generic Framework for Adding Semantics to Digital Libraries

Muhammad Ahtisham Aslam[1]([✉]), Naif Radi Aljohani[1], Rabeeh Ayaz Abbasi[1],
Miltiadis D. Lytras[2], and Muhammad Ashad Kabir[3]

[1] Faculty of Computing and Information Technology,
King Abdulaziz University, Jeddah, Saudi Arabia
{maaslam,nraljohani,rabbasi}@kau.edu.sa
[2] The American College of Greece, Athens, Greece
mlytras@acg.edu
[3] School of Computing and Mathematics,
Charles Sturt University, Sydney, NSW, Australia
akabir@csu.edu.au

Abstract. The World Wide Web (WWW) is emerging as the Web of Data, providing information on various domains. A vast number of scientific documents such as books, articles and journals can be found through many publisher's websites, portals and XML exports. The challenge here is that the data about these scientific documents can not be explored collectively, as they are published as a bounded group of sources organized by different publishers. To address these limitations, we have developed a generic framework termed as Linked Open Publications Data Framework (LOPDF) that facilitates crawling, processing, extracting and producing machine-processable data that is open and linked to other open datasets. We also demonstrate the RDF datasets produced by using LOPDF framework and describe statistics of different datasets entities.

1 Introduction

With the growth of the Web, it has become preferred platform on which to publish documents and organizational data [4]. Traditionally, data published on the Web has been made available in formats such as HTML, XML, CSV, and tables, resulting in loss of data's structure and semantics [3]. Moreover, a significant amount of information is encoded in structured forms [7] by using information templates. Specific to the scientific domain, information about scientific publications is encoded by using common terms such as *title, author, ISBN*, and structured by using various publisher-specific templates. This provides better representation and human understanding, yet it prevents the information from being processed by machines. As a result, data of scientific publications is silenced and fails to connect to scientific works put out by other publishers.

In response, a generic framework termed as Linked Open Publications Data Framework (LOPDF) is described in this paper. The LOPDF framework can be used to crawl, parse, extract and produce LOD of scientific publications. We

© Springer International Publishing AG 2017
I. Ciuciu et al. (Eds.): OTM 2016 Workshops, LNCS 10034, pp. 277–281, 2017.
DOI: 10.1007/978-3-319-55961-2_28

implemented and used the LOPDF framework to extract huge datasets of about three hundred million RDF triples providing information on over nine million scientific documents from *SpringerLink*[1] as source of data.

The remainder of this paper is organized as follows. Related work is discussed in Sect. 2. In Sect. 3 we describe the architecture of our framework. The knowledge extraction algorithm is discussed in Sect. 4. Section 5 demonstrates the results in terms of datasets extracted by using LOPDF framework. Finally, we conclude and outline future directions for our work in Sect. 6.

2   Related Work

For more than two decades, the semantic Web and LOD communities have been working on information integration [8] and semantic Web technologies [3]. This has led to the development of different frameworks and approaches for extracting and producing Linked Open Data (LOD). For example, a template-based extract transform load method is described in [2] to publish archaeological linked data from excavation archaeological datasets. The tool introduced in [2] minimizes the load to understand schema and mapping rules and maximizes the auto mapping of data to linked data. Another domain-independent framework for extracting linked data from tables is presented in [7]. The proposed framework can be used to interpret tables and thus produce linked data. Graphical models and probabilistic reasoning theories are used to extract the content of the columns and, to some extent, their data. DBpedia [6] is a key project, acting as the nucleus of the Web of open data. Datasets of the dbpedia knowledge base have been extracted using the dbpedia extraction framework, resulting in the addition of more than five million RDF triples to the Web of open data. A generic language (i.e. RML) for mapping relational databases to RDF is introduced in [5]. RML is basically an extension to R2RML and can be used to extract and map heterogeneous data to RDF.

3   Framework Architecture

Data on scientific publications is expressed by using terms (e.g. *title, ISBN,* etc.). Links between parent and child documents (e.g. link of a book with chapters) are established through publisher-specific templates. LOPDF architecture is designed to crawl across all parent/child documents and to extract and triplify metadata as well as links between documents. LOPDF architecture consists of four modules (as shown in Fig. 1) which are described below:

Crawler. The crawler is the main component of the LOPDF framework and it crawls through the data source in such a way that the relational information between documents is preserved. That is why, while crawling, if it finds that a document is a parent document (e.g. book or journal) that might have child

---

[1] http://link.springer.com/.

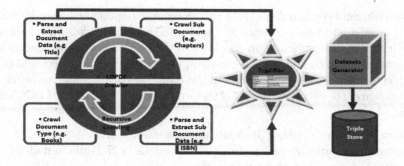

Fig. 1. *Linked open publications data framework (LOPDF)* architecture.

documents (e.g. chapters or articles), the crawler goes through all related child documents so that neither is left unprocessed.

Parser. This component is used to parse and extract metadata (e.g. *title, author, etc.*) about every document. Relational metadata is also parsed and extracted by this component to preserve the relational information between various entities. During the crawling process, when the crawler finds an information template, this component is activated to extract available information at that particular stage.

Triplifier. The triplifier component is used to process the information extracted by the parser, and to generate RDF triples for all metadata and to store them in to relevant data models. Before triplification, this component also takes care of the data types of the extracted data by considering the nature of values of properties as object or data type properties. The values of object properties are mapped to the relevant classes and values of data type properties are mapped to the appropriate literal data types.

RDF Generator. This component takes the data models created by the triplifier as its input and processes them to generate RDF datasets in N-Triple format. The resulting datasets contain complete information (as RDF triples) about metadata, as well as links between various entities, which enables researchers to put semantically enriched queries to these datasets through SPARQL endpoint.

4   Data Extraction Algorithm

The LOPDF data extraction algorithm adopts a recursive approach (as shown in Algorithm 1) to crawl, parse, extract and produce scientific publication's LOD. In its first step, the algorithm starts to traverse the data source from the first discipline (e.g. computer science, engineering, etc.) and crawls across every discipline.

In its next step, the algorithm starts crawling inside a particular content type (e.g. within a book or journal) and crawls through all documents with in a particular content type (e.g. all chapters in a book, all volumes, issues and articles in a journal, etc.). While crawling inside a particular content type, information about all documents that are part of a particular content type (i.e. relational information between content type and document) and metadata about a particular document (e.g. title, isbn, etc.) are extracted and added to the data model. Then recursive approach takes the extraction process back to the next content type, and then to the next discipline. By using this recursive approach, all disciplines, content types and document types are processed, and the data models are made ready for the triplification of the extracted data and the production of final datasets in N-Triple format.

Data: *Publisher's portal/ Web site* home as data source
Result: Semantically enriched publications data in N-Triple format
while *Not reach end of disciplines* **do**
> Crawl disciplines;
> **while** *Not reach end of content types (e.g. book, journal, etc.)* **do**
> > Crawl content types ;
> > **while** *Not reach end of content type with in a discipline* **do**
> > > Parse and extract content metadata (e.g. title, abstract, etc.) ;
> > > Add metadata information in to data model;
> > > Crawl sub-documents with in a particular content type;
> > > **while** *Not reach end of sub-documents* **do**
> > > > Extract metadata of sub-documents ;
> > > > Add metadata information in to data model;
> > > **end**
> > **end**
> **end**
> Triplify extracted information;
> Generate RDF datasets in N-Triple format;
end

Algorithm 1. *LOPDF* data extraction algorithm.

5   Results and Discussion

As a part of LOPDF implementation, we undertook minor customizations to the endpoint triggers of the generic framework and applied it to the extraction and production of semantically enriched data, using *SpringerLink* as our source of data. We were able to extract data from about nine million documents including 5.476 million articles, 3.24 million chapters, 0.478 million reference work entries. Resulting RDF datasets consist of about three hundred million RDF triples (all together) and are published on the project website[2] for download in .nt format. We also created a knowledge base (termed as SPedia [1]) by using these datasets and a SPARQL endpoint that can be used to put sophisticated queries to *SPedia* datasets, either by making use of semantic Web techniques or connecting the semantic Web browser to the SPARQL endpoint. Table 1 shows some sample statements from RDF datasets gernerated by using LOPDF framework.

---

[2] http://wo.kau.edu.sa/Pages-SPedia.aspx.

Table 1. Sample RDF statements from datasets generated by using LOPDF.

Subject	Predicate	Object
spedia:Coordinate_Metrology	spedia:has_Title	"Coordinate_Metrology".
spedia:Coordinate_Metrology	rdf:type	"Book".
spedia:Coordinate_Metrology	spedia:has_Online_ISSN	"978-3-662-48465-4".

6   Conclusion and Future Work

In this article we presented a generic framework that can be used to add semantics to digital libraries and produce LOD on scientific publications. We described the architecture of our framework and the generic recursive algorithm on which we implemented it. We outlined our results, comprised of RDF datasets that we extracted from *SpringerLink* as source of data. These datasets consist of about three hundred million RDF triples while providing information on about nine million scientific documents. As part of future enhancement, we are working on customizing the LOPDF framework to extract semantically enriched data from other well-known publishers as well.

References

1. Aslam, M.A., Aljohani, N.R.: SPedia: a semantics based repository of scientific publications data. In: Cui, B., Zhang, N., Xu, J., Lian, X., Liu, D. (eds.) WAIM 2016. LNCS, vol. 9658, pp. 479–490. Springer, Heidelberg (2016). doi:10.1007/978-3-319-39937-9_37
2. Binding, C., Charno, M., Jeffrey, S., May, K., Tudhope, D.: Template based semantic integration: from legacy archaeological datasets to linked data. Int. J. Semant. Web Inf. Syst. **11**(1), 1–29 (2015)
3. Bizer, C., Heath, T., Berners-Lee, T.: Linked data - the story so far. Int. J. Semant. Web Inf. Syst. **5**(3), 1–22 (2009)
4. Ceri, S., Bozzon, A., Brambilla, M., Valle, E., Fraternali, P., Quarteroni, S.: Web information retrieval. In: Chapter Publishing Data on the Web, pp. 137–159. Springer, Heidelberg (2013)
5. Dimou, A., Sande, M.V., Colpaert, P., Verborgh, R., Mannens, E., Van de Walle, R.: R.M.L: a generic language for integrated RDF mappings of heterogeneous data. In: Proceedings of the 7th Workshop on Linked Data on the Web, CEUR Workshop Proceedings, vol. 1184, April 2014
6. Lehmann, J., Isele, R., Jakob, M., Jentzsch, A., Kontokostas, D., Mendes, P.N., Hellmann, S., Morsey, M., van Kleef, P., Auer, S., Bizer, C.: Dbpedia - a large-scale, multilingual knowledge base extracted from wikipedia. Semant. Web **6**(2), 167–195 (2015)
7. Mulwad, V., Finin, T., Joshi, A.: A domain independent framework for extracting linked semantic data from tables. In: Search Computing Broadening Web Search, pp. 16–33 (2012)
8. Wiederhold, G.: Intelligent integration of information. In: Proceedings of the 1993 ACM SIGMOD International Conference on Management of Data, SIGMOD 1993, pp. 434–437. ACM, New York (1993)

Dynamic User Interface Architecture for Mobile Applications Based on Mobile Agents

Nikola Mitrović[1]([✉]), Carlos Bobed[1,2], and Eduardo Mena[1,2]

[1] Department of Computer Science and Systems Engineering,
University of Zaragoza, Zaragoza, Spain
`mitrovic@prometeo.cps.unizar.es`, {`cbobed,emena`}`@unizar.es`
[2] Aragon Institute of Engineering Research (I3A), Zaragoza, Spain

Abstract. Developing Graphical User Interfaces (GUIs) for mobile applications is a difficult task. Modern applications frequently need to interact with humans that use several devices with different characteristics (such as screen size or operating system). Any application that creates a specific GUI (surely designed for a certain device family) is likely to be rendered and/or behave incorrectly on many other user devices. Moreover, user interactions also need to be adapted to the preferences of each specific user and be learned from user context. The above challenges delegate every single application to have multiple versions of its GUI to be correctly executed on every possible device and operating system combination, in addition to consider user preferences and context.

In this paper, we propose an architecture based on mobile agents for developing adaptive user interfaces for multiple devices and applications. This architecture makes it possible to further separate GUIs from their underlying logic, allowing GUIs to be specified once and automatically be adapted to different platforms and user preferences without further development. Moreover, our architecture enables GUIs to be composed in a collaborative way by multiple agents and across different devices by automatically adapting them to each device capabilities and user preferences. Thus every application developer is relieved of considering these issues.

Keywords: Dynamic GUIs · Mobile cooperative agents · Mobile computing

1 Introduction

Adoption of mobile devices over the last decade has been significant: Just the number of mobile phones has exceeded world population in 2014[1]. Nowadays people rely on devices such as smartphones, tablets, laptops, smart watches, smart TVs, and PCs not only for practical and productivity tasks, but also to enhance social aspects of their lives. As the user adoption of these devices is increasing, the number of new platforms and devices is on the increase too.

---

[1] Definitive data and analysis for the mobile industry, https://www.gsmaintelligence. com/, last accessed 12th September 2016.

© Springer International Publishing AG 2017
I. Ciuciu et al. (Eds.): OTM 2016 Workshops, LNCS 10034, pp. 282–292, 2017.
DOI: 10.1007/978-3-319-55961-2_29

With the rising use of mobile devices, users' expectations of new applications and GUIs have risen too: Users frequently expect applications to be available on any device they own, regardless of the operating system or device features. Usability and flexibility of GUIs are more important than ever as interaction with the computer can happen anywhere and users dislike spending unnecessary time performing a task. Moreover, we are increasingly surrounded by sensors, sensing devices, computers which brings new dynamic and complexities. Users expect that all these devices and sensors will collaborate to learn about the user, predict users' needs, understand the context and help them complete tasks in the most efficient way. In this context, GUIs are required not only to be adapted to the specific device and platform combinations, but also to take into account users contexts.

Therefore, creating GUIs for collaborative and mobile applications that can work on multiple platforms and provide users, with experiences adapted to their context and preferences, is not an easy task. Different platforms or interaction modes (e.g., Android or Windows OS, smart watch, or smartphone applications) require different and separate GUI code. On the other hand, GUI adaptation to users preferences and context is typically custom developed for each GUI or application, which reduces the re-usability of the solutions. Every single application must have multiple versions of its GUI to be correctly executed on every possible device and operating system combination, in addition to consider user preferences and context, if its goal is to execute correctly in a wide spectrum of user devices with different capabilities and features. Even more, applications developed today are likely expected to be prepared, not adapted, to new incoming devices and operating systems. To solve all these problems we need (1) a way in which applications specify GUIs without compromising its flexibility to allow them to adapt to different devices and preferences, (2) an intermediate module that plays the role of interface between applications and user devices, alleviating the former from efforts to adapt their GUIs to user devices, preferences, and context.

Some approaches provide a certain level of GUI portability across one or two specific platforms (e.g., Android [1] or Xamarin [2]). However, such approaches do not automatically adapt the GUI to the device, require development of platform-specific GUI code, and do not offer automatic ability to adapt to the user preferences or context. Many approaches advocate using a *User Interface Definition Language (UIDL)* such as XUL [3], UIML [4], or UsiXML [5]. Such approaches allow re-using a single GUI design on multiple platforms but the GUI code is typically created and pre-compiled separately for different platforms [5]. As the code is specifically crafted for individual devices or platforms, it is hard to change and adapt to user or context once the application has been deployed to a target device. Some approaches use a client-server architecture [6] to adapt UIDL at run-time; these approaches can adapt GUI more easily across multiple devices. However, these approaches do not offer adapting to user preferences and context, and require the existence of client and server software (a fixed point in the network). Finally, it is important to note that GUIs in the above approaches are usually pre-defined and may take input from other devices or software; they are however seldom generated in a collaborative way, with multiple independent entities contributing to the GUI.

In this paper, we propose ADUS[2], an architecture based on mobile agents [7] for developing adaptive user interfaces for multiple devices and applications. This is achieved by adopting the use of UIDL specifications [4], which are processed by a network of agents who collaborate to both adapt the GUI to the local platform, as well as to learn from user interactions. By using the proposed architecture, application developers only have to specify their GUIs according to their functionality, which will be automatically adapted to each device and user at run-time.

The contributions of this paper can be summarized as follows:

1. We review the state of the art of GUI abstract definitions with specific focus on applicability to current mainstream mobile environments.
2. We introduce the ADUS architecture for GUI adaptation and its application in mainstream mobile computing environment.

The remainder of this paper is structured as follows. Section 2 introduces different existing GUI adaptation approaches, including different architectures and proposals based on mobile agents. In Sect. 3 we summarize the ADUS architecture and show how ADUS uses mainstream UIDLs. Finally, Sect. 4 concludes the paper giving a summary and an outlook.

2   Related Work

The development of GUIs has been and continues being a subject of intensive research, as they provide users with the means to interact with the computers (and applications). Up to this point, the different proposals to develop and generate GUIs can be broadly classified as follows:

1. *Design-time GUIs:* A tool is used to design the application GUI, the tool generates some skeleton to write the interaction code, and finally, the code is then compiled for a specific platform. This approach is presented in Sect. 2.1.
2. *Client-server GUIs:* In this approach, the client component renders the GUI to the specific device and the server component provides the business logic, GUI contents, and any adaptation. This approach is discussed in Sect. 2.2.
3. *Dynamic GUIs:* In this approach, GUIs can be defined at run-time and depend less on specific operating systems. Dynamic approaches are described in Sect. 2.3.
4. *Mobile agent-based GUIs:* Last but not least, the approaches in this category use mobile agent technology to provide mobility and enable collaboration and adaptation of GUIs to devices and user's context in run-time.

In the remainder of this section we will describe details of each of these broad categories of GUIs.

---

[2] ADUS stands for **AD**aptive **U**ser interface for mobile device**S**.

2.1 Design-Time

GUIs defined statically during the application design phase are one of the most common and popular approaches to GUI development. Using this approach, an *abstract* GUI is first defined using the abstract User Interface Description Language (UIDL) [4], and it is then compiled to a *concrete* user interface using a compiler or similar tool. The GUI is specifically designed for the target operating system or device.

The Design-time approaches are able to tailor and fine-tune GUIs to the specific of the target devices or operating systems. However, they require multiple versions of user interaction code to be developed (e.g., Xamarin [2]) or are able to serve only proprietary platforms (e.g., Apple Storyboards [8]). The GUI interaction code needs to be developed multiple times, and if the GUI was to be changed, the application needs to be re-developed and re-deployed to all devices. Software developers need to have significant expertise, know how to code for different devices, and how to work with their quirks. The resulting GUI has limited adaptability to contexts, events, or environments that have not been explicitly considered and developed by the software developer during the application design phase. For example, the software development would need to pre-program GUI code so to adapt to meet user's preferences whilst in a car or whilst at office. Besides, all GUI interaction is typically defined within the single application: GUIs are pre-defined and are not typically modified by other applications (i.e. GUIs are not generated in a collaborative way).

2.2 Client-Server GUIs

In this category of approaches, the client component usually renders the GUI to the specific device and the server component provides business logic, GUI contents, and any adaptation. This approach is very popular on the Internet; in fact, all web pages are delivered this way. In the case of web pages, the GUI is defined by the software developer using HTML [9] as the UIDL.

The client-server approach is very complex. HTML is not sufficient to describe and handle GUIs on its own and is almost always modified using Cascading Style Sheets (CSS) [9] and multiple JavaScript libraries [9] to achieve desired GUI. Client software (Web Browser) need to be developed for each device and existing Web Browser implementations interpret HTML, CSS, and JavaScript differently. Getting run-time insight for troubleshooting in client-server situations is very difficult too [9]. All of this makes client-server GUI difficult to develop and troubleshoot. Finally, the client-server approach relies on the availability of both the server and client component. If the server is 'off line' the GUI cannot be presented. For example, a Smart Watch does not have a Web Browser (the client) and so the HTML GUI cannot be displayed. More importantly, for complex interactions and applications, the GUI requires native code to be developed which, in turn, requires again multiple versions of code to be developed (specific to target operating systems or devices).

2.3 Dynamic GUIs

Some approaches allow GUIs to be defined and adapted as they are executed on the device. Examples of such approach include QML/QT [10]. Using this approach a developer can define GUI using QML notation and the code is bound to the GUI specification at the run time. However, as in the case of QML/QT, availability of the middleware script runtime for QT will be required for different devices or operating systems.

GUI specification languages in this category sometimes do not offer sufficient GUI abstraction level; for example, QML requires stronger widget positioning than other UIDLs. Although QML and QT are available for a number of different operating systems, it is restricted by some mainstream mobile devices (e.g., Apple) in such a way that all code must be statically packaged together, effectively making these approaches equivalent to design-time approach as described in Sect. 2.1. Dynamic GUI generation approach suffers from similar problems as the design-time approach when it comes to user context, device GUI adaptation, and goal orientation (see Sect. 2.4).

2.4 Mobile Agents and Agent-Based GUI Approaches

Mobile agents are autonomous software entities [7] that are capable of migrating from one device to another autonomously and continue their execution on the destination device. Mobile agents are goal oriented and social, i.e., in order to achieve their goal, they collaborate with other mobile agents. They have been used in the context of distributed computing [11] and are gaining popularity in fields such the Internet of Things (IoT) applications [12].

Because of their properties, mobile agents can provide good solutions for adaptive GUIs that are created in a collaborative way. Mobile agents can arrive at the users' device, check the device capabilities (i.e., its display size, the available interaction modes and GUI elements, etc.), and show their GUIs adapting it to the application goals. Thus, they can exploit different models of user interfaces on different and heterogeneous platforms. Due to their autonomy, mobile agents can handle communication errors (unreachable hosts, etc.) by themselves. Also, in contrast to the client-server model, they can move to the target device instead of accessing target devices remotely. For example, agents can be sent to a Windows desktop computer or they can play the role of a proxy server for a wireless device such as a Smart Watch that has limited processing capabilities. A number of researchers have adopted mobile agents technology for GUIs in order to address specific problems [13–15].

In our previous and preliminary work [16], we presented a previous version of our multi-agent system for generating GUIs. The system was using XUL as UIDL and mobile agents to deliver GUIs to different devices. However, the mainstream devices, platforms, and ecosystems have developed significantly over the last few years, and none of the approaches described in this section would be able to work on modern devices. The approach presented in this paper devises a new architecture and implementation that takes into consideration architectural challenges of the current mainstream devices and platforms.

3   ADUS Architecture Overview

ADaptive User interface for mobile deviceS (ADUS) is a system and architecture for generating adaptive GUIs. The ADUS is based on mobile agent technology (see Sect. 2.4) and the use of User Interface Description Languages (UIDLs) in order to achieve its flexibility. Its main goal is to adapt GUIs to devices with very different characteristics (e.g., fixed vs mobile devices, display sizes, input modes, ...).

In this section, firstly, due to their importance in our approach, we present a briefly mainstream UIDLs which we have analysed, and our choice for ADUS. Then, we present our mobile agent architecture which enables the development of adaptive GUIs.

3.1   User Interface Definition Languages

One of the basic aspects of GUI adaptation is the adoption of a User Interface Definition Language (UIDL) [4,5,17] to specify the desired GUI. Using this approach, an *abstract* GUI is first defined using the abstract UIDL, and it is then compiled to a *concrete* user interface. The abstract definitions can be pre-compiled as described in Sect. 2.1, or processed in a dynamic way at run-time (see Sect. 2.3).

We have compared several commercially available mainstream UIDLs [18] to establish their fitness for mobile application development. For space reasons, we focus here on three UIDLs based on their high level of adoption for mobile application development, namely, Android XML, Windows XAML, and Apple's Storyboards:

- **AndroidXML.** Android is by far the most widely used operating systems when it comes to mobile devices (i.e., smartphones and tablets) and the respective UIDL is Android XML [19]. Given the heterogeneity of Android devices, support for GUI adaptation to different devices is provided using layout elements and visual behaviour policies. It is, however, the developer who is in charge to develop and modify GUI so it is correctly adapted to different Android devices.
- **Storyboards (iOS).** Similarly to Android, Apple's iOS also adopts a XML-driven interface via *Storyboards* [8]. Apple's approach goes further than Android: Storyboards use *views* (similar to Android's *activities*), but they can also explicitly include navigation aspects of user interaction in the GUI specification. Thus, a storyboard provides a comprehensive model of the whole application and the workflow of interactions. Storyboards XML is clearly designed to be machine-generated and is not developer-friendly.
- **XAML.** (eXtensible Application Markup Language) [17] is the UIDL developed by Microsoft. XAML is at the core of Microsoft's effort to unify application development on different Microsoft devices and platforms (Unified Windows Platform, UWP) [17]. Such unified applications share a basic API and

GUI elements which are then extended and specialized for specific device families. Although XAML can be used on any Windows-based device, there is still a need to adapt GUIs to specific devices characteristics[3]; also adaptation to non-Windows devices is still required.

For developing the ADUS system, we decided to adopt Microsoft XAML as UIDL as it is most suitable for our use. Comparing with other mainstream and commercially available UIDLs, XAML offers very high abstraction level and is one of the less vendor-specific languages. XAML also offers good visual tools and most importantly native support across Microsoft's extensive ecosystem. XAML can be used as a native tool to develop for both Windows mobile phones, Windows desktop and laptop devices, and other Microsoft devices such as tablets or surface computers. It is important to note that our architecture (as we will see in Sect. 3.2) can use any abstract UIDL to generate adaptive GUIs.

3.2   ADUS Mobile Agent Architecture

In our system, mobile agents collaborate [7] in order to achieve their goal of adapting GUIs. In particular, as we can see in Fig. 1, the ADUS system contains several agents:

1. *Visitor Agent:* This mobile agent contains the core of the application functionality and the business logic used in the application. Apart from the application logic, this agent carries along with him the descriptions of all the different GUI elements (using a UIDL) that it needs to interact with the user.
2. *User Agent:* This static agent is in charge of storing and managing information about the user, her preferences, and the device at which this agent resides. For example, it provides profile and context information such as device type, location, or user's notification and font size preferences.
3. *ADUS Agent:* This static agent is in responsible for orchestrating all the required UIDLs adaptations and transformations, as well as for handling the user-computer interaction by creating the appropriate GUIs.
4. *(Optional) Knowledge agents:* These agents are specialised agents that can learn from collected information (e.g., GUI interaction events) and create knowledge that can be then either 1) passed to ADUS Agent to further adapt/transform the GUI or 2) passed to another agent for their use.

Using these agents and a UIDL to define the GUI, ADUS adopts an indirect generation architecture for generating and managing GUIs[4]. The detailed interaction among agents is as follows (see Fig. 1):

1. The Visitor Agent arrives (or is created) at the target device, carrying both the application code and a basic GUI specification using UIDL.

---

[3] Note that XAML is thus not used only for mobile devices, but for a broad family of heterogeneous devices (e.g., desktop computers, surfaces, consoles, ...).

[4] We refer the interested reader to our previous work [20], where a discussion about the benefits and drawbacks of other possible alternative agent architectures are presented.

2. The resident User Agent detects the Visitor Agent arrival, and creates a new ADUS Agent, which is specifically assigned to the recently arrived Visitor Agent.
3. The Visitor Agent sends the UIDL specification to the newly created ADUS Agent.
4. The ADUS Agent analyses the UIDL specification and passes it to the User Agent, which adapts such a specification to taking into consideration the user preferences and device features (i.e., it applies basic customisations such as font size and background color).
5. The ADUS Agent receives the adapted specification along with other user and device related information from the User Agent which might be relevant for the GUI (e.g., global properties such as when not to disturb the user with notifications).
6. The ADUS Agent generates a GUI for the specific device, reconciling it with the local device interface model and GUI available elements. Moreover, it handles all interaction events forwarding them appropriately to the Visitor Agent and calling its handling callbacks.
7. Each time the Visitor Agent processes a forwarded event, it responds accordingly presenting an updated GUI specification for ADUS' consumption (back to point 3).
8. As ADUS Agent processes interaction data, these data are collected and can be analysed. Such an information can be made available to any agent, e.g., User or Knowledge Agents. These agents can then analyse past interactions, learn from them, and create knowledge that can be applied to improve GUI or application usability. For example, input data could be saved and pre-populated on the next launch of the application. ADUS can use any tool set or learning techniques to enhance the GUI.

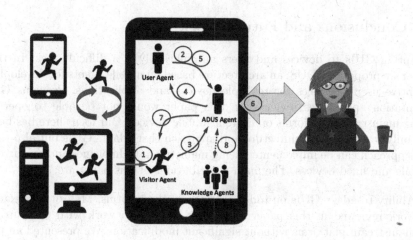

Fig. 1. ADUS: Indirect GUI generation architecture

By using the above method, the different elements of the GUI are created via an ADUS Agent. The GUI can be adapted to target device and to user preferences. In this way, the Visitor Agent does not have to know how to generate GUI or handle interactions with the specific device or user. Besides, note how the ADUS Agent is instantiated by the target platform, so the trust between the User and ADUS Agents is inherent. The trust relationship is important as agents that are not inherently trusted (e.g., the Visitor Agent) could generate GUI that is not appropriate or respecting users' preferences.

The user interactions are completely delegated to the ADUS Agent. The reason is twofold: (1) if the GUI was to be created by the User or Visitor agent, they would need to know how to interpret any GUI specification and create it on any device (this programming effort is put on the development of ADUS versions); and (2) if the User Agent was creating GUIs locally, it would quickly be overloaded by the possible multitude of applications and different tasks (ranging from learning about user and device to creating GUIs).

Finally, it is important to note that our approach allows collection of interaction data independently of the underlying platform. Collected data can be analysed at run time by learning algorithms and specialist agents so that GUI can be improved at the time of execution. The cooperation of agents when creating GUI in our approach is significant: the specification of a GUI is built collaboratively by agents with specialist roles allowing GUI to become truly dynamic and adapted to context and task at hand. For example, a Knowledge Agent can modify GUI specification so to make GUI more usable, and User Agent can help GUI be more adapted to users' preferences.

We have chosen this approach as it enables the creation of a functional, flexible, and trusted user interface. In addition, as multiple Agents collaborate to create a GUI, human computer interaction can be easily monitored and system load can be easily distributed.

4 Conclusions and Future Work

Adapting GUIs to devices and users automatically is a difficult task. In this paper we proposed ADUS, an architecture based on mobile agents for developing adaptive user interfaces for multiple devices and applications. Previous GUI adaptation approaches reviewed in this paper would not be able to operate using mainstream platforms on current mobile devices. Our focus here has been not only to create an architecture and approach that adapts GUIs but also that the approach can be implemented using mainstream technologies and on current mobile and fixed devices. The main contributions of this paper are:

1. Ability to adapt GUIs on today's devices and platforms. Majority of related work reviewed in this paper would not be able to work with the current mainstream platforms without significant modification. We presented an up-to-date architecture (based on mobile agents) for adapting GUIs that is usable for modern mainstream platforms and devices. Using our architecture GUIs

are specified once and automatically adapted to devices and user preferences at run-time.

2. Collaborative GUI. ADUS architecture allows GUIs to be created collaboratively by multiple agents (as opposed by a single entity or agent). Moreover, in ADUS architecture, agents collaborate in order to enhance GUIs at runtime. Our architecture allows monitoring of user behaviour and application of learning techniques to improve the GUI.

As future research we intend to improve content transformation and capturing of GUI events. Finally, we envisage including additional learning and re-targeting algorithms as well as more complex widgets in the prototype.

Acknowledgments. This work was supported by the CICYT project TIN2013-46238-C4-4-R and DGA-FSE.

References

1. Rogers, R., Lombardo, J., Blake, M.: Android Application Development. O'Reilly, Sebastopol (2009)
2. Xamarin: http://www.xamarin.com. Accessed 12 Sept 2016
3. Bullard, V., Smith, K.T., Daconta, M.C.: Essential XUL Programming. Wiley, Hoboken (2001)
4. Abrams, M., Phanouriou, C., Batongbacal, A.L., Williams, S.M., Shuster, J.E.: UIML: an appliance-independent XML user interface language. Comput. Netw. **31**(11), 1695–1708 (1999)
5. Michotte, B., Vanderdonckt, J.: GrafiXML, a multi-target user interface builder based on UsiXML. In: Proceedings of 4th International Conference on Autonomic and Autonomous Systems (ICAS 2008), pp. 15–22. IEEE Computer Society, March 2008
6. Coninx, K., Luyten, K., Vandervelpen, C., Van den Bergh, J., Creemers, B.: Dygimes: dynamically generating interfaces for mobile computing devices and embedded systems. In: Chittaro, L. (ed.) Mobile HCI 2003. LNCS, vol. 2795, pp. 256–270. Springer, Heidelberg (2003). doi:10.1007/978-3-540-45233-1_19
7. Gray, R.S., Kotz, D., Nog, S., Rus, D., Cybenko, G.: Mobile agents for mobile computing. Technical report TR96-285, Dartmouth College (1996)
8. Neuburg, M.: Progamming iOS 9. O'Reilly, Sebastopol (2015)
9. Weyl, E.: Mobile HTML5. O'Reilly, Sebastopol (2013)
10. Rischpater, R.: Application Development with Qt Creator, 2nd edn. Packt Publishing, Birmingham (2014)
11. Bobed, C., Ilarri, S., Mena, E.: Distributed mobile computing: development of distributed applications using mobile agents. In: Proceeding of the 16th International Conference on Parallel and Distributed Computing (PDPTA 2010), CSREA Press, pp. 562–568, July 2010
12. Leppänen, T., Liu, M., Harjula, E., Ramalingam, A., Ylioja, J., Närhi, P., Riekki, J., Ojala, T.: Mobile agents for integration of internet of things and wireless sensor networks. In: Proceedings of 2013 IEEE International Conference on Systems, Man, and Cybernetics (SMC 2013), pp. 14–21. IEEE Computer Society, October 2013

13. Liu, H., Lieberman, H., Selker, T.: A model of textual affect sensing using real-world knowledge. In: Proceedings of the 8th International Conference on Intelligent User Interfaces (IUI 2003), pp. 125–132. ACM, January 2003

14. Su, C.J., Chu, T.W.: A mobile multi-agent information system for ubiquitous fetal monitoring. Int. J. Environ. Res. Public Health **11**(1), 600–625 (2014)

15. Vassileva, J., Mccalla, G., Greer, J.: Multi-agent multi-user modeling in I-Help. J. User Model. User-Adap. Interact. **13**(1–2), 179–210 (2003)

16. Mitrović, N., Mena, E.: Adaptive user interface for mobile devices. In: Forbrig, P., Limbourg, Q., Vanderdonckt, J., Urban, B. (eds.) DSV-IS 2002. LNCS, vol. 2545, pp. 29–43. Springer, Heidelberg (2002). doi:10.1007/3-540-36235-5_3

17. Nathan, A.: Building Windows 10 Applications with XAML and C# Unleashed, 2nd edn. Sams, Carmel (2016)

18. Mitrovic, N., Bobed, C., Mena, E.: A review of user interface description languages for mobile applications. In: Proceedings of 10th International Conference on Mobile Ubiquitous Computing, Systems, Services and Technologies (UBICOMM 2016), ARIA XPS, October 2016

19. Morris, J.: Android User Interface Development. Packt Publishing, Birmingham (2011)

20. Mitrovic, N., Royo, J., Mena, E.: Adus: indirect generation of user interfaces on wireless devices. In: Proceedings of 7th International Workshop Mobility in Databases and Distributed Systems (MDDS 2004), Within 15th International Workshop on Database and Expert Systems Applications (DEXA 2004), Springer 1–5, September 2004

Learning by Tracking - Distributed Systems in Education

Michael Höding[✉]

TH Brandenburg, University of Applied Sciences,
Magdeburger Str. 50, 14770 Brandenburg/Havel, Germany
michael.hoeding@th-brandenburg.de
http://www.th-brandenburg.de

Abstract. Teaching distributed systems means to force the understanding of complexity and heterogeneity from different perspectives. The wide spectrum of legacy techniques and standards as well as up-to-date technology and future ideas is quite challenging. Learning science promises that personal experiences result in a deeper knowledge of problems and solutions in the field of distributed systems. For that we design a show case, managing a relay run (marathon) using android smartphones as relay batons and a web based infrastructure for data management. Whereas the system represents a quite small example it shows different problems, e.g., sensor data, energy management or evolution of smartphone operating systems or software development tools. Being part of the project, e.g. producing the tracking data as runner with an smartphone, students see the impact of own development steps made before. Also they can analyze their own sensor data after a run. Thus they are able to transfer this knowledge to integration or development projects in real enterprise scenarios.

1 Motivation

The development of distributed systems is an evolutionary process [11]. On one hand we have international organizations and communities which define clear and useful standards. Generally, this standardization process lasts some years. Therefore we have on the other hand independent approaches to solve a specific problem on implementing a distributed system. Whereas in the past these approaches were contradictory nowadays standardization processes include best practice examples from the real world. However we have to point out that the wide variety of standards, solutions and problems often result in heterogeneous systems. Students have to learn that a real system is generally not the perfect system that can be constructed with up-to-date standards und techniques. They have to consider that a system was developed in a specific time interval with available (legacy) technology and by developers with partially outdated knowledge. Whereas HTML5 now dominates the development of Web interfaces five year ago Adobe flash was the common, but often criticized approach. This effect can be boosted in a really dynamic area, like app development. For that teaching distributed systems has to cover.

I. Ciuciu et al. (Eds.): OTM 2016 Workshops, LNCS 10034, pp. 293–302, 2017.
DOI: 10.1007/978-3-319-55961-2_30

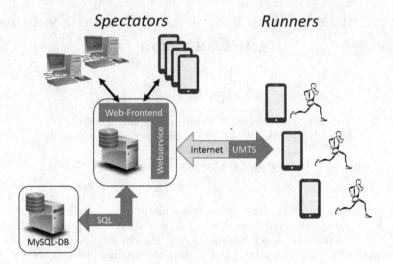

Fig. 1. Components of the distributed tracking system.

- up-to-date standards and techniques,
- legacy standards and techniques,
- awareness of problems and
- a tolerant attitude to heterogeneity

For that we design an annual experiment with the same task that illustrates many problems and solutions in mobile distributed systems. Smartphones are utilized as the baton for a marathon relay run. The smartphones send telemetry data in defined periods to the server. The audience can follow the running competition with a web frontend. Whereas this idea was relatively new in the first year today the smartphone based tracking is standard for sports or gaming. However the experiments covering development of frontend (smartphone app), backend and the application self (running) still produces valuable experiences for the participants.

2   System Architecture

The system architecture is sketched in Fig. 1. The central component is the webserver running. The webserver offers a web service for the tracking clients. The client app is deployed for android smartphones. The protocol is based an HTML and JSON messages [2,6]. The second interface is the website for spectators using HTML5 [10]. Not depicted is the connection to google map web services resp. open street map, which delivers the dynamic maps for the animation of tracks. The Webserver uses a SQL database on a different server in the internal network of the THB[1]. The reason for a separate server for the database are the

---

[1] Technische Hochschule Brandenburg - University of Applied Sciences Brandenburg.

restricted functions of the public webserver which can be connected from outside the university. This is also an example for unexpected constraints in the implementation of the distributed system.

Whereas the communication between spectator clients and central server or central server and database server is straight forward the connection from smartphone to central server is more critical. Here the transparent connection from cellphone network to internet shows sometimes an unstable behavior. This causes missing of telemetry packages or an uncertain delay.

3   Implementation and Preparation

The implementation of the systems addresses numerous skills from different courses. The design of the database is a repetition of SQL knowledge. The database schema is quite simple showing the single telemetry tuple associated with a team. In the mobile context we use the device ID of a smartphone for identification. To be flexible for future developments and for debugging we add a table collection all messages sent to the central server. Thus programming errors in the decoding part of the web service are less critical.

The implementation of the web service interface is based on HTTP GET using PHP [8]. This is well know from previous courses on database interface design. Moreover Android support HTTP objects in several development environments. The telemetry data is coded by JSON.

The very first running app was developed with the MIT App Inventor [12]. A very simple puzzle of clock, location and web components delivers tracking data to the server (see Fig. 2). However MIT App Inventor apps follow the android process state model. So an app falls to sleep when the smartphone screen switches to dark. Therefore the following versions were based on standard android development environments with Android SDK - first NetBeans, than the Android Studio. Also here the implementation is minimal. The thin client approach reduces the test of new versions on smartphone side.

The front end should visualize the run. For the live event we provide a map based on Google Maps [3] showing the position of the runner. The position is set by a periodic AJAX [5] request (every 5 s) without reload of the webpage

Fig. 2. Simple smartphone app using MIT app inventor.

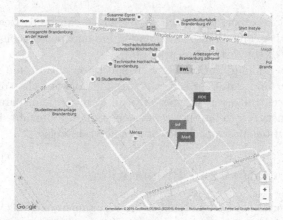

Fig. 3. Presentation of tracking data with Google maps - the position of active relays during the event.

containing the map. Because of the poll technique on the smartphone side and the spectator client side the shown position is not the current position of the runner (Fig. 4).

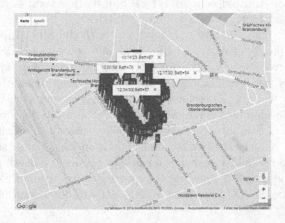

Fig. 4. Presentation of tracking data - the collected positions of one team.

The preparation or deployment phase is often underestimated by students. Whereas a tested stable release of the smartphone app is delivered a week before the competition we observe problems just before the event. Competitors bring their own device but have restrictions or special options for the usage of location providers or web access (see Fig. 3). This effect is enhanced in Android because the dynamic development of the operation system and the high number of existing versions. The poor but working solution for the organizer is to bring smartphones prepared especially for the run. Moreover the exact timing of app start and running is a problem. This is solved as shown before by a server based start event and an independent start of the smartphone app before the official start.

4   Lessons to Learn

This section sketches some exercises and problems connected with the project.

4.1   Timestamps and Delays

By theory the network is fast and we have latency times below one second. In practice we can measure the delay and the distribution with respect to the specific mobile network - generally students have different providers. Without network we can use the clock of the database server or the central server or the smartphone (see Fig. 5). The smartphone time is without delay whereas the server time is distorted by the transmission time. Otherwise smartphone clocks can differ. A simple straight forward implementation with database time shows problems when calculating the speed. However this can be hidden by inaccurate positions from the GPS sensors.

Questions, Discussions, Exercises
 – Which alternatives for timestamps of a track record are availbale?
 – How can we measure delays and identify patterns?

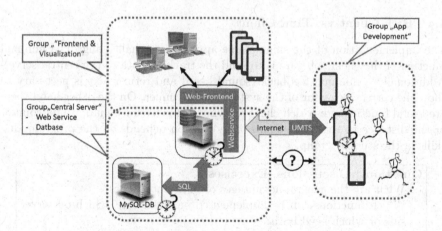

Fig. 5. Components and task for group work.

4.2   Database Structure

The database is the central infrastructure for logging telemetry data. Whereas we have several writing clients (the smartphones of the different teams) there is no concurrent writing (updating) of the same log entry. Parallel access in the web interface is only reading. Therefore redundant data structures are not critical.

> **Questions, Discussions, Exercises**
> - Do we need a normalized database structure? Is there parallel writing access resp. a need for ACID transaction?
> - How can we identify smartphones, teams, tracking entries or rounds?
> - How can we deal with flexibility for future developments?

4.3 Protocol for Web Services

The basic requirement for a protocol is that client and server use the same language. The first version of the systems used a own protocol with name value pairs. Of course, this approach is difficult to understand and has to solve problems like encoding of special characters. Here standards for web services can solve the common problems [7]. The experience to define an own protocol or use standard techniques, e.g. JSON or XML for the definition of the top level protocol is quite valuable. Therefore it is a perfect task for group discussion simulating a standardization process.

> **Questions, Discussions, Exercises**
> - Which standard formats can used for the telemetry data?
> - Which protocol stack is used for the transmission of smartphone data?

4.4 Rich Client vs. Thin Client

The implementation of the smartphone app is quite challenging. The minimal function of the client software is to send the tracking data to the central server. Additionally a minimal feedback (sound beep) and return text is necessary to show the correct behavior of the system to the runner. On the other hand there are useful functions for a rich client showing distance, track map, round counter or the distance to the other teams. The decision depends on the programming skills of the student group.

> **Questions, Discussions, Exercises**
> - What are the general advantages of both approaches?
> - Which functions can be implemented on client side, which on server side or which need both?

4.5 Accuracy of GPS-Signals

A location object in the Android SDK allows the transparent use of Android location services. Here the different location providers are possible, e.g. GPS or network [9]. GPS generally delivers positions with an accuracy of 10 m, sometimes less one meter. However with a moving object and GPS shadows of buildings the accuracy might be a problem. The replay of stored position data shows track point off the running course, as depicted in Fig. 6. After a run one can analyze the position data to find patterns. The visualization of a track delivers an easy approach to this subject.

Questions, Discussions, Exercises
- How can one find bad tracking points?
- Is there a dependency between smartphone, os version and accuracy?
- Which physical structures (buildings) cause errors?

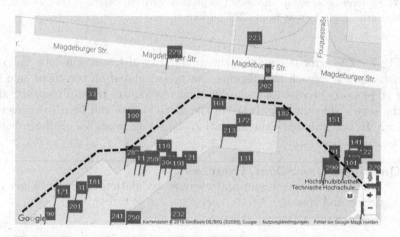

Fig. 6. The distribution of GPS positions offside the dashed line (real course) illustrate the general GPS accuracy problems.

4.6 Energy Consumption vs. Short Intervals

Energy consumption is a serious problem for smartphones [1]. The extensive use of energy consuming components like GPS sensor and network data transmission in a short interval is generally a problem for the four hour running event (see also Fig. 3 right). Otherwise short interval transmission (e.g. five seconds) delivers more data and a finer track.

Questions, Discussions, Exercises
- How can one measure power consumption?
- What is the difference between different periods?

4.7 Distance Measuring

The distance between two points can be calculated by Pythagoras. Due to bends of the track the calculated distance is generally shorter than the real distance

Fig. 7. Systematic error in distance calculation with 30 s steps - Left: real running course, rigth: track derived from GPS positions

(cf. Fig. 7). The error depends on the granularity of tracking points. Following the rich client approach the distance can be calculated on the client side with short steps every second and an additional mechanism to skip bad GPS data. On the server side the knowledge of the given course can help to correct the distance. In our example implementation the server sends the distance back to the client as a text string.

Questions, Discussions, Exercises
- What are the maximum and average calculation errors for a given period and speed?
- How can one minimize this errors?

4.8   Counting Rounds

Associated with distance measuring is the count of rounds. The round is measured before the event and has a known fixed distance. Thus finalizing a round helps to correct distance errors. Crossing the finish line means the difference between coordinates of the finish line and the runners move from negative to positive (or vice versa). In dependence of the running direction the calculation can be reduced to either longitude or latitude. The round information is also transmitted to the smartphone screen.

Questions, Discussions, Exercises
- How can the round counter minimize the distance errors?
- Which calculation method and period is appropriate for the specific course?

4.9   Smooth Animation

The animation of a current running event is the main application for the spectators side. Using a long period (e.g. 30 s) the flags of the runners jump in big steps
like 70 m. Because this is asynchronous the presented order might be different to
the real order. Here one can implement a soft animation using the speed of the
last step to estimate the position every second connected with the knowledge of
the exact course. This can be done on the server side (PHP) or in the browser
(Java Script).

> **Questions, Discussions, Exercises**
> - How can the position be estimated based on speed (last tracking
>   points) and course details?
> - Which advantages/disadvantages has the implementation in server or
>   in client (browser)?

4.10   Evolution of Operation System and SDK

Despite the restriction to focus only on Android we have to deal with evolution of
the operating system. Observing the period of five years now we see esp. changes
in rights management. The reason is an increased awareness of smartphone users
dealing with their personal data i.e. tracking information. This restricts the app
to a limited range of Android versions and requires software adaption every
year. Thus the adaption of the latest version of the smartphone app causes the
reflection of os evolution.

> **Questions, Discussions, Exercises**
> - Which SDK version is associated with which technology in rights
>   management?
> - Which Android version should be supported by the current smart-
>   phone app?

4.11   Reflecting Complexity in the Distributed System

The development of the system is done by different student teams. First they
have to develop their own component. For that they have to define the interface
to the components of other groups. This is a dynamic group negotiation process
restricted not only by technical aspects but also by emotions and persons. Moreover they have to deal with the legacy system of the last years work. Stepping
back this is a good playing ground to reflect the consequences of design decisions
and the complexity of the system.

> **Questions, Discussions, Exercises**
> - How does a new sensor attribute influence the system?
> - Which improvements, e.g. use of standards, can reduce side effects?

5   Conclusion and Outlook

The design and implementation of a distributed system is generally a task of many years. To simulate problems and to create a playing field close to real world scenarios we design an annual experiment covering smartphone app, database and web frontend. The system is used for the yearly running event at our university. The user experience is enhanced by the physical adventure being part of the run. Also test runs before the event are outstanding experiences showing the often unexpected behavior of a distributed system. Future work will analyze collected data in more detail and address the app development with newer android versions.

References

1. Biagioni, J., Musa, A.B.M., Eriksson, J.: Thrifty tracking: online GPS tracking with low data uplink usage. In: 21st SIGSPATIAL International Conference on Advances in Geographic Information Systems, SIGSPATIAL 2013, Orlando, FL, USA, 5–8 November 2013, pp. 486–489 (2013). http://doi.acm.org/10.1145/2525314.2525469
2. ECMA: The json data interchange format. July 2014 http://www.ecma-international.org/publications/files/ECMA-ST/ECMA-404.pdf
3. Google: Google maps APIs, July 2016. https://developers.google.com/maps
4. Hanus, M.D., Fox, J.: Assessing the effects of gamification in the classroom: a longitudinal study on intrinsic motivation, social comparison, satisfaction, effort, and academic performance. Comput. Educ. **80**, 152–161 (2015). http://dx.doi.org/10.1016/j.compedu.2014.08.019
5. Holzinger, A., Mayer, S., Slany, W., Debevc, M.: The influence of AJAX on web usability. In: Proceedings of the International Conference on e-Business, ICE-B 2010, Athens, Greece, 26–28 July 2010, ICE-B is part of ICETE - The International Joint Conference on e-Business and Telecommunications, pp. 124–127 (2010)
6. Kelly, S.: Speeding up AJAX with JSON, July 2006. http://www.developer.com/lang/jscript/article.php/3596836
7. Lemos, A.L., Daniel, F., Benatallah, B.: Web service composition: a survey of techniques and tools. ACM Comput. Surv. **48**(3), 33 (2016). http://doi.acm.org/10.1145/2831270
8. Mitchell, L.J.: Web Service Composition. O'Reilly, Sebastopol (2016)
9. Ranacher, P., Brunauer, R., Trutschnig, W., van der Spek, S., Reich, S.: Why GPS makes distances bigger than they are. Int. J. Geogr. Inf. Sci. **30**(2), 316–333 (2016). http://dx.doi.org/10.1080/13658816.2015.1086924
10. Schmitt, C., Simpson, K.: HTML5 Cookbook - Solutions and Examples for HTML5 Developers. O'Reilly, Sebastopol (2012). http://www.oreilly.de/catalog/9781449396794/index.html
11. Tanenbaum, A.S., Steen, M.V.: Distributed Systems: Principles and Paradigms, 2nd edn. Prentice-Hall Inc., Upper Saddle River (2006)
12. Walter, D., Sherman, M.: Learning MIT App Inventor: A Hands-On Guide to Building Your Own Android Apps. Addison Wesley, Reading (2014)

OnTheMove Academy (OTMA) 2016

The 13th OnTheMove Academy Chairs' Message

Last year's innovation was the addition of a collaborative paper clinic session integrating the idea of "Ph.D. student buddies" who review and help to improve one another's submission under the guidance of an OTMA faculty member. This fits very well with this year's innovation: post Academy proceedings. Participants now have the opportunity to improve their paper and publish the improved version.

The OTMA faculty members, who are well-respected researchers and practitioners, critically reflect on the students' work in a positive and inspiring atmosphere, so that the students learn to improve not only their research capacities but also their presentation and writing skills. OTMA participants learn how to review scientific papers. They also enjoy ample possibilities to build and expand their professional network thanks to access to all OTM conferences and workshops. OTMA Ph.D. students publish their work in a highly reputed publication channel, namely the Springer LNCS OTM workshops proceedings. And last but not least, an ECTS credit certificate rewards their hard work.

Crucial for the success of OTM Academy is the commitment of our other OTMA faculty members whom we sincerely thank:

- Josefa Kumpfmüller (Vienna, Austria), Student Communication Seminar
- Erich J. Neuhold (University of Vienna, Austria), OTMA Dean

The OTMA submissions were reviewed by an international programme committee of well-respected experts. We gratefully thank them for their effort and time:

- Galia Angelova (Bulgarian Academy of Science, Sofia, Bulgary)
- Christoph Bussler (Tropo Inc., USA)
- Paolo Ceravolo (Università degli Studi di Milano, Italy)
- Claudia d'Amato (Università degli Studi di Bari, Italy)
- Manu De Backer (University of Ghent, Belgium)
- Rik Eshuis (Technical University Eindhoven, The Netherlands)
- Claudia Jimenez (Universidad de los Andes, Chile)
- Frédéric Le Mouël (University of Lyon, France)
- Hervé Panetto (University of Lorraine, France)
- Erik Proper (Public Research Centre - Henri Tudor, Luxembourg)
- Rudi Studer (Karlsruhe Institute of Technology, Germany)

We also express our thanks to Christophe Debruyne (Trinity College Dublin) who again volunteered to be the OTMA 2016 "social media master".

This year, six papers were submitted by Ph.D. students. Two submissions" are published as regular papers, and two as short papers. We hope that you find the ideas of these upcoming researchers promising and inspiring for your own research.

October 2016

Peter Spyns
Maria-Esther Vidal

Exploring On-Demand Composition of Pervasive Collaborations in Smart Computing Environments

Markus Wutzler[✉]

Chair of Computer Networks, Technische Universität Dresden,
01062 Dresden, Germany
markus.wutzler@tu-dresden.de

Abstract. The increasing amount and interconnection of smart devices holds a high potential for complex collaborations. Smart computing environments will heavily rely on the collaboration of multiple of such systems but they also become more decentralized and volatile. Such collaborations cannot be managed centrally anymore as they emerge and disappear dynamically. The key challenges of such systems are specification of complex collaborations as well as decentralized discovery, composition and subsequent adaptation. We introduce the term *Pervasive Collaboration* which captures complex collaborations at run time as a dynamic set of distributed, loosely coupled, on-demand collaborating systems in decentralized environments. The concept of roles, which aims for loose coupling of abstract functionality and its actual performance, is utilized to ease both composition and reconfiguration of Pervasive Collaborations. We propose a middleware architecture for distributed adaptive role-based software systems which provides a decentralized discovery mechanism, on-demand composition and subsequent adaptation. We will evaluate our concept based on several case studies and failure scenarios as well as in terms of limitations, scalability and trade-off.

1 Motivation

Smart computing environments, e.g., Smart Cities, Smart Factories or the Internet of Things, will become more and more decentralized and volatile. Thus, a predefined central coordinator cannot be assumed. Additionally, such environments will heavily rely on spontaneous collaboration of multiple adaptive subsystems. Nowadays, for instance, smart devices already collaborate although never being specifically designed for each other, e.g., a smart tv acts as a display for a smart phone on-demand. The variety of interactions and continuously operating collaborations is limited – mostly to one-to-one collaborations or chains of such. The increasing number and interaction of smart systems holds a high potential of more complex on-demand collaborations, which will incorporate multiple systems in more complex relationships. How such complex collaborations in decentralized environments can be composed on-the-fly at run time, where no predefined central coordinator is available, is a question yet to be answered.

© Springer International Publishing AG 2017
I. Ciuciu et al. (Eds.): OTM 2016 Workshops, LNCS 10034, pp. 305–314, 2017.
DOI: 10.1007/978-3-319-55961-2_31

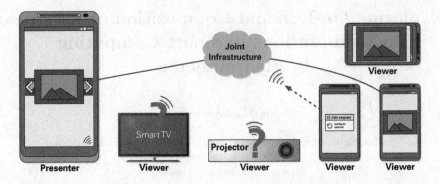

Fig. 1. Scenario: distributed slideshow collaboration.

A *Complex Collaboration* can incorporate multiple collaborators with the same capabilities simultaneously, i.e., it can bind multiple instances of the same type simultaneously, which is challenging in a decentralized environment. It supports relationships others than only one-to-one, multiplicities, constraints and (fully) meshed relationships, i.e., all collaborators are interconnected. The availability of a certain collaborator might be optional by purpose. Communication between collaborating systems will be asynchronous and bidirectional, thus, there is no assumption on a predefined control flow. Collaborations will be composed *on-demand*, i.e., an event causes the system structure and its interconnection to be created on-the-fly at run time. Thus, we introduce the term *Pervasive Collaborations* which captures complex collaborations at run time as a dynamic set of distributed, loosely coupled, on-demand collaborating systems. Pervasive Collaborations are composed on-demand and can be recomposed over time, which leads to adaptivity in the sense of structural reconfiguration. Additionally, Pervasive Collaborations are considered to operate in environments, where no predefined central coordinator can be assumed.

Consider a distributed on-demand slideshow (Fig. 1): You are in a bar and want to share some photos with your friends. Instead of handing around the smart phone, which makes other people snooping for photos they should not see, the photos should be displayed on devices having the (photo) displaying capability. The presenter is initiating and coordinating the decentralized slideshow. Smart devices having the (photo) displaying capability can join and leave the composition over time. All devices must be attached to a joint infrastructure, e.g., an ad-hoc network. In this example a one-to-many relationship exists between the presenter and its viewers. The environment is decentralized and volatile as devices can (dis-)appear over time. Communication is asynchronous and bidirectional as viewers might be able to switch back and forth without affecting other participants or give feedback to the presenter. For the sake of simplicity, we rely on this use case in the remainder of this paper. However, the presented approach is not limited to such simple scenarios.

Pervasive Collaborations lead to distributed adaptive software systems. Centralized or distributed approaches for Self-Adaptive Software System are infeasible as they always require a predefined central instance [9]. Decentralized approaches rely on dependency-based composition [2,4,13] of individual components but do not support complex collaborations due to missing specifications. In summary, run-time composition of Pervasive Collaborations remains challenging because existing approaches do not support either complex collaborations or automated discovery, composition and subsequent adaptation.

To tackle these challenges, we propose a middleware architecture for distributed adaptive role-based software systems which provides a (1) decentralized discovery mechanism, and (2) on-demand composition and subsequent adaptation of Pervasive Collaborations. We utilize the concept of roles to ease both composition and reconfiguration of such systems. Preliminary explorations have been presented in [17]. In this paper we introduce the notion of *Pervasive Collaborations*, explain our understanding of roles, elaborate on the conceptual part and refine the research questions and hypothesis.

As foundation of our approach, we first introduce the concept of roles in Sect. 2 followed by our research questions, hypothesis and goals in Sect. 3. Section 4 discusses related work continued by Sect. 5, which presents our approach. In Sect. 6, we explain the evaluation of our approach. Finally, Sect. 7 concludes this paper and provides an outlook on future work.

2   Concept of Roles

The concept of roles used in this paper conforms to the informal definition given by Boella and Steimann [1], in which a role encapsulates an abstract functionality which will be utilized in collaboration with other roles. The actual performance of the role's abstract functionality is delegated to the role's player which is bound dynamically. Roles can specify requirements for their players (e.g., class restrictions, provided methods or contextual properties) which allows for dynamic binding of roles and players at run time. Additionally, they define a collaboration as "a structure of collaborating roles" [1].

Kühn et al. derived a list of 26 features [11] classifying role-based modeling and programming languages concerning their relational and context-dependent nature. This resulted in a formal foundation for relational context-dependent roles [10], which is intended to become the formal foundation of our concept. The separation between abstract functionality and concrete performance, combined with the ability to loosely couple roles, makes this concept interesting for easing composition and adaptation of loosely coupled systems. Hereafter, we use the following terminology:

Collaboration. A collaboration specifies a self-contained set of collaborating roles, which in turn defines a consistent system configuration.

Role. A role encapsulates abstract functionality (method interface and abstract implementation). It provides a collaborative interface, an interface which can be accessed by other roles within the same collaboration. The *role type* refers to the specification of the role within the specification of the collaboration, whereas the role instance refers to the instantiation acquired by the player.

Player. A player provides the actual performance of a role by means of complementing the partial implementation of the role's behavior.

Adaptive (Sub-)System. An instantiated collaboration is considered as an adaptive system because its structure can be recomposed at run time. The subsystem refers to a run time providing a player (and respective role instance) which is adaptive because it could acquire new or drop existing roles.

3   Research Hypothesis and Questions

The concept of roles was introduced as a promising abstraction for easing composition and adaptation of loosely coupled systems. From our initial research question, how complex collaborations in decentralized environments can be composed on-the-fly at run time, we derive the following research questions:

RQ 1. Are role-based models expressive enough to represent complex collaborations at run time?

RQ 2. Do role-based models allow for dynamic composition and subsequent adaptation of distributed, loosely coupled systems at run time?

RQ 3. What are the limitations of enforcing (partial) application structures in decentralized, loosely coupled, on-demand collaborating systems?

RQ 4. What is the trade-off, respectively?

Our approach is based on the hypothesis that, *at run time, role-based collaboration models are more flexible and expressive than existing composition models concerning on-demand composition and subsequent adaptation of loosely coupled systems in decentralized environments.* Concerning the first two questions a research artifact and corresponding case studies will be developed. Our goal is to compute all information, necessary for run-time composition, from the role-based collaboration specifications modeled at design time. We will evaluate the research artifact in terms of limitations and trade-off based on the case studies and to a baseline provided by related approaches (cf. Sect. 4.2), respectively.

4   Related Work

This section discusses approaches that address the challenges of run-time composition of Pervasive Collaborations. First, role-based composition approaches in Sect. 4.1 are analyzed. Subsequently, Self-Adaptive Software System, which tackle the challenge of adaptive applications, are discussed in Sect. 4.2.

4.1   Role-Based Composition

In literature, two different perspectives on the concept of roles exist: player-centric and organization-centric [3]. In the player-centric view, roles are attached to a player (core object) in order to add, remove or manipulate behavior. *Smart*

Application Grids (SMAGs) [12] uses role-based composition to compose adaptive software systems. In *SMAGs*, a role is an instance of a *provided port*, i.e., it adapts the behavior of one component to comply with another component. *LyRT* [14,15] provides a dynamic instance binding for loose coupling of roles and players on a local run-time as well as a mechanism to add new roles to the system at run time in order to improve modularity and variability.

In the organization-centric view, roles exist independently of their players, are linked together and found a self-contained organization. Players can be exchanged in order to perform the role in a different manner. The *Helena Approach* [7] provides a formal foundation for modeling distributed systems by teaming up roles into ensembles, which are "groups of active entities that collaborate to perform a certain task." [7] Players in this approach have no intrinsic behavior, thus, exchanging player does not result in different performance of a role. *Macodo* [6] provides a conceptual model for dynamic collaborations of distributed service-oriented architectures by means of functional decomposition of business processes into smaller units in order to improve modularity and reusability. Roles in *Macodo* are an abstraction of underlying systems to comply with the business process. *Macodo* is a design-time approach, which does not focus on run-time aspects of roles. *Role Oriented Adaptive Design* [3], focuses on adaptability, but does not support distributed applications; however, this proves the applicability of roles to build adaptive non-distributed systems. A collaboration in our approach denotes a self-contained specification, thus, our approach primarily adopts the organization-centric view.

4.2 Self-Organizing Software System

Recently, Krupitzer et al. [9] investigated the research landscape of Self-Adaptive Software System. Only a few approaches address decentralized control, which corresponds to Weyns et al. [16] who conclude that "state-of-the-art self-adaptive frameworks lack support for a growing class of systems in which central control is not an option." These few systems belong to the group of Self-Organizing Software System(SOSSs) [5], which achieve complex behavior through interactions among individual, autonomous subsystems.

A key concept of SOSSs is to match provided and required ports based on service dependencies. Fulfilling such dependencies is usually limited to binding one instance of a type to one instance of another type even if multiple instances are available. *MetaSelf* [4] provides a software architecture and development method for engineering SOSSs. It relies on self-describing components, services, or agents and a coordination/emptyadaptation service. As parts of the architecture can be only distributed but not replicated, full decentralization is not supported. *FlashMob* [13] is a decentralized algorithm for self-assembly. It uses the gossip protocol for aggregating and distributing state information. *State* represents *active* dependencies that describe a system configuration of multiple components. This improves scalability by reaching an agreement on a particular solution in a logarithmic number of steps with respect to the size of the network. *GoPrime* [2] is a decentralized middleware for adaptive self-assembly of distributed services. Each peer can perform tasks, but could require services offered by other peers to carry them out. Required and provided services are matched using a joint ontology and quality-of-service attributes. In *Distributed Emergent Ensembles of Components* (DEECo) [8] component communication and bindings are extracted from the implementation and implicitly specified in an ensemble specification. Data is obtained from the component by a middleware layer and shared with other components. Each component solely relies on its local data. Components are considered to be autonomous, thus, there is no explicit interaction between them. Roles in *DEECo* are a specification for provided data attributes. Except *DEECo*, no SOSS supports *complex collaborations*. *DEECo* itself supports a more complex structure, but collaborations are limited in a way that roles in *DEECs* have no behavior, i.e., no methods and corresponding implementations.

5   Middleware Architecture and Approach

The high-level middleware architecture, running on each adaptive subsystem, is depicted in Fig. 2[1]. Our main focus is on decentralized discovery, coordinated composition and subsequent adaptation of collaborations. Adaptive subsystems (smart phone) know their roles (slideshow host/presenter) and how they can utilize them in collaboration with other subsystems (photo displaying smartphone). Further we assume that an (user) event triggers a certain subsystem to initialize collaborations with others. Each subsystem has a repository containing collaboration specifications and their respective triggers.

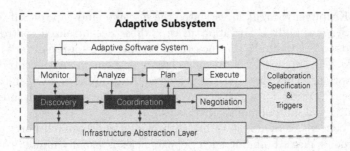

Fig. 2. High-level middleware architecture.

Our middleware architecture consists of a *discovery module* to gather knowledge about the infrastructure and a *Coordination* module primarily responsible for composing collaborations in a coordinated manner, which will be presented in more detail in the remainder of this section. The *Negotiation* module will solve ambiguities and run-time errors. To abstract from the network infrastructure

---

[1] Colors indicate scope of research: dark blue – in scope, light blue – partial, white – out of scope.

the modules for discovery and coordination are connected to an *Infrastructure Abstraction Layer*. This layer is responsible for abstraction of and communication with other autonomous subsystems.

5.1   Discovery

The *Discovery* module extracts discovery information from role-based collaboration specifications and acquires information about systems in the infrastructure.

We consider the role-based collaboration specification[2] to be self-contained, i.e., the collaboration is specified as a whole, including all roles and their interconnections. Additionally, the specification can declare context features for both the collaboration and its roles as required. From this specification, we derive an abstract implementation, including collaboration structure, (partial) role implementations and placeholders for context features. The abstract implementation must be complemented by the developer, providing an implementation of at least one player (including values for context features).

Since the player knows its provided role, the role knows its collaboration and the collaboration is aware of its complete structure, basic discovery information can be derived this way. Every subsystem publishes its role information to the *infrastructure abstraction layer*. Maintaining a global view of all available subsystems and roles will be unnecessary as a single subsystem only needs information about other roles in potential collaborations. Adding new subsystems – or a new role to a local subsystem (e.g., using LyRT [14]) – enables incorporation of new functionality, since players can perform roles in new ways.

5.2   Coordinated Composition and Subsequent Adaptation

We propose a protocol, depicted in Fig. 3, to achieve coordinated composition of Pervasive Collaboration in decentralized environments. The *Coordination* module intercepts the local feedback loop and receives events. This event will be processed by the *Composition Management*, which selects the respective collaboration specification. Thereafter, the planning component enriches the selected specification with infrastructure knowledge obtained from the *Discovery* module. Consequently, the computed composition (binding) instructions will be processed and the composition will be set up. In order to achieve a consistent composition (all or nothing), a commit protocol, e.g., two-phase commit protocol, needs to be applied. As the event-consuming subsystem is responsible for setting up the composition, it gains the position of a *Virtual Coordinator* node within the Pervasive Collaboration. We assume that a collaboration will stop working, as soon as the collaboration's initiator fails or stops.

To deal with subsequent adaptation, the *Coordination* module of the virtual coordinator receives the responsibility to monitor changes in the infrastructure

---

[2] We consider a domain specific language as specification. TRoML is a textual modeling language based on [10], which currently does not support loose coupling of roles and players as well as specifying context features.

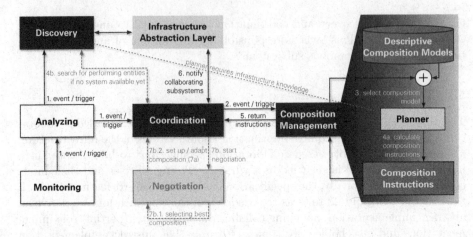

Fig. 3. Protocol for coordinated composition of pervasive collaborations.

and adapt the collaboration as necessary. Reconfiguration will depend on both infrastructural and contextual changes. In Fig. 4, an instantiated collaboration of the initial example is depicted. Among the five smart phones, #1 has the presenter role, #2–#5 have viewer roles, #3 is leaving and #5 wants to join the collaboration. In this case, smart phone #1 monitors the infrastructure, analyzes the configuration and context features and adapts the collaboration if needed.

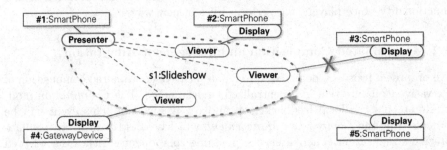

Fig. 4. Instantiated collaboration of distributed slideshow scenario.

6   Evaluation

Our main research goal is to show that role-based collaboration models (1) are more flexible and expressive than existing composition models concerning their run-time advantages, and (2) allow for dynamic composition in decentralized environments without additional run-time management overhead. We prove our concept by defining a couple of case studies. A second scenario considers a tech-enhanced classroom setting in which the lecturer wants to use the students' devices as second screen and a projector. In this scenario, it should be possible to move the presenter role of the lecturer to any of the students.

Hence, we implement these case studies and evaluate our middleware architecture in terms of functional correctness, addressing RQ 1 and RQ 2. We validate functional correctness by exposing the prototypes against several failure scenarios, e.g., node failure or partitioned subnets. Concerning RQ 3, we want to analyze both conceptual (e.g., specification) and run-time (e.g., scalability) limitations. RQ 4 will be answered, comparing our approach against a baseline provided by a recent SOSS, e.g. *GoPrime* [2].

7   Conclusion

In this paper we presented the challenges of On-Demand Composition of Pervasive Collaborations in Smart Computing Environments. So far, existing role-based approaches, i.e., [3,6,8], support Pervasive Collaborations to a certain degree, but fail in terms of run-time composition in decentralized environments. On the contrary, Self-Organizing Software System [2,4,13] perform well in decentralized composition but cannot enforce a more complex system structure.

We tackle these issues by providing a middleware architecture for self-assembly of distributed role-based software systems. The main contributions of this work are a specific discovery mechanism for role-based systems in decentralized environments as well as a protocol for coordinated composition and subsequent adaptation of Pervasive Collaborations.

In the future, we will elaborate on a more sophisticated concept for consistent adaptations within an instantiated collaboration. As mentioned, a subsystem is adaptive, thus, changes on this system could have tremendous side effects on the collaboration as a whole. Besides, we will broaden the variety of case studies to emphasize the advantages of role-based software systems. A current limitation of our approach is that only one Virtual Coordinator per instantiated collaboration is allowed. For the future we will consider multiple of such coordinators, e.g., for replication. Finally, we will investigate, how to incorporate legacy systems using the concept of roles.

Acknowledgements. This work is funded by the German Research Foundation (DFG) within the Research Training Group "Role-based Software Infrastructures for continuous-context-sensitive Systems" (GRK 1907).

References

1. Boella, G., Steimann, F.: Roles and relationships in object-oriented programming, multiagent systems and ontologies. In: Cebulla, M. (ed.) ECOOP 2007. LNCS, vol. 4906, pp. 108–122. Springer, Heidelberg (2008). doi:10.1007/978-3-540-78195-0_11
2. Caporuscio, M., Grassi, V., Marzolla, M., Mirandola, R.: GoPrime: a fully decentralized middleware for utility-aware service assembly. IEEE Trans. Softw. Eng. **42**(2), 136–152 (2016)
3. Colman, A.W.: Role oriented adaptive design. Ph.D. thesis, Swinburne University of Technology (2006)

4. Di Marzo Serugendo, G., Fitzgerald, J.: MetaSelf: an architecture and a development method for dependable self-* systems. In: Proceedings of the 2010 ACM Symposium on Applied Computing, SAC 2010 (2010)

5. Di Marzo Serugendo, G., et al.: Self-organisation: paradigms and applications. In: Di Marzo Serugendo, G., Karageorgos, A., Rana, O.F., Zambonelli, F. (eds.) ESOA 2003. LNCS (LNAI), vol. 2977, pp. 1–19. Springer, Heidelberg (2004). doi:10.1007/978-3-540-24701-2_1

6. Haesevoets, R., Weyns, D., Holvoet, T.: Architecture-centric support for adaptive service collaborations. ACM Trans. Softw. Eng. Methodol. (TOSEM) 23(1), 2–40 (2014)

7. Hennicker, R., Klarl, A.: Foundations for ensemble modeling – the HELENA approach. In: Iida, S., Meseguer, J., Ogata, K. (eds.) Specification, Algebra, and Software. LNCS, vol. 8373, pp. 359–381. Springer, Heidelberg (2014). doi:10.1007/978-3-642-54624-2_18

8. Keznikl, J., Bures, T., Plasil, F., Kit, M.: Towards dependable emergent ensembles of components: the DEECo component model. In: 2012 Joint Working IEEE/IFIP Conference on Software Architecture and European Conference on Software Architecture, pp. 249–252. IEEE (2012)

9. Krupitzer, C., Roth, F.M., VanSyckel, S., Schiele, G., Becker, C.: A survey on engineering approaches for self-adaptive systems. Pervasive Mob. Comput. 17, 184–206 (2015)

10. Kühn, T., Böhme, S., Götz, S., Aßmann, U.: A combined formal model for relational context-dependent roles. In: Proceedings of the 2015 ACM SIGPLAN International Conference on Software Language Engineering, SLE 2015, pp. 113–124 (2015)

11. Kühn, T., Leuthäuser, M., Götz, S., Seidl, C., Aßmann, U.: A metamodel family for role-based modeling and programming languages. In: Combemale, B., Pearce, D.J., Barais, O., Vinju, J.J. (eds.) SLE 2014. LNCS, vol. 8706, pp. 141–160. Springer, Heidelberg (2014). doi:10.1007/978-3-319-11245-9_8

12. Piechnick, C., Richly, S., Götz, S., Wilke, C., Aßmann, U.: Using role-based composition to support unanticipated, dynamic adaptation-smart application grids. In: The Fourth International Conference on Adaptive and Self-Adaptive Systems and Applications, ADAPTIVE 2012 (2012)

13. Sykes, D., Magee, J., Kramer, J.: FlashMob: distributed adaptive self-assembly. In: Proceedings of the 6th International Symposium on Software Engineering for Adaptive and Self-Managing Systems, pp. 100–109. ACM, New York, May 2011

14. Taing, N., Springer, T., Cardozo, N., Schill, A.: A dynamic instance binding mechanism supporting run-time variability of role-based software systems. In: Companion Proceedings of the 15th International Conference on Modularity, MODULARITY Companion 2016, pp. 137–142. ACM, New York (2016)

15. Taing, N., Wutzler, M., Springer, T., Cardozo, N., Schill, A.: Consistent unanticipated adaptation for context-dependent applications. In: Proceedings of the 8th International Workshop on Context-Oriented Programming, COP 2016, pp. 33–38. ACM, New York (2016)

16. Weyns, D., Malek, S., Andersson, J.: On decentralized self-adaptation: lessons from the trenches and challenges for the future. In: Proceedings of the 2010 ICSE Workshop on Software Engineering for Adaptive and Self-Managing Systems, pp. 84–93. ACM, New York, May 2010

17. Wutzler, M.: Composing adaptive software systems in decentralized infrastructures. In: Proceedings of the MobiSys 2016 PhD Forum, MobiSys Ph.D. Forum 2016. ACM, June 2016

Employing Aviation-Specific Contexts for Business Rules and Business Vocabularies Management in SemNOTAM

Felix Burgstaller[(⊠)]

Department for Business Informatics - Data & Knowledge Engineering,
Johannes Kepler University Linz, Linz, Austria
felix.burgstaller@jku.at

Abstract. SemNOTAM is a knowledge and rule-based semantic filter system for safety and time critical announcements of temporary changes to flight conditions (NOTAMs). The relevance and importance of NOTAMs to a specific situation is determined by business rules (BRs). In SemNOTAM, many BRs apply across several situations and thus can be collected into super-situations. To support an incremental BR elicitation process, required by their number, and later maintenance of BRs, an adequate BR management system is vital. However, current systems provide mostly simple organisation techniques insufficient for SemNOTAM.

Many research fields, e.g., library information science, manage large information bases by utilising problem-specific contexts. These contexts may be hierarchically structured. Similarly, we propose aviation-specific contexts to manage BRs and their associated business vocabularies in SemNOTAM. To implement the proposed management system we employ design science. In this paper we present the method, preliminary results, and the evaluation planned to this end.

Keywords: Context models · Business rule management · Business vocabulary management

1 Introduction

NOTAMs (c.f. Table 1 for examples) are vital to flight operations personnel such as pilots, air traffic controllers, or ground control. Nevertheless, flight operations personnel often consider more than 40% of the NOTAMs provided to them as irrelevant to their situation [6,7]. For instance, a helicopter pilot is not interested in a runway (RWY) closure but an airplane pilot on the other hand is. Furthermore, the provided NOTAM sets are often unstructured [20]. This causes information overload, stress, and an increased risk of missing vital information. Thus, a system providing effective intelligent filtering is needed [7,12].

1.1 SemNOTAM

SemNOTAM is such a system enabling fine-grained semantic filtering of NOTAMs [1]. It uses a new XML-based data model for NOTAMs that has

© Springer International Publishing AG 2017
I. Ciuciu et al. (Eds.): OTM 2016 Workshops, LNCS 10034, pp. 315–325, 2017.
DOI: 10.1007/978-3-319-55961-2_32

been introduced by the FAA and EUROCONTROL to enable intelligent filter systems: the Aeronautical Information Exchange Model 5.1. This model allows many flexible constructs, e.g., the compound expression in *N1*. These flexible constructs make applying standard techniques like data mining difficult as the number of input features can vary.

The requirements collected and identified by the authors [1,2,20] can be grouped into functional and non-functional requirements. Functional requirements are: determining relevant NOTAMs regarding time, space, flight plans, aeronautical features (e.g. aerodromes), aircraft characteristics, or any logical combination thereof; importance annotation of NOTAMs; grouping by user-defined criteria; ordering by proximity; and high precision while maintaining 100% recall, i.e., NOTAMs considered relevant to a scenario by flight operations personnel or laws must not be omitted. Non-functional requirements are: customisation without redevelopment, redesign, or redeployment; accountability of results; scalability; and reasonable response times.

The relevance, importance, and groups of a NOTAM depend on the specific situation. Thus, how to determine them is currently tacit knowledge of flight operations personnel. This knowledge can be explicated as BRs using aeronautical business terms (cf. Table 1 for examples). Thus, in each situation specific BRs apply. Many of these BRs apply to more than one situation.

Table 1. Sample NOTAMs and BRs (spatial and temporal relevance omitted).

NOTAM (natural language)	*NOTAM (Simplified objectLogic)*
N1: Due to snow RWY 16/34 at VIE is restricted to wingspan <115 ft and total weight <45t on 8.11.2016	N1: NOTAM[feature-> rwy16_34, restr-> Expr, type->RWYRest, loc-> VIE, valid-> "8.11.2016"]
N2: RWY lighting outage on RWY 16/34 at VIE on 8.11.2016	N2: NOTAM[feature-> rwy16_34, type-> LightOut, loc-> VIE, valid-> "8.11.2016"]
Partial rules (natural language)	*Partial rules (simplified objectLogic)*
R1: A NOTAM is irrelevant if aircraft width is below NOTAM width limit	irrelevant(?N):- aircraft[width-> ?wa], ?N: NOTAM[widthLim-> ?wn], ?wa<?wn
R2: A RWY lighting outage NOTAM is crucial if pilot flies VFR	crucial(?N) :- ?N: NOTAM, flight[type-> VFR], ?N: RwyLightingOut
R3: A RWY lighting outage NOTAM is nice to know if pilot flies IFR	addInfo(?N) :- ?N: NOTAM, flight[type-> IFR], ?N: RwyLightingOut
IFR ... Instrumental flight rules	*VFR ... Visual flight rules*

As a result, SemNOTAM is a rule-based system [1]. The F-logic derivate ObjectLogic provides object-oriented knowledge representation and scalable reasoning well suited for semNOTAM [1]. Consequently, BRs and business terms are represented using ObjectLogic in SemNOTAM (cf. Table 1 for examples).

SemNOTAM supports or satisfies the functional requirements regarding filtering by providing an abstract query interface, the interest specification [1]. An interest specification consists of basic interests combined by conjunctions and disjunctions. Each basic interest is one of the functional filter requirements time, space, aeronautical features, or aircraft characteristics. By combining them using conjunctions and disjunctions flight plans can be represented.

1.2 Problem Description

The large number of situations to be covered requires an incremental BR elicitation process. This was also confirmed in first BR elicitation workshops with passenger pilots. Furthermore, these workshops revealed that the number of BRs necessary for a filter system like SemNOTAM goes into the thousands. Many of these BRs apply not just to a single situation but to several. Consequently, it is possible to arrange situations and their corresponding BRs into hierarchies. For instance, *R1* in Table 1 applies to all situations whereas *R2* applies only to situations where VFR is used. If VFR is used in a situation *R1* as well as *R2* apply. In SemNOTAM the use of flight rules is just one of many attributes describing the different situations.

To support incremental addition, revision, and revocation of BRs, business terms, and situation attributes, an adequate management tool for situations as well as their BRs and associated business vocabulary is required. This management tool must support or satisfy the requirements identified for SemNOTAM. Of particular interest are the requirements *determining relevant NOTAMs* and *customisation*. The former requires automatic determination of the BRs applying in a specific situation. The latter causes an increase in situations, e.g., different flight crews may be interested in different groupings of NOTAMs. Furthermore, customisation includes export of situation subsets to different SemNOTAM systems. A BR management system satisfying these requirements must furthermore be scalable and support reasonable response times. From a user perspective, such a system must support search, browsing, and berrypicking [8]. Berrypicking is an "evolving search with expansion and side-tracking" [8, p. 7] during which the information need, in contrast to search, can change. An example is searching for all BRs and business terms necessary to evaluate a specific BR.

Furthermore, the system must be able to organise existing BR sets. Given an unorganised BR set the system should suggest a potential organisation into situations. The user can then accept or modify this suggestion. Subsequently, the BRs contained in the given set will be collected into the different situations.

Current systems for managing BRs collect BRs into sets regarding one or multiple attributes. Due to the number of attributes necessary to describe a situation, organisation along a single criteria is insufficient. The systems supporting multiple attributes have fixed generic attributes, e.g., BR type, or do not support hierarchy semantics (e.g. inheritance of BRs) or determination of the BRs to be applied in a specific situation. The OMG standard Semantics of Business Vocabulary and Business Rules 1.3. explicitly excludes BR management [16].

In library information science faceted topics are used to manage large information bases [8]. A similar concept are contexts which are described as "any information that can be used to characterize the situation of an entity" [5, pp. 3–4] in one of the most used context definitions. In case of SemNOTAM, the entities are the BRs to be applied in a specific situation; a context would be, for instance, flight rules, a context value IFR. An advantage of faceted topics and contexts is that they can be used to form hierarchies with inheritance semantics. This is particularly useful for the situation hierarchies in SemNOTAM. Consequently, we propose a system based on aviation-specific contexts to manage BRs and their associated business vocabularies in SemNOTAM.

To develop such a system, we employ design science, a framework designed to support creation, understanding, execution, and evaluation of research artefacts. Regarding creation and execution, the language suited most has still to be determined. Most likely, this will be a knowledge representation language such as F-logic. For the evaluation, different measures will be necessary, e.g., classification measures such as accuracy for evaluating whether the right BRs have been determined.

2   Related Work

Two approaches for managing BRs have been identified in the literature: collecting BRs into sets regarding one attribute and regarding multiple attributes.

An example for the former approach are Rai and Anantaram [18] who identify six BR types with the dual purpose ease of decision making and efficient rule processing. Hamza and Fayad [9] classify constraints (one class of BRs, c.f. [3]) into five categories regarding the objective of the constraint. These approaches are insufficient as situations, and thus BR sets, in SemNOTAM are described by many attributes.

An example for the latter approach are Schäfer and Kreher [19]. They suggest situation adequate enclosing of BR sets regarding business criteria but do state any details. Butleris and Kapocius [4] propose a parameter driven approach where BRs are characterised by several attributes. Nevertheless, hierarchies and inheritance are not supported; nor are semantics for addition, revision, or revocation of attributes. Other multiple attribute approaches for BRs organisation use different but fixed attributes [10,14,17] and thus cannot be adapted for Sem-NOTAM. Neither of the found approaches supports determination of the BRs to be applied in a specific situation nor do the mention business vocabularies.

Enhanced versions of the multiple attribute approach, e.g., having value hierarchies for each of the attributes, are used in other research areas. Homola et al. [13] for instance, introduce description logic based contextualised knowledge repositories for the Semantic Web. Similar concepts are used in library information science, e.g., polyhierarchies or faceted topics [8]. Neither of these approaches has been applied to BRs yet, nor do they define semantics for attribute changes.

Besides research papers, actual BR management systems like Oracle Business Rules, JBoss Drools, or IBM's Operational Decision Management exist. These usually comprise a BR repository, a BR engine, and tools for managing and defining BRs. A BR repository consists of several BR sets into which BRs are organised, most often along a single criterion. Some BRMSs also support definition and organisation of business vocabulary. Like the other approaches they do not support determination of BRs to be applied in a specific situation.

3   Research Hypotheses

Besides the requirements identified in the problem description, several hypotheses regarding our proposed BR management system based on aviation-specific contexts for SemNOTAM have been derived.

H1. The system returns for given situations the NOTAMs considered relevant by flight operations personnel and regulations, as well as the importance and groups of these NOTAMs.

H2. The time between providing an interest specification and being returned relevant NOTAMs as well as their importance and groups is lower compared to single, multiple, and enhanced multiple attribute approaches.

H3. The definition length of BRs and business terms is lower compared to existing approaches.

H4. The suggested contexts for organising existing BRs into situations are close to manually determined ones, i.e., at least 75% of the manual contexts are also represented in the suggested contexts.

4   Material and Resources

To test H1, BRs for determining relevance, importance, and groups for many different situations are necessary. Furthermore, for each of these situations NOTAM sets need to be annotated with the correct classifications by flight operations personnel. Subsequently, interest specifications corresponding to these situations need to be created. So far, about 300 BRs in natural language with 400 associated business terms have been elicited in workshops with passenger pilots. These are subsequently translated into ObjectLogic by the project members. As the BRs elicited so far cover only a few situations, further BR elicitation workshops with other flight operations personnel groups are planned.

None of the found approaches uses its organisation structure to reduce the number of BRs to be evaluated. Thus, to test H2, a simple BR evaluation system is needed to compare our approach to. Therefore, the elicited BRs need to be adapted as the information now encoded in the situation description needs to be encoded in the BRs themselves. As the BRs and corresponding vocabulary are already available in ObjectLogic, we will use ObjectLogic for this.

To test H3, the BRs elicited for H1 will be adapted to the different approaches identified in the related work. To test H4, manual determination of situations and their describing contexts is necessary. Section 6 presents preliminary contexts describing situations in SemNOTAM.

To test whether the BRs are collected into the correct situations, we employ the BRs prepared for H1 and H2. BRs prepared for H2 are unorganised and thus will be used as input; BRs prepared for H1 are organised by situations and thus can be used to evaluate H4.

5   Methods/Work Plan

The aim of this research is to create a management system based on contexts for BRs and their associated business vocabulary in SemNOTAM. Design science creates and evaluates IT artefacts to solve problems [11]. Consequently, design science, with its iterative process of assessing and refining the artefact at hand, is an appropriate approach to pursue our aim. This implies that the seven research guidelines of design science: design as an artefact, problem relevance, research contribution, design evaluation, research rigour, design as a search process, and communication of research are followed.

First, current literature regarding contexts will be analysed. In particular, we are interested in characteristics of contexts, methods and functions of contexts and situations, context and context value relationships and their consequences, and how contexts are modelled. Subsequently, we will decide, based on our problem description, which characteristics, methods, functions, and relationships are relevant for contexts in the aeronautical domain.

Thereafter, we will create a conceptual model of the aviation-specific contexts in SemNOTAM. Therefore, we need to identify the relevant contexts and context values describing situations in the aeronautical domain. These are known by flight operations personnel. To externalise this knowledge we deem a case-by-case study design with problem-centered expert interviews (open and semi-structured) [15] the most suitable research design. Especially, as the authors have only limited experience in the aeronautical domain and creating the conceptual model requires an in-depth analysis of the situations and their contexts.

Once the conceptual model is known, we will implement it. Therefore, an appropriate language needs to be chosen supporting the concepts used in the model. Next, the component suggesting aviation-specific contexts and context values for existing unorganised BR sets and the component collecting existing BRs into the corresponding situations are to be designed and implemented. Subsequently, the hypotheses will be tested and the artefact evaluated.

6   Preliminary Results

A few steps of the proposed work plan have already been accomplished in [3]. In this paper we identify characteristics, methods, functions, and relationships of contexts. Subsequently, we argue which of them are relevant to managing BRs and business vocabulary. Based on this argumentation and knowledge gained by analysing the literature, we created an interview guideline for the expert interviews. This interview guideline was then used in three interviews with passenger pilots. Figure 1 depicts the contexts and context values identified. A specific situation contains for example spatial relevance BRs for an IFR passenger flight of a specific Airline under VMC for a pilot departing his/her aerodrome.

Based on the literature analysis and the contexts and context values identified so far, we developed a conceptual multi-level UML model for context-based BR mangement [3]. The upper-most layer models generic contexts and situations. The second layer instantiates the generic contexts and situations to domain-specific ones, e.g., the aviation-specific contexts for SemNOTAM. On the lowest layer, the domain-specific context values as well as situations and their associated BRs and business vocabulary are instantiated. Figure 2 displays three exemplary situations, their contexts, and context values for the BRs shown in Table 1.

IFR_Pilot_Sit contains the BRs to be applied in situations where *IFR* are used and the requesting user's role is *pilot*. This situation inherits the terms and BRs defined in *AnyFlightRule_AnyRole_Sit*, as indicated by the relationship. Given the interest specification *MyIntendedFlight*, the proposed approach is able to determine the correct situation *IFR_Pilot_Sit*. This can be derived from the fact that the given interest specification is a flight plan filed by a pilot and this pilot wants to fly IFR. Consequently, by the inheritance relationship, also BRs and terms of *AnyFlightRule_AnyRole_Sit* need to be considered. Subsequently,

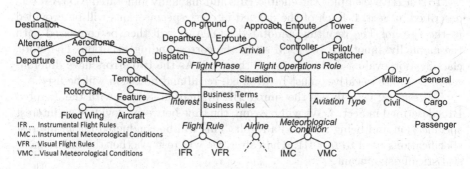

Fig. 1. Aviation-specific contexts, context values, and relationships identified so far.

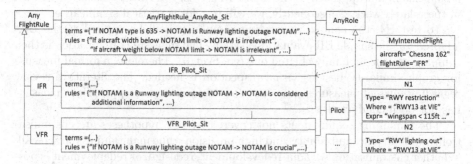

Fig. 2. Sample aviation-specific situations, contexts, and BRs in SemNOTAM.

the determined BRs can be applied to the two given NOTAMs. *N1* is rendered irrelevant as both width and weight of a Chessna 162 are below the limits. *N2* is considered additional information due to *R3* (*IFR_Pilot_Sit*).

A first prototype, realising the most important features of the approach described in [3], is being implemented using Flora-2, an open-source F-Logic derivate. Furthermore, first steps regarding the component suggesting aviation-specific contexts and context values have been made. The basic idea is that situations are identified by their values for several contexts. This can also be expressed as an *and* connected sequence of *ctx = value*. Consequently, contexts and their context values describe expressions often occurring in BRs. Therefore, by transforming BRs into conjunctive normal form and counting the occurrences of the different expressions, potential contexts and context values can be identified. To determine hierarchies of context values and thus situation hierarchies, the business vocabulary needs to be considered. Except for the determination of hierarchies this idea has been implemented in a first prototype using Python.

7   Evaluation

Before we can test our hypotheses, we need to decide how to evaluate them. Furthermore, in concordance with design science, our proposed artefact needs to be evaluated regarding the identified requirements.

To test H1, we employ the elicited BRs and manually annotated NOTAM sets described in Sect. 4. Each of the defined interest specifications will be provided to the system. The resulting annotated NOTAMs will then be compared with the manually annotated NOTAM set of the corresponding situation. Therefore, classification evaluation measures will be used. As the two errors have different costs, i.e., false-negatives must be avoided, recall and precision will be used.

To test H2, we will use the simple BR evaluation system with the adapted BRs described in Sect. 4. We will measure the time between providing an interest specification and being returned a result. This will be conducted for all interest specifications used to test H1. Thereafter, we will test whether the difference is statistically significant.

To test H3, we compare the number of operands necessary for BRs and business terms in our approach to the number necessary in the approaches identified in the related work. Subsequently, we will test for statistical significance.

To test H4, the context suggesting component will be applied to the BRs adapted for the simple BR evaluation system. The suggested organisation is then compared to the manually elicited one (c.f. Sect. 6). Therefore, a formal measure for graph similarity besides visual inspection is needed. The literature review regarding current measures necessary for determining an appropriate measure has not been conducted yet.

The remaining requirements not covered by our hypotheses are customisation, scalability, accountability, and high precision while maintaining 100% recall. Whether customisation without redevelopment, redesign, or redeployment is possible is inherent to the used multi-level approach. Thus, logical argumentation based on the model of the proposed approach (c.f. Sect. 6) will be used for evaluation. To test the scalability of our approach, the test of H1 will be repeated with different NOTAM set sizes and different numbers of BRs. Accountability can either be covered by the used BR engine or needs to be integrated into the BRs. Similarly, 100% recall depends on the BRs themselves and not on the system. Thus, an evaluation of these requirements does not permit for conclusions on the system and consequently is not performed.

In concordance with the assess and refine cycle of design science, any hypotheses falsified or any requirement not satisfied will be investigated. Based on the results of these investigations we will refine our system and assess it again.

8   Conclusion and Future Work

In this paper we identified a lack of suitable BR and business vocabulary management systems (BRVMS) for the aeronautical domain, in particular SemNO-TAM. The concept of contexts used in other research fields addresses these lacks. Consequently, we propose a BRVMS based on aviation-specific contexts.

These aviation-specific contexts describe aeronautical situations. A situation contains BRs and business vocabulary to be applied when this situation occurs. Consequently, maintenance is eased as for each BR the situation in which it holds is explicitly defined. Furthermore, the proposed system is able to determine, for a given interest specification, the correct situations and thus BRs. As only a subset of all BRs needs to be evaluated, this approach is presumably faster than other approaches found. Analogously, debugging is eased. Furthermore, the number of operands needed to define BRs and business terms is lower as some of them are already encoded in the situation's contexts and context values. Thus, the readability of BRs and business terms increases.

To increase the usefulness of the proposed system, existing BR sets need to be (semi-)automatically organised by aviation-specific contexts. Therefore, we propose a component analysing a given BR set, suggesting contexts and context values and thus a potential organisation into situations. Once the user has modified and accepted the organisation, the BRs will be organised accordingly.

Future work includes a full implemenation of the conceptual model introduced in [3]. Furthermore, the implementation of the component suggesting aviation-specific contexts and context values needs to be completed. Once these implementations have been completed, our hypotheses can be formally evaluated. Application and adaptation of the approach to other domains, e.g., the promising domain of laws and insurance contracts, is future work as well.

Acknowledgments. This industry-collaborative research (e.g. Frequentis AG, Eurocontrol) is supported by the Austrian Ministry of Transport, Innovation, and Technology in program TAKE OFF under grant FFG-839006 (SemNOTAM - Semantic-NOTAMs: Ontology-based Representation and Semantic Querying of Digital Notices to Airmen). Moreover, I would like to thank my supervisor Michael Schrefl and my colleagues Ilko Kovacic and Dieter Steiner for their help.

References

1. Burgstaller, F., Steiner, D., Schrefl, M., Gringinger, E., Wilson, S., van der Stricht, S.: Airm-based, fine-grained semantic filtering of notices to airmen. In: Integrated Communication, Navigation, and Surveillance Conference (ICNS), pp. D3-1–D3-13 (2015)
2. Burgstaller, F., Steiner, D., Neumayr, B., Schrefl, M., Gringinger, E.: Using a model-driven, knowledge-based approach to cope with complexity in filtering of notices to airmen. In: Proceedings of the Australasian Computer Science Week Multiconference, ACSW 2016, pp. 46:1–46:10. ACM (2016)
3. Burgstaller, F., Steiner, D., Schrefl, M.: Modeling context for business rule management. In: 2016 IEEE 18th Conference on Business Informatics (2016). tbp, doi:10.1109/CBI.2016.37
4. Butleris, R., Kapocius, K.: The business rules repository for information systems design. In: Research Communications of 6th East European Conference ADBIS, pp. 64–77 (2002)
5. Abowd, G.D., Dey, A.K., Brown, P.J., Davies, N., Smith, M., Steggles, P.: Towards a better understanding of context and context-awareness. In: Gellersen, H.-W. (ed.) HUC 1999. LNCS, vol. 1707, pp. 304–307. Springer, Heidelberg (1999). doi:10.1007/3-540-48157-5_29
6. EUROCONTROL: Digital NOTAM (phase 3 p-21) (2014). https://www.eurocontrol.int/articles/digital-notam-phase-3-p-21
7. EUROCONTROL: FAA: Digital notam event specification 1.0 (2011). http://www.aixm.aero/public/standard_page/digital_notam_specifications.html
8. Frické, M.: Logic and the organization of information. In: Frické, M. (ed.) Logic and the Organization of Information, pp. 277–282. Springer, New York (2012)
9. Hamza, H., Fayad, M.: A novel approach for managing and reusing business rules in business architectures. In: 2013 ACS International Conference on Computer Systems and Applications (AICCSA), pp. 973–978 (2005)
10. Herbst, H., Myrach, T.: A repository system for business rules. In: Meersman, R., Mark, L. (eds.) Database Applications Semantics, pp. 119–139. Springer, Boston (1995)
11. Hevner, A.R., March, S.T., Park, J., Ram, S.: Design science in information systems research. MIS Q. **28**(1), 75–105 (2004)
12. Hoeft, R., Jentsch, F., Kochan, J.: Freeing NOTAMs from teletype technology. Flight Saf. Digest **23**(4), 1–35 (2004)
13. Homola, M., Serafini, L., Tamilin, A.: Modeling contextualized knowledge. In: Proceedings of the 2nd Workshop on Context, Information and Ontologies (CIAO), vol. 626 (2010)
14. Kardasis, P., Loucopoulos, P.: Expressing and organising business rules. Inf. Softw. Technol. **46**(11), 701–718 (2004)
15. Mayring, P.: Einführung in die qualitative Sozialforschung: Eine Anleitung zu qualitativem Denken. Beltz Verlag, Weinheim (2002)
16. Object Management Group: Semantics of Business Vocabulary and Business Rules (SBVR), v1.3 (2015). http://www.omg.org/spec/SBVR/1.0/PDF/
17. Prakash, N., Sharma, D.K., Prakash, D., Singh, D.: A framework for business rules. In: Parsons, J., Chiu, D. (eds.) ER 2013. LNCS, vol. 8697, pp. 68–73. Springer, Heidelberg (2014). doi:10.1007/978-3-319-14139-8_9
18. Rai, V.K., Anantaram, C.: Structuring business rules interactions. Electron. Commer. Res. Appl. **3**(1), 54–73 (2004)

19. Schäfer, A., Kreher, M.: Wie strukturiere ich meine Business Rules für eine effektive Pflege und Steuerung von kritischen, komplexen und dynamischen Geschäftsprozessen. In: GI Jahrestagung, no. 1, pp. 213–218 (2010)
20. Steiner, D., Kovacic, I., Burgstaller, F., Schrefl, M., Friesacher, T., Gringinger, E.: Semantic enrichment of DNOTAMs to reduce information overload in pilot briefings. In: 2016 Integrated Communications Navigation and Surveillance (ICNS), pp. 6B2-1–6B2-13 (2016)

Characterization of Dynamic Resource Consumption for Interference-Aware Consolidation

Markus Hähnel[(✉)]

Chair for Computer Networks, Faculty of Computer Science,
Technical University of Dresden, 01062 Dresden, Germany
markus.haehnel1@tu-dresden.de

Abstract. Nowadays, our daily live concerns the usage of Information Technology, increasingly. As a result, a huge amount of data has to be processed which is outsourced from local devices to data centers. Due to fluctuating demands these are not fully utilized all the time and consume a significant amount of energy while idling. A common approach to avoid unnecessary idle times is to consolidate running services on a subset of machines and switch off the remaining ones. Unfortunately, the services on a single machine interfere with each other due to the competition for shared resources such as caches after the consolidation, which leads to a degradation of performance. Hence, data centers have to trade off between reducing the energy consumption and certain performance criteria defined in the Service Level Agreement. In order to make the trade off in advance, it is necessary to characterize services and quantify the impact to each other after a potential consolidation. Our approach is to use random variables for characterization, which includes the fluctuations of the resource consumptions. Furthermore, we would like to model the interference of services to provide a probability of exceeding a certain performance criterion.

Keywords: Dynamic workload · Characterization · Resource consumption · Consolidation · Interference · Energy-efficient computing · HAEC

1 Introduction

In their daily lives, citizen all over the globe increasingly use cloud-based information and communication technology services. As a result, a huge amount of data has to be processed by an ever-growing multitude of power consuming servers in data centers. At the same time, using data centers is an effective approach to combine all the competence of building, managing, maintaining, etc. the infrastructure. Nevertheless, the data center has to provide a certain quality to his costumers which are paying for the service. In the context of Information Technology (IT) these demands are specified by a Service Level Agreement

© Springer International Publishing AG 2017
I. Ciuciu et al. (Eds.): OTM 2016 Workshops, LNCS 10034, pp. 326–332, 2017.
DOI: 10.1007/978-3-319-55961-2_33

(SLA) between the costumer and the data center [1]. Commonly, the SLA contains limits of some performance criteria such as latency or response time of the hosted applications.

However, data centers consume a significant amount of energy unproportional to the workload [14]. Therefore, in order to improve the energy efficiency (work done per energy) in the data centers, different approaches have to be taken. The addressed points divide mainly into two aspects, namely IT itself and the periphery. First, the periphery like cooling must be minimized. Modern examples of Facebook and Google show that it is possible to reduce the proportion for the periphery to less than 10% of the data center's overall power consumption [2]. Second, the way the machines are utilized has to be optimized for best energy efficiency. The overall power consumption should be proportional to the workload but servers consume up to 50% of their peak power when they are idling. Hence, the best energy efficiency is reached only when the running servers are all fully utilized. Nevertheless, a data center has to perform accordingly to the current demands even if the amount of workload fluctuates over the time (see Fig. 1 [6]). To satisfy the rare high demands, it is designed to accomplish a certain degree of peak performance. However, the average utilization is much lower, for instance, only 10% for a university data center or 25% for Wikipedia [14]. Furthermore, when a service is running, it does not fully utilize a system. An approach for avoiding underutilized servers is to consolidate the currently running services on a subset of machines [3,4,11,15]. Thanks to several live-migration-techniques with very low downtimes the migration can be suitable even for very high SLAs [10]. Afterwards, this subset of machines operates more efficiently because of a higher utilization. Subsequently, the remaining systems which are idling can be switched off. The energy savings exceed the migration costs after only a short period [10].

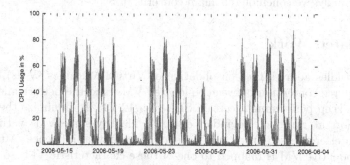

Fig. 1. Fluctuations of the workload (represented by the example of the overall CPU usage) over the time [6]. Variation between day (high workload) and night (low workload), for instance, are addressed by workload consolidation to a subset of servers.

After consolidation, the services will be affected by each other. For instances, even when a service was assigned exclusively to one core of a processor, it will be influenced by the services running on the other cores due to the limited size of shared last level cache (LLC). Obviously, the contention of different services, called interference, depends on several parameters because CPU, memory, disk, and network do not operate independently from each other. For example, all reads and writes to the disk are cached in the memory. Unfortunately, unlike the CPU which can be utilized from 0 to 100%, there is no common measure to quantify the activity to memory for instance. If we want to consolidate services with different resource demands to maximize the entire utilization of the target system, we have to answer the following two questions.

Research Question 1: Which parameters characterize a service in terms of its resource consumptions?

Furthermore, the service consolidation represents a optimization problem. On the one hand, the data centers would like to power on only as few as possible servers to save energy. On the other hand, the service consolidation introduces interference, and hence affects the SLAs. Due to the time required for rebooting additional servers and re-migrate a service, the data center has to trade off between energy savings and performance in advance. Therefore, it is necessary to estimate the influence and resulting performance decrease. This leads to Research Question 2.

Research Question 2: What is the impact on the performance of one service to another after consolidation?

We are going to address the characterization as well as the estimation of interference with random variables. This enables to describe the dynamic of services while the services are consolidated. Furthermore, the mathematical formalism for describing random variables can yield criteria for the SLA. The rest of the paper is organized as follow: In Sect. 2 we summarize a few exemplary publications with related work. Afterwards we discuss our approach and methods in Sect. 3. Finally, we conclude our main concerns in Sect. 4.

2   Related Work

Several studies address the consolidation of Virtual Machines (VMs), particularly, resource contention between co-located VMs, and the performance degradation to keep performing a certain SLA [7–9,12,13]. To minimize the computation effort at runtime, Govindan *et al.* [7] identify some VMs with characteristic interference signature and measure their mutual influence. Afterwards, every productive VM is mapped to one of these characteristic VMs so that the performance after consolidation can be predicted. This strategy needs a low computation effort at runtime, but requires to define a set of characteristic VMs and discard details of productive VMs by mapping them to this limited set.

Another approach is done by Srinivasan and Bellur [12]. They model immediately the job completion time. Independent of the concrete combination of consolidated VMs they rely on a general parameter, namely the CPU utilization. It is split into an independent and dependent part because the duration of a task does not depend only on the CPU utilization. An advantage of this approach is the possibility to model the power consumption based on the CPU utilization. Additionally, they include the current frequency of the processor for their model.

Roytman et al. [9] observe that the CPU independent part of performance degradation comes mainly from the contention in shared caches and memory band widths. Again, all active VMs are mapped to a finite number of classes to predict the degradation. Afterwards, they introduce a metric for the costs of consolidation: Degradation of VMs divided by the number of VMs. In the performance mode (minimize resource costs under performance constraints), they calculate this metric for all combinations, order them in descending order, and locate the VM sets to the servers. Considering all combinations include the optimal solution, but due to the mapping to a predefined characteristic VMs this optimal solution is only approximated, again. The performance mode yield an energy saving of 30% by switching of the remaining unused servers. Alternatively, they introduce an eco mode (minimize degradation under cost constraints). VMs are iteratively permuted until no improvement could be achieved or a limit of permutations is reached.

Another characterization is used by Verboven et al. [13]. They classify each workload by CPU utilization, cache hit/miss-rate, and disk-I/O. Unfortunately, network-I/O is omitted and only one vCPU per VM is used as common assumption in literature. First, they measured each VM running alone and afterwards co-locate evermore VMs. Therefore, they describe the performance lost of consolidation. Finally, they propose a scheduling algorithm as consequence. The characterization by generic parameters belonging to the VM makes the mapping to a finite predefined set of VMs obsolete. On the other hand, the effect of a VM on another VM has to be separately considered for each of them.

As discussed above, interference depends strongly on the cache and the memory. Hence, Kim et al. [8] focus their investigation on the LLC and the memory bus. They observe that the runtime consists of calculation time and the access times of the cache levels and memory. The latter one can be estimated by the LLC misses. Both the number of LLC-misses and the memory access time increases when two services were consolidated. Thus, Kim et al. [8] define the interference intensity and the interference sensitivity. The intensity is described by the LLC-misses, LLC-references, and the execution duration. It is a measure of how strong the service impacts another service. The sensitivity is described by the ratio of number of cycles waited for memory and overall cycles. It is a measure of how strong the service is impacted by another one. Finally, they co-locate services having a high interference intensity and services having a low interference sensitivity.

All of these approaches consider only static parameters and static states of services. Dynamic workload, and hence varying utilizations of hardware is neglected. Therefore, SLAs can be violated while peaks of high workload and energy can be wasted while weak utilization.

3   Methods

We wish to minimize the power consumption of a data center by consolidating services to make the power consumption proportional to the workload [5]. But consolidation creates contention between services, which in term may degrade performance and increase power consumption. Therefore, we wish to develop a strategy to measure contention, called interference. We propose a stochastic model to identify and model interference. We employ performance indicator parameters such as CPU utilization, cache miss rate, cache hit rate, instructions retired, etc. for our stochastic model. The model covers the dynamic of a service. For example, most of the services do not have static workload. A web service becomes active only when a user initiates a request. Also, the degree of resource utilization varies; sometimes just a few users access the web service (e.g. a home-page) and sometimes many users put requests to the service. In this example, the requests are a random workload. In Fig. 1 is shown that it is possible to pre-dict the workload changes within a time window of one day (e.g. weekday and weekend). A bit more fine-grained prediction can also be done for night and day. In contrast to this, it is not possible to deduce the upcoming workload based on the workload before for the time scale of one hour. As a result, all perfor-mance indicator parameters, such as CPU utilization, fluctuate. The idea is to describe such a changing value as random variable, denoted by X. There are several descriptive formalisms for random variables: expectation value, cumula-tive distribution function (CDF), probability density function (p.d.f.), etc. The expectation value $E\{X\}$ gives the average of the random variable. Of course, we are interested in a more detailed description which is given by the CDF $F_X(x)$. It gives the probability P that the random variable is lower or equal to a certain value x: $F_X(x) = P\{X \le x\}$. The derivation of the CDF is called p.d.f. $f_X(x)$. The p.d.f. gives the probability $f_X(x)\,dx$ that X is in the interval $[x, x + dx]$. Because of the probability of 1 that X is anywhere, the p.d.f. is normalized: $\int f_X(x)\,dx = 1$.

As mentioned in Sect. 1 it is not always possible to describe the resource utilization only by a single parameter. Especially, the memory utilization rely on the number of different events like retired instructions and LLC misses. The stochastic formalism enables us to combine such performance indicator para-meters described by random variables, including their dynamic expressed by the p.d.f. Furthermore, we can estimates the degree of contention after con-solidation. As a simple example, we consider the CPU utilizations X and Y of two independent services (see Fig. 2). The statistics of the random variables X and Y can be obtained by data mining before the consolidation. For run-ning example, we approximate the usual complex p.d.f. by a normal distribution $f_X(x) = N(\mu_X = 45\%, \sigma_X = 15\%)$ and $f_Y(y) = N(\mu_Y = 30\%, \sigma_Y = 10\%)$, respectively. After consolidation of both services on a server which was idling before, we would expect an overall CPU utilization of $Z = X + Y$ with the p.d.f.

$$f_Z(z) = \frac{1}{\xi} \int f_X(x) \cdot f_Y(z - x)\,dx = N(\mu_X + \mu_Y, \sigma_X + \sigma_Y).$$

The ξ is just a normalization factor to preserve the normalization of the obtained p.d.f. After integration of $f_Z(z)$, we obtain the CDF $F_Z(z)$ which yields the probability $1 - F_Z(100\%) = 15.6\%$ that the server is overloaded after the consolidation. In this case, the CDF can be used as a SLA.

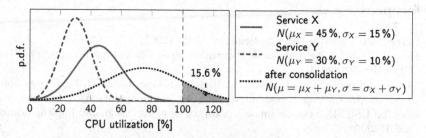

Fig. 2. Distribution functions of CPU utilization of Service X and Service Y before consolidation, and the expected overall CPU utilization after consolidation.

In the first step, we identify suitable parameters and patterns of their dynamic to characterize services regarding to their resource consumption. As second step, we investigate the dependencies and contentions of different resources. Finally, we try to estimate the performance decrease of services with resource consumptions characterized as complementary based on the interferences that we have found.

Our approach will serve as new metric for the optimization problem between saving energy by service consolidation and introduced interference. It defines a new optimal solution which has to be compared to already existing consolidation strategies and their implementations.

4   Conclusion

The significant contribution of data centers to the world energy consumption makes it necessary to improve their efficiency as much as possible. A common strategy is to scale the number of running systems to the current demands by consolidating the active services on a subset of servers and switching off entirely the remaining idling systems. However, even these machines are running efficiently for themselves only when they are fully utilized. This includes a minimization of idle times as well as utilizing other resources than the CPU such as memory, disk, and network. Current models of characterization assume only static aspects of resource consumption. We aim to find an approach which also includes the dynamic of a service by describing varying values as random variables.

Further, we wish to model the contention of different resources to estimate, based on our service characterization, the interference after consolidation. Thus, it will be possible to consolidate services with respect to both full utilization of all resources of the server system for best efficiency, and SLAs.

Acknowledgement. This work is supported by the German Research Foundation (DFG) within the Collaborative Research Center SFB 912 – HAEC. Special thanks to my supervisor Dr. Waltenegus Dargie and my colleague Frehiwot Melak Arega for their constructive feedback and inspiring discussions.

References

1. Berger, T.G.: Service Level Agreements. VDM (2007)
2. Brown, A.S.: Keep it cool! inside the world's most efficient data center. The Bent of Tau Beta Pi (2014)
3. Chen, G., He, W., Liu, J., Nath, S., Rigas, L., Xiao, L., Zhao, F.: Energyaware server provisioning and load dispatching for connection-intensive internet services. In: USENIX Symposium on Networked Systems Design and Implementation (NSDI) (2008)
4. Elnozahy, E.N.M., Kistler, M., Rajamony, R.: Energy-efficient server clusters. In: Falsafi, B., Vijaykumar, T.N. (eds.) PACS 2002. LNCS, vol. 2325, pp. 179–197. Springer, Heidelberg (2003). doi:10.1007/3-540-36612-1_12
5. Fettweis, G., Nagel, W.E., Lehner, W.: Pathways to servers of the future: highly adaptive energy efficient computing (HAEC). In: Conference on Design, Automation and Test in Europe (DATE 2012) (2012)
6. Gmach, D., Rolia, J., Cherkasova, L., Kemper, A.: Workload analysis and demand prediction of enterprise data center applications. In: IEEE International Symposium on Workload Characterization (IISWC) (2007)
7. Govindan, S., Liu, J., Kansal, A., Sivasubramaniam, A.: Cuanta: quantifying effects of shared on-chip resource interference for consolidated virtual machines. In: 2nd ACM Symposium on Cloud Computing (2011)
8. Kim, S.G., Eom, H., Yeom, H.Y.: Virtual machine consolidation based on interference modeling. J. Supercomput. 66(3), 1489–1506 (2013)
9. Roytman, A., Kansal, A., Govindan, S., Liu, J., Nath, S.: PACMan: performance aware virtual machine consolidation. In: 10th International Conference on Autonomic Computing (ICAC 2013) (2013)
10. Rybina, K., Dargie, W., Umashankar, S., Schill, A.: Modelling the live migration time of virtual machines. In: Debruyne, C., et al. (eds.) On the Move to Meaningful Internet Systems: OTM 2015 Conferences. LNCS, pp. 575–593. Springer, Cham (2015). doi:10.1007/978-3-319-26148-5_39
11. Srikantaiah, S., Kansal, A., Zhao, F.: Energy aware consolidation for cloud computing. In: Power Aware Computing and Systems (2008)
12. Srinivasan, S.P., Bellur, U.: Watttime: novel system power model and completion time model for DVFS-enabled servers. In: IEEE 21st International Conference on Parallel and Distributed Systems (ICPADS) (2015)
13. Verboven, S., Vanmechelen, K., Broeckhove, J.: Black box scheduling for resource intensive virtual machine workloads with interference models. Future Gener. Comput. Syst. 29(8), 1871–1884 (2013)
14. Zhang, W., Rajasekaran, S., Wood, T.: Big data in the background: maximizing productivity while minimizing virtual machine interference. In: Workshop on Architectures and Systems for Big Data (2013)
15. Zhu, Q., Zhu, J., Agrawal, G.: Power-aware consolidation of scientific workflows in virtualized environments. In: ACM/IEEE International Conference for High Performance Computing, Networking, Storage and Analysis (2010)

Exploring Appraisals and Rewards in the Context of Business Process Orientation

Aygun Shafagatova[✉]

Department of Business Informatics and Operations Management, Ghent University,
Ghent, Belgium
Aygun.Shafagatova@UGent.be

Abstract. An increasing attention to Business Process Orientation (BPO) brings new challenges in terms of how to motivate employees to become more process-minded and to perform better in order to enjoy full benefit of business processes. Appraisals and rewards have been proven to be powerful techniques in influencing employee behavior and performance in the human resource management (HRM) literature. Hence, new opportunities arise for researching what can make appraisals and rewards more process-oriented. This paper will address such opportunities by conducting an explorative and interdisciplinary study on how to motivate employee performance and behavior in process-oriented organizations. With the help of case studies and a Delphi study, we intend to develop and evaluate a process-oriented appraisals and rewards framework with guidelines.

Keywords: Business Process Orientation · Appraisals · Rewards · Business Process Management · Human resource · Motivational theories · Performance

1 Introduction

In recent years, there has been growing interest in BPO, which is a more holistic approach to Business Process Management (BPM). While BPM can be defined as "a body of principles, methods and tools to design, analyze, execute and monitor business processes (e.g. an order fulfillment process)" [1, p. 26], BPO is seen as broader concept that entails the alignment of structure and culture of organization around business processes [2–4]. McCormack [2, p. 52] defines a "process-oriented organization as one that emphasizes horizontal business processes rather than hierarchy, and that places special emphasis on outcomes and customer satisfaction", instead of focusing on a functional structure. Although considerable body of research exists on the technical aspects of BPM (e.g. process modeling, optimization, execution) [1], current research suffers from limitations mainly concerning the people aspects, in particular how to build a process-oriented culture and how to motivate employees to perform better in process-oriented organizations.

For example, fulfilling a certain customer order (e.g. ordering a car) involves a complex set of interdependent steps that runs through different departments and requires the close coordination and cooperation of the sales, accounting, production and other departments (Fig. 1).

© Springer International Publishing AG 2017
I. Ciuciu et al. (Eds.): OTM 2016 Workshops, LNCS 10034, pp. 333–339, 2017.
DOI: 10.1007/978-3-319-55961-2_34

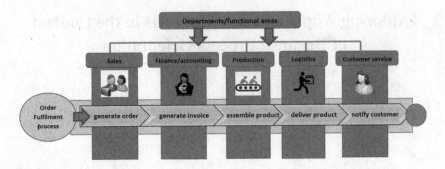

Fig. 1. An illustrative example of cross-functional, end-to-end business processes

While these departments are traditionally organized vertically, end-to-end business processes run horizontally and cross-functional which has implications for employee performance and behavior. The people from different departments that participate in these processes are thus responsible for the process results and performance. However, if they are still appraised and rewarded according to narrow departmental objectives and tasks, they will be less interested in the results and performance of the entire business process, instead they will focus on their individual objectives and tasks. For example, if sales is focused on selling more cars, and disinterested in customer satisfaction and service quality, that would be a narrow view that ignores the process goals which would have a negative impact in the long run.

Including the process goals and performance measures (e.g. time target or customer satisfaction in the case of the order fulfilment process) and competences/behaviors relevant to process orientation (e.g. customer orientation, process knowledge) to the appraisal process of each process participant could refocus the employees' attention to the whole process. Moreover, tying rewards to these appraisals could motivate them to perform better and improve the process performance as a whole (Fig. 2). Thus, a business is also challenged on how to evaluate and reward employees according to a process-oriented structure.

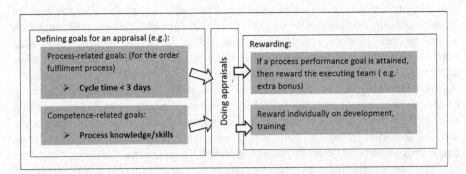

Fig. 2. An example of possible process-oriented appraisals and rewards mechanism

Interestingly, the HRM literature related to appraisals and rewards is mainly concerned with the functional and individual perspective of appraising and rewarding employees [5], and tends to ignore the horizontal character of business processes requiring a cross-functional, and mostly team-based approach. Hence, we intend to conduct an explorative and interdisciplinary study which will combine concepts from the BPM/BPO and HRM disciplines to examine how to appraise and motivate employee performance and behavior for end-to-end business processes in order to build a process-minded culture and to improve process performance. We will specifically analyze how traditional appraisals and rewards can be more process-oriented and thus more supportive for business (process) performance.

The remainder of the paper is structured as follows. Section 2 summarizes related work. Then, Sect. 3 identifies the research questions and proposes our methodology. Finally, preliminary concluding remarks will be highlighted in Sect. 4.

2   Related Work

2.1   Appraisals and Rewards in the HRM Literature

Fletcher [6, p. 473] defines performance appraisals as "a variety of activities through which organizations seek to assess employees and develop their competence, enhance performance and distribute rewards". The most relevant underpinning theory on appraisals is the **goal setting** theory which emphasizes the importance of setting goals for employees against which performance can be measured and managed [7]. The framework of Armstrong [8] is interesting as well in this context which deals with different dimensions of evaluating employees by combining the performance (outcomes) and behavior/competence (input) dimensions of employee in a multidimensional assessment matrix.

Rewards (which are most of the times based on performance appraisals) are considered to influence behavior, increase employee motivation, satisfaction and performance which in turn help realize organizational goals [6, 9, 10]. The most relevant theories for explaining the link between individual behavior, rewards, motivation and performance are: (1) **the expectancy theory**, and (2) the '**line of sight' model**. First, the expectancy theory postulates that motivation is generated when employees expect valence and instrumentality in rewards [5, 11, 12]. Secondly, the 'line of sight' model builds upon the expectancy theory by stating that individuals will only be motivated if they can make a clear link between what they do (effort/performance) and what they will get for doing it (reward) [5, 10, 11]. While these well-established appraisals and rewards theories represent generic approaches, they don't cover the process-orientation dimension. Moreover, they lack the insights on how to link business process performance goals with employee appraisals and rewards, and on which appraisals and rewards techniques and practices better suit process-oriented structure.

As processes are executed most of the times by teams, team-based appraisals and rewards seems to be a relevant perspective for our study [3, 13]. Although research on team performance and rewards provides little guidance so far, the HRM literature suggests that performance can be more accurately and reliably assessed on team level when individual tasks are mostly interdependent [5, 10, 13]. However, it remains challenging to reward teams as a whole and distribute rewards among team members, since the **equity theory** states that rewards may be perceived as unfair if the inputs of teammates differ, yet the rewards or outcomes are distributed equally [11]. Although limited research on team-based appraisals and rewards mostly focus on equity/equality issues, it does not yet pay attention to a process-orientation dimension.

2.2 Appraisals and Rewards in the BPO Literature

Appraisals and rewards have been mentioned in BPO literature from two perspectives. First, BPM/BPO maturity models measure/define how mature an organization is in establishing BPM/BPO. Van Looy et al. [4] conducted an extensive research on existing maturity models resulting in a comprehensive framework with six main areas of capabilities needed for BPM/BPO. Appraisals and rewards have been included within the culture dimension of this framework together with values, attitude and behaviors, and top management commitment [4]. Thus, most of the maturity models mention that if an organization wants to level up its BPM/BPO maturity, it has to modify its appraisals and rewards to serve the process needs, but without elaborating on it further.

Secondly, several academic studies [3, 14–16] have identified the importance of having appraisals and rewards which meet process needs and recognize process performance as a whole. They mention the need of linking incentive systems to process performance measurement and by focusing on cross-functional, process-based teams when rewarding in order to focus an individual's attention to the process instead of personal objectives. These studies confirm that applying BPM/BPO implies changes to the traditional approach of appraisals and rewards and thus emphasize the importance of process-oriented appraisals and rewards, albeit without going deeper.

To conclude, there is a lack of research in both the HRM and BPM/BPO literature regarding process-oriented appraisals and rewards. HRM generically focuses on mostly functional and individual dimensions while ignoring process dimension. Further, team-based appraisals and rewards could be relevant to process-orientation, but are less researched. Moreover, BPM/BPO literature mentions the importance of and need for having appraisals and rewards that support process orientation but without going into detail on how to realize it. Thus, there is a need for research that would combine both perspectives and elaborate on an appraisals and rewards framework that is process supportive.

3   Research Questions and Methodology

In line with the above-mentioned limitations, we intend: to conduct a research to explore the theoretical and empirical evidence on process-oriented appraisals and rewards practices; then to develop a possible framework with guidelines that could help organizations to add a business process dimension to their appraisals and rewards system by combining relevant concepts from two disciplines (HRM and BPO). The following research questions are proposed to shed light on the topic:

RQ1. Which appraisals and rewards practices and techniques can be used in a BPO context?

RQ2. How to realize/build process-oriented appraisals and rewards in process-oriented organizations (i.e. building guidelines)?

RQ3. What is the impact of process-oriented appraisals and rewards on process performance and organizational performance (e.g. testing guidelines)?

This study is situated within the behavioral-science paradigm[1], since our intention is to contribute to a theory for introducing process-oriented appraisals and rewards in specific organizations in the sense of building and testing guidelines or best practices rather than building a process-oriented appraisal and rewards system as an IT artefact.

Regarding RQ1, a literature review will be conducted to study all relevant papers. Secondly, exploratory case studies [17] will be conducted to find HRM-related best practices in organizations with high BPM/BPO maturity levels (i.e. level 4 or more on the scale of Lockamy and McCormack [18]). We assume that only high mature organizations might have developed such best practices regarding process-oriented appraisals and rewards. We will not focus on specific domains or sectors given the study's explorative character. The HRM theories on appraisals and rewards will be of importance to recognize possible patterns and reasoning behind current practices.

Next, to respond to RQ2, we will conduct a Delphi study (i.e. consensus-seeking decision-making) [19] to check the comprehensiveness of the approaches found in RQ1 and discuss them to reach consensus. The subject-matter experts will be HRM and BPM scholars, as well as HRM managers, process managers. They will be asked to give their feedback in several rounds until there is a consensus. Delphi study will also function as a mean of validating the findings. The intention is to build a framework with guidelines or steps to facilitate the introduction and realization of process-oriented appraisals and rewards. Hence, the existing knowledge of BPO and HRM will be combined to define new dimensions for appraisals and rewards. The most prominent challenge is gaining insight on how to link performance appraisals to process performance results and how rewards can be tied to it on both a team and an individual level. Henceforth, it is expected that the guidelines will be rather an addition to or modification of existing appraisal and reward systems instead of requiring a totally new system.

For RQ3, we will possibly apply action research [20] or reality check case studies in order to evaluate our developed guidelines from RQ2 in partner organizations interested in applying the new dimension of appraisals and rewards in their existing HRM system. Our initial proposition is that rewards and appraisals, which are tailored to process needs and are supportive for BPO, will have a positive effect on process performance and eventually organizational performance, and can help reinforce a process-oriented way of thinking. The unit of analysis is organizations since the organizational perspective will be studied.

---

[1] The behavioral science paradigm seeks to develop and verify theories that explain or predict human or organizational behavior [21].

4 Conclusion

This study is explorative and interdisciplinary in character by combining relevant concepts from HRM and BPO. HRM research agrees on the importance of appraisals and rewards to influence employee behavior and performance [5, 10–12]. Besides, process orientation requires different performance measurement and targets than in a traditional (i.e. more individual and functional-based) organizations [3, 14, 15]. Therefore, HRM and BPO perspectives of appraisals and rewards can be combined to motivate employees more accurately in process-oriented organizations and to reinforce them to think in terms of end-to-end business processes. However, the initial literature study showed that comparatively little attention has been paid to this issue indicating a need for more research on the topic. To this end, we will build upon the above-mentioned theories and methodologies in order to develop a framework with guidelines for possible process-oriented appraisals and rewards and to provide empirical evidence of its impact on overall performance.

Acknowledgements. This Ph.D. project will be funded by Ghent University (Belgium) under the supervision of Prof. Dr. Manu De Backer (administrative promoter) and Prof. Dr. Amy Van Looy (daily supervisor).

References

1. Dumas, M., La Rosa, M., Mendling, J., Reijers, H.A.: Fundamentals of Business Process Management. Springer, Heidelberg (2013)
2. McCormack, K.P.: Business process orientation: do you have it? Qual. Prog. **34**, 51–58 (2001)
3. Armistead, C.: Principles of business process management. Manag. Serv. Qual. Int. J. **6**, 48–52 (1996)
4. Van Looy, A., De Backer, M., Poels, G.: A conceptual framework and classification of capability areas for business process maturity. Enterp. Inf. Syst. **8**, 188–224 (2014)
5. Armstrong, M.: A Handbook of Human Resource Management Practice. Kogan Page Publishing, London (2006)
6. Fletcher, C.: Performance appraisal and management: the developing research agenda. J. Occup. Organ. Psychol. **74**, 473–487 (2001)
7. Locke, E.A., Latham, G.P.: Building a practically useful theory of goal setting and task motivation. a 35-year odyssey. Am. Psychol. **57**, 705–717 (2002)
8. Armstrong, M.: Handbook of Reward Management Practice: Improving Performance Through Reward. Kogan Page Publishing, London (2010)
9. Den Hartog, D.N., Boselie, P., Paauwe, J.: Performance management: a model and research agenda. Appl. Psychol. Int. Rev. **53**, 556–569 (2004)
10. Lawler, E.E.: Effective reward systems: strategy, diagnosis, design, and change. Cent. Eff. Organ. E **6**, 1–43 (1993)
11. Agarwal, N.C.: Reward systems: emerging trends and issues. Can. Psychol. **39**, 60–70 (1995)
12. Hendry, C., Woodward, S., Bradley, P.: Performance and rewards: cleaning out the stables. Hum. Resour. Manag. J. **10**, 46–62 (1999)
13. DeMatteo, J.S., Eby, L.T., Sundstrom, E.: Team-based rewards: current empirical evidence and directions for future research. Res. Organ. Behav. **20**, 141-183 (1998)

14. Hernaus, T.: Process-based Organization Design Model: Theoretical Review and Model Conceptualization. FEB Working Paper Series, vol.385, pp. 1–17 (2008)
15. Kohlbacher, M.: The effects of process orientation: a literature review. Bus. Process Manag. J. **16**, 135–152 (2010)
16. Kohlbacher, M., Gruenwald, S.: Process orientation: conceptualization and measurement. Bus. Process Manag. J. **17**, 267–283 (2011)
17. Yin, R.K.: Case Study Research: Design and Methods. Sage Publications, Thousand Oaks (2009)
18. Lockamy, A., McCormack, K.: The development of a supply chain management process maturity model using the concepts of business process orientation. Supply Chain Manag. Int. J. **9**, 272–278 (2004)
19. Dalkey, N., Helmer, O.: An experimental application of the Delphi method to the use of experts. Manag. Sci. **9**, 458–467 (1963)
20. Gilmore, T.: Action based modes of inquiry and the host-researcher relationship. Consult. Int. J. **5**(3), 160–176 (1986)
21. Hevner, A.R., March, S.T., Park, J., Ram, S.: Design science in information systems research. MIS Q. **28**, 75–105 (2004)

Author Index